PENGUIN BOOKS

BATTLESHIP

On a visit to France and Belgium in 1967 Martin Middlebrook was so impressed by the military cemeteries on the 1914–18 battlefields that he decided to write a book describing just one day in that war through the eyes of the ordinary men who took part. The book, *The First Day on the Somme*, was published by Allen Lane in 1971 and received international acclaim. Martin Middlebrook has since written other books that deal with important turning-points in the two world wars; these are *The Kaiser's Battle, Convoy, The Peenemünde Raid, The Battle of Hamburg, Battleship* (with Patrick Mahoney), *The Schweinfurt-Regensburg Mission, The Nuremburg Raid, The Bomber Command War Diaries* (with Chris Everitt), *Task Force: The Falklands War, 1982, The Berlin Raids, The Fight for the 'Malvinas', The Somme Battlefields* (with Mary Middlebrook) and *The Battle of Arnhem* (1994). Many of his books have been published in the United States and Germany, and three of them in Japan, Yugoslavia and Poland.

Martin Middlebrook is a Fellow of the Royal Historical Society. Each summer he takes parties of visitors on conducted tours of the First World War battlefields.

Patrick Mahoney was born in Portsmouth in 1927. After leaving school at the age of fourteen he became a messenger boy with Cable and Wireless. He served with the Royal Artillery in Germany during the years 1947 to 1948. In his career as an overseas telegraphist Patrick Mahoney was stationed in Bermuda, Aden, Amman, Jerusalem, Geneva and Ndola. He says he has always held a morbid fascination for the First World War and the war in the Far East.

Martin Middlebrook
and Patrick Mahoney

Battleship

The Loss of the Prince of Wales
and the Repulse

Penguin Books

For James Kyle

with the compliments of my
friend and co-author,
Patrick Mahoney
and with my best wishes,

Martin Middlebrook

PENGUIN BOOKS

Published by the Penguin Group
Penguin Books Ltd, 27 Wrights Lane, London W8 5TZ, England
Penguin Books USA Inc., 375 Hudson Street, New York, New York 10014, USA
Penguin Books Australia Ltd, Ringwood, Victoria, Australia
Penguin Books Canada Ltd, 10 Alcorn Avenue, Toronto, Ontario, Canada M4V 3B2
Penguin Books (NZ) Ltd, 182–190 Wairau Road, Auckland 10, New Zealand

Penguin Books Ltd, Registered Offices: Harmondsworth, Middlesex, England

First published by Allen Lane 1977
Published by Penguin Books 1979
10 9 8 7 6 5 4

Printed in England by Clays Ltd, St Ives plc
Set in Monotype Bell

Contents

List of Maps and Text Figures

List of Plates

Introduction

At 11.00 on Wednesday, 10 December 1941, the crews of a formation of Japanese Navy Mitsubishi Type 96 aircraft sighted two large warships escorted by three destroyers steaming on an easterly course some fifty miles off the coast of Malaya. One merchant ship could also be seen near by, but there was no sign of any aircraft protecting the warships. The two larger ships were both British; they were the battleship H.M.S. *Prince of Wales* and the battle cruiser H.M.S. *Repulse*. Two of the escorting destroyers were also Royal Navy ships, but the third was Australian. It was only the third day of the war that Japan had started in the Far East. The weather was fine and clear. Lieutenant Yoshimi Shirai, the pilot of the leading Mitsubishi, ordered his formation to attack.

That night there were great parties at two Japanese-held airfields near Saigon to celebrate a momentous victory against the hated British.

This is not the first book to be written about the loss of the *Prince of Wales* and the *Repulse*, but history is a subject that takes many years to unfold, both in the increasing availability of documents and in the continuing repercussions of events and the gradual realization of their implications. In particular, the publication in 1969 by the Japanese of their Official History and the release in 1972 of the British Second World War documents at the Public Record Office have thrown new light on this decisive action and justify a fresh study.

This book will aim to pass fairly quickly over those aspects of the subject which are common knowledge or are not controversial; it will concentrate more on those areas which earlier writers may not have been able to cover in depth. An attempt will also be made to tell the reader not just what happened on that sunny morning off Malaya, but what it was like for the men involved. One hundred and ninety-three officers and men who were serving in the warships attacked have been traced, together with others who were stationed at Singapore or other relevant places at the time of the disaster. We are fully aware of the pitfalls of relying on the human memory for descriptions of an episode full of confusion and emotional stress – an episode furthermore that occurred more than thirty years ago. But the basic framework of the book has been formed from reliable contemporary records; the participants in the battle provide descriptions of smaller incidents never included in the official records and, perhaps more importantly, tell of their emotions at that dramatic time. The contributions of these men put flesh on the bare bones of the story and bring it more to life.

Our choice of title may need some explanation. We realize that the *Repulse* was a battle *cruiser* and that battleships and battle cruisers were designed for different roles in the event of a fleet action, but on 10 December 1941 neither the *Repulse* nor the *Prince of Wales* was operating in the strict role for which it had been built. Our title – *Battleship* – has been chosen for other reasons. Since 1918 the leaders of most of the world's navies had been under pressure, sometimes in the bitterest of circumstances, to accept the argument that heavily gunned and armoured capital ships – what may be called battleships, whether true battleships or dreadnoughts or battle cruisers – had outrun their useful lifespan and that new weapons and their means of delivery – the torpedo, the bomb, the submarine, the aircraft – had rendered the battleship obsolescent. In Britain this argument had been put even before 1914. But in no country had the theory been fully accepted and vast quantities of money from national budgets had continued to be spent on battleships.

The clearest warning of all had been given by a famous American, Brigadier-General Billy Mitchell, Assistant

Chief of the U.S. Army Air Corps between 1919 and 1925. After the First World War the U.S. Navy had wanted to re-equip with a fleet of new battleships. Mitchell argued, as forcefully as he could, that aircraft could sink by bomb or by torpedo any ship afloat. He proved it, though not to the U.S. Navy's satisfaction, in trials during which his aircraft sank two empty ex-German warships – a battleship and a cruiser – in 1921, and then three old American battleships during the next two years. The experiments were naturally followed with great interest by other naval powers, but Mitchell and the other anti-battleship critics did not prevail. Billy Mitchell continued to agitate until exiled to a remote command for pressing his ideas too strongly, and then was court-martialled and suspended from duty for publishing his views in the press without permission. At least thirty-four battleships were launched and completed after this time at a cost of around £250–300 million or $1,000 million, and many more of the older battleships were refitted and modernized at further massive cost. Most of the countries engaged in this battleship bonanza started their wars in 1939 or 1941 desperately short of aircraft carriers and anti-submarine vessels.

The action started by Lieutenant Shirai on 10 December 1941 proved conclusively that the battleship could no longer live with the bomb, the torpedo and the aircraft. The validity of this theory, so hated and resisted by traditionalist naval officers of so many countries, had taken a remarkably long time to find its proof.

The tenth of December 1941 was the end of the battleship era.

PATRICK MAHONEY
MARTIN MIDDLEBROOK

1

'A Sword at Our Hearts'

In the years following the First World War, the victorious but exhausted Allied nations took stock of the much-changed world over which they held virtual rule. There were at least three urgent tasks to be undertaken: clear up the mess in Europe, exact suitable penalties from the defeated Germans and Austrians, and plan for the future. There was a genuine and sincere desire by the victors to make sure that the four-year holocaust just ended would never need to be repeated. To unscramble the tangled web of new allegiances, the thirsts for vengeance, the debts to be honoured and secret promises to be kept, to rebuild anew the delicate balances of power and spheres of influence – these were the daunting tasks facing the statesmen. Events twenty years on were to show that the decisions reached, so often achieved by compromise between politicians whose national desires overcame their grasp of the world's needs, were the wrong decisions. The conferences and treaties of the five years or so following 1918 are as good a starting point as any to the story of the *Prince of Wales* and the *Repulse*.

The Pacific was hardly touched by the First World War, but the role of Japan in that war should be studied. Britain had had a friendship and mutual aid alliance with Japan since 1902, and when she found herself fighting Germany in August 1914, the Japanese had honoured the treaty and joined Britain in attacking the German-held colony of Tsingtao on the coast of China. Tsingtao fell quickly, but this proved to be the limit of the Japanese Army's support; the mutual-aid clauses of the alliance only covered India and the Far East. No Japanese troops were ever sent to France or any other front where British troops were fighting. The Japanese Navy did, however, send warships in 1917 to help the hard-pressed Royal Navy on convoy escort work in the Mediterranean.

The Japanese had meanwhile taken advantage of the great powers' preoccupation with the European war by gaining important footholds in mainland Asia. The conquered German colony of Tsingtao was retained and China was forced to give up other land in the area. Further moves into China were blocked by British and American political pressure, but the Japanese were allowed to move into southern Manchuria to extend their existing control of Korea. Finally, when the ex-German island colonies in the Pacific were being divided among the victors after 1918, the Japanese had to be given the Marianas, the Carolines and most of the Marshall Islands in return for the naval help given to Britain in 1917 – a typical example of the settling of debts that took place after the war.

So, for the modest outlay of possibly a battalion of infantry at Tsingtao in 1914 and a few escort vessels in 1917, Japan had gained important footholds in mainland Asia and the Pacific Islands. Japan was one of the few countries to do well out of the First World War. She also showed that her aims were expansionist. The Japanese Empire was clearly on the move.

This Japanese attitude posed a dilemma for two of her wartime Allies, Britain and the United States. Communications to important members of the British Empire – Australia, New Zealand, New Guinea, Borneo and Malaya – could be threatened by an expanding Japan, and the United States' interests in the Philippines were similarly at risk. Both countries were also heavily dependent upon South-East Asia for two essential commodities: Malaya and the Dutch East Indies produced three quarters of the worlds' raw rubber and two thirds of its tin. The political and commercial consequences of Japanese moves into this area were immense. The American and British dilemma was how to check the Japanese without directly antagonizing their former ally.

The threat to Britain and the United States was closely bound up with sea power; political and military progress by the Japanese away from mainland Asia could be achieved with naval cover. At the end of 1921, the United States, using her new-found influence as a major world power, invited the other four naval powers – Britain, France, Japan and Italy – to a joint conference. This meeting, the Washington Naval Conference, took only a few weeks to reach agreement. The outcome was that the existing strengths should not be altered, nor existing spheres of influence be extended by the construction of new bases outside the old spheres.

No doubt to the relief of Britain and the United States, the Japanese signed, without demur, this agreement which limited their naval strength to 60 per cent of that of both the Royal Navy and the United States Navy while forbidding them to build bases in their newly acquired island possessions in the Pacific. Although the British were not permitted to build a new base at Hong Kong nor the Americans one in the Philippines, they could do so in Malaya or Hawaii. This question of bases was all-important. The Pacific was so vast that a naval power could only expand within certain distances from proper bases.

The Washington Naval Agreement had limited the Japanese dream of expansion – at least for the moment.

The post-war period posed particular problems for the British Admiralty. The old enemy, Germany, had lost her navy and was no longer a threat in European waters; the old ally, Japan, now posed a potential threat in the Far East and the Pacific. Britain had enough warships but no base in the Far East with a dry dock capable of taking the largest capital ships; and even if these docks had existed, it would be an expensive burden to maintain permanently an Eastern Fleet which contained battleships. The Admiralty solution was to press the government to build a new base in the Far East but to retain all the battleships in the Home and Mediterranean Fleets. The British naval presence would be made up, as in the past, of cruisers and smaller vessels; capital ships would make no more than the occasional flag-showing visits. It was hoped that if ever war in the East threatened, capital ships could be rushed out in time to meet that threat. The proposed new base would service and repair these ships both on arrival and during subsequent operations. This combination of a permanent modern base in the Far East and rapid reinforcement by capital ships from England was to be the cornerstone of British and Empire defence policy in the area for exactly twenty years.

The British Cabinet accepted the Admiralty plans and also the choice of a site for the base. Hong Kong was soon dismissed as too isolated and vulnerable, and Trincomalee, in Ceylon, as too remote from the area to be defended. Singapore and Sydney were both given more serious consideration, but the final choice fell on Singapore as having the better strategic position. At the Imperial Conference of 1921 Mr Arthur Balfour, representing the British government, said:

We have come to the conclusion that one of the pressing needs for Imperial defence is that Singapore should be made into a place where the British Fleet can concentrate for the defence of the Empire, of our trade interests in the East, our interests in India, our interests in Australia, our interests in New Zealand, our interests in the small possessions there and for that purpose it is absolutely necessary to undertake works at Singapore. *

It is interesting to note that this decision had been taken in June 1921, five months before the Washington Naval Conference was convened. Britain was thus able to agree at the conference that no new naval bases would be built by her 'east of the 110 degrees meridian'. Singapore was just west of this line.

There were two possible sites at Singapore for the great new base: at the existing small naval base at Keppel Harbour, among the commercial wharves just south of

* Public Record Office WO 106/2530.

Singapore city, or at a new site in the remoter northern part of the island on the Johore Strait. The Admiralty asked for the Johore Strait site since it was remote enough from the open sea to be free from the danger of naval bombardment, and also because it would be clearer of commercial shipping. The Admiralty's recommendation was approved, and it was also decided to construct an air and seaplane base at near-by Seletar.

The next thing to be settled was how the base should be protected from enemy attack, and here an unhappy story begins, the main ingredients of which are well known. It was at this time that the Royal Air Force was striving to establish itself as the third major service and to get the principle accepted that air power would be a major factor in any future war. The 1920s and 1930s were difficult economic times, and the allocation between the three services of the limited defence budgets was bitterly contested. The R.A.F. did have some friends in British governments of the time, but not enough. Of the £1,938 million in the defence budgets for the fifteen years from 1920 to 1934, the Navy received the lion's share of 47 per cent, the Army 40 per cent, and the R.A.F. only 13 per cent.

When the defence of Singapore was being considered in the 1920s, belief was almost unanimous that any threat would come from naval bombardment, possibly followed up by a landing directly on the island of seaborne troops; the jungle-covered mainland of Malaya to the north was believed to be impenetrable. The R.A.F. contended that the best defence against naval attack was the presence at Singapore of a strong force of torpedo bombers protected by fighters, but the Navy and the Army believed that heavy-calibre guns in fixed positions would provide a better defence. The 'big-gun' lobby won and Singapore's main line of defence was entrusted to artillery in fixed emplacements and capable of covering all sea approaches to Singapore, but most being unable to train back on to the mainland of Malaya.

The actual work of building the base and its defences was slow to start. The newly elected Labour government of 1924 decided to abandon the scheme completely, but Labour were out of office again within the year and their Conservative successors reinstated the plan. So it went on for several years, with successive governments slowing down or speeding up construction according to financial pressures, political outlook or changing world events. The main work was not completed until 1938, but the result was the fine, modern Singapore Naval Base. The 1,006-foot King George VI Graving Dock and the 858-foot No. 9 Floating Dock were both capable of dry-docking the largest Royal Navy ships then afloat or planned, while a smaller floating dock would care for destroyers and other small vessels. There were great towering cranes, workshops and stores to cater for a whole fleet, huge oil tanks and the F.S.A. (Fleet Shore Accommodation) with facilities for housing up to 3,000 men when their ships were undergoing major repair. The total area of the base covered one and a half square miles and there were twenty-two square miles of anchorages. The final cost came to more than £60 million.

This fine outpost of the Empire was formally opened on 15 February 1938 by Sir Shenton Thomas, Governor of the Straits Settlements, in the presence of many distinguished visitors. It is recorded that Mr Okamoto, the Japanese Consul-General in Singapore, attended the opening ceremony but left before the reception. Eighteen naval vessels made a fine sight with the cruiser H.M.S. *Norfolk* flying the flag of the Eastern Fleet and the United States and the Indian Navies were each represented by three ships. But no battleships were present. The new Singapore Naval Base stood ready to receive these should the British Empire in the Far East ever be threatened.

The Japanese were not happy. The Singapore Naval Base, which the British saw as a vital link in the *defence* of the Empire, appeared to the Japanese to be more a base for aggression against them – or, at least, that was the public line they took in the 1930s.

Relations between Britain and Japan had undergone great changes after 1918. The alliance and solidarity that had existed between the two nations for almost twenty years had begun to crumble even before the end of the First World War. Britain's belief in Japanese good faith had been shaken by the Japanese moves in China and Manchuria while the attention of most of the world was still concentrated on the fighting in Europe. Japan's expansionist policy had provoked not only the 1921 Washington Naval Conference – which, as already described, limited her naval strength – but also two political treaties: the Four-Power Treaty, defining and regulating the positions in the Pacific of Britain, the United States, France and Japan; and the Nine-Power Treaty, which was intended to protect China from Japanese aggression. At the same time, Britain informed Japan that she would not be renewing the long-standing Anglo-Japanese Alliance, giving as the main reason the view that the new League of Nations rendered such alliances obsolete. All these changes were undertaken while Japan was under a government where civilians dominated and whose outlook was commercial rather than military. This government accepted all these great changes without demur.

The treaties of the 1920s were to keep the peace for eight years, but a succession of seemingly isolated events meanwhile gradually eroded the post-war stability of Japan's civilian government. Japan was accorded the status of a major power by the League of Nations and a permanent seat on the League's Council, but the League failed to pass Japan's requested declaration of racial equality, mainly on opposition from Australia's prime minister, Billy Hughes. A great earthquake in 1923 caused the deaths of approximately 100,000 people in Yokohama and Tokyo. Hot on the heels of this disaster came a widely circulated rumour that Communists and Korean Nationalists were combining to overthrow the government; this caused a bloody witch-hunt and badly rocked the government. Then, Crown Prince Hirohito was photographed in western clothes playing golf with the Prince of Wales while on a visit to England – a seemingly innocent event, but one which upset the traditionalists in Japan. In 1924, the United States government passed a Bill banning further immigration from oriental countries, which caused the Japanese Ambassador in Washington to threaten 'grave consequences' to this second racial insult to his country. These were just some from an intricate series of events that rocked the stability of Japan in the 1920s. The final blow came when Japan suffered more severely than most countries from the world slump of 1927 and its government fell in 1928; a new party, the Seiyukai, came to power with General Tanaka Giichi as prime minister.

General Tanaka's party had strong support from the young army officers, the traditional malcontents in any country emerging slowly to full democratic status. What did they see around their country? They found the West classifying them as 'inferior orientals', their naval strength being limited to a level well below that of other world powers, their expansion on the mainland of Asia and their desire to build an empire deliberately blocked by countries that had already built their own empires, their centuries-old standards and traditions threatened, their trade in ruins, their civilian government failed. And how had Britain, their old ally, behaved? Britain had torn up the alliance which had been so useful in gaining Japanese help in the First World War. Britain had connived with the United States to keep Japan in an inferior naval position and was now building this great new base at Singapore, the only reason for which could be distrust of Japan. A proud nation had been deeply hurt. The Singapore Naval Base, it was said, was 'a sword at our hearts'.

The situation deteriorated fast in the 1930s. Japan renewed her expansion in Manchuria in 1931 and in China the following year. A full-scale military attack on China was undertaken in 1937. The Western Powers were

appalled by the savagery with which the Japanese treated
the captured Chinese cities, but were unable to stop the
fighting. When the League of Nations protested, the
Japanese withdrew from the League. Japan then refused
to renew the conditions of the Washington Naval Conference when these came up for renewal in 1934 and commenced a great modernization and expansion of her navy,
though details of how this was implemented were largely
kept secret. At home in Japan, personal freedom and
democracy went and the country moved towards a military
dictatorship that the Emperor seemed powerless to check.
The behaviour of the Japanese during these years matched
closely that of the Germans under Hitler and the Nazis.
These two countries, although so dissimilar in character,
were taking almost parallel paths to outright aggression,
to the military alliance of the Axis – and to their own
eventual self-destruction in 1945.

The Japanese made no secret of their intentions. A
remarkable book written by an officer of the Imperial
Japanese Navy, *Japan Must Fight Britain*, was translated
into English in 1936 and sold at least 11,000 copies in
Britain. The English publisher's introduction stated:

The Pan-Asia movement to establish Tokyo as the pivot of an
empire 1,000,000,000 people strong . . . The author discusses the
inevitable war between the two powers, detailing the relative
strengths and weaknesses of their Army, Navy, Air Force, a com-
parison from which Britain emerges as definitely the weaker. He
claims that the Singapore Base is an insult to Japan, that the
Dominions are apathetic and of little material aid in the event of war,
that the British Navy is decadent . . . He urges Britain to realize the
terrible disadvantages under which she would labour in such a
struggle, and to avoid it by making such concessions as will satisfy
Japan, concessions that will assure Japan's domination of the Pacific.
If she will not give way, then war is inevitable, and the result will be
that the British Empire will be broken up for ever.*

* Tota Ishimaru, *Japan Must Fight Britain*, Paternoster Library,
London, 1936.

The whole point of the book, of course, was to persuade the British government, through public opinion, to stand aside in China and the Pacific while Japan created her empire.

The governments of Britain and the Empire were well aware of the Japanese threat, but the mid and late 1930s were difficult years with threats to peace from many other quarters – Italy invaded Abyssinia (now Ethiopia), there was the Civil War in Spain, Germany had reoccupied the Rhineland. Britain was ill-prepared to meet the danger of a new war. She was only slowly recovering from the terrible years of the Depression; a constitutional crisis culminated in the abdication of Edward VIII; and public sentiment had far from forgotten 1914–18 – 'the war to end all wars'. But, as that decade moved on, Britain did reluctantly start to rearm and the Far East qualified for part of the expenditure.

The Singapore Naval Base continued to be regarded as the vital position in the Far East and further attention was given to its defence. More heavy coastal guns were installed; two more military airfields were built in the north of Singapore Island at Tengah and Sembawang; and a further five airfields were built up-country in Malaya. The purpose of these last airfields was to extend air cover out over the sea. When they were planned in 1935 and 1936, any Japanese attack was still expected to be purely seaborne and directed only on Singapore Island. It was not until 1937 that Major-General W. G. S. Dobbie, General Officer Commanding in Malaya, came to the conclusion that the jungle on the mainland was not after all impassable to well-trained troops and that the Naval Base could one day be threatened by a Japanese landing on the east coast of Malaya and by a subsequent attack on Singapore from the north. A paltry £60,000 was thereupon allocated to General Dobbie for the construction of ground defences on a stretch of coastline a hundred miles long.

Britain's naval policy for the Far East remained almost

unaltered throughout these years. The defence of the homeland would come first; the Mediterranean, with its vital oil and other trade communications, took second priority; and a threat by Japan came only third. By the late 1930s it was hoped that Japan would keep quiet at least until the completion of the five new battleships and six aircraft carriers of the emergency building programme. The main strength of the Royal Navy's capital ships continued to be retained in the Home Fleet and the Mediterranean Fleet; nothing larger than a cruiser was allocated to the Far East. The policy remained unchanged: in the event of trouble a squadron of capital ships would be sent immediately to Singapore. To make sure that this reinforcement could still be carried out if the Mediterranean or the Suez Canal became closéd, extra fuelling facilities were constructed at Freetown, Sierra Leone, and at Simonstown in South Africa.

Over and over again during these years the Admiralty was pressured to change this policy and to station capital ships permanently at Singapore. Australia and New Zealand were constant petitioners; the Australians once considered building their own battleships, but nothing came of it. British Ambassadors in Far Eastern capitals wrote many reports asking for battleships to be sent on prolonged cruises, or, even better, to be stationed permanently at Singapore – anything to impress the Japanese. The Foreign Office passed the correspondence on to the Admiralty. The Navy's answer remained the same. It could not spare battleships for the Far East; Europe and the Mediterranean came first; Germany and Italy were the more likely to attack first. Perhaps, when the new battleships and aircraft carriers were completed, the situation would be more favourable.

Germany put an end to some of the uncertainty in September 1939 by invading Poland and starting the long-anticipated war in Europe. Britain's Far East Empire was now in extreme danger, with every possibility of an opportunist Japanese attack while her main forces were tied up by the Germans. Singapore would have to rely on Britain being able to release heavy naval forces in time and get them out to the Naval Base; if the Japanese arrived before the capital ships, then Singapore's coastal guns, and the slender Army and R.A.F. strength would have to hold off the Japanese until the Royal Navy arrived.

2

'Sinister Twilight'

There were to be just two and a quarter years of war in
Europe before the conflict spread to the Far East. What
therefore were the principal actions in which capital ships*
became involved in European waters during the period
between the German invasion of Poland in September
1939 and the early days of December 1941?

Britain started the war with a seemingly impressive
strength of capital ships: twelve battleships, three battle
cruisers and six aircraft carriers. These twenty-one ships,
with five French battleships and one French carrier, faced
five German battleships and battle cruisers. These were
odds well in favour of the Allies, though the summer of
1940 would add six Italian battleships to the Axis strength
while the French fleet would be as good as lost to the
Allies. But it was not just a question of relative numbers;
of the fifteen British battleships and battle cruisers, only
three – *Nelson*, *Rodney* and *Hood* – were post-1918 ships,
and *Hood* was only just so. The carriers, too, were an
assorted lot, mostly converted to this role after being laid
down and partly built as battleships. All the German and
most of the Italian ships were of modern construction, and
these countries also had the great advantage of being
Continental powers with the ability to feed and supply
themselves from the mainland of Europe for many years
without need for overseas trade. They could keep their
ships in harbour until ready to strike while the Royal Navy
had to guard a huge arc from the Red Sea round to Scan-
dinavia against enemy attacks on the overseas trade shipping that kept Britain alive. Britain's main hope for the
future lay in five modern battleships and four aircraft

* Capital ships are taken here to include aircraft carriers as well
as battleships and battle cruisers.

carriers which started to come into service after the outbreak of war. The Germans were building only two battleships – the powerful *Bismarck* and *Tirpitz* – and one
carrier, the *Graf Zeppelin*, though this ship would never be
completed.

How had capital ships fared in their encounters before
the Japanese joined in this deadly game of war?

After the sinking of the *Prince of Wales* and the *Repulse* in
action in December 1941, one of the leading questions was
whether the admiral in charge of the operation had been
justified in risking the two ships in an area where friendly
air cover could not be guaranteed and over which enemy
aircraft were likely to be operating. Although it became
painfully obvious after the event that some of the admiral's
decisions were misjudged, an examination by him of the
main actions in which capital ships had been involved up
to that time would not have led him to that conclusion
before the event. Twelve capital ships were in fact sunk
between the opening of the war in September 1939 and the
end of November 1941.

17 September 1939. The British aircraft carrier *Courageous*
was torpedoed off Ireland by the German submarine, U.29.
The *Courageous* would probably have outrun the submerged
U-boat, whose presence was not suspected, had the
carrier not turned to 'fly on' her aircraft and given the
U-boat captain a lucky shot.

14 October 1939. The British battleship *Royal Oak* was
torpedoed at anchorage in Scapa Flow by U.47. The
defences of Scapa Flow against submarine entry were not
yet complete and the attack was made with great skill.

17 December 1939. The German battleship *Admiral Graf
Spee* was caught by three cruisers – H.M.S. *Exeter* and
H.M.S. *Ajax* and H.M.N.Z.S. *Achilles* – off the River Plate
while commerce raiding and seriously damaged. The *Graf
Spee* put into Montevideo for repairs but was then scuttled
on the order of Hitler.

8 June 1940. The British aircraft carrier *Glorious,* with only two escorting destroyers, was caught off Norway by the German battle cruisers *Scharnhorst* and *Gneisenau.* For reasons not known, the *Glorious* was not flying reconnaissance air patrols at the time. All three British ships were soon sunk by shellfire, but not before one of the destroyers, *Acasta,* had damaged *Scharnhorst* in a torpedo attack.

3 July 1940. The French battleship *Bretagne* blew up in Oran harbour when French warships were bombarded by the Royal Navy to prevent them being used by the Germans.

12 November 1940. Three Italian battleships – *Littorio, Conte Di Cavour* and *Caio Duilo* – were torpedoed in a night attack by Fleet Air Arm Swordfish aircraft while moored in Taranto Harbour. All three sank in shallow water.

24 May 1941. The British battle cruiser *Hood* blew up and sank after a surface gun action with the German battleship *Bismarck* and the cruiser *Prinz Eugen* in the North Atlantic. H.M.S. *Prince of Wales* also took part in this battle and scored two hits on the *Bismarck* before herself being hit and forced to break off the action.

27 May 1941. After being damaged by *Prince of Wales,* then hit by torpedoes of three Fleet Air Arm aircraft and two more fired by destroyers, the *Bismarck* was crippled by the battleships *King George V* and *Rodney* and finally finished off by the cruiser *Dorsetshire*'s torpedoes.

13 November 1941. The British aircraft carrier *Ark Royal* sank in the Mediterranean after one torpedo, fired by U.81, struck her engine room.

25 November 1941. The British battleship *Barham* was torpedoed in the Mediterranean by U.331 and her magazines blew up at once.

Twelve capital ships were thus lost between the beginning of the war and the end of November 1941 – four to submarine attack, four to surface gun action, three (the Italian battleships) sunk in harbour by Fleet Air Arm torpedo-carrying aircraft and one (the *Bismarck*) succumbing to a combination of shells and torpedo hits.

It therefore seemed at the time that the main danger to capital ships remained the gunfire of other capital ships. It might have been reasonable to assume that the four ships lost to submarine attack had all been unlucky – *Royal Oak* at anchor at Scapa Flow, *Courageous* turning into the U-boat's sights to fly on her aircraft, *Ark Royal* and *Barham* sunk by single torpedo hits which caused disproportionate damage. At least four other battleships – *Nelson*, *Barham* (in an earlier attack), *Scharnhorst* and *Gneisenau* – had shrugged off torpedo hits by submarines. It was still believed, and correctly so, that a battleship could elude most submarine attacks if she kept up her speed, and that her armoured belt or watertight compartments could usually survive any but the most unfortunate hit if torpedoes did strike home.

Attack by aircraft had not yet loomed large as a danger to capital ships. None had as yet succumbed to bombing attacks, though plenty of smaller ships, including five British cruisers and twenty-eight destroyers, had done so, while the British battleships, *Barham* and *Warspite*, had withstood direct hits by bombs while at sea, and the German ships, *Scharnhorst* and *Gneisenau*, had done the same while in port. The British aircraft carrier *Illustrious* had sailed on in the Mediterranean after being hit by six heavy bombs and near-missed by three more. Torpedo bombers had been active since the outbreak of war, but, apart from the Taranto Harbour action, had achieved no outright sinkings of capital ships.

Any survey carried out in early December 1941 might thus have come to the following three conclusions:

First, capital ships were at risk when faced with a superior force of enemy capital ships.

Secondly, capital ships were vulnerable to submarine

attack only if they slackened speed or suffered unlucky hits in vulnerable spots.

Thirdly, and despite the forecasts of Billy Mitchell and his like, no capital ship, Allied or Axis, had yet been sunk at sea by any form of aircraft attack.

These are important and not unreasonable conclusions for that time. But, more than this, there had been several occasions when the vigorous use of capital ships by both sides had brought positive success. The sending of *Warspite* with a party of destroyers into the enclosed waters of Narvik Fjord in April 1940 had led to the destruction of eight German destroyers and a U-boat, the only outright British success of the Norwegian campaign. Three battle-ships – *Warspite* again, *Barham* and *Valiant* – had, with the aircraft carrier *Formidable*, humiliated the Italian Fleet at the Battle of Cape Matapan and sunk three cruisers without loss. The Germans, too, had had their triumphs. Their fast, modern battleships and battle cruisers had claimed the *Glorious* and the *Hood*, and the bold use of their capital ships as commerce raiders had resulted in the sinking or capture of fifty-one merchant ships, though they had paid for this with the loss of the *Graf Spee* and the *Bismarck*.

The new war in Europe did not seem to have altered the basic nature of naval warfare. The battleship still appeared to have a future.

This second European war in twenty-five years was again a golden opportunity for the Japanese, hungry as always, to expand their empire. Britain was by now almost totally involved in Europe; the United States were watchful but still neutral. When Holland and France fell to the Germans in the summer of 1940, the Far East possessions of these two countries lay almost defenceless. The Japanese could be excused for thinking that before long Britain would also be defeated and another Far Eastern empire could become theirs for the taking. So the Japanese were able to continue their conquests of China and to start actively planning to

take over rich European possessions. An even more
military-dominated government came to power in July
1940 with General Tojo as Army Minister. A Tripartite
Pact was signed with Germany and Italy later that year,
and a Neutrality Pact with Russia early in 1941.

The Japanese were not yet ready for outright war with
a Western country, but they made steady progress in other
ways. The Dutch were persuaded to step up raw-material
exports from the Dutch East Indies to Japan, though not
by as much as the Japanese would have liked. The British
were pressed to close the Burma Road along which most of
American war aid entered China, and also to withdraw the
British garrisons from Tientsin and Shanghai. The British
did close the Burma Road for three months, but only during
the monsoon season when the road would have suffered
from heavy lorries. And the small garrisons at Tientsin and
Shanghai were withdrawn, but for the excellent military
reason that, in the event of war, they would have been
eliminated in a few hours anyway; the troops could be
better employed elsewhere and were moved to Singapore.

Within weeks of the fall of France in 1940, the Japanese
demanded that Japanese troops in China be allowed to move
into the northern part of French Indo-China. The French
Governor-General had to agree, and in April 1941 the
Vichy government in France, under German as well as
Japanese pressure, had to allow the Japanese the use of air
and naval bases in southern Indo-China. Without firing a
shot, the Japanese had secured bases only 450 miles from
Malaya and 700 miles from Singapore itself. The British
possessions were now well within range of Japanese
bombers.

Even before the war, doubts about the speed at which
capital ships could reinforce Singapore from England had
led to a warning that the island might, in the event of
attack, have to hold out for ninety days rather than the
earlier estimate of seventy days. At the outbreak of war in
1939, Royal Navy strength in the Far East consisted only
of the old aircraft carrier *Eagle*, four cruisers, nine

destroyers and some submarines; and most of these were soon withdrawn to Europe. After the crisis of the Battle of Britain had passed in 1940, the Far East situation was again reviewed. The commanders of the three services there were asked for their assessment of the minimum military and air force strength needed to hold Singapore until the Navy could arrive. This 'Singapore Defence Conference' was held in October 1940, with Vice-Admiral Sir Geoffrey Layton, Commander-in-Chief China Station, in the chair. (Layton would later be involved, though in a minor way, with the *Prince of Wales* and *Repulse* affair.) Lieutenant-General L. V. Bond and Air Vice-Marshal J. T. Babbington represented the Army and R.A.F. Commander A. C. Thomas, the American Naval Attaché at Bangkok, was sent by his government to Singapore, ostensibly to consult a doctor, though he attended the conference in civilian clothes.

The truth was that the British were in a pathetic position just over one year before full-scale war would begin in the area. The Japanese were known to have occupied two French military airfields near Saigon, to have over 400 land-based aircraft and 280 carrier-based aircraft available for operations, and to be expanding this strength fast. The combined strength of the British and U.S. Navies in South-East Asia was weaker now than the British strength alone had been before the war. The conference decided that, with the Japanese now in Indo-China, the potential danger to Singapore was no longer from a sea attack but from a land advance through Siam and down the Malayan peninsula. The conference also decided that it would now be most prudent for the main defence of Singapore to rely on a strong force of aircraft, and so asked for 582 modern aircraft to be provided. Given these, together with additional Australian and Indian army units earmarked for Malaya, it should be possible to hold off a Japanese offensive until the Navy arrived. The actual air strength in Singapore and Malaya was at that time only eighty-eight aircraft, of which only forty-eight were modern machines.

The vast majority of those 582 aircraft was never provided. They existed, in England, but the recent experiences of the Battle of Britain and the London 'Blitz', coupled with the desire of the R.A.F. leaders, with Churchill's full support, to create a huge bomber force with the hope of bombing Germany into defeat, kept them at home. When the Japanese eventually did strike just over a year after the Defence Conference, Malaya and Singapore would only have 158 operational aircraft, the best of them being a slow American fighter, the Brewster Buffalo, and the Bristol Blenheim bomber – hardly modern aircraft in 1941. At that moment, the R.A.F. would have at least a hundred squadrons of modern fighters in England, very much under-employed since the main Luftwaffe strength would have been moved to Russia and the Mediterranean. Only three months after Singapore fell, R.A.F. Bomber Command would mount the first of its Thousand Bomber Raids on Germany. But such errors are easy to see in hindsight.

Immediately after the Singapore Conference, a new command system for the Far East was instituted. For the first time a joint commander for the British forces in the area was appointed. Air Chief Marshal Sir Robert Brooke-Popham, who had retired from the R.A.F. in 1937 to become Governor of Kenya, but who was now back on the active list, was in November 1940 appointed as Commander-in-Chief, Far East. His imposing title gave him command of all British army and air units in Burma, Malaya, Singapore and Hong Kong. It was a measure of the reliance now being placed on the R.A.F. to defend Singapore until the Navy's battleships could arrive that the choice for this important post should fall on an air force and not an army officer. But the Royal Navy's ships in the Far East were expressly excluded from his joint command!

The second of the future participants in the tragedy of the *Prince of Wales* and the *Repulse* had thus arrived on the scene. Pity poor Brooke-Popham, whose parent service allowed him to go out to carry this burden in the Far East but which kept its aircraft at home.

The five-month period from July to November 1941 was destined to be the last period of peace in the Far East and the Pacific. During these months three of the Western powers with interests in the area finally said 'No' to further Japanese expansion, even at the risk of provoking a war which two of them certainly could not afford. For Winston Churchill, the Japanese threats made these months a period of 'sinister twilight' in the Far East. The crunch came over a country and over a commodity that, by coincidence, were both to threaten world stability in entirely different circumstances a quarter of a century later. This country was Indo-China, part of which is now Vietnam, and the commodity was oil.

In July 1941 the Japanese Ambassador to the Vichy government in France was instructed to inform the French that Japan demanded further military and economic concessions in Indo-China. Such an extension of the Japanese sphere of influence would bring Japanese army units much closer to the Americans in the Philippines and the British in Malaya. The Americans had succeeded in deciphering the radio instructions from Japan to her Ambassador at Vichy and informed Britain that the United States was not prepared to let Japanese troops move south in Indo-China and would stop all trade with Japan if it happened. Before taking this drastic step, the United States proposed to Japan that Indo-China should be regarded as neutral, but this proposal was ignored. Vichy soon submitted to the Japanese demands and the Japanese troops did march into southern Indo-China. The Americans immediately stopped all trade with Japan and froze Japanese assets in the United States. The British and Free Dutch followed suit, wanting to keep in step with the Americans at all costs, but desperately alarmed at the prospect of war if the Japanese refused to withdraw from Indo-China.

The Japanese were appalled at this firm American action,

which was entirely unexpected. Their main problem was oil. Japan produced a mere 10 per cent of her own oil needs; 80 per cent of her oil imports came from the United States and 10 per cent from the Dutch East Indies. Although she had stockpiled oil steadily over the past ten years, these reserves could only last for three years, even with the strictest economies. For this modern industrial country, striving hard to build up its forces for a later confrontation with the West at the same time as continuing the war in China, the American and Dutch oil embargo was intolerable. The Japanese decided that they could take one of three courses: (a) back down and withdraw their army units from southern Indo-China; (b) attempt to negotiate with the Americans; or (c) take the ultimate step and prepare for an all-out war in which they could invade the oil-rich countries of South-East Asia and set up their much desired 'Greater East Asia Co-Prosperity Sphere' – the Japanese dream of a federation of Asiatic countries under Japanese leadership.

The proud Japanese had suffered enough insults at the hands of the West over the years; they were not prepared to lose face further and refused to withdraw from Indo-China. Instead, a negotiating team was sent to Washington in the hope that the Americans might relax the trade embargo. At the same time, however, preparations were made for war if the Americans would not cooperate. It is interesting to note that it was the Army in Japan which was keenest for war while the Navy wanted to continue negotiations. There was no separate air force and the civilian politicians and the Emperor were now without influence. As it turned out, neither side was prepared to offer any real compromise.

On 5 November a decision was taken in Tokyo: if no agreement could be reached with the Americans by the 25th, Japan would launch surprise attacks on the Americans, the British and the Dutch at many points, the operations to start as soon as possible after 1 December. Time was now of the essence for the Japanese; with each day that passed her oil reserves were being run down, her potential enemies were reinforcing their garrisons, the monsoons expected at the end of November would make more difficult the operations being planned.

British and American naval plans of twenty years' standing were about to be put to the test. It would be very much a naval war and the battleships would soon be in action.

3

'A Decisive Deterrent'

No large British warship had visited the Far East since long before the war, but with the Battle of Britain safely weathered in 1940, the *Bismarck* sunk in May 1941, and the new King George V Class battleships coming into service, the Admiralty decided upon a long-term plan to assemble a force of heavy warships in the Indian Ocean; then to send it to Singapore as Britain's third fleet – the 'Eastern Fleet'. Public Record Office documents reveal that this fleet was to consist of no less than seven battleships or battle cruisers, one aircraft carrier, ten cruisers and twenty-four destroyers. Together with the American Pacific Fleet based at Pearl Harbor, this force would be a formidable deterrent to Japanese aggression.

But there were several weaknesses in the Admiralty plan. The battleships selected were *Nelson* and *Rodney* with the four old and slow R Class ships, *Ramillies*, *Resolution*, *Revenge* and *Royal Sovereign*, and the equally old but faster battle cruiser *Renown*. No King George V Class ship was included; quantity rather than quality would be the keynote. Then, it was found necessary to refit or repair many of the ships chosen, and also to fit them with the latest radar. And finally, the destroyers could not yet be released from the Home and Mediterranean Fleets or from convoy work. The earliest date given by the Admiralty for the assembly of the Eastern Fleet was March 1942. This document is undated, but undoubtedly refers to the Admiralty policy for the summer of 1941 after the *Bismarck* had been sunk.*

Alas, events would move too fast for this paper fleet ever to become a reality. The next move came on 11

* The document is Public Record Office A D M 199/1149.

August 1941, while the Prime Minister was attending the Atlantic Conference with President Roosevelt in Newfoundland, having been taken across the Atlantic by the battleship *Prince of Wales*. Roosevelt had informed Churchill that the American attitude to Japan, which had already led to the trade embargo, was about to be stiffened further and that war in the Far East might result. Churchill immediately signalled this information to his planners in London.

Even while Churchill was still in Newfoundland, work began. On 12 August the Joint Planning Staff started to prepare a plan for the immediate reinforcement of the Far East with a force 'including capital ships'. The twentyyear-old-plan to send battleships out to the Singapore Naval Base was about to be put into effect. The proposal was passed to the Naval Staff, and they met the following day, presumably under the First Sea Lord, Sir Dudley Pound. The naval leaders produced a plan which became the basis of their policy for the next two months – until, in fact, they were argued out of it by the politicians. This was that only the old battle cruiser *Repulse*, now more easily available than *Renown* of the previous plan, and the four old R Class battleships be sent to the Indian Ocean. This plan reflects the great reluctance of the Admiralty to let any of their modern battleships leave European waters. Their fear was that the fast German battleship *Tirpitz*, or the battle cruisers *Scharnhorst* and *Gneisenau*, might sail to attack the Atlantic trade convoys; it was a good example of the way a handful of German capital ships was able to tie down the Royal Navy for years without actually leaving harbour.

These deliberations in August 1941 were taking place at a time when the Americans were quietly taking over some responsibility for the protection of North Atlantic convoys. Sir Dudley Pound and the Naval Staff decided to lay down their terms for the release of a modern British battleship for the Eastern Fleet. At the First Sea Lord's meeting at the Admiralty on 20 August, it was concluded that should the U.S.A. provide a sufficiently strong striking force of modern battleships capable of engaging *Tirpitz* and be prepared to allow one of these ships to replace one of our own King George V Class if damaged, then it would be possible to send one of the King George V Class to the Far East or Indian Ocean in addition to *Nelson*, *Rodney*, four R Class and *Renown*.*

In other words, if the Americans were prepared to send not just escort vessels to protect convoys but several modern battleships to Scapa Flow to serve with the British Fleet at a time when the United States was not at war with Germany, then the Admiralty would send one modern British battleship to the Far East to defend Singapore in the event of a Japanese attack. It was a condition that the Admiralty knew could hardly be met, and amounted to a virtual refusal to release a modern battleship.

Churchill was back in London by the end of the month, and soon made his views known to the First Sea Lord in one of his celebrated 'Action This Day' personal minutes.

It should become possible in the near future to place a deterrent squadron in the Indian Ocean. Such a force should consist of the smallest number of the best ships. The most economical disposition would be to send *Duke of York* as soon as she is clear of constructional defects, via Trinidad and Simonstown to the East. She could be joined by *Repulse* or *Renown* and one aircraft carrier of high speed. This powerful force might show itself in the triangle Aden-Singapore-Simonstown. It would exert a paralysing effect upon Japanese Naval action. The *Duke of York* could work up on her long voyage to the East, leaving the C.-in-C. Home Fleet with two K.G.V.s which are thoroughly efficient. It would be in my opinion a more thrifty and fruitful use of our resources than to send *Prince of Wales* from regions where she might, though it is unlikely, meet *Tirpitz*.†

Several implications of this important minute should be looked at more closely. Churchill clearly wanted a small fleet of quality – a fast, hard-hitting combination of battleship, battle cruiser and aircraft carrier. In later documents on the same subject it becomes clear that Churchill did not

* Public Record Office ADM 199/1149.
† Public Record Office PREM 163/3.

fear a direct Japanese attack on Singapore or Malaya, seeing the greatest potential danger as coming from Japanese ships attacking British trade shipping in the Pacific and Indian Oceans. Churchill therefore wanted a fast *offensive* or 'hunting-down' force on the lines of that which had so recently destroyed the *Bismarck*. The Admiralty wanted a larger *defensive* force of ships to protect Malaya and Singapore. Churchill's choice of *Duke of York* is an interesting one. This was the third of the five King George V Class battleships, only recently completed, and Churchill was obviously saying to the Admiralty, 'Give me one aircraft carrier and this latest, unready, King George V Class battleship and I will leave you with *Nelson*, *Rodney* and the two more experienced modern battleships, *King George V* and *Prince of Wales*, to look after any German ships coming out into the Atlantic.'

Churchill was badly in error over two major parts of his reasoning. First, the Japanese were already planning an attack on Malaya and, through it, on Singapore; and secondly, had the Japanese limited themselves to raiding actions against British shipping, just three British ships would have been of very little use against the Japanese Navy with its strong force of battleships and aircraft carriers. His reference to the exertion by his three ships of a 'paralysing effect upon Japanese Naval action' was soon to look a little ludicrous, but Churchill was not the only one in these months to so seriously underestimate Japanese intentions and capabilities.

Churchill's note was followed three days later by a long reply from Sir Dudley Pound in which the Admiralty put forward many, quite valid, reasons why all three King George V battleships should remain at home and repeated their intention of building up the larger force of older ships in the East. Churchill did not accept this without a counter-blast on the following day. It contained no new views, but several powerful arguments in support of his original position. It is worth recording in full the contents of this minute, for not only does it set out fully Churchill's policy which eventually resulted in the dispatch of the *Prince of Wales* and the *Repulse* to the Far East, but is also a good example of the vigorous way Churchill set about his service leaders, without mincing words:

1. It is surely a faulty disposition to create in the Indian Ocean a fleet considerable in numbers, costly in maintenance and manpower, but consisting entirely of slow, obsolescent or unmodernized ships which can neither fight a fleet action with the main Japanese force nor act as a deterrent upon his modern fast heavy ships, if used singly or in pairs as raiders. Such dispositions might be forced upon us by circumstances but they are inherently unsound in themselves.

2. The use of the four R's for convoy work is good as against enemy 8-inch cruisers. But if the general arrangements are such that the enemy is not afraid to detach an individual fast modern battleship for raiding purposes, all these old ships and the convoys they guard are easy prey. The R's in their present state would be floating coffins. In order to justify the use of the R's for convoy work in the Indian and Pacific Oceans, it would be necessary to have one or two fast heavy units which would prevent the enemy from detaching individual heavy raiders without fear of punishment. No doubt the Australian Government would be pleased to count the numbers of old battleships in their neighbourhood, but we must not play down to uninstructed thought. On the contrary, we should inculcate the true principles of naval strategy, one of which is certainly to use a small number of the best ships to cope with a superior force.

3. The potency of the dispositions I ventured to suggest in my minute M 819.1 is illustrated by the Admiralty's own extraordinary concern about the *Tirpitz*. *Tirpitz* is doing to us exactly what a K.G.V. in the Indian Ocean would do to the Japanese Navy. It exercises a vague, general fear and menaces all points at once. It appears, and disappears, causing immediate reactions and perturbations on the other side.

4. The fact that the Admiralty consider that three K.G.V.s must be used to contain *Tirpitz* is a serious reflection upon the design of our latest ships, which though being undergunned and weakened by hangars in the middle of their citadels, are evidently judged unfit to fight their opposite number in a single ship action. But, after making allowances for this, I cannot feel convinced that the proposal to retain the three K.G.V.s in the Atlantic is sound, having regard (a) to the American dispositions which may now be counted upon and (b) to the proved power of aircraft carriers to slow down a ship like

Tirpitz if she were loose. It also seems unlikely that *Tirpitz* will be withdrawn from the Baltic while the Russian Fleet remains in being; and further, the fate of the *Bismarck* and all her supply ships must surely be present in the German mind. How foolish they would be to send her out, when by staying she contains the three strongest and newest battleships we have, and rules the Baltic as well! I feel therefore that an excessive provision is being made in the Atlantic, and one which is certainly incomparably more lavish than anything we have been able to indulge in so far in this war.

5. The best use that could be made of the R's would be, even at this late date, to have them re-armoured against aircraft attack and used as a slow-moving squadron which could regain for us the power to move through the Mediterranean and defend Malta indefinitely.

6. I must add that I cannot feel that Japan will face the combination against her of the United States, Great Britain and Russia, while already preoccupied in China. It is very likely she will negotiate with the United States for at least three months without making any further aggressive move or joining the Axis actively. Nothing would increase her hesitation more than the appearance of the force mentioned in my minute M 819-1, and above all a K.G.V. This might indeed be a decisive deterrent.

7. I should like to talk these matters over with you.

W.S.C. 29.8.41*

These views were sent to the First Sea Lord, but, strangely, the talk that Churchill wished to have on the subject does not seem to have materialized. It was nearly seven weeks before the issue was raised again. During these weeks it was the Admiralty plan for the collection of the force of old battleships in early 1942 that was quietly being proceeded with.

By the middle of October, no one could ignore further the developing events in the Far East. The Americans had kept their British friends informed of all diplomatic moves, and British Intelligence had gleaned a few items from the Japanese side, even though the Japanese were making their preparations under conditions of unprecedented secrecy. As early as 3 June, a British naval intelligence officer at

* Public Record Office PREM 163/3.

Cape Town had reported a considerable increase in Japanese cipher cable traffic between Tokyo and Japanese consuls as far afield as Singapore, Mombasa and Beirut. Another intelligence officer, at Mombasa, reported that Japanese businessmen in Kenya were selling off their businesses and belongings at prices well below their true value and leaving for home. Reports from elsewhere in August and September told of Japanese merchant ships having all their sailing schedules cancelled, painting out all house flags and national markings and being gathered in large numbers at Japanese ports. Japanese naval reservists were being called up and were reporting for duty at naval bases. All Japanese shipping had disappeared from the Indian Ocean. These sundry reports are all recorded in naval documents; no doubt there were many other intelligence hints that the Japanese were actively preparing for war.

On 16 October, a new government with General Tojo as Prime Minister took power. All over the world, diplomats warned their governments that this event had brought war appreciably nearer. The British War Cabinet met the following day to hear the views of Anthony Eden, the Foreign Minister. Eden asked that the possibility of sending capital ships to the Far East be once more examined. No firm decision was taken at this meeting, and there was not much more than the restating of old views. Churchill, supported by Eden, and also by Clement Attlee, the Labour leader in Churchill's Coalition government, all wanted one modern battleship of the King George V Class as a deterrent, Churchill quoting to the sailors how,

we had before us the example of the battleship *Tirpitz* which now compelled us to keep on guard a force three times her weight in addition to the United States forces patrolling the Atlantic. The presence of one modern capital ship in Far Eastern waters could be calculated to have a similar effect on the Japanese Naval authorities, and, thereby, on Japanese foreign policy.*

* Public Record Office CAB 69/2.

Mr A. V. Alexander, First Lord of the Admiralty (equivalent to Navy Minister), pointed out that the two situations cited by Churchill were not comparable; it was not Britain's intention to go raiding Japanese trade convoys as the *Tirpitz* was threatening to do in the Atlantic. This piece of logic was ignored. The First Sea Lord, Admiral Sir Dudley Pound, was not present, and the Admiralty's views were put by Vice-Admiral Sir Tom Phillips, the Vice-Chief of the Naval Staff. Phillips merely repeated the long-held Admiralty view that the older battleships should be sent East. Churchill heard Phillips out, then said he was not going to impose a decision on the Admiralty in the absence of Sir Dudley Pound, but, 'in view of the strong feeling of the committee', he 'invited' the Admiralty to consider the proposal to get one King George V battleship and one aircraft carrier out to Singapore as quickly as possible to join the old battle cruiser *Repulse*, already on her way to the Indian Ocean. Churchill hoped 'that the Admiralty would not oppose this suggestion', which would be finally debated at the committee's next meeting three days hence. There is no record of the Army or R.A.F. leaders, General Sir John Dill and Air Chief Marshal Sir Charles Portal, expressing an opinion on this naval matter.

And so, at 12.30 p.m., on Monday, 20 October 1941, what was to be a fateful meeting of the War Cabinet's Defence Committee took place at 10 Downing Street. Admiral Sir Dudley Pound was present. Sir Tom Phillips, who had represented Pound at the previous meeting, was also there, knowing already that he would command whatever fleet was established as a result of this protracted debate.

Churchill started on a belligerent line. He had clearly heard quite enough of the *Tirpitz* and the Admiralty's desire to keep three King George Vs at home in case the *Tirpitz* came out into the Atlantic. 'The War Cabinet', Churchill said, 'are quite prepared to face the loss of shipping which might take place if the *Tirpitz* comes out into the Atlantic.' Sir Dudley Pound restated the Admiralty position at length. While his statement contained little that was new, he took care to 'note that the War Cabinet are prepared to face this responsibility' – for shipping losses caused by *Tirpitz* should a King George V battleship be sent East. (The King George V battleship now under consideration was *Prince of Wales*; it had been accepted that *Duke of York* was too new and unready.) Anthony Eden backed Churchill. 'From the political point of view there is no doubt as to the value of our sending a really modern ship. The weakness of our political position at present is that the Japanese are not faced with the certainty that the United States and ourselves will act, if, for example, they go into Thailand (Siam) or attack Russia.'*

The absence of any reference by Eden to a danger to Malaya shows how he, like Churchill, had little idea of Japanese intentions, or of how mightily audacious would be the opening Japanese moves.

It is difficult to interpret the full force of emotion through the recorded, written record of the discussion. The Prime Minister said that he did not believe that the Japanese would go to war with the United States and ourselves. He would like to see the *Prince of Wales* sent and the situation reviewed when the *Nelson* had been repaired. It seems innocent enough, and the War Cabinet secretaries have probably condensed Churchill's full statement for the minutes, but it must have been said with enough emphasis for Sir Dudley Pound to know that he was beaten and the Admiralty overruled.

The First Sea Lord's surrender was couched in the form of a compromise. He would send *Prince of Wales* to Cape Town so that the full publicity value of its arrival there, ostensibly *en route* to the Far East, could be gained, but he would not authorize any further movement by *Prince of Wales* to the East until that time so that the current

* Public Record Office CAB 69/8.

situation could then be assessed. Nothing had been said at the meeting about an aircraft carrier to accompany *Prince of Wales*. Like the dispatch of the battle cruiser *Repulse*, this had been taken for granted, and the committee had confined itself to debating the one outstanding item of disagreement between the two sides: that of the type of battleship to be sent. In fact it was planned that H.M.S. *Indomitable*, a new aircraft carrier then working up in the West Indies, would be included in the force.

So the decision was taken. The Navy were to dispatch as quickly as possible H.M.S. *Prince of Wales* and H.M.S. *Indomitable* to Cape Town, and a decision would then be taken about the advisability of sending these two ships into the Indian Ocean to join H.M.S. *Repulse* and proceed to Singapore. Only three people Churchill, Eden and Sir Dudley Pound, had taken part in the discussions; once again, the Army and the R.A.F. had remained silent. The Committee proceeded to its next item of business, which was to consider 'Operation Crusader', General Auchinleck's proposed offensive in the North African desert.

There was one strange and, so far, unexplained sequel to the decision. Although Pound's proviso was that the *Prince of Wales* should not proceed past Cape Town without further consideration, Admiralty orders to various headquarters on the day following the meeting announced that *Prince of Wales* would be sailing for Singapore, with no mention of Cape Town. This has always been one of the small mysteries of the *Prince of Wales* and *Repulse* story. Churchill, sending out his round of telegrams to the Empire governments, was quoting the Cape Town plan. Perhaps the Admiralty's references to Singapore as the destination were deliberately spread around in the hope that the Japanese would pick up the information and be suitably impressed that the British meant business.

It should be emphasized that the Public Record Office documents show quite clearly that Churchill, well backed up by Eden and the Foreign Office, had insisted on sending this force of only three ships, from three widely separated points, to Singapore in the belief that it would persuade the Japanese to make no further moves in South-East Asia. Churchill and Eden clearly did not consider Malaya and Singapore to be threatened by direct attack. The Admiralty had concurred with the general intention of this move, but had consistently opposed, until overruled, the inclusion of the King George V Class ship in this force on the grounds that its dispatch would encourage the *Tirpitz* to come out. In fact the Admiralty were probably more realistic in their assessments of the danger to Malaya, though they did not make much of this argument.

Time was running out. Within a week of the War Cabinet decision, Naval Intelligence was reporting that the Imperial Japanese Navy had fully mobilized on a war footing and was concentrated at Sasebo Naval Base in southern Japan.

4

Force G

Even under the pressure of imminent war in the Far East, it would take several weeks to assemble the three large ships of Force G and their attendant escorts. The *Prince of Wales* was at Scapa Flow, having only recently returned from operations in the Mediterranean. The new aircraft carrier *Indomitable* was three days out into the Atlantic from Greenock on her way to the quiet waters of the Caribbean. Once there, she would complete the working up of her ship's company and Fleet Air Arm squadrons before proceeding round the Cape of Good Hope to join the remainder of Force G. Only the battle cruiser *Repulse* was even part-way to Singapore, having arrived in the Indian Ocean earlier in the month. There were in the Far East only the ships of the China Station, with Headquarters ashore at Singapore, and nothing heavier than three old light cruisers. The Eastern Fleet could come into being only when the various ships of Force G reached Singapore.

H.M.S. *Repulse* was just a quarter of a century old, having been launched at John Brown's Clydebank yard on 8 January 1916 and being completed ready for service in August of that year. It was originally intended that she would become one of the seven R Class battleships, the first of which were already under construction in 1914, but it was decided to alter drastically the design of two of this class from battleships to battle cruisers. Hence *Repulse* and her only sister ship, *Renown*, finished up more lightly protected and less heavily gunned but a clear 8 knots faster than the R Class battleships. *Repulse*'s main armament consisted of six 15-in. guns in two double turrets forward and one aft, and the secondary armament consisted of nine 4-in. guns. Her weight was 32,000 tons – 36,800 fully loaded – and the top speed was 32 knots. As usual with capital ships built at that time, underwater bulges up to fourteen feet wide were built outside the main hull to absorb the force of a torpedo hit.

With her graceful lines and slim beam, this fast battle cruiser was pleasing in appearance. She and the *Renown* were certainly the most elegant big ships in the Royal Navy at the time and, with the *Hood*, built two years later, remained so for many years. In the summer of 1916 *Repulse* reported for service with the Grand Fleet at Scapa Flow just after the Battle of Jutland. As three battle cruisers had been blown up under German shellfire in the battle, the new arrival was immediately sent back for more armour plating, even though battle cruisers were intended to have a fast, roving commission in war and should not have been expected to withstand the slogging match of a fleet action on Jutland lines. Before the First World War ended, *Repulse* did manage to take part in one brief, inconclusive action with German ships in the engagement off the Horn Reefs in the Heligoland Bight in November 1917. She covered the retirement of a squadron of British light cruisers and her 15-in. guns scored a hit on the German cruiser *Königsberg*. That single hit was destined to be the only one scored by *Repulse*'s great guns in her whole career.

From 1918 to 1939, *Repulse* lived the typical peacetime life of a Royal Navy capital ship with a mixture of home service and foreign cruising. She took Edward, Prince of Wales, to South America and South Africa in 1925, and another voyage included a call at Singapore, many years later to be the starting-point of *Repulse*'s last voyage. There were two extensive refits costing over £2 million in all; these kept *Repulse* in good shape for the next war, but she was never re-engined like the *Renown*, although her ageing machinery was still capable of producing a useful 29 knots when required. During her last refit, *Repulse* had been fitted with special accommodation to take the newly crowned King George VI and Queen Elizabeth on the 1939

Royal Visit to Canada, but a last-minute decision not to allow the battle cruiser to leave European waters in that year of crisis meant that she could do no more than escort the King and Queen on the first part of their voyage aboard the liner *Empress of Australia*.

So the coming of war in September 1939 found the *Repulse* ready, in sound condition and still fast, with a powerful armament and accommodation fit for a king. If she had one drawback other than the thin armoured protection of all battle cruisers, it was the quantity and quality of her anti-aircraft armament. This was composed of just six hand-operated high-angle 4-in. guns and three sets of eight-barrelled 2-pounder 'pom-poms'.

Repulse was at sea within four days of the outbreak of war, serving on the Northern Patrol between Scotland and Iceland, guarding against German naval units trying to get out into the Atlantic and among the British merchant shipping there, and also against blockade-running merchant ships trying to reach Germany. When German raiders did get into the Atlantic, *Repulse* sailed as heavy escort with trade convoys and formed part of the escort for the convoy of five liners which brought the 20,000 soldiers of the 1st Canadian Division safely to England in December 1939. Then, in 1940, she took part in the naval operations off Norway, but without making contact with any German ships. More Northern Patrol and convoy work followed, and in 1941 *Repulse* narrowly missed being in action with the *Bismarck* when sent out with the rest of the Home Fleet in the hunt for the German battleship. A combination of tired engines and shortage of fuel eventually forced her to break off and put into Newfoundland while other ships had the satisfaction of finishing off *Bismarck* and revenging the *Hood*.

Just as *Repulse* was a representative of the pre-war Royal Navy, so were most of her crew. The ship had recommissioned early in 1939 after a long refit, and the crew had been bitterly disappointed to miss the glamour of the Royal Visit to Canada that summer. This 1939 crew, a large proportion of whom were still aboard *Repulse* when she sailed East in 1941, had been provided by the Devonport Manning Depot at Plymouth. It is said that when the Navy had first come to Devonport many years earlier, the sailors were much impressed by the local peoples' appetite for Devonshire cream and 'Tiddley Oggies' (Cornish pasties), and had ever since called the Devonport people 'Guzzlers'. The naval base thus became 'Guz', and *Repulse* what is known in the Royal Navy as a 'Guz ship'.*

Repulse had been built for a crew of 1,181 men with extra accommodation for an admiral's staff of twenty-four if required. Like all wartime ships, she had been forced to take more men aboard for extra weapons and equipment. She would eventually sail into action with sixty-nine officers and 1,240 petty officers and ratings. The increase of 104 over her intended capacity was much less than in many wartime ships, so *Repulse*'s men probably had as spacious and comfortable accommodation as any ship in service at that time. Since she had better ventilation than *Prince of Wales*, she would not be so troubled by a voyage to the tropics.

Captain E. J. Spooner had commanded *Repulse* for the first years of war, but was then posted to Singapore as Rear-Admiral, Malaya, where he would soon be welcoming his old ship to the Naval Base. Spooner was succeeded by Captain W. G. (Bill) Tennant, a tall grey-haired officer of fifty-three, seemingly stern and reserved in character but found on closer acquaintance to be a warm-hearted man and a fine leader. By reputation he was one of the Navy's finest navigators. Captain Tennant had done well at Dunkirk, where he had served ashore as Senior Naval Officer throughout the evacuation and been one of the last to leave. The *Repulse* men were quite proud of their new captain's exploits at Dunkirk and called him affectionately 'Dunkirk Joe'.

* Of the other two manning depots, Portsmouth is known as 'Pompey' and Chatham as 'Chats'.

Repulse's Heads of Departments when she sailed East in 1941 were as follows:

The Commander: Commander R. J. R. Dendy

Gunnery: Lieutenant-Commander C. H. Cobbe

Torpedo and Electrical: Lieutenant-Commander K. R. Buckley

Navigation: Lieutenant-Commander H. B. C. Gill, D.S.C.

Engineering: Engineer-Commander H. Lang

Medical: Surgeon-Commander D. A. Newbery, M.R.C.S., L.R.C.P.

Supply: Paymaster-Commander L. V. Webb

Royal Marines: Captain R. G. S. Lang

Chaplain: Reverend Canon C. J. S. Bezzant

Repulse's more junior officers were quite typical of large naval ships at this time, being mainly a mixture of regular officers and R.N.V.R.s, with three Royal Marine and three Fleet Air Arm officers, the latter for the ship's two Walrus amphibian reconnaissance aircraft. An unusual element among the midshipmen were five Australians who had been sent to join the Australian cruiser *Australia*. On arrival in England in February 1941, they found that their intended ship had departed to the Indian Ocean, and they were posted instead to *Repulse*, then on the Clyde.

It is a little difficult to remember exactly one's impressions on that particular afternoon of joining one's first ship. Naturally to a Midshipman she looked enormous, impressively powerful, and capable of high speed. It was not possible to comprehend how we would ever find our way about or fit into the organization, and one had the inevitable feeling of apprehension about the future, from the personal aspect rather than from operational activities. On arrival we were welcomed by the 'Snotty's Nurse' – then Lieutenant Joc Hayes – and Sub-Lieutenant Dicky Pool, Sub of the Gunroom. (Midshipman G. R. Griffiths) *

* Ranks used in this and the following quotations are those held in December 1941. The 'Snotty's Nurse' was the officer in charge of midshipmen.

Probably 60 to 70 per cent of *Repulse*'s lower deck were pre-war regulars, the remainder being recalled reservists or 'Hostilities Only' men. There were about 130 Royal Marines, and the usual complement of 120 or so of the sixteen- and seventeen-year-old boy seamen carried by all capital ships and cruisers. It is clear, from contact with many of the men who served in her, that *Repulse* was a well-disciplined and happy ship under a popular captain. Not one criticism of any aspect of the ship's equipment or organization was to be heard. Rather there was immense pride in the old ship, especially in her gunnery – 'we could straddle any battle practice target at 26,000 yards' – and also in the fact that their ship was one of the élite battle cruisers and not just a 'common' battleship. There was pride also in the fact that *Repulse* had protected many a convoy in her 30,000 miles of steaming since 1939 and had not lost a single ship from those convoys or had otherwise let down any ship in which she had been in company. But there was regret that her main armament had yet to be fired in this war, and it was the great desire of *Repulse*'s ship's company that they would soon meet an enemy warship against which to try out those six 15-in. guns.

While his ship was undergoing a short refit at Rosyth in August 1941, Captain Tennant was summoned to London and told that *Repulse* was now destined for the Indian Ocean as one of the first members of the new Eastern Fleet. On 28 August, *Repulse* received her orders to sail as senior ship of the escort of Convoy WS. 11,* carrying troops and military equipment for Suez via the Cape. On the last day of the month, *Repulse* slipped quietly out of the Clyde to join her convoy and commence her voyage to the East.

The five ships of the much-vaunted King George V Class of battleships formed part of Britain's emergency rearmament

---

* Each regular convoy run was identified by initials, usually denoting the starting or finishing points of that run. The WS. Convoys were an exception; the initials stood for 'Winston's Specials'.

programme of the late 1930s and were the first battleships
to be built since *Nelson* and *Rodney* had been launched in
1925. The Royal Navy was no longer building battle
cruisers; battleships could now achieve almost 30 knots,
so these new vessels had the best of both worlds – armour
and speed. The biggest drawback to the new battleships
was the limitation on their tonnage and on the size of their
main gun armament imposed by the latest naval treaty.
The London Naval Treaty of 1936 had restricted ships to
a weight of 35,000 tons and their guns to 15-in. calibre,
and Britain had complied. Germany on the other hand, who
had also signed, was designing the battleships *Bismarck*
and *Tirpitz* which would eventually turn out at 45,000 tons
and 56,000 tons respectively and be armed with 15-in.
guns; and the Japanese, who had refused to sign at all,
were soon to build their two Yamato Class monsters of
64,000 tons with 18-in. guns! It was such adversaries that
the King George Vs might one day be called upon to fight.

But the King George Vs did have some advantages,
especially in their main armament. Each ship had ten guns.
The original design had even envisaged twelve, but the
tonnage limitation had posed the choice of armour plating
or guns, and two guns had been dropped to give more
armour. The 14-in. guns were also of an advanced design,
had a range of 36,000 yards (over twenty miles) and a
higher rate of sustained fire – two shells per gun per
minute – than had ever been achieved before. The weight
of shell that could be delivered in a stand-up fight would
thus still be formidable. There were few doubts about the
King George Vs' secondary and anti-aircraft armament.
They had four twin 5·25-in. turrets mounted on each side
of the main deck, each gun being capable of firing eighteen
rounds a minute at either a ship or aircraft target. These
5·25-in. guns had a highly sophisticated control system
and were reckoned to be the last word in anti-aircraft
armament. The close-range anti-aircraft armament varied
slightly from ship to ship, but *Prince of Wales* carried six
sets of eight-barrelled 2-pounder pom-poms, a 40-mm.

Bofors gun and a number of Oerlikon light cannons and Lewis machine guns.

The anti-torpedo bulge of the older battleships and battle cruisers had now been replaced in the King George V Class by a sophisticated system of bulkheads and water-tight compartments intended to limit any flooding follow-ing a torpedo hit to very small areas. Out of a total weight of 35,000 tons, no less than 12,500 tons was armour plating, but most of this was above the waterline. Unofficial propaganda claimed that the King George Vs were unsinkable.

THE KING GEORGE V CLASS BATTLESHIPS

King George V: launched 21 January 1939

Prince of Wales: launched 3 May 1939

Duke of York (originally named *Anson*): launched 24 February 1940

Anson (originally named *Jellicoe*): launched 28 February 1940

Howe (originally *Beatty*): launched 9 April 1940

It is interesting to note that three of the class had their names changed before being launched; it was perhaps thought that Jellicoe and Beatty were names involved in too recent and controversial an action – Jutland – to be used so soon. The Prince of Wales and the Duke of York were the two sailor sons of the old King George V, who had died in 1936 while the class named after him was being planned. There may have been some embarrassment at the choice of name for H.M.S. *Prince of Wales* when the prince became King Edward VIII in 1936, then abdicated in the same year over his proposed marriage to the American divorcee Mrs Simpson, but the choice of name was allowed to stand.

Prince of Wales was laid down on New Year's Day 1937 by Cammell Lairds at their Birkenhead shipyard, and the hull took just over two years to build. She was launched on

4 May 1939 by the Princess Royal in glorious spring
weather and before a crowd of 50,000. At the luncheon
following the launching, the Princess Royal, who had
launched the *Rodney* from the same yard fourteen years
earlier, said she now had 'two splendid God-children',
and Mr R. S. Johnson, Managing Director of Cammell
Lairds, said: 'If I were in Hitler's shoes and heard about
the wonderful work and speed with which we are turning
out new ships, I believe I would turn on my "Axis" and
think twice before coming to grips with this country.' *

But the building and subsequent fitting-out period was
not a happy one and the new and complicated design of hull
and equipment caused difficulties. After the war started, a
heavy German bomb burst between *Prince of Wales* and
the quay of the fitting-out basin during the 1940 Liverpool
Blitz and caused leaks in the hull; dockyard officials and
naval officers were much concerned at the amount of water
that entered the ship, causing a list which one observer
stated to be 14 degrees, though this was probably an over-
estimate. It was the first of many incidents that were to
bring *Prince of Wales* a reputat on for bad luck.

It was decided to get *Prince of Wales* away from Liverpool and the danger of further German bombs as soon as
possible. She was commissioned on Sunday, 19 January
1941, but her departure for Rosyth the following day was
delayed when her four tugs pulled her on to an unsuspected
sandbank before she could even get under her own power.
Prince of Wales then sailed with two of her four screws
lashed down to the upper deck; there had been no time to
fit them at Liverpool. There were more unhappy incidents
at Rosyth – a pom-pom crew fired two rounds in error
while reloading and a nearby dockyard worker was injured,
though not seriously; small fires broke out three times in
the shell room of B Turret, but were soon extinguished;
two men had bad falls and were injured.

The Admiralty had obviously selected with care the

* *Liverpool Daily Post*, 5 May 1939.

officer to command one of its precious modern battleships. Captain John C. Leach was a tall, broad-shouldered West Countryman, sometimes called 'Trunky' on account of a large nose. He was a superb athlete – Racquets, Squash and Tennis Champion of the Navy in the late 1920s – a good cricketer, keen fisherman and gardener. As with Captain Tennant of *Repulse*, there have been no adverse comments on Captain Leach's qualities of leadership. His naval specialist occupation was that of gunnery and, like many gunner officers, he was slightly deaf. Leach had served in battleships in the First World War, had commanded the cruiser *Cumberland*, flagship of the China Fleet, before the Second World War, and then served, appropriately for a future battleship captain, as Director of Naval Ordnance at the Admiralty.

Captain Leach's Heads of Departments in December 1941 were as follows:

The Commander: Commander H. F. Lawson

Navigation: Commander M. Price*

Gunnery: Lieutenant-Commander C. W. McMullen

Torpedo and Electrical: Lieutenant-Commander R. F. Harland

Engineering: Commander (E) L. J. Goudy, D.S.O.

Medical: Surgeon-Commander F. B. Quinn, M.B., B.Ch.

Supply: Paymaster-Commander A. J. Wheeler

Royal Marines: Captain C. D. L. Aylwin

Chaplain: Reverend W. G. Parker

Paymaster-Commander Wheeler found that his son, John, was appointed to *Prince of Wales* as a midshipman, but did not think that father and son should serve together and persuaded the Admiralty to move his son. The two Wheelers were one of the few father and son combinations

---

* Commander Price was also Navigation Officer on Admiral Phillips's staff.

to have served in the same Royal Navy ship in the Second World War.

Prince of Wales would sail into action with 110 officers, including an admiral's staff, and 1,502 men. The crew were provided by the Devonport Manning Depot, so, like *Repulse*, *Prince of Wales* was a 'Guz' ship, but a far higher proportion of *Prince of Wales*'s crew were 'Hostilities Only' men. The best-known rating in the crew was undoubtedly the Manchester-born boxer Johnny King, the reigning British and Empire Bantamweight Champion. Among the 180 or so boy seamen were two sets of twins.

There was no hanging about for *Prince of Wales*. Within two months of sailing from Rosyth for Scapa Flow, she was pitchforked into action even though she had not completed her working-up period: there were still numerous defects in her equipment and dockyard workmen were still aboard. Several books have been written about the dramatic engagement between *Hood*, *Prince of Wales* and the German battleship *Bismarck* and heavy cruiser *Prinz Eugen*. When the Germans were sighted, Vice-Admiral L. E. Holland, in command aboard *Hood*, turned towards the enemy. The range at this time was about on the 36,000-yard limit for *Prince of Wales*'s 14-in. guns, but not yet inside the range of *Hood*'s eight 15-in. guns. Admiral Holland ordered a new course that would converge on that of the Germans, but this would only allow the forward guns of his two ships to bear. For fifteen minutes, *Hood* and *Prince of Wales* closed the range without opening fire, not even when *Hood* did come within range.

It has been suggested that Admiral Holland, who died a few minutes later, was unwilling to try a long-range action in case the unarmoured deck of *Hood* were to be exposed to the plunging fire of German shells when an engagement at shorter range would result in shells arriving with a flatter trajectory. Admiral Sir John Tovey, Commander-in-Chief of the Home Fleet, who was at sea in his flagship *King George V*, was aware of what was happening and nearly sent a signal ordering *Prince of Wales* to take the lead so that her more heavily armoured deck could take the brunt of the German fire. But he was reluctant to interfere, the signal was never sent and Admiral Holland kept *Prince of Wales* tucked in close astern of *Hood*.

During the lengthy run-in, Admiral Holland ordered both ships to aim at the left-hand enemy ship. This was the *Prinz Eugen*, mistaken by Holland for the *Bismarck*. The *Prince of Wales*'s gunnery officers, however, had been training their guns on the more important target of the *Bismarck* and ignored the order. Holland only realized his mistake at the last moment and hurriedly amended the aim to *Bismarck* when all four ships opened fire at the comparatively close range of 26,000 yards.

It was a sorry story. The German ships obtained the correct range almost at once, while *Prince of Wales*'s first five salvoes all fell beyond the *Bismarck*. One of her 14-in. guns developed a fault after the first round and never fired again, and, because of the angle of Admiral Holland's approach, the four guns of the rear turret could not open fire at all. No one is certain where *Hood*'s opening salvoes landed, but they were not on the enemy. The Germans were firing full broadsides. *Hood* was hit almost at once, then again, and this fine ship blew up and disappeared only seven minutes after the first shell of the action had been fired. Three men out of the 1,419 aboard were later picked up by a destroyer. *Prince of Wales* continued to fight on and scored two hits on *Bismarck*, but was herself hit seven times by German shells, one of these making a bloody shambles of her bridge. The four-gun turret aft was now bearing on the enemy, but soon broke down and could not fire.

With the loss of Admiral Holland, *Prince of Wales* had come under the command of Rear-Admiral W. F. Wake-Walker in the cruiser *Norfolk*. He decided that *Prince of Wales* should discontinue this one-sided fight and join the cruisers shadowing the enemy until the main strength of the Home Fleet came up. Although *Prince of Wales*'s log showed that she did open fire again later that day while shadowing, the action was as good as over for this ship.* She buried her dead at sea and was detached to Iceland to land her wounded. Among the thirteen dead were two midshipmen and one boy seaman, none aged more than eighteen years; and one of the wounded officers was Esmond Knight, a well-known actor who was blinded though he later recovered the sight of one eye.

The men on the *Prince of Wales* felt they had done well in this their first action. Despite the technical failures caused by teething troubles in unproved equipment and their own inexperience, they had identified *Bismarck* before *Hood*, their guns had hit the *Bismarck* twice and their ship had withstood the effects of German gunfire. One of their hits on the *Bismarck* had affected the German ship by causing a serious oil leak, which later made the German admiral give up the idea of raiding in the Atlantic and was a major link in the chain of events that led to the *Bismarck's* own destruction three days later. Unfortunately, none of this was known at the time and *Prince of Wales* was not credited with the hits. Her crew were very bitter at the way they had been prevented from using the greater range of their guns and believed that the *Hood* had been unwilling to allow another ship the privilege of opening fire first.

When we put into Iceland to patch up the shell holes in our hull and take in fuel, we were naturally feeling unhappy about the inconclusive nature of our *Bismarck* encounter, but worse was yet to come. Knowing that we had been obliged to act under the orders of two admirals throughout the crucial part of the engagement, we could hardly blame ourselves for failing to sink the *Bismarck* on our own initiative. We went into action as ordered, opened fire when ordered, and withdrew only when the *Hood* had been blown out of the water and we (by then heavily damaged) would have been inviting a similar fate had we not sensibly lengthened the range.

Unfortunately this simple interpretation of the facts was not available to the rest of the fleet, who could only darkly deduce what had

---

* *Prince of Wales*'s log for the *Bismarck* action is Public Record Office ADM 53/114888.

occurred from such cryptic signals as were intercepted from the
battle area. Thus, when the cruiser *Kenya* secured alongside us that
day, we found ourselves on the receiving end of some extremely hurt-
ful and unfounded accusations of being unduly cautious in the presence
of the enemy. Some of *Kenya*'s marines were misguided enough to
couch these comments in blunter terms and in the ensuing skirmishes
our marines amply proved that their zeal for combat was still unim-
paired. Even so, it was a bitter experience. It was bad enough having
to watch such a promising encounter with the enemy's prize battleship turn into a total disaster without having to stagger back with
our dead and wounded and be blamed for decisions we had never
made. (Leading Telegraphist B. G. Campion)

But *Hood* had been an extremely popular ship in the
Navy, and although the charge was completely without
foundation, *Prince of Wales* was felt to have let *Hood* down
and immediately took on the reputation of being a 'Jonah'.

After *Prince of Wales*'s battle damage had been repaired,
she was chosen to take Mr Churchill across the Atlantic
for the famous meeting with President Roosevelt in Newfoundland at which the Atlantic Charter was drawn up.
Churchill's choice of a battleship recently scarred by battle
made quite an impression on the Americans; President
Roosevelt came in a cruiser. After bringing Churchill
home, *Prince of Wales* was soon in action again, this time
in the Mediterranean on 'Operation Halberd' in which a
convoy of merchant ships carrying vital reinforcements and
supplies from Gibraltar to the besieged island of Malta was
escorted by no less than three battleships – *Prince of
Wales*, *Nelson* and *Rodney* – the aircraft carrier *Ark Royal*,
five cruisers and eighteen destroyers. It was a major naval
operation designed to fight the convoy through at all costs.
There were numerous air attacks in which *Prince of Wales*'s
anti-aircraft armament had plenty of opportunity to take
part. The guns and gun crews performed well and at least
two Italian torpedo bombers were shot down by *Prince of
Wales*, but unfortunately one of the *Ark Royal*'s fighters
followed up too closely and was also shot down. The Italian

Fleet was reported to be at sea, and *Prince of Wales* and *Rodney* were detached to give battle; *Nelson* had to be left behind, having been hit by an aerial torpedo. *Prince of Wales* worked up to 31½ knots in this chase, but the Italian ships, as so often, turned back and were never seen. The merchant convoy eventually reached Malta, with the exception of only one ship hit by a torpedo bomber in a moonlight attack. *Prince of Wales* returned to Gibraltar and thence home.

'Operation Halberd' may not have made a big impact on naval history, but it was of considerable significance to *Prince of Wales* in the light of her own last operation, now a mere ten weeks away. Here was a convoy, albeit well protected, that had withstood and fought off repeated bombing and torpedo attacks by aircraft, and the Italians were certainly neither inept nor cowardly in their attacks. It was realized that *Ark Royal*'s aircraft had been an important factor in the defence, but there was still no hint that well-fought battleships had much to fear from aircraft. The torpedo hit on *Nelson*, which had done little more than slow her down slightly, tended to confirm this.

There was another aspect of this operation that attracted attention. Soon after returning to Scapa Flow from 'Operation Halberd', the Commander-in-Chief, Home Fleet, was warned by the Admiralty that *Prince of Wales* was to be sent out to the East. Admiral Tovey protested to the Admiralty that:

the recent operations in the Mediterranean made it clear that, when under way, ventilation in King George V Class is most inadequate in a hot climate and health and efficiency of ship's company will be seriously affected, which will be aggravated by lack of awning and side screens in harbour. Evaporator power is inadequate for long periods at sea and there is every reason to expect failure of V.S.G [Variable Speed Gear] Pumps for 14-inch turrets which is liable to have a serious effect on the efficiency of the main armament. *

It is unlikely that any newly commissioned battleship had

* Public Record Office ADM 199/2232.

ever been worked so hard in the first months of her service as the *Prince of Wales*, but the ship had survived without serious harm, at least not to her structure, but there is some evidence that the morale of her crew was not all it might have been. The lack of time allowed to work up the ship peacefully, the trauma of seeing the *Hood* blown to pieces, the recurring mechanical defects for which time for proper rectification was never allowed, few opportunities for leave – all these had impaired the settling down of the crew. Much has been made of this by other authors; it has been strongly contested by some *Prince of Wales* men, but supported by others. Perhaps this view by one of her crew may be a fair summing up of what the lower deck felt.

When we joined the ship originally at Scapa, starry-eyed and idealistic, straight from initial training, we soon formed the impression that it wasn't a well-run-in ship. It had never been given a chance. I was also conscious that there was not that confidence between the officers and senior ratings – nostalgic for peacetime Navy manning perhaps – on the one hand and the predominantly 'hostilities only' crew on the other, many of whom came from that stratum of society which had good cause to resent the 'gaffers' and upper class generally. I often wondered just what one of my friends from the Liverpool slums was 'fighting to defend'.

The Navy had never had to face this sort of problem on so large a scale. Given a lot of time and training and the elimination of mechanical faults, all would have been O.K., but the ship was hustled from one commitment to another, with petty, demoralizing setbacks. Discipline and *esprit de corps* were no better but no *worse* than could be expected. In the *final* analysis everyone knew the job expected of him and did it. (Ordinary Seaman D. F. Wilson)

We will leave *Prince of Wales* at Scapa Flow in October 1941 so as to look at the remainder of the proposed Force G.

The third of the major ships allocated to Force G was the aircraft carrier *Indomitable*, commanded by Captain H. E. Morse, D.S.O. This was one of the modern 23,000-ton Illustrious Class carriers, and she had only been launched at Vickers Armstrong's Wallsend-on-Tyne yards the previous year. *Indomitable* was still not fully worked up and had just been sent to the West Indies to complete her working-up period at Bermuda and Kingston, Jamaica. There were four Fleet Air Arm squadrons on board: 800 Squadron with twelve Fulmars, 827 and 831 Squadrons each with twelve Albacores and 880 Squadron with nine Hurricanes. With these aircraft and her speed of 31 knots, *Indomitable* would have been an ideal partner for *Prince of Wales* and *Repulse*.

But on 3 November, only one week after *Indomitable* reached Bermuda, the Admiralty received the following signal from the aircraft carrier:

REGRET TO REPORT SHIP GROUNDED AT 16.21R/3 WITH STEM IN POSITION 174 DEGREES 600 FEET FROM RACKUM CAY BEACON. WAY WAS NEARLY OFF BUT SHIP IS FAST FROM STEM FOR ABOUT 100 FEET. AM LIGHTENING SHIP. NO TUG AVAILABLE HERE. WEATHER AND SEA CALM. NO WIND.

Indomitable had run aground on the reef just before entering Kingston harbour. It must have been a badly charted area as the tiny corvette *Clarkia*, escorting *Indomitable*, also went aground at the same spot. *Indomitable* managed to get off the reef by her own efforts the next morning and went into Kingston for an inspection by divers. The hull plating was found to be badly torn, and, once her aircraft had flown off to a local airfield, *Indomitable* was ordered to the United States for dry-docking and repair. She reached Norfolk, Virginia, within the week and became Job No. S.139 in the U.S. Navy Dockyard there.

The Americans were to do a fast job on *Indomitable*, and she would be away again twelve days later. After picking up her aircraft at Kingston, she would set off for the Cape of Good Hope and Singapore, but it would be too late. By the time she reached the Indian Ocean the Japanese would have attacked and *Prince of Wales* and *Repulse* be beyond the help of *Indomitable*'s aircraft. *

The composition of the destroyer escort allocated to Force G would eventually change from that originally ordered by the Admiralty. The first members were the E Class ships *Express* and *Electra*, 4·7-in. guns, 1,375 tons, 35 knots, modern ships built in the mid-1930s. *Electra* (Commander C. W. May) and *Express* (Lieutenant-Commander F. J. Cartwright) were detached from the Home Fleet at the same time as *Prince of Wales*, and would sail out from England with the battleship. Both destroyers had already had an eventful war. On the very first day, *Electra* had helped to rescue survivors when the liner *Athenia* was sunk by a German submarine; and it had been *Electra* that picked up *Hood*'s three survivors in the *Bismarck* action. *Express* had served at Dunkirk, and later in 1940 had her bows blown off by a mine when a flotilla of British destroyers ran into a German minefield off the Dutch coast; two other destroyers, *Esk* and *Ivanhoe*, were lost in that incident, but *Express* returned to have new bows fitted at Hull.

The Mediterranean Fleet was ordered to give up two of its destroyers to join Force G later in the Indian Ocean. Those chosen were *Encounter* (Lieutenant-Commander E. V. St J. Morgan), another E Class ship, and *Jupiter* (Lieutenant-Commander N. V. J. T. Thew) of the slightly

---

* *Indomitable* was diverted to the Sudan and took on a further fifty Hurricanes as belated reinforcements for the R.A.F. in the Far East. These were later flown off from a safe position south of Java and flew to Singapore by way of Batavia, but they arrived too late in Singapore to have any great effect on the outcome of the fighting there. *Indomitable* gave honourable service during the remainder of the war, mostly in the Far East and the Mediterranean. She was seriously damaged by bombs dropped by German aircraft off Sicily in 1943, and in 1945 a Japanese Kamikaze suicide aircraft bounced off her deck without exploding. The Illustrious Class – *Illustrious, Indomitable, Implacable, Indefatigable, Victorious* and *Formidable* – were lucky; they all survived the war.

larger J Class. The choice of these two was ostensibly that they were recent arrivals in the Mediterranean Fleet and were more easily spared than older members, and also that most of the Mediterranean Fleet's destroyers were F Class ships, so an 'E' and a 'J' could be more easily spared. It was later said, however, that the Mediterranean Fleet had given up its poorest destroyers. Both ships were later plagued with mechanical troubles, and neither was to be available to sail out with *Prince of Wales* and *Repulse* from Singapore.

Since there was already a naval command system in existence at Singapore – that of the China Station with Vice-Admiral Sir Geoffrey Layton as Commander-in-Chief – it might have been expected that, because of his knowledge of local conditions, this officer would take command of the Eastern Fleet that would come into being when Force G reached the Far East. As we have seen, however, the Admiralty had someone else in mind, someone who had had far more contact with the realities of modern war: Rear-Admiral Sir Tom Spencer Vaughan Phillips, K.C.B., then Vice-Chief of the Naval Staff. In this position he had attended the two important War Cabinet meetings that had made the decision to send *Prince of Wales* and *Indomitable* to join *Repulse* in the Far East. It may be assumed that Phillips had supported his chief, Sir Dudley Pound, in opposing so bitterly the inclusion of *Prince of Wales* in this force.

Sir Tom Phillips was fifty-three years old and had been a naval officer for thirty-seven of those years. His early speciality had been navigation, so often in the Royal Navy a stepping stone to high rank. He had served in the First World War as a lieutenant in the cruiser *Bacchante* at the Gallipoli landings in 1915, but had missed the great naval action at Jutland in 1916. He was a captain and in command of his own ship before the war finished. After the war, a spell at the Staff College was followed by a variety of staff positions, mostly of some importance. He was

Assistant Director of Plans at the Admiralty, Chief of
Staff to Commander-in-Chief, East Indies, and finally
Director of Plans at the Admiralty from 1935 to 1939.
Then came his first big command position: Commodore
Commanding Home Fleet Destroyer Flotillas.

Just before the outbreak of war, Phillips had come to the
important post of Deputy Chief of the Naval Staff, a post
redesignated Vice-Chief of the Naval Staff in 1940. In this
position, for the whole of the German war to date, he had
acted as immediate deputy to the First Sea Lord with
special responsibility for operational matters, and would
certainly have been well up on all the latest operational
principles and thinking. Phillips had also been very close
to Churchill, First Lord in 1939 and Prime Minister from
1940, but their relationship had cooled after disputes over
the effectiveness of the R.A.F.'s heavy bombing of
German cities – Phillips did not place a high value on this
as a means of waging war – and over the decision to go to
the aid of Greece, which Phillips opposed. Phillips had
always shown an interest in the Far East and was realistic
about the danger from Japan. He had supported the
Admiralty plan to create an Eastern Fleet, although one to
be composed of older battleships only, and had long been
earmarked as Commander-in-Chief of such a Fleet when it
could be assembled. Churchill was probably not too sorry
to see him leave the Admiralty.

Much has been written about this officer. His intellect
and determination had always been recognized as first
class. He liked to take firm, centralized control of any
situation, did not delegate much, and was a stickler for
detail. He was a man of small stature, and his nickname in
the Navy was 'Tom Thumb' Phillips. In general, it
might be said that he was well experienced in naval
strategy, highly respected but not unduly popular and
certainly not an easy man to get on with.

There were at least two reservations to be made about
the appointment of Sir Tom Phillips to command the
Eastern Fleet. First, he had seen no action since 1917 and

had not been to sea since 1939. Secondly, he had no great opinion of the effectiveness of the modern aeroplane or the danger it posed to warships. We have already seen how no capital ship had yet been sunk, or even seriously damaged, by aircraft while at sea and Phillips's views on the many smaller ships that had succumbed to aircraft attack was that they had been unlucky to be caught alone or had not been properly handled. But Phillips was clearly not the only Royal Navy officer to underestimate the danger of aircraft, and later events in the Pacific would soon show that the Royal Navy was not the only navy to contain such officers. Yet it is probable that Phillips's views were considerably more out of touch and mistaken than those of most of his contemporaries.

The following illuminating quotation is by General Lord Ismay – in 1941 Major-General Sir Hastings Ismay, Chief of Staff in the office of the Ministry of Defence and a participant in many of the discussions leading up to the dispatch of Force G. Before studying it, the reader must take into consideration the fact that these views are those of an army officer and an R.A.F. officer about a naval officer and may be touched with anti-naval prejudice. The Arthur Harris mentioned in the passage became Commander-in-Chief of Bomber Command in 1942, and when he worked with Ismay and Phillips before the war had certainly objected to the huge expenditure on the Navy between the wars and the failure to recognize the R.A.F. as an equal service. Here is what Hastings Ismay wrote after the war:

After a good deal of discussion with the Admiralty, it was decided that an Eastern Fleet would be formed and consist of the *Prince of Wales*, the *Repulse* and the aircraft carrier *Indomitable*. This Fleet was to be under the command of Admiral Sir Tom Phillips. We had worked together for many years in peace and war and I had always greatly admired his courage, industry, integrity and professional competence. His whole heart and soul were in the Navy, and he believed that there was nothing that it could not do. In particular, he refused to admit that properly armed and well-fought ships had anything to fear from air power. Nor was he alone in that opinion. Even Winston Churchill, whose forecasts were not often at fault, was one of the many who did not 'believe that well-built modern ships properly defended by armour and A.A. guns were likely to fall a prey to hostile aircraft'.

The battles royal which raged between Tom Phillips and Arthur Harris when they were Director of Plans in their respective departments were never-ending and always inconclusive. On one occasion, when the situation which would arise in the event of Italy entering the war on the side of Germany was under discussion, Tom Phillips insisted that our Fleet would have free use of the Mediterranean however strong the Italian Air Force might be. Bert Harris exploded, 'One day, Tom, you will be standing on a box on your bridge (Tom was diminutive in stature) and your ship will be smashed to pieces by bombers and torpedo aircraft; as she sinks, your last words will be, 'that was a . . . great mine!'

Tom Phillips came to say goodbye to me before he sailed. He was blissfully happy at the prospect of flying his flag after so many years in Whitehall. As he left the room I suddenly felt sad. I am not psychic, nor am I given to having presentiments. But for some unaccountable reason I had a feeling that I would not see him again. *

It should not be thought that Harris and Phillips were enemies; they were the greatest of friends, sharing the same 'diggings' in London. Harris was also a friend of Captain Leach of the *Prince of Wales*; they had met while Harris was at the Staff College at Camberley.

Admiral Phillips would be taking his own staff out to Singapore. His Chief of Staff was Rear-Admiral A. F. E. Palliser, a former gunnery specialist. There would be the usual team of experts and their assistants, including a strong team of communications and cypher officers and ratings. The assembly of this staff was codenamed 'Party Piano', and they were to sail in *Prince of Wales* with Admiral Phillips. A batch of eight R.N.V.R. sub-lieutenants of the Paymaster Branch, newly commissioned from H.M.S. *King Alfred* at Hove, were chosen as cypher officers,

* Lord Ismay, *The Memoirs of General The Lord Hastings Lionel Ismay*, Heinemann, London, 1960, p. 240.

and the communications ratings came from the Wireless School at Chatham.

Prince of Wales had been at Scapa Flow when the War Cabinet decided at its lunchtime meeting on Monday, 20 October, that the battleship should become part of Force G. No time was lost, and before the afternoon was out Captain Leach was summoned to *King George V* to receive preliminary orders from Admiral Tovey. That evening the first ammunition lighter was alongside *Prince of Wales*. For the next two and a half days, the crews of *Prince of Wales* and those of the destroyers *Electra* and *Express* worked to fill their ships with ammunition, water and stores for the long voyage east. At dawn on Thursday the three ships sailed out of Scapa Flow, making for Greenock, where Admiral Phillips and 'Party Piano' would come aboard. Greenock was reached on Friday morning and *Prince of Wales* moored out in the river where a succession of ships topped her up with oil, water and stores. A group of R.A.F. men, probably taking passage for Freetown or South Africa, also came aboard, and a last-minute consignment of Oerlikon light anti-aircraft cannons with ammunition arrived. Admiral Phillips and his staff duly arrived and the Admiral's flag was hoisted in the new flagship.

Two men, one of the newly commissioned cypher officers and the other an older reservist rating recalled for war service, remember what it was like arriving in *Prince of Wales* before she sailed:

There were eight Cypher officers aboard *Prince of Wales*. I think two lived in the Gun Room and the rest of us in the Ward Room. She was not a particularly happy ship. We seemed to be shunned by the other officers in the Ward Room. We had to sling our hammocks even though there were many empty cabooses. We kept our kit in our suitcases until we 'purloined' chests of drawers. (Sub-Lieutenant H. J. Lock)

Our draft fell in outside Greenock Station and marched straight down to the Dockyard where a trawler was already being loaded with our bags and hammocks. We made a last effort to send a message back home but failed and found ourselves packed on board the trawler, on the water once again. As we cleared the entrance to the break-water, quite a number of ships came into view – naval and merchant – and included one big battleship, H.M.S. *Prince of Wales*, and it was towards this that the trawler steered – much to our disgust for most of us, at least our little gang, were reservists or pensioners and had no wish to join up with the 'Real Navy'.

We found everyone on board knew no more than we did and, until they saw the tropical helmets attached to our kit, had been expecting a trip to Northern Russia. The crew had not had much leave during the previous eighteen weeks although many rumours had been cir-culating concerning a long leave whilst the ship docked, so that our coming aboard smashed their hopes. (Telegraphist C. V. House)

5

The Voyage East

At 13.08 hours on Saturday, 25 October 1941, *Prince of Wales* hauled up anchor and steamed down the Clyde towards the open sea; it was only six days, almost to the minute, since the War Cabinet had decided to send this ship to the Far East. It was 'a good Scottish day, one could see for miles'. The battleship had three destroyers as escort – *Electra* and *Express*, her permanent escort, and *Hesperus* (Lieutenant-Commander A. A. Tait), loaned by Western Approaches to provide additional protection for the first part of the voyage. There were mixed emotions among those aboard the ships and those ashore who knew their destinations. The lower deck of the battleship were not particularly happy at the prospect of going 'foreign' without the usual leave; the destroyer crews did not even know that they were setting out on such a long voyage. One young officer in *Prince of Wales* remembers:

I was not alone amongst the young, fired with enthusiasm to do our bit, who thought we were being sent away from the fighting war – and our families – to take part in a 'Fleet-in-being' containment of the Japanese along with the Americans. We were a bit cheesed off. I reacted by embarking some personal luxuries, extras like shotgun, cricket gear, some decent personal oddments – studs, links etc. Others did too. More fool us?

I dare say that those higher up saw the future differently. Admiral Noble said to my father, then a Rear-Admiral on his staff in the Western Approaches Command, as we sailed from Greenock, 'I'm very sorry for those chaps.' He didn't know that his Rear-Admiral's son was on board *Prince of Wales*. As one who had recently been in command in the Far East, I expect he read the tea leaves successfully and rightly. (Lieutenant D. B. H. Wildish)

Admiral Sir Percy Noble had been Commander-in-Chief China Station until September 1940. His Western

Approaches Command was responsible for the sailing arrangements of *Prince of Wales* from Greenock.

The four warships, now known as Force G, made out to the west, passing north of Ireland and getting well out into the Atlantic before turning south to avoid long-range German aircraft operating from France. Because the through passage of the Mediterranean was too dangerous at this time, Freetown in Sierra Leone would be the *Prince of Wales*'s first port of call. The battleship settled down to a steady 18 to 20 knots, any greater speed would have caused the destroyers to use too much fuel. Various patterns of zig-zag were steamed to confuse the aim of any German U-boat that might be lucky enough to find itself ahead and try a long-range torpedo shot; no U-boat could travel fast enough, submerged or surfaced, to catch up from astern. The crews soon dropped into the shipboard routine of a long voyage – four hours duty on, eight hours off, many practice Action Stations, two hours' gun drill every day, much vigilance by lookouts and radar, all incoming signals decoded but radio silence observed and no outgoing signals. The occasional long-range Coastal Command aircraft – Sunderlands, Catalinas or Liberators – turned up to give added protection. Most of the men believed they were off on a prolonged 'flag-waving exercise', and on *Prince of Wales* Admiral Phillips was looked upon as 'a supernumerary and a very much respected nuisance'.

Prince of Wales's log gives details of one or two incidents on the first leg of the voyage. On the first day out from Greenock *Express* caused a stir when she opened fire and signalled 'submarine in sight' but her 'submarine' turned out to be a large floating spar. Two days later a fourth destroyer H.M.S. *Legion* (Commander R. F. Jessel), joined the escorts; *Legion* had been detached from a Gibraltar–U.K. convoy to cover *Prince of Wales* while *Express* and *Electra* went off to refuel from a tanker at Ponta Del Garda in the Azores. Later that night, while *Express* and *Electra* were away, what appeared to be the track of a torpedo was seen passing astern of *Prince of Wales*, but the War Diary of the German U-boat Head-quarters does not record any attack by one of their boats; perhaps it was an Italian submarine or perhaps a mistake by the *Prince of Wales* lookout. If it was a torpedo, it is fascinating to speculate what the future course of events in the Far East or *Prince of Wales*'s own fortunes might have been if the submarine commander had calculated his target's speed more accurately and put a torpedo into *Prince of Wales*. This would probably have done no more than damage the battleship but it would have meant a period of repair and would certainly have delayed the ship's arrival in the Far East by weeks if not by months.

Express and *Electra* returned the following day, and the *Hesperus* and *Legion* parted company for Gibraltar; their involvement with Force G was now over.*

Mr Churchill was kept informed at the progress of Force G and complained to the Admiralty at the comparatively slow speed *Prince of Wales* was making, urging that she push on faster. Churchill also wasted no time in informing the heads of various governments that he was sending Britain's most modern battleship to deter the Japanese, and a spate of his famous 'personal telegrams' was soon on its way. Looked at in the light of subsequent events, Churchill's hopes at the time seem a little optimistic. As Stalin was informed:

With the object of keeping Japan quiet, we are sending our latest battleship *Prince of Wales*, which can catch and kill any Japanese ship, into the Indian Ocean and are building up a powerful battle squadron there. I am urging President Roosevelt to increase his pressure on

* *Hesperus* went back to her normal convoy work and sank a U-boat, U.93, off Portugal in January 1942; she survived the war, though her captain, Lieutenant-Commander Tait, later a successful Escort Group Commander in the Battle of the Atlantic, was lost when his next ship, *Harvester*, was torpedoed in March 1943. *Legion* returned to Force H at Gibraltar, but was sunk by German aircraft off Malta in March 1942 with the loss of eleven men.

the Japanese and keep them frightened so that the Vladivostok route will not be blocked.

And President Roosevelt was told:

As your naval people have already been informed we are sending that big ship you inspected into the Indian Ocean as part of a squadron we are forming there. This ought to serve as a deterrent on Japan. There is nothing like having something that can catch and kill anything. I am very glad we can spare her at this juncture. It is more than we thought we could do some time ago. The firmer your attitude and ours, the less chance of their taking the plunge.

I am grieved at the loss of life you have suffered with *Reuben James* [an American destroyer lost in the Atlantic]. I salute the land of unending challenge.*

Churchill addressed himself to a wider audience on 10 November when he spoke at the Lord Mayor's inaugural luncheon at the Mansion House, the traditional evening banquet of pre-war years having been dropped as a war-time economy. In a rousing speech, Churchill referred to the 'splendid new battleship and aircraft carriers of the largest size' coming into service, and went on to announce that 'a powerful naval force of heavy ships' was being pro-vided for service in the Indian and Pacific Oceans. 'Should the United States become involved in war with Japan, the British declaration will follow within the hour.' This was fully reported, as Churchill intended it should be, and was all part of the plan to persuade the Japanese not to go to war.

On 5 November, eleven days out from Greenock, *Prince of Wales* with her two destroyers put into Freetown. This was one of the intermediate refuelling points established by the Admiralty well before the war in the event of the Mediterranean being blocked to the safe passage of a fleet being sent to Singapore. Although Force G was hardly a fleet, this was a good example of the steady unfolding of the twenty-year-old plan to reinforce the Far East. Some

* Both these documents are from Public Record Office CAB 65/24.

shore leave was given in Freetown that night, and a few men failed to return to *Prince of Wales* when the battleship sailed next day.

Sunderland flying boats of 95 Squadron, based in Sierra Leone, flew further anti-submarine patrols until the range became too great. Sergeant Fowler was a signaller in the last Sunderland to escort Force G.

I recall our last moments with the battleship. She looked a magnificent sight and, despite wartime livery, her lines, armament and decks stood out giving an impression of speed, strength and impregnability. As was our practice on leaving a big ship, we 'beat up' her bows at low level – probably about 100 feet – making two or three runs and then informally waved to the crew. We had been under a tightly enforced communications silence throughout these patrols; however, prior to our final departure we flashed by Aldis lamp to the battleship, 'Good Luck KG5', meaning King George the Fifth. The response was an immediate, 'Thank You – but we are the POW.' We were highly amused at being caught out, although the two ships were very similar in every way. We then gave the POW a final 'beat up' and turned for our base.

Soon after leaving Freetown, the traditional 'Crossing the Line' ceremony was performed for the many men on board who had never before crossed the Equator, but conditions on board were by now becoming extremely uncomfortable in the hot climate because of the ship's poor ventilation.

Conditions inside the ship were getting rather trying by then. Our mess deck had no portholes and was just above one of the boiler rooms so that the constant temperature was about 95 to 100 degrees. The only time my skin was dry was when I got onto the upper deck. The hammock soon became impossible – unable to sleep with pillow and bedding damp with perspiration. Conditions were much the same in the wireless office and reading signals was a sticky job. My hands suffered with prickly heat in the shape of small blisters spread all over them but, as most of the ship's company were suffering from the same complaint, it was just a case of carrying on. (Telegraphist C. V. House)

Surgeon-Commander F. B. Quinn, the Fleet Medical

Officer, had earlier warned Admiral Phillips of the dangers
of heat exhaustion and asked that ratings in positions
between decks should not be kept closed up at Action
Stations for long periods unless it was absolutely essential.
Many men took to sleeping on deck, but, while on duty,
they were subject to great hardship, particularly the engine
and boiler-room men, and several stokers collapsed despite
the introduction of two-hour spells of duty in the hotter
compartments.

Just before reaching Cape Town, the second port of call,
rough weather was encountered. A man on *Express*
records that the seas were the heaviest he ever met in six
years of naval service, and one member of the destroyer's
crew was washed overboard and lost. The two destroyers
certainly had to slow down because of the weather, and
Prince of Wales pressed on alone. The battleship's crew
were told that a number of shore-based aircraft would
carry out dummy air attacks as their ship approached Cape
Town to exercise the gun crews, but the 'attackers' could
not locate *Prince of Wales* in poor visibility and the exercise
was abandoned. *Prince of Wales* came into Table Bay soon
after breakfast time on 16 November, having taken ten
days to steam from Freetown. *Electra* and *Express* put into
the near-by Simonstown Naval Base that afternoon.

It had been intended that Force G would remain at
Cape Town for a week. Churchill wanted Admiral
Phillips to meet Field-Marshal Smuts, the Empire states-
man whose opinion and support Churchill valued so
highly. He also wanted Smuts to visit *Prince of Wales*.
There was, besides, the promise to the Admiralty to reconsider the future movements of *Prince of Wales* at this point.
Finally, the crew would have benefited from a period of
rest. Alas, it was not to be. Phillips did meet Smuts, but
only briefly at Pretoria where Phillips flew by air with his
secretary and valet. After the meeting, Smuts sent a
telegram to Churchill which showed that, of the two, the
South African had a clearer insight into the Far East
situation.

ADMIRAL TOM PHILLIPS HAS BEEN HERE FOR MOST
USEFUL TALKS AND WILL REACH CAPE TOWN
BEFORE NOON TODAY. HE HAS MUCH IMPRESSED
ME AND APPEARS ADMIRABLE CHOICE FOR MOST
IMPORTANT POSITION . . . IN PARTICULAR, I AM
CONCERNED OVER PRESENT DISPOSITION OF TWO
FLEETS, ONE BASED ON SINGAPORE AND OTHER
ON HAWAII, EACH SEPARATELY INFERIOR TO
JAPANESE NAVY WHICH THUS WILL HAVE AN
OPPORTUNITY TO DEFEAT THEM IN TURN. THIS
MATTER IS SO VITAL THAT I WOULD PRESS FOR
REARRANGEMENT OF DISPOSITIONS AS SOON AS
WAR APPEARS IMMINENT. IF JAPANESE ARE
REALLY NIPPY THERE IS HERE OPENING FOR
FIRST CLASS DISASTER.*

No records have been released giving details of the
promised reconsideration whether *Prince of Wales* should
now proceed to Singapore. At home the naval situation
was quiet, while the situation in the Far East continued to
deteriorate. If there had been close cooperation between
Germany and Japan at this time – which there was not –
the Germans could have caused real difficulties by making
threatening moves with *Tirpitz* which might have induced
the Admiralty and Churchill to bring *Prince of Wales* back
to Europe. However, nothing of the sort took place and,
after only a two-day stay instead of the proposed week,
Admiral Phillips was ordered by the Admiralty to leave
Cape Town.

It had still been a very happy two days for the men of
Prince of Wales and the two destroyers. The *Prince of
Wales* had arrived on a Sunday and an estimated 600 cars
had been waiting at Cape Town harbour to carry away the
crew to private homes, farms and sightseeing trips; most
men had at least one night ashore and the survivors of the
Prince of Wales cannot speak too highly of the hospitality

* Public Record Office PREM 3 163/3.

shown to them. For the many men who were not to survive, this South African hospitality was their last taste of
civilian conviviality.

Some events planned for the Cape Town visit had to be
rushed or cancelled. Workmen fitted the four Oerlikon
light anti-aircraft guns put aboard at Greenock, two near
the bridge and two on the quarterdeck. It had been
arranged that selected officers and ratings would be inter-
viewed by the local press, but this was cancelled, as was a
visit to the ship by press photographers. The local papers
were allowed to report the visit the day after *Prince of
Wales* left and to identify the battleship by name, though
the local censor only allowed vague references to the ship's
future movements.

The censor had earlier been ordered to treat Force G's
visit as 'Most Secret' and to arrange that all cables in
cypher to Japan, France and Spain be held up for seven
days. The local police were also alert, and picked up the
radio operator of a Greek merchant ship who had broken
regulations and taken a photograph of *Prince of Wales*.
The Greek was charged at the Cape Town court and sen-
tenced to three weeks in prison or a fine of £10.

Prince of Wales took on thirty-nine fresh ratings, most
of whom were naval prisoners who had 'jumped' previous
ships visiting South Africa. Captain Leach welcomed these
men to *Prince of Wales*, promised them a fresh start and
let it be known that their previous bad records would not
henceforth be mentioned. The battleship sailed on the
afternoon of 18 November, short once again of a few crew
members who had deserted. Ironically, the aircraft carrier
Hermes had that morning come into Simonstown Naval
Base for a refit after recent service in the Indian Ocean.
Although *Hermes* was the smallest of the Royal Navy's
carriers, with room for only fifteen aircraft, it is strange
that no consideration at all seems to have been given to
attaching her to Force G as a replacement for the recently
damaged *Indomitable*. *Hermes* was not performing any
vital duty in the Indian Ocean and she could eventually

have refitted at Singapore as well as at Simonstown. She would certainly have added to the deterrent effect of Force G. But no changes were made, and *Prince of Wales* sailed out of Cape Town even as what was virtually a spare aircraft carrier sailed into Simonstown a few miles away.

It took another ten-day voyage for Force G to reach Colombo. It was, again, a cruise under the hot weather conditions that were such a trial to the crew. *Prince of Wales*'s Engineering Officer, Commander L. J. Goudy, and her Meteorological Officer, Instructor-Lieutenant T. W. Smith, took readings of the temperatures in some of the worst-ventilated positions. These are some examples of the temperatures found:

Engine Rooms – 105 to 122 degrees
Boiler Rooms – 125 to 136 degrees
X and Y Action Machinery Rooms – above 150 degrees when machines run for more than four hours.
Stores and Workshops – considerably above 100 degrees
Torpedo Working Spaces – 100 to 110 degrees
Mess decks – 95 degrees
Officers' Cabins – 75 to 80 degrees*

The voyage to Colombo was broken by short calls at Mauritius and at Addu Atoll (now known as Gan) so that Force G could refuel. Ashore at Addu Atoll was a small detachment of Royal Marines. Sergeant Eric Winter tells how pleased they were to see *Prince of Wales*.

We had been here for something like two months building defences and installing emplacements for 6-inch guns, living on hard-tack biscuits with tins of herrings, sardines, tomatoes and powdered egg. Our water ration was two pints a day for drinking and washing. The *Prince of Wales* did us proud; they cooked us a Christmas dinner, sent ashore fresh bread, fruit, meat, vegetables and other fresh food. Not only that, they sent beer and a tot of Navy Rum; this proved too much for some of those who drank and dined too well; most of them

* The temperature readings report is from Public Record Office ADM 199/1149.

went down with dysentery and diarrhoea. I was one of the few left standing the following day.

Repulse was waiting at Ceylon; the battle cruiser had been out in the Indian Ocean, killing time by escorting convoys off the East African coast and holding gunnery practices. There was a certain amount of shuffling around of the two ships between Colombo and Trincomalee, and orders had been given to the press that *Repulse* was not to be mentioned by name; she was to be reported only as 'a large warship'. This order, originating from the Admiralty, caused much resentment among *Repulse*'s crew. They viewed the arrival of *Prince of Wales* and the prospect of serving in her company with considerably less than enthusiasm. The battleship's 'Jonah' reputation among the lower decks of the Royal Navy had preceded her and the crew of the old battle cruiser, who thought their ship's gunnery the best in the Royal Navy, did not care to be serving under the orders of an admiral in such a recently commissioned and apparently unlucky battleship. One man from *Repulse* recollects that 'there was an instant and bitter rivalry between the two ships'.

The reason for the decision not to mention the *Repulse* by name was a wish to conceal from the Japanese both the strength and the quality of the force about to sail for Singapore. The Admiralty had earlier suggested that not only *Repulse* but also *Revenge*, which was also available in the Indian Ocean, should accompany *Prince of Wales* to Singapore, but Admiral Phillips had given his opinion that *Revenge* should not go.

The two fast battleships in Singapore would cause Japan concern but would be regarded by her as a raiding force rather than as an attempt to form a line of battle against her.

The addition of one 'R' Class battleship might give the impression that we were trying to form a line of battle but could only spare three ships, thus encouraging her.*

It is curious to see this old-fashioned phrase, 'a line of

* Public Record Office ADM 119/1149.

battle', used as late as November 1941. And so the old and slow *Revenge* remained behind in the Indian Ocean to survive the war while the old but fast *Repulse* went on to Singapore. The destroyers *Encounter* and *Jupiter* were expected to arrive shortly from the Mediterranean, but Admiral Phillips was ordered by the Admiralty not to wait for them but to fly on immediately to Singapore to discuss the latest Japanese situation with the commanders there and, if possible, with Admiral T. C. Hart, Commander-in-Chief of the American Asiatic Fleet in Manila. The day after the arrival of *Prince of Wales* in Ceylon, Admiral Phillips flew on to Singapore in a Catalina flying boat.

Prince of Wales herself was to stay little longer. The Admiralty was now urging that *Prince of Wales* and *Repulse* get to Singapore as soon as *Encounter* and *Jupiter* arrived. Several fresh ratings were put aboard both ships to fill various gaps. One *Prince of Wales* telegraphist had been given permission to visit his sister in up-country Ceylon and missed his ship when the sailing time was brought forward; he hoped then to be given a comfortable shore job in Ceylon, but was packed off on another ship and later rejoined *Prince of Wales* just before she sailed from Singapore into action. He survived. One of *Jupiter*'s stokers, Tom Cairns from Liverpool, missed his ship by a few minutes and just had time to be put aboard *Prince of Wales*. He never went back to *Jupiter* and did not survive. After *Prince of Wales* sailed, Captain Leach congratulated his ship's company on the fact that, for the first time since leaving Greenock, there had been no desertions from shore leave.

On 29 November, *Prince of Wales* sailed with *Electra*, *Express*, *Encounter* and *Jupiter* from Colombo, and *Repulse* left Trincomalee. What would soon become known as Force Z assembled at sea and set a south-easterly course for Singapore. With Admiral Phillips absent, Captain Tennant was now senior officer, so *Repulse* preceded *Prince of Wales* on this occasion, much to the satisfaction of *Repulse*'s crew.

There were no incidents of note during this last stage of the voyage. Singapore was reached three days later on the afternoon of 2 December, and the impressive line of ships steamed up Johore Strait and entered the Naval Base. It was without doubt a historic moment. The years of naval planning and the vast expenditure of money spent on the Base had at last borne fruit.

Singapore had been warned that, should Japan attack, it would probably have to hold out for ninety days before the Navy could get there. Now, with the judicious decision of the War Cabinet and the subsequent hard driving by Churchill and the Admiralty, this new fleet had arrived before the first shot had been fired.

6

Singapore

Prince of Wales, being the flagship, was given the best berth alongside the West Wall of the Naval Base, opposite the main office buildings. *Repulse* was left moored out in the stream like the poor relation. Sir Tom Phillips had watched the berthing of *Prince of Wales* and was first of the large welcoming party up her gangplank. It had been announced publicly the previous day that Phillips had been promoted to full admiral and was to be Commander-in-Chief of the new Eastern Fleet.

The arrival of the ships, long heralded in the world's press, caused much interest at Singapore. The Naval Base, officially H.M.S. *Sultan*, was also manned from Devonport, and many men there soon renewed old friendships in *Prince of Wales* and *Repulse*. It had been decided that the exact composition of the new fleet should remain a secret, and local newspapers were directed to refer to the arrival of *Prince of Wales* 'with other heavy ships and auxiliary vessels'. The identity of *Repulse*, the only other 'heavy ship' nearer than Ceylon, was once more concealed – much to the disgust of her crew when they bought local papers.

Only a few press reporters were initially allowed into the Naval Base, and the remainder had to be content with a long-distance view from vantage points outside the base and the handouts of the Naval Press Officer. These restrictions were bitterly criticized in some local newspapers and the authorities relented two days later when *Prince of Wales* threw a big party in the wardroom for the general body of the press. Officers were asked to be particularly friendly to the reporters on account of the earlier 'social error' in not allowing better press facilities. It was all part of the dream world in which the men from wartime Britain found themselves.

The local newspapers gave enthusiastic coverage to the Fleet's arrival.

It is big news not only for Singapore and Malaya but for the whole of the democratic countries bordering on the Pacific; it is bad news for Japan which may begin to see the shattering of her hopes for an unopposed naval advance to the south. *

The *Malaya Tribune*'s military correspondent, Major Fielding Eliot, wrote on the same day:

A Far Eastern detachment [of the Royal Navy] of the size suggested would not be able to seek out the Japanese Navy in Japanese waters and force it to battle, but neither would the Japanese Navy dare venture into the South China Sea . . . In fact, the arrival of some British battleships at Singapore would render the Japanese naval problem in the Pacific quite hopeless . . . Naval aviation is, of all its departments, that in which the Japanese fleet is weakest as compared with the American, and Japanese aircraft production is so small as to be utterly unable to replace the losses of war . . . The Japanese are caught in a trap of their own making and neither by land nor sea nor in the air do they have even a glimmer of a chance of victory if they now appeal to arms against the preponderant forces which encircle them.

Yet Japan had built 5,088 military and naval aircraft in 1941 alone! Such unrealistic optimism was not confined to naval and air prospects. The *Singapore Free Press* had sent a reporter to visit Australian troops preparing positions in northern Malaya against a possible Japanese landing and informed the people of Singapore that

an enemy force invading this area has a poor chance of escaping complete ruin . . . A back-door entrance to Singapore will be closed to the enemy with the same determination which has characterized the fighting of Australians in other spheres of the present war.

The reporters were keen to talk to the recently arrived sailors. One *Prince of Wales* man was found to be 'itching for someone to start something so that we can show him what we have on board'. Much interest was shown in

* *Singapore Free Press*, 3 December 1941.

Johnny King, the Bantamweight Champion in *Prince of Wales*, who was recognized 'in spite of his huge growth of beard' and was found 'eager to fight in Singapore provided permission is given by my Commander'; but Johnny admitted that he was now over the weight for his old class and would have to fight as a lightweight.

By day the crews of *Prince of Wales* and *Repulse* were kept hard at work taking on stores and overhauling boilers and engines after the long voyage from England, though at night there was plenty of shore leave. *Repulse* was standing by to sail to Australia, but the crew of *Prince of Wales* could get to Singapore city fifteen miles away – a 30-cent bus ride or $2 by taxi (there were nine Malayan dollars to the £ at the time). Although a State of Emergency had been declared in Malaya and Singapore the day before the fleet arrived, social life in the city was proceeding as normal. Those men who had never been in the Far East before found it fascinating to walk through the noisy, smelly, but lively Chinese quarter. Many comment that, while the Chinese and other local races were friendly enough, the Europeans were not, in stark contrast to the hospitality the sailors had so recently been shown by the white South Africans. One young sailor wrote to his mother: 'The English-speaking people are very wealthy and won't have anything to do with the Servicemen who are out here to defend them, but we get on very well with the natives.'

There were opportunities a-plenty in Singapore for the sailors to enjoy themselves.

THE HAPPY CABARET
Charming, Happy Girls Ready to Greet and Dance with You
Miss Venus Chong – An Overnight Sensation
Nowhere else such Cheerfulness and Friendliness
Carnival Night in Honour of the Military
Non-stop Dance 8–12pm Nightly

NEW WORLD CABARET
Singapore's Premier Dance Palace De Luxe

And, possibly for officers only:

THE CATHAY RESTAURANT

The Finest Ballroom in the East – Air Conditioned Orchestral Concert by the Band of the Gordon Highlanders (by kind permission of Lt.-Col. W. J. Graham, M.C., and officers). Followed by Dancing to Harry Hackmire's Band with Lisette the popular vocalist.

RAFFLES HOTEL

Dinner and Dance Tonight
Saturday – Tiffin-Time Orchestral Concert

SEAVIEW HOTEL

Tonight – Romantic Night
Dinner Served in the Moonlight
Dancing in the Ballroom

And were any of the sailors invited to the Singapore Rotary Club Meeting at the Adelphi Hotel to hear Dr J. W. Scharff speak on 'Vegetables For All'?

At various cinemas were showing films such as *Blood and Sand* with Tyrone Power and Linda Darnell, *International Squadron* with Ronald Reagan, *Belle Star* with Gene Tierney and Randolph Scott, *A Woman's Face* with Joan Crawford and Mervyn Douglas.

The *Prince of Wales* men certainly enjoyed themselves in those few days of peace at Singapore. There were the usual troubles, including a fight at the Union Jack Club involving sailors, Australian soldiers and the Gordon Highlanders, and thirty men finished up in the Alexandra Military Hospital. Captain Leach had to talk to the ship's company of *Prince of Wales* about the publicity their ship was receiving and warned them not to get 'swollen-headed', particularly when in company with the men from the *Repulse*, which had seen more war service than *Prince of Wales*, or from the old cruisers *Danae*, *Durban* and *Dragon*, which had been doing dull local patrol duties for many months. Captain Leach also warned against rumours that *Prince of Wales* might soon return home. The captain who commanded *Prince of Wales*'s Royal Marines remembers this time.

Viewed from home, Singapore would appear to be remote from war and I believe officers and ship's company alike were looking forward to settling down to a peacetime routine. I had been given to understand that the purpose of *Prince of Wales*'s presence in the Far East was largely political. It was also rumoured that public morale in Australia was at a rather low ebb and the presence of substantial naval reinforcements at Singapore was intended to bolster it up.

So the ships' companies present had visions of goodwill cruises to Sydney and other Australian ports, Manila in the Philippines, and various ports in the Netherlands East Indies. Certainly the vast quantity of champagne, red and white wines and 10,000 bottles of beer that were embarked and stored in the wardroom wine store during the first few days at Singapore gave credence to this idea. The Commander set about having a quarterdeck awning made in the dockyard. The seeming remoteness of air raids would permit a quarterdeck awning to be spread to shelter from the tropical sun those who walked it. (Captain C. D. L. Aylwin)

The diners, dancers and cabaret singers, sailors and soldiers, the Rotary Club members and all at Singapore were about to find a veritable whirlwind blowing through their well-ordered lives.

When negotiations between the United States and Japan approached their climax in November 1941, the Japanese had already taken the decision that, should no agreement be reached by the 25th, they would go to war as soon as possible after 1 December. In the event, Japan extended the deadline to the 29th, but the extra few days made no difference; there was no agreement of any kind. A so-called Imperial Conference was held in Tokyo on 1 December, and no one disagreed when General Tojo insisted there was no option but for Japan to go to war. Because she was unwilling to give up her ambitions in China and other parts of Asia, because she could not live with the resulting economic embargo – especially that on oil – and because she was tired of being treated as an inferior power by the white nations, Japan was prepared to take on the United States, the British Empire and the

Dutch. The Japanese decided that their attacks were to commence on 8 December. *

The scale and boldness of the proposed Japanese attacks can only be described as breathtaking. No less than five separate operations, or groups of operations, were planned to commence on that first day.

1. *Pearl Harbor:* The United States Pacific Fleet was stationed at this naval base in Hawaii. A Japanese force of six aircraft carriers protected by battleships, cruisers, destroyers and submarines was to launch 360 aircraft to carry out what was hoped to be a surprise attack on the American warships in Pearl Harbor. It was known that the Pacific Fleet usually returned to port at the weekend, and the timing of this attack, at dawn on Sunday, 7 December, governed the whole timetable of the Japanese attacks elsewhere.

2. *The Philippines:* Air attacks from airfields in Formosa were planned to cripple the aircraft strength on the American airfields in Luzon. These air strikes were to be followed almost immediately by the full-scale invasion of the Philippines.

3. *Guam, Wake Island and the Gilbert Islands:* These American island-outposts, situated between Pearl Harbor and the Philippines, were to be first attacked by air and then occupied by troops. Airfields were then to be built to cut off the Philippines from seaborne reinforcements from Pearl Harbor or the United States.

4. *Hong Kong:* This isolated British outpost on the coast of that part of China already occupied by Japan was to be attacked by Japanese troops.

5. *Siam, Malaya and Singapore:* A Japanese naval force was

* Because of the International Date Line, the first attacks would occur on 7 December by United States and British times, but on the 8th in Japan and South-East Asia. The times used here will be the local times for the location involved unless otherwise stated.

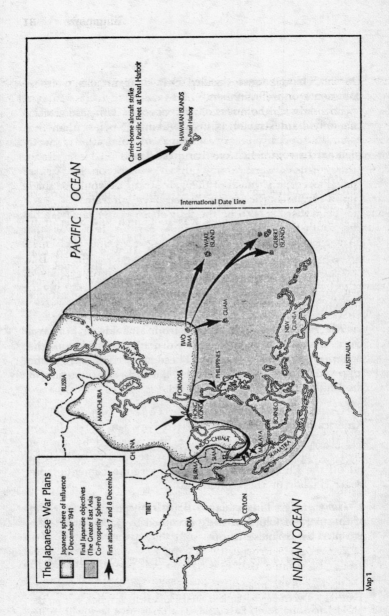

The Japanese War Plans

☐ Japanese sphere of influence
7 December 1941

▨ Final Japanese objectives
(The Greater East Asia
Co-Prosperity Sphere)

➤ First attacks 7 and 8 December

Carrier-borne aircraft strike
on U.S. Pacific Fleet at Pearl Harbor

HAWAIIAN ISLANDS

Pearl Harbor

PACIFIC OCEAN

International Date Line

WAKE ISLAND

GILBERT ISLANDS

GUAM

IWO JIMA

BONIN

RUSSIA

MANCHURIA

KOREA

CHINA

FORMOSA

PHILIPPINES

NEW GUINEA

AUSTRALIA

HONG KONG

INDO-CHINA

SIAM

BURMA

MALAYA

SINGAPORE

SUMATRA

BORNEO

JAVA

TIBET

INDIA

CEYLON

INDIAN OCEAN

Map 1

to land troops at several points in Siam and northern Malaya as a preliminary to the advance down the Malayan peninsula with the eventual aim of eliminating the British naval and air bases on Singapore Island.

For these attacks, excepting only that on Hong Kong, the Japanese were completely dependent on the use of naval forces, and much of their air strength would be made up of carrier-borne or land-based naval aircraft.

This, then, was to be the first phase of the Japanese bid in South-East Asia. Their only serious fear was that American or British warships might escape the initial attacks and break up the various invasion fleets. But, provided the first objectives were successfully achieved, the Japanese planned to go into a second phase and invade New Guinea, Borneo, the Dutch East Indies and Burma. It was calculated that all of these, except Burma, could be taken within 150 days of the opening attack. In less than six months, the Japanese intended to dispossess the United States, Britain and Holland of their entire colonial territories in South-East Asia. There could have been few outside Japan who, if they had known of the Japanese intentions, would have credited that such a grand plan was possible, especially since the Japanese were already fighting a major war in China. But the Japanese, by daring and skill coupled with a savagery that their national code encouraged but which the rest of the world found loathsome, were to prove capable of achieving most of these aims.

Looking back on the whole affair, however, it seems incomprehensible that the Japanese should have expected to hold on permanently to what they called their 'Greater East Asia Co-Prosperity Sphere'. It was reasonable for them to assume that German-occupied Holland could do little to regain the Dutch possessions, but Britain was far from being beaten by the Germans and the vast resources of British India were right on the border of what would become the Japanese outpost of Burma. And did the

Japanese really expect the Americans to retreat into their shell on the mainland of North America without any attempt to make a comeback in South-East Asia? Did the Japanese, who themselves placed so much store on national prestige and 'face', really believe that the Americans had so little of these qualities? Japanese judgement in these matters was clouded by a hatred of the West so deep that they seemed incapable of realizing the consequences of their actions.

It was not going to be any ordinary war.

The Japanese intended to put ashore strong forces of troops at the narrowest part of the Malaya–Siam peninsula with three aims in view: to cut communications between Burma and Malaya, to develop the attack on Singapore to the south and, later, the attack on Burma to the north. Siam was militarily a weak country, so the landings there were not expected to be resisted strongly, but Malaya and Singapore would be a different matter.

The Japanese army units to be involved do not much concern us here. Most had seen active service in China, where they had carried out several previous amphibious landings and had since been trained in jungle warfare. They would perform their task well and were destined to appear at the gates of Singapore a few weeks later.

The naval units involved had been on the move since 21 November. The arrival at Singapore of *Prince of Wales* and *Repulse* had become known to the Japanese, as Churchill intended it should, and had been confirmed by a Japanese reconnaissance aircraft which had flown over Singapore on 3 December. Although there is no evidence that the last-minute appearance of these two ships at Singapore led the Japanese to reconsider their decision to go to war, it did cause them much concern as all their aircraft-carrier force had been committed to the Pearl Harbor operation 5,000 sea miles away to the east and the best of the Japanese battleships were also committed elsewhere.

The Malaya–Siam operation was the responsibility of Vice-Admiral Nobutake Kondo's Southern Force. Kondo himself would keep a distant watch both on the Malaya–Siam landings and on the Philippines operation. He had two battleships in Southern Force: the old ships *Kongo* and *Haruna*, both launched before 1914. The *Kongo* had actually been designed and built by the British during the long period when the two countries had been friendly, and the remainder of the Kongo Class, of which *Haruna* was one, had then been built in Japanese yards to the same design. Both ships had been modernized between the wars, were armed with eight 14-in. guns and were capable of making 30 knots, though they were not reckoned by the Japanese to be a match for *Prince of Wales* and *Repulse*. The closer protection of the Japanese landing forces was provided by Vice-Admiral Ozawa's 'Malaya Unit', and he had nothing heavier than Takao Class 8-in. gun cruisers.

To help to counter the threat posed by *Prince of Wales* and *Repulse*, the Japanese made three amendments to their plans. Two minelayers, the *Tatsumiya Maru* and the *Nagasa*, were sent south to lay a minefield between the island of Tioman and the Anamba Islands – in other words, across the direct route that *Prince of Wales* and *Repulse* might take if they came out from Singapore to attack the Japanese invasion fleets. The two minelayers accomplished their task and laid 1,000 mines during the night of 6/7 December, forty-eight hours before the outbreak of war.

The next move was to dispatch every submarine available in the area to form patrol lines north of the minefield. The ten submarines concerned sailed from Hiroshima and Sasebo late in November, and by 2 December were formed up in three patrol lines while two more submarines were on station near the approaches to Singapore. A further four submarines are believed to have arrived as reinforcements on 8 December.

The third step taken by the Japanese to protect the

invasion convoys from *Prince of Wales* and *Repulse* was to reinforce the air units assigned to the area. Since there was no separate Japanese Air Force, an earlier plan had called for army planes to cover the landings. Yet the Japanese Navy had no confidence in the Army to provide the necessary scale of air cover, and Admiral Yamamoto, Commander-in-Chief of the Japanese Navy, had ordered the 22nd Koku Sentai – the 22nd Air Flotilla – to move from its airfields in Formosa to Indo-China. Rear-Admiral Sadaichi Matsunaga, the 22nd Flotilla's commander, had moved his headquarters to Saigon and his aircraft had followed. The Genzan Kokutai – the Genzan Air Corps – flew into Saigon airfield with thirty-six twin-engined Mitsubishi Navy Type 96 G3M2 bombers, and the Mihoro Air Corps, with another thirty-six aircraft of the same type, flew into Tu Duam airfield north of Saigon. Thirty-six fighters and six reconnaissance aircraft at Soc Trang to the south of Saigon completed the concentration of Admiral Matsunaga's flotilla. But, when the arrival of the two large British ships at Singapore became known, Admiral Yamamoto decided to strengthen this force by taking part of the Kanoya Air Corps away from the 21st Air Flotilla in Formosa. In this way, twenty-seven Mitsubishi Navy Type 1 G4M1s flew into Saigon just in time for the new war.

This redeployment of the Kanoya aircraft was at the expense of the forces supporting the Philippines attack. The aircraft of Kanoya Air Corps became the most modern and effective of the aircraft supporting the Malaya operations, and Admiral Matsunaga now had a total of ninety-nine bombers, thirty-six fighters and six reconnaissance planes with which to protect the landings.

There are several points concerning these Japanese naval air units that ought to be clarified at this point. The Japanese word *kokutai* is normally translated as 'Air Corps', but this is unfortunate as the English 'corps' is usually a much larger unit than the Japanese *kokutai*. The English word 'wing' – a unit containing two to four squadrons – would have been better, but, to avoid confusing readers who have become used to seeing these Japanese naval air units described as 'air corps', we will continue to use that translation. It should be borne in mind, however, that these 'air corps' contained only three or four squadrons, normally of nine aircraft each.

The Japanese did not have different ranks for their Army and Navy. In our translations we use the nearest equivalent to Royal Navy ranks. This will solve most problems, though American readers will know the 'Sub-Lieutenant' and 'Midshipman' better as 'Lieutenant (Junior Grade)' and 'Ensign'. The Japanese warrant officer and petty officer system is a complicated one with many subsidiary grades, and the general term 'petty officer' will be used here for all these.

The British and the Americans code-named all the Japanese aircraft types with English Christian names. The Mitsubishi Type 96 G3M2 became known as the 'Nell' and the Mitsubishi Navy Type 1 G4M1 became the 'Betty'.

There are considerable differences between various sources, including the British Official History,* over the exact number of bombers in the three Japanese air corps, and many works give higher figures. Details quoted above are from the Japanese Official History† and are partly confirmed by the number of aircraft recorded as taking part in subsequent operations. It is possible that the larger strengths quoted elsewhere were the full establishment of the units and that some of these aircraft had been left behind at home bases.

The title of each air corps is derived from the name of its home base. Genzan and Kanoya are in Japan and Mihoro is in Korea.

• • • •

* S. Woodburn Kirby, *The War Against Japan*, vol. 1, H.M.S.O., London, 1957; subsequently referred to throughout the text as the British Official History.

† Japanese Defence Agency, Research Section, *The Book of Military History: The Malayan Area*, Tokyo, 1969; subsequently referred to throughout the text as the Japanese Official History.

The Japanese plans were based on the hope that the landings and subsequent army operations in northern Malaya would rapidly draw into battle the R.A.F.'s aircraft and that the Mitsubishi Bettys and Nells – whose crews had been thoroughly trained in torpedo as well as in bombing work – could, with the two Japanese battleships, take care of *Prince of Wales* and *Repulse* if the British ships ever got past the minefield and the submarine patrols. The main fear of the Japanese was that their invasion convoys might be spotted *en route* to the landing areas, and that the British ships would come out to intercept the convoys before the Japanese actually started hostilities.

Soon after dawn on 4 December, the main convoy of nineteen troop transports with an escort of cruisers and destroyers left Hainan for the four-day voyage to the area of operations. Nine more transports sailed from Saigon and other Indo-Chinese ports on the 5th and the 7th. These twenty-eight merchant ships, together with no less than thirty-five warships giving close and distant cover, sailed on to the south and then west around Cape Cambodia. The troop transport convoys were then to sail north-west towards Bangkok as a feint before coming to the splitting point in the middle of the Gulf of Siam. It was the earnest hope of every man aboard those ships, and of every other Japanese connected with this operation, that Allied reconnaissance aircraft or ships would not sight the invasion convoys. Should this happen, and should the Allies decide to jump the gun and attack first, the whole Japanese invasion plan would be in jeopardy.

The Allies had been aware of many of the Japanese moves, but it is clear that there was still a great reluctance to accept that war was inevitable. A few realistic decisions were taken in those last few days of peace, but many more moves were made on the assumption either that everything would turn out all right in the end or that more time was available than was actually the case. This attitude was the product of two factors: the first-class security being practised by the Japanese and the continuing underestimate by the Western nations of their true ability and potential. To the average European the Japanese were seen as buck-toothed, short-sighted, physically poor specimens with inferior equipment and a clumsy attitude to mechanical devices. The thought of such a people seriously challenging the sophisticated nations of Great Britain and the United States was not a serious consideration in the minds of many of the men making decisions at that time. It was not just a matter of faulty intelligence, but also of an attitude of mind rooted deep in generations of colonial rule and military supremacy. (Dare one mention the more recent underestimate by the French and then by the Americans of the people of Vietnam?)

The following paragraphs detail the various moves made by the Allies during the first week of December 1941, particularly those that would affect the fortunes of the British ships which arrived at Singapore on the 2nd.

Monday, 1 December

A State of Emergency was declared in Malaya. The Admiralty sent a signal to Admiral Phillips, who had just arrived at Singapore by air from Colombo, suggesting that either *Prince of Wales* or *Repulse*, or both ships if possible, should leave Singapore soon after their arrival and cruise in waters east of Singapore. The purpose of this was ostensibly 'to disconcert the Japanese', but there was probably also a fear that the two ships might be caught in harbour at Singapore by a surprise Japanese air attack which would cripple the new Eastern Fleet igno-miniously before it ever sailed on operations.

Tuesday, 2 December

American patrol aircraft from the Philippines sighted twelve Japanese submarines off Indo-China; all were pro-ceeding south and it was thought likely that the submarines were bound for the Singapore area to keep watch on the movements of the capital ships just arrived. Other Allied intelligence reports stated that twenty-one transport vessels were seen in Camranh Bay, a large anchorage north of Saigon, and that there were now no Japanese merchant ships in the whole of the Pacific, Atlantic or Indian Oceans and that Japanese air strength in southern Indo-China had reached 180 aircraft, including ninety heavy bombers.

Wednesday, 3 December

The Admiralty again signalled Phillips, suggesting that *Prince of Wales* and *Repulse* should be got away from Singapore. This second urging was probably because of the possibility that the Japanese submarines sighted off Indo-China might reach Singapore and attack the capital ships as they came out in the event of war. The Admiralty also urged Admiral Phillips to ask Admiral Hart, commanding the U.S. Asiatic Fleet at Manila, if the eight American destroyers then in the Dutch East Indies and Borneo areas could be moved to Singapore to strengthen the British naval forces there. This last suggestion is interesting and shows how British policy was always to attempt to involve the Americans in any outbreak of war and to show the Japanese that an attack on one was an attack on both. The British were certainly prepared to join with the Americans in the event of war; they probably still had doubts about reciprocal American willingness.

Admiral Phillips informed the Admiralty that he was soon to visit Admiral Hart and would discuss the destroyer suggestion there, and also that he intended to sail *Repulse* on a short visit to Darwin in Australia. This would at least get one of his two ships away from Singapore. Phillips also asked the Admiralty if the old battleships *Revenge* and *Royal Sovereign* as well as *Ramillies* and *Resolution*, previously earmarked for his Fleet, could now be sent to Singapore; he also asked if *Warspite*, which was due to return to England from repair in the United States, could call in at Singapore and remain one week to give a further impression of strength. He informed the Admiralty that he was anxious to commence 'Fleet training of battleships'.*

Thursday, 4 December

Admiral Phillips with two members of his staff left Singapore by air for Manila to meet Admiral Hart and General MacArthur and to plan for future cooperation. This meeting was intended to be the first of several with the Americans and the Dutch to draw up a long-term plan for mutual naval aid in South-East Asia.

Friday, 5 December

Repulse sailed from Singapore for Darwin, accompanied by the destroyers *Vampire* and *Tenedos* (Lieutenant R. Dyer). The crews of all three ships were delighted at the prospect: the *Repulse* and the *Tenedos* for the opportunity to visit Australia and the *Vampire* because she was an Australian ship. It was hoped by the crews that this trip to Darwin was only the start of a longer visit to Australia and there was some talk of being in Sydney for Christmas. The true purpose of the voyage was twofold: *Repulse* could be got away from Singapore, as the Admiralty had twice requested, and Admiral Phillips was hoping to persuade the Australians to send H.M.A.S. *Hobart*, one of their cruisers, to join the Eastern Fleet. Phillips had earlier been counting on receiving H.M.A.S. *Sydney*, another Australian cruiser, but this ship had just been lost with her entire crew in an action with a German raider, the *Kormoran*, off the coast of Western Australia. But the dispatch of *Repulse* to a destination well outside the potential war area shows how little the proximity of war was appreciated at Singapore.

Admiral Phillips met Admiral Hart at Manila on this day and the two discussed the possibility that the British Eastern Fleet might do well to join the Americans at Manila, which would make a suitable base for combined

* Public Record Office ADM 199/2234.

offensive operations in the event of war against Japan. This view, a little over forty-eight hours before the Japanese struck in the Pacific and South-East Asia, again illustrates the naïvety of Allied thinking. The two admirals agreed that this joining of their fleets would have to remain a long-term plan dependent upon more British aircraft being sent to replace the Navy and protect Singapore.

Saturday, 6 December

Admiral Hart and Admiral Phillips continued their talks in Manila. Admiral Hart agreed to send the four ships of his Destroyer Division 57 (Commander E. M. Crouch) from Balikpapan in Dutch Borneo to join Phillips's ships at Singapore if Phillips would call into Singapore the three British destroyers stationed at Hong Kong. It was agreed. The four Americans – U.S.S.s *Whipple* (Lieutenant Commander E. S. Karpe), *John D. Edwards* (Lieutenant Commander H. E. Eccles), *Edsall* (Lieutenant J. J. Nix) and *Alden* (Lieutenant Commander L. E. Coley) – were told to prepare to sail from Balikpapan, ostensibly for Batavia for their crews to have shore leave, but in reality for Singapore. Admiral Phillips must have agreed in principle to moving the Hong Kong destroyers, though they were nominally part of China Station and so still under Vice-Admiral Layton's command, because two of them, *Scout* (Lieutenant-Commander H. Lambton) and *Thanet* (Lieutenant-Commander B. S. Davies), proceeded to Singapore on the outbreak of war. This was hard luck on Hong Kong, but its position was regarded as indefensible and its garrison as good as written off should war break out. The third Hong Kong destroyer, *Thracian* (Commander A. L. Pears), was under repair and remained at Hong Kong.*

This was the last item discussed at Manila before an

---

* *Thanet* and *Thracian* were both sunk within the next few weeks, although *Thracian* was later salvaged by the Japanese and used by them as a patrol boat. *Scout* survived the war. The four American destroyers will be met later in this narrative.

American officer brought a dramatic message into the meeting. A convoy of Japanese merchant ships, previously located by air reconnaissance at Camranh Bay, had now been spotted at sea by an Australian-crewed Hudson aircraft flying from Malaya. The Hudson's captain, Flight Lieutenant J. C. Ramshaw, had reported seeing, first, three Japanese ships steaming south, and then what Ramshaw estimated to be a convoy of no less than twenty-five merchant ships escorted by one battleship, five cruisers and seven destroyers (Ramshaw's 'battleship' was actually a heavy cruiser). This convoy was well south of Saigon and steaming a westerly course. The ships Flight Lieutenant Ramshaw had seen could only be making for Siam, which was still neutral, or Malaya. If this was not war, then it was as near as one could get to war without it actually breaking out. *

There was a flurry of action. The four American destroyers at Balikpapan were ordered to sail at once and were on their way to Singapore within twenty-four hours. Admiral Phillips sent a signal to his Chief-of-Staff, Rear-Admiral Palliser, ordering that *Repulse* should be recalled, but Palliser had already done this. Within an hour or so, Phillips was himself on the way back to Singapore by air, departing so hurriedly that one member of his aircraft's crew who was out in Manila city was left behind. More sightings of Japanese ships at sea came in, and three convoys had now been spotted, believed to contain twenty-nine merchant ships and to be guarded by a similar number of warships.

These sightings by Allied aircraft of the invasion convoys were the last thing the Japanese wanted at this stage, but their luck still held. Now was undoubtedly the time for the British to throw their warships and aircraft at the Japanese convoys, but Admiral Phillips had been in Manila, *Repulse* had been steaming south towards Australia

* Flight Lieutenant Ramshaw was to be killed in action on the first day of the Japanese War.

and the convoys were still beyond the range of most of the obsolete British aircraft in Malaya. In addition, there was the deep-rooted desire by the British to believe that this was not yet war and they were certainly unwilling to take the first step and attack the convoys. But, if Admiral Phillips and all his ships had been at Singapore, and if he had sailed at once for the Gulf of Siam, the appearance of these ships might well have persuaded the Japanese to turn back their vulnerable convoys, which would at least have upset their whole timetable.

The R.A.F. were ordered to fly more air patrols from Malaya, but low cloud and bad weather prevented any more sightings that day.

Sunday, 7 December

Admiral Phillips arrived back at Singapore in the early hours and found waiting to consult him the First Naval Members of both the Australian and the New Zealand Naval Boards. This was about the last thing the harassed British admiral wanted, but he did meet his visitors, if briefly, in company with Dutch and American naval liaison officers.

There was much relief at Singapore when *Repulse* and her two escorting destroyers arrived back after a high-speed run. The British cruiser *Exeter* (Captain O. L. Gordon), with a convoy in the Bay of Bengal, was ordered by the Admiralty to make for Singapore at her best speed.

More air reconnaissance sorties were flown, but the weather had become even worse with the low clouds and tropical downpours of the north-east monsoon. Several fleeting glimpses were obtained of Japanese ships, however, although the reports were so scattered that no clear picture of the Japanese movements could be deduced. As a last resort, two Catalinas of 205 Squadron were sent even farther to the north to examine the bays on the western coast of Indo-China in case the Japanese convoys had put in there. One Catalina returned without having sighted anything useful, but the second was never seen again. A Japanese fighter had shot it down. Its crew were all killed, the first casualties of this new war.

The town of Kota Bharu is situated near the mouth of the Kelantan river at the most north-easterly point of Malaya. The beach, six miles away, was defended by the Indian troops of the 3/17th Dogra Regiment. Just after midnight of 7/8 December the Indians spotted three large merchant ships anchoring two miles off their beach, and a few minutes later were being shelled. The sea was rough, and some of the Japanese troops drowned, but this did not prevent their main force from reaching the beach in landing craft. The invaders were the veteran soldiers of the Japanese 56th Infantry Regiment. The Dogras were mostly young recruits, not fully trained, who had never before been in action. The fighting was fierce and the Japanese eventually gained a firm foothold ashore.

The timing of this Japanese landing, at 00.45 hours local time, was probably dictated by the need to land in the dark and at high tide. It was actually the very first open attack of the new war, preceding the attack on Pearl Harbor by seventy minutes. This was a considerable risk for the Japanese; had news of the Kota Bharu landing been flashed around the world, the American defences at Pearl Harbor might have been alerted. Yet the Japanese guessed correctly that the information could not be passed on so quickly. (In London, Winston Churchill was furious on hearing of the landings; his advisers had repeatedly told him that once the north-east monsoon on this coast started such landings would be impossible until spring.)

What the Japanese were really after at Kota Bharu was the airfield. It lay half-way between the town and the invasion beach and was the home of the R.A.F.'s 36 Squadron, with twelve ancient Vildebeeste torpedo bombers, and of No. 1 Australian Squadron, with thirteen Hudson bomber–reconnaissance aircraft. It is a measure of the Japanese awareness of air power and the vulnerability of their ships at sea that this airfield was their first objective. The Australian Hudsons took off almost at once, and in the bright moonlight they, and the army artillery firing from the shore, managed to hit all three Japanese merchant ships and some of the landing craft. But, when daylight came, the Japanese troops started advancing inland and Japanese aircraft from Indo-China bombed and machine-gunned the airfield. The Indian troops fought well, but there was panic among the ground personnel at the airfield. Disheartened by the constant strafing by the Japanese aircraft and by stray bullets whizzing out of the near-by jungle across the airfield, the R.A.F. men set fire to buildings and equipment, although no order to do so had been given, and departed in lorries. Soon afterwards the eighteen aircraft that had survived the Japanese air attacks were ordered to leave and the army gave up trying to defend the airfield. The airfield in Malaya which was best placed for aircraft to operate against the Japanese invasion convoys had fallen in less than twenty-four hours.

The action at Kota Bharu was typical of the Japanese successes that day. At Pearl Harbor the Japanese aircraft carrier fleet approached undetected, the warnings of a U.S. Army radar station which picked up the Japanese aircraft 130 miles out having been ignored. The Japanese swept in and caused tremendous havoc. Their torpedoes and bombs sank or crippled all eight battleships of the American Pacific Fleet together with several other smaller vessels. One hundred and eighty-eight American aircraft were destroyed, parked wing-tip to wing-tip and mostly caught on the ground. The Japanese lost twenty-nine aircraft. It was a brilliant stroke, marred only by the fact that the three American aircraft carriers were not in harbour and escaped to fight another day. It was much the same story on a smaller scale in the Philippines, in Siam and at Hong Kong. Despite the great risk to the Japanese of committing so many of their forces to slow seaborne convoys, some of which had been sighted several days earlier,

the Allies had failed to act quickly enough and the first
Japanese moves were everywhere successful.

Singapore was the target of one of the earliest Japanese
strikes. Some of the aircraft from the Japanese naval air
units at the airfields around Saigon had spent the past few
days flying long reconnaissance patrols over the sea to
give warning if the British capital ships left Singapore.
Others had stood by, loaded with bombs or torpedoes in
case that did happen. There had been intense dismay
among the Japanese airmen when it was reported that
their troop convoys had been spotted on 6 December, and
amazement that no air attack developed either on the ships
at sea or on their own airfields and that there was no sign
of the British ships coming out of Singapore. When this
strained period of waiting had passed safely, the Japanese
aircrews were able to revert to their main role for the first
day of the open war: the bombing of Singapore.

Fifty-four Mitsubishi bombers of the Mihoro and
Genzan Air Corps were loaded with bombs for the first
strike, the targets being the airfields at Tengah and
Seletar. Once again, the attempt to neutralize British air
strength was seen as having paramount importance. The
attack was to be carried out in the bright moonlight of
early morning of the 8th, partly because Singapore was
beyond the range of any Japanese fighter aircraft and
partly because the Japanese wanted to get this first raid in
before the British were fully alerted by other Japanese
operations.

But the Singapore operation did not go as planned.
Heavy cloud and turbulent conditions forced all of the
Genzan and some of the Mihoro aircraft to turn back, and
only seventeen of the Mihoro crews struggled through to
find themselves in the clear sky over Singapore soon after
04.00. Because the defence system at Singapore had never
practised joint operations between night fighters, searchlights and anti-aircraft guns, the defence of the island was
left to searchlights and guns only, and the night-fighter
crews, who had been alerted by radar while the Japanese

were still 140 miles away, were forbidden to take off. The Japanese were picked up by searchlights and thousands of people on the ground watched the neat formation fly steadily over the island. Many bombs were dropped around the airfields, but no serious damage was caused by the bombing at any of the airfields. Some bombs were dropped into the middle of Singapore city, where the blackout did not function until after the raid was over, and 200 people, most of them Chinese, were killed or wounded. The Japanese aircraft flew away; not one had been hit by the anti-aircraft fire.

The crews of *Prince of Wales* and *Repulse* were among the spectators of the raid.

I had been ashore with some of my mates on the Liberty boat to the big wet canteen at the Naval Base. We had been drinking Lion or Tiger beer – I forget which – and had had plenty. When I got back to the ship I went to sleep on the upper deck. I was woken up by gunfire and the sirens ashore and heard the bugle calling us to Action Stations. For a moment I wondered where I was and what was going on. 'Blimey. What am I doing here?' (Able Seaman S. E. Brown, H.M.S. *Repulse*)

I was returning to the ship following a pleasant, sociable day in Singapore. It was a night of quiet, warm and peaceful calm, when all hell let loose and all the guns and sirens sounded off. We watched *Prince of Wales* in action as we ran back – a little surprised to see the multiple pom-poms firing away at the minuscule high-level targets. I remember our absolute astonishment at the time. (Lieutenant D. B. H. Wildish, H.M.S. *Prince of Wales*)

I can remember quite clearly various areas of the Dockyard blacking out whilst others remained fully lit. As one area was blacked out, so another would be switched on, and this continued for a considerable time, during which people were forever running hither and thither, presumably looking for some sort of shelter. (Able Seaman R. H. James, H.M.S. *Prince of Wales*)

We had turned in, very merry from a Canteen Leave and not very worried, and were awakened by the almost forgotten sound of wailing air-raid sirens in the Dockyard followed by distant gunfire. This could only mean Japs? My waking thoughts were merely, 'Damn it! The silly blighters have gone and started it!' How our little world was bound to change. I watched very high-flying planes lit by searchlights – far too high to be hit by the wasteful volume of Ack-Ack. Strangely, they dropped no bombs near the Dockyard. (Ordinary Seaman D. F. Wilson, H.M.S. *Prince of Wales*)

In fact the Japanese aircraft had been within range of *Prince of Wales*'s high-angle 5·25-in. guns, and after 'the raid the battleship was moved away from the quayside so that these guns could operate more freely in any future air raid.

The crews of *Prince of Wales* and *Repulse* had already seen much of the war, and this new development was soon accepted by them if not by the civilian population of Singapore. The recent arrival of the two capital ships and the presence on the island of so many aircraft and troops, coupled with the poor opinion that the Europeans at least held of the Japanese, had led the civilians to believe that their peaceful existence in this tropical haven would continue undisturbed. Now, Japanese aircraft had appeared from nowhere, bombed the city, caused many deaths, and flown off undamaged. The shattering event was to be followed by a whole string of disastrous news items during the hours ahead.

At 06.30 a special Order of the Day was published by all military units and civil authorities in the British possessions of the Far East.

Japan's action today gives the signal for the Empire Naval, Army and Air Forces, and those of their Allies, to go into action with a common aim and common ideals.

We are ready. We have had plenty of warning and our preparations are made and tested. We do not forget at this moment the years of patience and forbearance in which we have borne, with dignity and discipline, the petty insults and insolences inflicted on us by the Japanese in the Far East. We know that those things were only done because Japan thought she could take advantage of our supposed weakness. Now, when Japan herself has decided to put the matter to a sterner test, she will find out that she has made a grievous mistake.

We are confident. Our defences are strong and our weapons efficient. Whatever our race, and whether we are now in our native land or have come thousands of miles, we have one aim and one only. It is to defend these shores, to destroy such of our enemies as may set foot on our soil, and then, finally, to cripple the power of the enemy to endanger our ideals, our possessions and our peace.

What of the enemy? We see before us a Japan drained for years by the exhausting claims of her wanton onslaught on China. We see a Japan whose trade and industry have been so dislocated by these years of reckless adventure that, in a mood of desperation, her Government had flung her into war under the delusion that, by stabbing a friendly nation in the back, she can gain her end. Let her look at Italy and what has happened since that nation tried a similar base action.

Let us all remember that we here in the Far East form part of the great campaign for the preservation in the world of truth and justice and freedom; confidence, resolution, enterprise and devotion to the cause must and will inspire every one of us in the fighting services, while from the civilian population, Malay, Chinese, Indian, or Burmese, we expect that patience, endurance and serenity which is the great virtue of the East and which will go far to assist the fighting men to gain final and complete victory.

> R. Brooke-Popham, Air Chief Marshal,
> Commander-in-Chief, Far East
>
> G. Layton, Vice-Admiral,
> Commander-in-Chief, China*

This document had actually been prepared several months earlier so that it could be translated into the various languages spoken in the Far East, but, in the light of what had happened and what was about to happen, it reveals a failure by the British leaders in the area to appreciate the strength of their new enemy.

When the Admiralty in London had heard of the sightings of the Japanese convoys at sea two days earlier, a signal had been sent to Admiral Phillips asking what action he proposed to take. It was a good question. The sending of

* Quoted in the British Official History, p. 525.

the two capital ships to Singapore had always been
intended as a political deterrent and no detailed planning
had taken place about what was to be done if that deterrent
failed.

The overall Commander-in-Chief of the Far East forces,
Air Chief Marshal Sir Robert Brooke-Popham, was due
for routine replacement when events put him in the un-
enviable position of having to cope with the Japanese
attacks. Despite his title, as we have seen, Brooke-
Popham exercised command only over the Army and the
R.A.F. units in the Far East; the Admiralty had insisted
that their ships remain purely under naval command.
And even in this independent naval command there was
an element of ambiguity. Admiral Phillips had been
appointed Commander-in-Chief Eastern Fleet on his
arrival at Singapore, but there still remained Vice-
Admiral Sir Geoffrey Layton, who was Commander-in-
Chief China Station. The Admiralty had ordered that
Phillips would take over command and administration of
China Station at 00.30 on 10 December, two days hence.
Admiral Layton was to strike his flag that evening, and
had planned to sail at once for England on a liner. He is
reputed to have been very disappointed at not being given
command of the new Eastern Fleet, and the imminent
departure at this critical time of an officer so experienced
in local conditions was a great waste. As soon as the
Japanese opened their attacks, however, Admiral Phillips,
by prior order of the Admiralty, brought forward the take-
over from Layton. Poor Admiral Layton does not appear
to have been much consulted by Admiral Phillips in the
momentous decisions about to be taken, though in the
event it is unlikely that the outcome would have been
much different if he had been. However, Layton was not
yet out of the story.

On the relationship between Brooke-Popham and
Phillips, there is clear documentary evidence of their
respective positions since both had received detailed direc-
tives from London on 2 December. Brooke-Popham's

position as Commander-in-Chief Far East was reaffirmed and he was told that he was to be 'jointly responsible with Commander-in-Chief Eastern Fleet to H.M. Government for the conduct of our strategy in the Far East'. Phillips was similarly directed to become 'jointly responsible with the Commander-in-Chief Far East to H.M. Government for the conduct of our strategy in the Far East'.* In other words, because the Admiralty was unwilling to place its ships under a unified command and under an R.A.F. officer, even though one of higher rank, the war in the Far East was to be fought under divided command. Admiral Phillips, who had spent not much more than a few days in the Far East and only a few hours at Singapore, need only *consult* Brooke-Popham and was then completely free to decide on the action to take in the naval side of the war.

It is known that Phillips and Brooke-Popham met for a short while at the Naval Base in the late evening on 7 December, just two hours before the Japanese landed in northern Malaya, and discussed the latest situation. Soon after this meeting Phillips sent the following signal to the Admiralty:

IF THE RELATIVE STRENGTH OF THE ENEMY FORCE PERMITS, ENDEAVOUR WILL BE MADE TO ATTACK THE EXPEDITION BY NIGHT OR BY DAY. IF WE ARE INFERIOR IN STRENGTH A RAID WILL BE ATTEMPTED AND THE AIR FORCE WILL ATTACK WITH BOMBS AND TORPEDOES IN CONJUNCTION WITH OUR NAVAL FORCES.†

It is probable that this signal was not sent until after the Japanese actually landed and that it merely represents Phillips's preliminary intentions. There is one aspect of the signal which is of interest. During his years as Vice-Chief of the Naval Staff, Phillips had seen many examples

* British Official History, pp. 485 and 487.
† Public Record Office ADM 199/1149.

of the Admiralty taking detailed control of operations at
sea; indeed, he had probably exercised such control in the
name of the First Sea Lord on numerous occasions.
Although London was now half a world away, it was quite
possible that the Admiralty might try the same methods
here; they were certainly asking to be informed of every
move. It is only conjecture that the vague wording of this
signal reflects the desire of Phillips to retain as much
freedom of action as possible, but this aspect will be met
again.

By midday of the 8th, with the war now nearly twelve
hours old, more news of the widespread Japanese moves
had come in to Singapore. Information from more distant
areas was still lacking in detail but it had become quite
clear that the Japanese had landed in northern Malaya and
at several points in Siam and that units of the Army and
the R.A.F. were involved in heavy fighting. It was time
for Phillips to decide what the Royal Navy should do. At
12.30 Admiral Phillips opened a meeting aboard *Prince of
Wales*. Besides the admiral and his immediate staff, there
were Captain Leach of *Prince of Wales*, Captain Tennant
of the *Repulse*, and the captains of several destroyers. No
representative of Air Chief Marshal Brooke-Popham's
Far East Headquarters was invited, and nobody from the
local R.A.F. command. It was purely a naval occasion. No
minutes were kept of this council of war, but there is little
doubt of how it went.

Admiral Phillips had already counted up the strength of
warships available to him. The Admiralty were now
making desperate efforts to get more ships to Singapore,
but these would take days or even weeks to arrive. Fortunately Phillips's two capital ships, *Prince of Wales* and
Repulse, were free of any serious defect and ready to sail
within an hour or so of receiving orders. There were also
four cruisers in the Naval Base at Singapore. Three of
these were *Durban* (Captain P. G. L. Cazalet), *Danae*
(Captain R. J. Shaw) and *Dragon* (Commander D. H.
Harper) of the China Station force which Phillips had

taken over that morning, but they were old ships built for patrol and scouting work and not for hard fighting, though each carried six 6-in. guns and had the speed to keep up with *Prince of Wales* and *Repulse*. Only one of them, however, the *Durban*, was actually ready to sail. The fourth was a more modern cruiser, the *Mauritius* (Captain W. D. Stephens), with twelve 6-in. guns. She was undergoing refit, and although orders were issued to hurry this along as fast as possible, she could not be available for some time. The *Exeter*, a powerful eight 8-in. gun cruiser, was on the way from the Indian Ocean at top speed and was expected to arrive within thirty-six hours, as was the Dutch 5·9-in. gun cruiser *Java*, coming up from the Dutch Indies.

The destroyer situation was not much better. Two of the four that had escorted *Prince of Wales* and *Repulse* into Singapore were out of action with defects. These were the two ships provided by the Mediterranean Fleet, and while *Encounter* would be ready in three days' time, *Jupiter*, described by Phillips in a signal as 'a notorious crock', would take three weeks to complete repairs. However, *Express* and *Electra*, the two destroyers provided by the Home Fleet, were both fit for action. There were two other destroyers on hand at Singapore: H.M.A.S. *Vampire* (Commander W. T. A. Moran) and H.M.S. *Tenedos* (Lieutenant R. Dyer). Moran and Dyer were both in Phillips's cabin, surprised, perhaps, to find their old First World War destroyers being considered for a major fleet action with these glamorous capital ships fresh out from England. Another local destroyer, H.M.S. *Stronghold* (Lieutenant-Commander G. R. Pretor-Pinney), had recently completed repairs and was also available. Moreover, if Admiral Phillips could wait two more days, he would have the four American destroyers from Balikpapan and the two British destroyers that had been sailed from Hong Kong that morning as they could do little to decide the outcome there.

So, when Admiral Phillips surveyed the warships available that morning, he found that he had one battleship, one

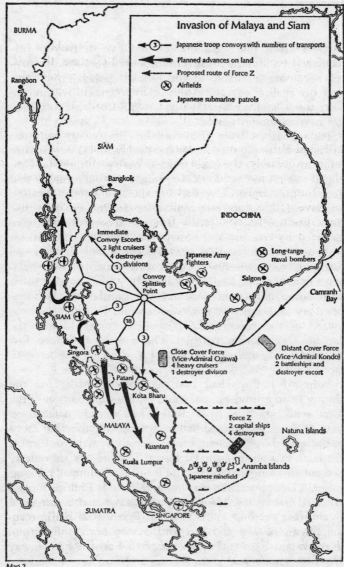

Map 2

battle cruiser, one light cruiser and five destroyers immediately on hand, with several more cruisers and destroyers becoming available in the following days. But there was no chance of capital-ship reinforcement within the next week, and no aircraft carrier could become available for an even longer period.

It is obvious from the available documents that the British were in possession of remarkably sound intelligence on many of the Japanese moves, partly through a U.S. Naval radio unit at Honolulu, which was monitoring and deciphering Japanese naval signals, and partly through effective R.A.F. air reconnaissance during the past few days. Phillips knew that the Japanese troop convoys were escorted by cruisers and destroyers, and that there was a covering force of heavier warships containing at least one Kongo Class battleship. (There were actually two battleships of this class, *Kongo* and *Haruna*.) Phillips also knew with some degree of accuracy the number of Japanese bombers and fighters stationed around Saigon, and was aware of the recently laid Japanese minefield and the Japanese submarine patrols. There were therefore few gaps in his knowledge of what his ships might have to face.

Admiral Phillips had two decisions to make: on the timing of any move he made and on the composition of the force with which he made it. He had already decided on both of these points, and had summoned the meeting more to inform those present of his decision than to consult them. It was an undramatic scene. The officers sat quietly around the long mahogany table in the Admiral's dining cabin. The atmosphere was hot and humid; Phillips looked strained and weary. He quietly announced that he intended to sail that evening in his flagship *Prince of Wales* in company with *Repulse* and just four destroyers – the faithful *Express* and *Electra* that had escorted Force G all the way from Greenock, and with *Tenedos* and *Vampire* of the local ships to complete the destroyer screen. The cruiser *Durban* was to be left behind. It would be a small but fast striking force. His intention was to sail north into the Gulf of Siam and, on the morning of 10 December, attack the Japanese shipping carrying out landings on the coasts of Malaya and Siam.

Phillips then asked for opinions on his plan, though it is unlikely that he expected serious argument from professional naval officers, and unlikely also that this determined personality needed the reassurance of juniors. The question was a formality and was treated by those present as such. Captain Tennant of *Repulse* was the first to support the decision. Hardly anyone else spoke.

There were, in any case, only two real alternatives to Phillips's proposed course of action: first, that the Eastern Fleet should remain at Singapore to see how the situation developed and gather further strength, but at the same time risking an air attack like the one which had finished off the American battleships in Pearl Harbor that same morning; or, secondly, that it should sail for safer waters and await events. With the Army and the R.A.F. fighting for their lives in northern Malaya, however, these were not really valid alternatives.

During the research for this book it was possible to contact the last two men still alive who had been among those present at the meeting.

The atmosphere was calm and quietly thoughtful – fatalistic perhaps. To the best of my recollection I remember Admiral Phillips saying, 'Gentlemen, this is an extremely hazardous expedition and I would liken it to taking the Home Fleet into the Skagerrak without air cover. Nevertheless, I feel that we have got to do something.'

There was a very long silence after this and I suspect that others were feeling the same as I at the time. My own thoughts were 'Yes, indeed you have got to do something but this is quite against your own reasoning and the position in which you find yourself must be laid at Churchill's feet.' I suppose we were all thinking of ourselves and forgetting other priorities, the North Atlantic, Mediterranean, Home Defence and so on. (Lieutenant R. Dyer, H.M.S *Tenedos*)

After all the discussion was over, Admiral Phillips summed up in words something like this. 'We can stay in Singapore. We can sail away to the East – Australia. Or we can go out and fight. Gentle-men, we sail at five o'clock.' (Lieutenant-Commander F. J. Cart-wright, H.M.S. *Express*) *

The meeting had lasted half an hour at the most, and those present returned to their ships or duties ashore to prepare for sailing. Even before the meeting, Admiral Phillips had sent a signal to the Admiralty stating that he intended to sail that evening and to attack Japanese shipping off Kota Bharu on the morning of the 10th. Now he turned his attention to the question of air cover. There are several references to discussions that day between Admiral Phillips or his staff and the R.A.F. over air support for the coming operation, but there are no documents recording what was actually said because most of the Singapore headquarters war diaries and signal files were later lost. It is probable that Air Vice-Marshal C. W. H. Pulford, Air Officer Commanding Malaya, had earlier indicated that the R.A.F. would do its best and asked for the Navy's specific requirements. After the meet-ing on *Prince of Wales*, one of Phillips's staff officers put the naval requirements into writing and this was delivered to Air Vice-Marshal Pulford:

1. Reconnaissance 100 miles northward of the force at daylight on the 9th December,

2. Reconnaissance off Singora at first light on 10th December,

3. Fighter protection off Singora during daylight of the 10th December.†

It is of interest that Admiral Phillips had already in-formed the Admiralty that he intended to attack Japanese shipping at Kota Bharu; now he was telling the local R.A.F. command that his target was the Japanese shipping off Singora, 120 nautical miles farther into the Gulf of Siam. Up-to-date intelligence had probably indicated that

* Unfortunately Lieutenant-Commander (later Captain) Cart-wright died before this book was ready for publication.
† Public Record Office ADM 199/1149.

the Singora landings were more serious than those at Kota
Bharu, though Phillips was now planning a more ambitious
operation than the one he had signalled to the Admiralty
that morning. But in this new theatre of war the fortunes
of the R.A.F. were already running low. The obsolete aircraft of their squadrons were being battered to pieces on
the ground or shot to pieces whenever they took to the air.
The forward airfields were being evacuated under Japanese
attack, and the R.A.F. was fast diminishing as a major
element in the defence forces of the Far East. There is no
need to labour the point that the Air Ministry had consistently failed to send any modern aircraft to Malaya
and that their men out there were now paying the penalty.

It is not easy to be certain about the precise developments following the arrival of this message at R.A.F.
Headquarters. The airmen were well aware of the risks the
sailors were taking if they ventured into the Gulf of Siam
without air cover, and they were becoming more aware by
the hour of how difficult it would be for the needed aircraft
to be found. It would look very bad for them simply to say
that air cover could not be provided; it would look even
worse later if they allowed the ships to sail and then could
not provide the requested air cover, particularly in two
days' time when the ships would be closest to the known
Japanese air bases in Indo-China.

It is probable that Air Vice-Marshal Pulford talked with
Air Chief Marshal Brooke-Popham about his dilemma, and
it is still believed in Singapore that there was an argument
that afternoon between Brooke-Popham and Phillips, presumably with Brooke-Popham warning Phillips that the
operation was in danger and that the R.A.F. would not be
able to fulfil all the Navy's demands. But, with the divided
command at Singapore, Brooke-Popham, although Commander-in-Chief Far East, could not order Phillips to give
up the operation. There is also evidence, albeit hearsay,
that one of Brooke-Popham's staff, Group Captain L.
Darvall, was dispatched on a special visit to *Prince of
Wales* that afternoon 'to make it quite clear to him that he

could not have or expect shore-based air cover. Admiral Sir Tom Phillips, therefore, having been left in no doubt, took a calculated risk and sailed.' These words were spoken by Darvall to a colleague later in the war, but Darvall (later an Air Marshal) is now dead and they cannot be verified.

His difficulties with the R.A.F. made no difference to Admiral Phillips's resolve to sail, though he would still be free to cut short the operation between the time of sailing and the arrival in the area of maximum danger in thirty-six hours' time. Yet some sympathy is due to the tired admiral on that afternoon. Given time, much that was not yet clear would have become so. More ships would be arriving. Indeed, if Phillips had waited only forty-eight hours, the expedition could have sailed with two cruisers and four extra destroyers. It would then also have been a true Allied force, with American and Dutch as well as British ships; whether Phillips would have thought that an asset cannot be guessed, but the anti-aircraft defences of such an increased force would have been far stronger. But time was the one element Tom Phillips did not have. With every hour that passed the Japanese were securing their landings in the north. Also, as one naval officer rightly comments, the effect on morale in Singapore if the ships had remained in harbour would have been 'devastating'. True, there was danger from the air, but how great was that danger? It is said that Phillips did not believe that any Japanese torpedo bomber had the range to fly the 400 miles from Saigon to the area off Siam he was heading for. If this was Phillips's belief, then he did not realize that the Japanese aircraft that had bombed Singapore the night before had flown nearly twice the distance and that these same aircraft could operate as torpedo bombers when required.

But perhaps Admiral Phillips let his thoughts wander over the various capital ships that had been sunk since 1939 and dwelt on how not one had succumbed to air attack while at sea. Mines, submarines and old Japanese battleships he would face as a matter of course. He could steer clear of the area where the mines were believed to be. He could steam fast enough to outrun any submarine. His ships could stand up to any of the Japanese warships known to be in the area. And, if he could get into the right position, the big guns of *Prince of Wales* and *Repulse* could inflict a veritable slaughter on the Japanese merchant ships off the invasion beaches. If he could achieve this, then it would be a great victory for the Royal Navy and for British interests in the Far East.

In retrospect, it might have been better to have proceeded more cautiously, but there are few who will say that, on the evidence available, Phillips actually went wrong. Retrospectively again, it might have been better if Air Chief Marshal Brooke-Popham had been in overall command and, with his airman's sense of reality, could have imposed a decision on Phillips and made him wait. But the Admiralty had demanded its freedom of action in operational matters, and it was this freedom which Phillips was now exercising.

There remained only a few hours before the ships sailed. For signal purposes it was decided to call the squadron 'Force Z', an unhappy choice which had a ring of finality. Admiral Phillips's Chief-of-Staff, Rear-Admiral A. F. E. Palliser, was ordered to remain ashore to provide Phillips with a link between the ships at sea and the various headquarters at Singapore during the operation. Palliser was to keep his chief as fully informed as possible, by signal, of any developments after Force Z sailed, but Phillips would want to maintain radio silence for as long as possible and the two must have discussed the various moves that Phillips might make in the event of changing circumstances. The degree to which Palliser could read Phillips's mind after the ships had sailed would be of great importance.

The two capital ships were completely ready and could have sailed at once, but Admiral Phillips wanted an evening departure to conceal the sailing from possible Japanese agents on the island. An officer in *Prince of Wales* remembers the afternoon as being filled with 'much preliminary scampering of staff officers'.

There was more work still to do on the destroyers, particularly on the *Express*:

Prior to 8 December, the ship's company had been busy de-ammunitioning ship to enter drydock for urgent repairs. When the order was given to reverse the whole operation and prepare for sea – shells half in and half out of portholes – you can imagine the verbal chat that followed. 'Do these idiots know what they are doing?' The intense heat didn't help. Shipshape and Bristol fashion, we were soon ready to leave harbour to head for all sorts of mysterious adventures as rumour had it – communication hadn't been invented then. One version was we were heading home. Bloody good job! (Able Seaman J. M. Farrington)

An Admiralty press officer, Lieutenant Horace Abrahams, reported aboard *Repulse*, complete with camera. Two civilian journalists, O'Dowd Gallagher of the *Daily Express* and an American, Cecil Brown of the Columbia Broadcasting System, followed, having been offered an 'unknown assignment' lasting up to five days. Many of the pressmen at Singapore had turned down this offer; only Gallagher had had a hunch that it might be something big and had persuaded his friend Brown to keep him company.

Captain Leach of the *Prince of Wales* managed to get ashore that afternoon and met his son whose own ship was refitting at the Naval Base.

I saw little of my father that day, but we did manage to meet at the Base swimming pool in the late afternoon. I am a poor swimmer and merely splashed about to get cool but I remember my father saying, 'I am going to do a couple of lengths now; you never know when it mightn't come in handy', a remark which in retrospect was both prophetic and consistent. Afterwards we had a final Gin Sling (the popular local drink at the time subsequently to be replaced by Gin and Tonic) and he introduced me to Captain Bill Tennant of the *Repulse*, a charming, kindly man. The two were good friends and clearly saw very much eye to eye. We then parted, my father to the

Prince of Wales and I to the shore accommodation that is now called
H.M.S. *Terror*. I never saw him again. (Midshipman H. C. Leach,
H.M.S. *Mauritius*)

It is difficult to generalize about the morale and feelings
of the men aboard the six ships preparing to sail. Most had
been involved in dozens of wartime sailings, and no one
had yet told the lower deck one word of what was happening, although many must have had some idea that they
were off to look for the Japanese.

Only two quotations are needed to round off this
chapter. Surgeon-Commander F. B. Quinn, the Fleet
Medical Officer who was sailing aboard *Prince of Wales*,
later prepared a report commenting on the physical state
of the ship's company following the long, high-speed
voyage from England in a badly ventilated ship and then
the strenuous working while at Singapore.

Though the morale of the ship's company was good, I am of the
opinion that the men were fatigued and listless and their fighting
efficiency was below par. *

And Ordinary Seaman Cecil Jones, a New Zealander
stationed ashore at the Naval Base, recollected:

I was on one of the many working parties from the Fleet Shore
Establishment and other ships who helped to provision *Repulse* and
Prince of Wales before they sailed. I remember them sailing, as it
was with deep regret that I did not get a draft on to one of them.
Only two N.Z. seamen did so; one survived.

The ships left the Dockyard with our honest thoughts that they
were unsinkable.

* Public Record Office ADM 199/1149.

7

The Sweep

'Close all scuttles and deadlights. Special seadutymen close up.' Over the Tannoy loudspeakers of four warships came these instructions alerting the crews that they would soon be putting to sea. A third call, 'Hands fall in for leaving harbour', then set in motion the procedure that most of the sailors had gone through so often before.

The Australian destroyer *Vampire* was first away at 17.10, followed closely by another destroyer, *Tenedos*. Then came *Repulse* and *Prince of Wales*. *Electra* and *Express* had been out exercising their minesweeping gear since mid afternoon, and would rendezvous outside the boom off Changi Point. As the two capital ships left the Naval Base, an official photographer took photographs of each but not of the escorting destroyers. All the ships flew the Royal Navy's White Ensign, but from the main mast of *Prince of Wales* also flew a red cross of St George on a white background – the flag of a full admiral taking his fleet to sea. It was a fine but hot evening, already starting to grow gloomy, and the sun was near to setting behind the palms and low hills of Singapore Island. When the ships turned east to steam away down Johore Strait towards the sea, there were many spectators on shore to wave them on their way. With this new war not yet twenty-four hours old, it was a sight to stir any breast, and there can have been few among the onlookers who did not believe that they were watching these warships deliberately going out to find and fight the Japanese. Six warships: one new battleship that had already been involved in a dramatic battle, one battle cruiser that had not fired her big guns in action since 1917, two destroyers that had been in constant action since the war began and two more which had passed just as many peaceful months in the East and whose crews must have been still in a daze over being plunged so suddenly into action.

Once clear of the land, Force Z formed into its cruising pattern for the first night. *Prince of Wales* had overtaken and passed *Repulse* and the battle cruiser was now in position four cables (800 yards) astern of the flagship. On reaching the open sea, *Express* moved ahead to take up a position well in front of *Prince of Wales* and streamed her high-speed minesweeping gear, but this broke down almost at once and *Electra* had to take her place. The six warships steamed on into the night at $17\frac{1}{2}$ knots.

Many men have recorded their feelings on this first evening at sea with the prospect of action within days or, possibly, hours. There was every point of view between the extremes of blind optimism and a belief in imminent doom.

I experienced that tense awareness of one's heart beating; that rather pleasurable, bittersweet enjoyment – I wonder is it pleasure? It's difficult to say, for I am quite sure no man gets any kick out of being shelled or bombed. I certainly don't, but I do know that these occasions give you an intense comradeship with your shipmates and a rather selfless exaltation which appears to be pleasurable.

We went to routine Dusk Action Stations and then many of us stood on deck talking long after darkness had fallen. What was ahead of us? How did the Japs fight? Were they truly fanatical? Did they make suicidal attacks? (I recalled the last time I personally had seen a Jap – he was playing snooker at Edinburgh.) I talked to an old friend of mine, who had joined the ship at Singapore, and we watched the escorting destroyers winking a few signals at us, then went through the screen into the bright, chattering Wardroom for a drink. (Surgeon Lieutenant-Commander E. D. Caldwell, H.M.S. *Prince of Wales*)

We had been led to believe that the Japs would be quite unorthodox and not nearly equal to the German Air Force. We should be able to pick them off like pigeons. The only misgivings I had were the small rumours which had come up from the 'Plotting Tables' that things were not as coordinated as they would like them to be during some of the practice shoots. But putting all doubts on one side we quietly eased away to meet the tropical darkness and silence. (Ordinary Seaman W. E. England, H.M.S. *Prince of Wales*)

We had left Singapore in glorious weather but I had this premonition that the *Prince of Wales* would never again return to Singapore or any other port. I had this feeling that this was the end as far as the ship was concerned. (Boy Seaman W. S. Searle, H.M.S. *Prince of Wales*)

This uneasy feeling of trouble ahead was even stronger on the *Repulse*.

It was a funny thing, I don't know if anyone else has memories of this but a 'buzz' seemed to go round the ship that this was one trip we wouldn't be coming back from, this stemming from the fact that we were in company with the *Prince of Wales* who was generally considered by many as a 'Jonah'. (Ordinary Seaman H. J. Hall)

We all knew that with the *Prince of Wales* with us we were never coming back again in one piece. (Chief Petty Officer E. L. Smith)

Many other men in *Repulse*, however, would say that this gloomy talk was not prevalent and that the greater number of men on the battle cruiser were only too anxious to see their ship in action at last and had no doubts about the outcome.

The feelings of the British sailors about their enemy was that there was really nothing to fear.

Well, here we come you Jap bastards. Get ready!

The popular conception was that the Japanese were pushovers.

Afraid? Not really; perhaps excited is the word. After all, this is the battle cruiser *Repulse* and they are only Japs.

Their ships were supposed to be old and top-heavy, liable to roll over if they fired a full broadside; their aircraft were even slower than our old Swordfish, so what had we to worry about?

We talked quite a lot of sharks and jokingly said they are going to have a beanfeast – on Japs.

We didn't really know what we were up against and just passed them off as slant-eyed so-and-so's.

Eight hours after sailing, the first of several signals sent by Rear-Admiral Palliser in Singapore was received in *Prince of Wales*. It was not a signal to increase Admiral Phillips's confidence.

TO C IN C E.FLEET   FROM CHIEF OF STAFF
                                                E.FLEET

IMMEDIATE

MY 2253/8TH PART 1 BEGINS. R.A.F. RECON-NAISSANCE TO A DEPTH OF 100 MILES TO THE NORTH WESTWARD OF YOU WILL BE PROVIDED BY 1 CATALINA FROM 08.00 ONWARDS 9TH.

(II) IT IS HOPED THAT A DAWN RECONNAISSANCE OF COAST NEAR SINGORA CAN BE CARRIED OUT ON WEDNESDAY 10TH.

(III) FIGHTER PROTECTION ON WEDNESDAY 10TH WILL NOT, REPEAT NOT, BE POSSIBLE. MY 2253/8TH PART 1 END. PART 2 FOLLOWS.

MY 2253/8 PART 2

(IV) JAPANESE HAVE LARGE BOMBER FORCES BASED SOUTHERN INDO-CHINA AND POSSIBLY ALSO IN THAILAND. C IN C FAR EAST HAS RE-QUESTED GENERAL MACARTHUR TO CARRY OUT ATTACK WITH HIS LONG RANGE BOMBERS ON INDO-CHINA AERODROMES AS SOON AS POSSIBLE.

(V) KOTA BHARU AERODROME HAS BEEN EVACU-ATED AND WE SEEM TO BE LOSING GRIP IN OTHER NORTHERN AERODROMES DUE TO ENEMY AIR ACTION.

(VI) MILITARY POSITION NEAR KOTA BHARU DOES NOT SEEM GOOD BUT DETAILS ARE NOT AVAILABLE. *

* Public Record Office ADM 199/1149. Further operational signals will be from the same Public Record Office reference unless otherwise stated.

Palliser was telling his chief in as clear a manner as possible that the R.A.F. could supply limited reconnaissance support but there was no chance at all of fighter cover on the 10th, the day on which Force Z would be most at risk from the Japanese air units known to be in Siam. The R.A.F. had been blamed many times from Dunkirk onwards for leaving the Army or the Navy in the lurch without air cover; on this occasion they were leaving the Navy in no doubt that if their ships ventured too far north then it must be entirely at the Navy's risk.

There was one factor to this affair that Admiral Phillips did not then know. On 8 December, the previous day, Japanese aircraft had made a successful air attack on Clark Field, Manila, and destroyed half the American B-17 Flying Fortresses there; these were the American aircraft that Air Chief Marshal Brooke-Popham had asked General MacArthur to use in bombing attacks on the Japanese airfields near Saigon. The American air attack referred to in Palliser's signal was thus never to take place.

The signal placed a further heavy burden of decision on Admiral Phillips's shoulders. It is believed, however, that he did not anguish for long and his mind was soon made up. The earlier fine weather had now broken and there was low and heavy cloud with frequent rain squalls. Phillips would continue to sail north throughout the next day, the 9th, and then, if the bad weather continued to shield his ships from Japanese reconnaissance aircraft, he could still turn west and make the intended dash at high speed to one of the Japanese invasion areas at dawn on the 10th. After attacking whatever Japanese shipping could be found, Force Z could then retire at speed to the south and fight off whatever air or surface vessel attack the Japanese could mount while it was withdrawing. But, if the Japanese spotted his ships during the daylight hours of the 9th, Phillips could always give up the operation and return to Singapore. In retrospect it seems as prudent a course as was possible in the circumstances.

One account says that Admiral Phillips did not do much

more than shrug his shoulders over the 'no fighter cover' signal and declared that it was 'best to get on with it'. But this is probably a simplification and the decision taken was certainly the product of some careful thought. Admiral Phillips decided there was no need to reply to this signal and thus break wireless silence; he assumed that Palliser would realize that no signal meant the operation was proceeding.

There is one important point to be emphasized. The R.A.F. had not abandoned the Navy altogether in the matter of fighter support. Although their fighter squadrons were being drawn into the land battle in northern Malaya, No. 453 (Australian) Squadron, with their Brewster Buffalo fighters at Sembawang airfield on Singapore Island, was earmarked to support Force Z. There was no question of this handful of aircraft providing permanent air cover over the British ships, but they would remain at readiness throughout the hours of daylight for as long as the naval operation continued. Whether the Australian pilots would be able to intervene in the event of a Japanese air attack on the British ships depended on how much advance warning they would receive and how far north the attack on the ships took place.

It was a quiet night free of any incident. Dawn came at around 06.00 and there was much satisfaction when it was found that the low cloud, rain showers and generally misty conditions that so favoured the concealment of the British ships from air reconnaissance showed no signs of breaking up. Force Z had now been at sea for almost twelve hours and had covered 220 nautical miles of the proposed route to the area of action. There still remained 520 miles to steam in the whole of the coming day and night. Admiral Phillips believed that he had avoided being spotted by the Japanese and everything now depended upon his ability to remain concealed for the coming fourteen hours or so of daylight. When dawn broke, Phillips ordered that a zig-zag course be adopted with a

speed of 17½ knots. This speed would achieve the arrival
in the area of the Japanese landings in twenty-four hours'
time, while the combination of speed and zig-zag would
prevent a Japanese submarine getting off anything but a
lucky snap torpedo shot. The course was still the north-
easterly one needed to pass east of the Anamba Islands and
avoid the Japanese minefield. *Electra* was still ahead of the
big ships, sweeping for mines, but there were none on this
route.

There was a moment of alarm soon after daylight had
broken when *Vampire* signalled the flagship that she had
sighted an aircraft. Immediately came this reply from
Prince of Wales:

TO VAMPIRE   FROM C IN C

ARE YOU CERTAIN OF AIRCRAFT SIGHTING.
REPORT ALL DETAILS.

This incident was obviously of paramount importance and
Phillips's inquiry must have been followed by some close
questioning of the lookout who had spotted the plane and
much consultation of aircraft recognition books aboard the
Australian ship because it took Commander Moran thirty-
eight minutes to draft his reply.

TO C IN C   FROM VAMPIRE

YOUR 06.21. AIRCRAFT WAS SEEN BY ONE RELIABLE
LOOKOUT FOR ONE MINUTE, BEARING 135 DEGREES,
ANGLE OF SIGHT 8, AND THEN DISAPPEARED INTO
CLOUDS. TYPE NOT RECOGNIZED.

Admiral Phillips had now to assess whether his force
had been spotted by a Japanese aircraft and, if so, decide
whether to continue or abandon the operation. Again,
there are no documents to support Phillips's decision, but
it is obvious that he decided that the aircraft may not have
been Japanese and that, even if it had been, the sighting
was so brief that the aircraft may not have seen the ships.
It is possible that *Prince of Wales*'s radio room was also

consulted and asked whether it had picked up a signal near by. Phillips weighed the evidence, decided that Force Z had not been spotted and took no action. He was right to do so. The identity of the aircraft is not known; if it was a Japanese, it did not see the warships.

At 07.13, Force Z at last 'turned the corner' to the east of the Anambas and settled on to a new course of 330 degrees. The next two hours were incident free and allowed everyone to have breakfast. The dawn Action Stations had been relaxed to 'Second Degree of Readiness' with all guns still loaded and at least partially manned but some men off duty, sleeping, reading, writing letters, playing cards, 'someone playing the old guitar'. It was important that the crews be given as much rest as possible at this stage, particularly in the poorly ventilated *Prince of Wales*; a later emergency or the action expected on the morrow night required that First Degree of Readiness of full Action Stations be maintained for hours on end.

There were a few medical incidents. In *Repulse*, an R.N.V.R. officer missed his footing on a ladder while changing watches at the Air Defence Position, fell to the deck below and had to be taken to the Sick Bay with a broken arm and several bruised ribs. In *Prince of Wales* a young gunnery rating had recently been operated on for appendicitis. The ship's doctors advised that he should not serve at his action station in one of the 5·25-in. turrets because the scar would still be weak and the sailor was ordered to remain below decks in the event of action. Both the officer and the young gunner were later caught below when the action did come. It is also known that Admiral Phillips was in some pain on this day. When Boy Seaman Millard reported for duty that morning as Admiral's Messenger, he was told by the coxswain to 'be very quiet and not make any noise because the Admiral was suffering from a severe bout of toothache'. Phillips sought no treatment for this, but may have asked for a few aspirin or codeine tablets.

The six British ships steamed on through the damp,

claggy weather. Lookouts strained hard but more reliance
was placed on the various radar sets aboard *Prince of
Wales* and *Repulse*. The British radar sets could detect
surface vessels at ranges up to twenty-five miles, depend-
ing on the size of the ship involved, and could pick up a
high-flying aircraft eighty miles out or lower aircraft at
closer ranges, though these were still early days for radar
and the sets did not always function satisfactorily. Japanese
ships and aircraft had no operational radar at all at this
time. The Asdic sets of the four British destroyers could in
theory pick up submarines, but Asdic was a very imperfect
device and could only cover a small arc in front of each
destroyer; a submerged submarine more than 2,500 yards
away was fairly safe from detection. On balance, however,
the conditions of that morning of 9 December could not
have suited the British purpose more admirably.

At 09.06 the quiet was broken, but only by a long signal
flashed out by *Repulse*'s signal lamp to the flagship.

TO C IN C   FROM REPULSE

A VERY CONVENIENT SKY TO PREVENT US BEING
SPOTTED. AT WHAT SPEED WILL YOU OPERATE AT
DAWN TOMORROW. PRESUMABLY WE SHALL BE
CLEAR OF ALL MINEFIELDS. WOULD IT HELP IF
TENEDOS SPENT TOMORROW WELL TO THE SOUTH
EASTWARD AT ECONOMICAL SPEED, SHE MIGHT
THEN BE AVAILABLE TO SWEEP US HOME. PRO-
POSE TO HAVE ONE AIRCRAFT FUELLED AND AT
SHORT NOTICE TO FLY FOR SPOTTING IF ANY-
THING WORTH OUR METAL APPEARS. AIRCRAFT,
IF FLOWN OFF, TO LAND AT PENANG OR ELSE-
WHERE. SHOULD BE VERY GRATEFUL FOR ANY
INFORMATION YOU MAY HAVE DURING THE DAY
ABOUT JAPANESE OPERATIONS ON THE SIAM—
MALAYA COAST.

It is always useful to try and read between the lines of
signals, and this one is full of interest. The message

Captain Tennant had sent to Admiral Phillips was almost a public one in that it could be seen and read by anyone on *Prince of Wales* who understood Morse Code. Tennant's message had opened with a chatty comment on the weather in true English style, but had then gone on to make several major suggestions and ask pointed questions about the future of the operation, questions to which Captain Tennant might normally have expected to receive answers as a matter of course later in the day. It is only conjecture that Captain Tennant was feeling a little left out of things on *Repulse* and might have imagined that Captain Leach on *Prince of Wales* was being frequently consulted by Admiral Phillips on the future course of the operation and Tennant wished to put his experience and thoughts also at the disposal of the overall commander. What is evident from the signal is that Captain Tennant was showing no apprehension about the danger of air attack on nearing the Japanese airfields. Tennant had seen many Royal Navy ships sunk by German aircraft at Dunkirk, but, if he was having qualms about the danger of the current operation, he would certainly not reveal these in a signal that so many people could read.

Captain Tennant had to wait nearly two hours for this brief reply to his signal.

TO REPULSE   FROM C IN C

YOUR 09.06. POLICY SIGNAL IS BEING MADE SHORTLY.

What followed next was not a policy signal but several exchanges about the possibility of *Repulse* refuelling *Tenedos* and *Vampire*. *Repulse* reported that speed would have to be reduced to 8 knots to refuel *Tenedos* because of the nature of this old destroyer's equipment, but that *Vampire* could be refuelled at 11 knots. In each case it would take about one and a half hours to refuel. Admiral Phillips decided to take no action; he was unwilling to reduce speed and lose time in this way and the problem of his destroyers' fuel endurance would have to be solved in another manner.

Soon after midday a Catalina flying boat appeared over *Prince of Wales* and, having been identified as friendly, came in low and flashed a message by Aldis lamp. This message is reputed to have read:

JAPANESE MAKING LANDING NORTH OF SINGORA.

But no copy of this signal has been found in the Public Record Office. It is unlikely that the Catalina had itself been to Singora, way up north in the Gulf of Siam. It was probably the aircraft detailed (requested by Admiral Phillips before leaving Singapore) to provide reconnaissance a hundred miles ahead of Force Z during this day. It is not known why this method of relaying information from Singapore to Admiral Phillips was used. The Catalina disappeared into the mist to continue its reconnaissance.

Force Z had recently altered course to 345 degrees and was now keeping farther to the east than the intended route, presumably to keep well away from the more obvious direct route of approach to the Gulf of Siam which the Japanese might be searching. The half-way mark from Singapore to the area where Japanese shipping might be found was passed at 13.00. Admiral Phillips had still to make up his mind on the exact course of action to take that night and on the next morning, and a decision would have to be taken shortly about *Tenedos*, whose fuel position would not allow her to keep up the present speed much longer. Force Z was now only 360 miles from the airfields around Saigon and within very easy range of the Japanese aircraft there. Every hour's steaming took them nearer to this danger and to the many Japanese warships guarding the invasion routes but, thanks mainly to the weather conditions, the British ships had still not been spotted.

The Japanese had drawn up three incomplete patrol lines of submarines to cover the routes from Siam to the invasion areas. The most easterly submarine in the second of these patrol lines was I.65. This submarine was actually the command boat of the 30th Submarine Flotilla and was carrying the flotilla commander, Captain Masao Teraoka, as well as the boat's own captain, Lieutenant-Commander Hakue Harada. At 15.15 by Tokyo Central Time (one and a half hours ahead of the time by which the British were working), I.65's officer of the watch caught a glimpse through his periscope of the dim shapes of two ships to the east and almost at the extreme limit of visibility. The Japanese assumed that the two ships were destroyers and immediately called the two senior officers. Both looked carefully through the periscope, but had difficulty making a surer identification as the two ships kept disappearing into the mist and squalls and rain kept dashing over the periscope's outer lens. Eventually, after much staring and consulting of identification books, Captain Teraoka decided that the ships he was looking at were not destroyers but a British battle cruiser and a more modern type of battleship. To save time, Teraoka ordered the following signal to be transmitted:

TWO REPULSE TYPE ENEMY BATTLESHIPS SPOTTED.
THEIR POSITION KO.CHI.SA11. COURSE 340. SPEED 14 KNOTS.*

This was a good piece of work by I.65, and a fairly accurate assessment; the British ships were then steaming 345 degrees at 18 knots. The Japanese submarine waited for them to pass, came to the surface and settled down to shadow the British ships for as long as it could.

This was the cruellest of luck for the British. If their course had carried them just a few miles more to the east, *Prince of Wales* and *Repulse* would not have been spotted.

* All Japanese signals quoted here are from the Japanese Official History. The position given is part of the Japanese naval grid reference system.

As it was, Force Z was so far from I.65 that the four destroyers were invisible to the submarine.

There is no doubt that, from the very beginning, the Japanese commanders in the Malaya–Siam operation had been extremely apprehensive about the two big British ships known to have arrived at Singapore. The elaborate Japanese war plans had not allowed the release of aircraft carriers or modern battleships from the Pearl Harbor operation, and the Japanese would have to take care of the British ships with the two old battleships keeping a distant watch on the landing areas, with the collection of cruisers and destroyers giving close escort or support to the troops and supply ships and with their aircraft and submarine forces. Although the Japanese warships were numerous, no individual ship or group of ships had anything like the combination of speed and gun power of *Prince of Wales* and *Repulse*. The landings on the Malayan and Siamese coasts may have been progressing well, but every Japanese commander had the fear in the back of his mind that the British capital ships might intervene.

During most of 9 December the Japanese had had no idea that the British were at sea. A reconnaissance plane had flown over Singapore on the previous afternoon and spotted the two ships still in harbour. There had been surprise among the Japanese that the British ships had not put to sea to catch their invasion forces in the first critical hours of the landings. Then, on the morning of the 9th, another Japanese aircraft flew high over Singapore and its pilot thought that he could see the British capital ships still in harbour. He radioed this report to Saigon. Until this moment the Japanese had been particularly concerned over their landing at Kota Bharu. The landings farther north had all gone according to plan, but the vigorous action of the Australian-crewed Hudsons and the army artillery battery in attacking the Japanese ships off the Kota Bharu beaches had thrown the timetable there into some confusion. Now Vice-Admiral Ozawa received two

vital messages. One told him that during the past night
the main landings at Kota Bharu had been successfully
completed, and the second told him that the British capital
ships still appeared to be at Singapore. The Japanese
Official History tells of the Japanese satisfaction at this
stage.

Since a British aircraft had spotted our invasion fleet [before the
landings] Vice-Admiral Ozawa judged that it was highly likely that
the British naval force would make a preventive attack on our forces
and thus he paid the greatest attention to this possibility. However,
the British had failed to attack and our units had now succeeded in
landing at various points. At this moment only a small amount of
resupplying was continuing. Even if the British attacked from now
onwards, there would be no damage done to the military units
already landed and any damage would only be to empty ships and to
a small quantity of supplies. In other words, the British naval force
had lost their best chance and the critical time for our naval units had
already passed without serious difficulty.*

The Japanese were now free to plan the next stage of
their operations, and once again their audacity and speed
were breathtaking. The troops ashore were left almost to
their own devices to fight their way into Malaya with a
bare minimum of resupplying and reinforcement. The
Japanese had no need for the huge logistical build-up
considered essential in Western armies. At around midday
on the 9th, Vice-Admiral Ozawa issued his next orders.
Most of his warships were ordered back with the empty
transports to Camranh Bay in Indo-China to take on fresh
troops for the invasion of Borneo. Only a few light warships were left behind to protect the invasion beaches. The
air units at Saigon and the submarines were left with the
main responsibility for dealing with the British warships
at Singapore. At 13.30, while *Prince of Wales* and *Repulse*
were steaming steadily north, and just before I.65 sighted
the British ships, Admiral Ozawa's orders had gone out
and many Japanese warships would soon be on their way

* Japanese Official History, p. 247.

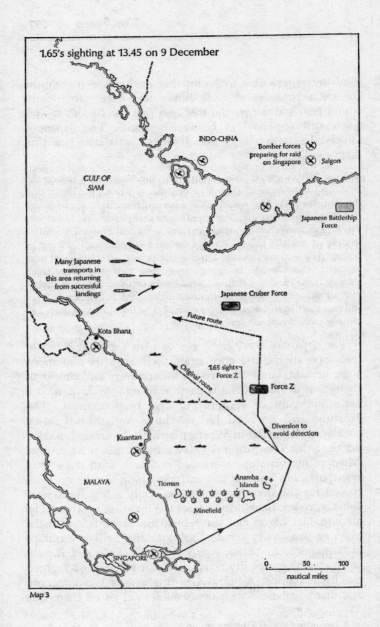

1.65's sighting at 13.45 on 9 December

INDO-CHINA

GULF OF
SIAM

Bomber forces
preparing for raid
on Singapore   Saigon

Japanese Battleship
Force

Many Japanese
transports in
this area returning
from successful
landings

Japanese Cruiser Force

Future route

Kota Bharu

Original route

1.65 sights
Force Z

Force Z

Diversion to
avoid detection

Kuantan

MALAYA   Tioman   Anamba
Islands

Minefield

SINGAPORE

0   50   100

nautical miles

Map 3

east, steaming directly into the area towards which Force Z was heading.

The false news that the British ships were still in harbour at Singapore had been received by the Japanese airmen at Saigon.

Everybody relaxed; our troopships were free of the threat of the big British guns. Although we had nothing to fear from the warships as long as they remained in Singapore, at any moment the British might move the ships out to sea where they would be in a position to attack.

Rear-Admiral Matsunaga called a staff conference in his headquarters to determine the feasibility of our bombers making a mass torpedo attack against the warships while they remained within the base.

All pilots and aircrew members were in high spirits. We had found the battleships, and the opportunity to gain even more glorious fame than the men who had successfully attacked Pearl Harbor beckoned to us. Everybody was busy investigating the water depths at the Singapore Naval Base, the best directions from which to attack, and the most advantageous flight formations to utilize. (Lieutenant Sadao Takai, Genzan Air Corps)*

Of the 138 Mitsubishis at the airfields near Saigon, nine were away attacking the British airfield at Kuantan and three more were flying reconnaissance sorties. Ground crews were working hard on the remaining aircraft, preparing them for what the Japanese airmen hoped would be a second Pearl Harbor in the morning.

But while the ground crews sweated on the airfields, the Japanese were suffering a major setback elsewhere. I.65 was just managing to keep in visual touch with the two ships she had spotted, but at 15.50 a squall obscured the view and contact was lost. Although the British ships were seen once more an hour later, the contact was lost for good at 18.00 when a seaplane approached the Japanese submarine as though to attack. Lieutenant-Commander

* This and further quotations by Lieutenant Takai are from *Zero, The Story of the Japanese Naval Air Force*, Cassell, London, 1957.

Harada dived, and when he came back to the surface half an hour later he could see nothing of the British ships. The aircraft which forced him to dive had, ironically, been a Japanese scouting seaplane from the cruiser *Kinu* which was acting as a flagship to some of the Japanese submarines.

Unfortunately for the Japanese, there had been a two-hour delay before I.65's sighting signals had been received – a delay that became the subject of some comment in the Japanese Official History. It seems that only *Kinu* and *Yura*, another cruiser acting as a submarine flagship, together with a unit described as the '81st Communications Unit', were tuned to I.65's wavelength. Either through poor radio reception conditions or by confusion in the signals arrangements, nobody at all picked up I.65's signals for an hour and a half, and it was two hours before *Kinu* managed to pass on to Vice-Admiral Ozawa the vital news that a British battleship and a battle cruiser were at sea and steaming north.

When it did arrive, I.65's signal startled Ozawa. Thinking that the British were still at Singapore, he had released most of his warships from their escort duties with the transports and they were now steaming in non-battle formation back to Camranh Bay. The air units at Saigon were mostly loading bombs for the air raid next morning on Singapore. Now, here were two powerful British ships almost into an area full of Japanese shipping with only a few hours of daylight left. No doubt the Japanese admiral roundly cursed the two-hour delay in receiving I.65's signal, and cursed still further when the submarine reported that it had lost contact with the British ships.

The first thought of the Japanese was that I.65 had been mistaken and that the British really were still at Singapore. It was an easy matter to clarify this. A reconnaissance aircraft just about to land at one of the outlying airfields at Saigon was ordered instead to land at Saigon itself, and the photographs it had taken over Singapore were rushed to the developing room. They showed a large floating dock, possibly mistaken by the aircrew for a battleship, some cruisers and a large merchant ship – no battleships! I.65's report must be true.*

The Japanese reacted quickly to this alarming situation. Vice-Admiral Ozawa, in his flagship the cruiser *Chokai*, was himself only about 120 miles from the reported position of the British ships and decided on the simple expedient of ordering every available Japanese warship to search for the British during the four remaining hours' of daylight and on during the coming night, despite the fact that a hastily prepared night action can be the most confusing of naval engagements. Once more Ozawa's orders went out by radio. Scouting planes from *Chokai* herself and from *Mogami*, *Mikuma*, *Kumano* and *Suzuya* – the four cruisers of the 7th Cruiser Squadron – were ordered to be catapulted off and to rediscover, if possible, the British ships. Unknown to Ozawa, a sixth cruiser, the *Kinu*, the submarine flagship already referred to, also sent off its seaplane. The nearest warships were then pulled into some sort of order and it was found that there were seven cruisers and at least five destroyers to join in the hunt for the British.

Vice-Admiral Kondo's battle squadron, with the old battleships *Kongo* and *Haruna*, were farther north, but these could not arrive until the early hours of the following day. A further six cruisers and several more destroyers would also be able to join in the morning. The nearest submarines were also ordered to the sighting area. The transports off the invasion beaches were ordered to stop unloading immediately and to scatter to the north. A further Japanese ploy was to order the frequent use of the

* I.65 will not be met again in this book. She was renumbered I.165 in May 1942 and remained in service as an operational boat until December 1944, sinking several Allied ships. She then served for a few months as a training boat, but in April 1945 was equipped to carry two Kaiten midget submarines; the Kaitens were the naval equivalent of the Kamikaze suicide aircraft. It was while on a Kaiten mission that I.165 was sunk with all her crew off Saipan by U.S. Navy aircraft on 27 June 1945.

radios in those of their warships which were well out to sea in a deliberate attempt to lure the British to battle and away from the invasion beaches. But there is no British record that any of these radio signals were picked up.

Hurried new plans were also made at the Saigon airfields, and Rear-Admiral Matsunaga decided on his own initiative to prepare his aircraft to join in this grand hunt that evening. The last reported position of the British ships had been only 300 miles from Matsunaga's airfields. Once more there was a delay because the aircraft had mostly been loaded with bombs and these now had to be taken out and replaced with torpedoes. Once more the ground crews sweated and heaved to get the attacking aircraft ready.

The first aircraft to get away were four reconnaissance planes which were ordered to take off at once and search for the British ships. Three formations of fifty-three attack aircraft managed to take off in the late afternoon and early evening. There had been no time to remove the bombs from nine of these aircraft, but all the others were armed with torpedoes. Local army units near Saigon had heard of what was happening and a large group of Japanese army officers came out to Saigon airfield and cheered the airmen on their way.

The position, then, in the early evening of 9 December, was that *Prince of Wales*, *Repulse* and the four destroyers were still on their northerly course, unaware as yet that they had been sighted by I.65. Attempting to find them were several more submarines, six Japanese scouting sea-planes from the cruisers, and the four search aircraft from Saigon. Intending to attack the British ships if they could be found again, were seven Japanese cruisers, at least five destroyers, several submarines, forty-four torpedo-carrying aircraft and nine bomb-carrying aircraft.

At 18.09 the sun would set. At 22.38 the moon would rise. At dawn Admiral Phillips hoped he would have the Japanese shipping off the invasion beaches under his guns.

. . .

It had been an afternoon of planning and preparation for the British. Following his earlier decision to persist with the operation, providing the Japanese did not detect the presence of his force, Admiral Phillips had finalized his plans for the coming night and for the critical first hours of daylight on the following day. Five signals had blinked out from *Prince of Wales*, some addressed to the captains of ships, some intended for every man in the crews of the ships.

TO FORCE Z   FROM C IN C E.F.

1. BESIDES A MINOR LANDING AT KHOTA BHARU WHICH WAS NOT FOLLOWED UP, LANDINGS HAVE BEEN MADE BETWEEN PATANI AND SINGORA AND A MAJOR LANDING 90 MILES NORTH OF SINGORA.

2. LITTLE IS KNOWN OF ENEMY FORCES IN THE VICINITY. IT IS BELIEVED THAT KONGO IS THE ONLY CAPITAL SHIP LIKELY TO BE MET. THREE ATAGO TYPE, ONE KAKO TYPE, AND TWO ZINTU TYPE CRUISERS HAVE BEEN REPORTED. A NUMBER OF DESTROYERS POSSIBLY OF FLEET TYPE ARE LIKELY TO BE MET.

3. MY OBJECT IS TO SURPRISE AND SINK TRANS-PORTS AND ENEMY WARSHIPS BEFORE AIR ATTACK CAN DEVELOP. OBJECTIVE CHOSEN WILL DEPEND ON AIR RECONNAISSANCE, INTEND TO ARRIVE OBJECTIVE AFTER SUNRISE TOMORROW 10TH. IF AN OPPORTUNITY TO BRING KONGO TO ACTION OCCURS THIS IS TO TAKE PRECEDENCE OVER ALL OTHER ACTION.

4. SUBJECT TO C.O.'S FREEDOM OF MANOEUVRE IN AN EMERGENCY, FORCE Z WILL REMAIN IN CLOSE ORDER AND WILL BE MANOEUVRED AS A UNIT UNTIL ACTION IS JOINED. WHEN THE SIGNAL 'ACT INDEPENDENTLY' IS MADE OR AT DISCRE-TION OF C.O. REPULSE WILL ASSUME FREEDOM MANOEUVRE REMAINING IN TACTICAL SUPPORT

BUT ENGAGING FROM A WIDE ENOUGH ANGLE TO FACILITATE FALL OF SHOT.

5. INTEND TO OPERATE AT 25 KNOTS UNLESS A CHASE DEVELOPS AND SUBSEQUENTLY TO RETIRE AT MAXIMUM SPEED ENDURANCE WILL ALLOW.

6. CAPITAL SHIPS SHOULD ATTEMPT TO CLOSE BELOW 20,000 YARDS UNTIL FIRE IS EFFECTIVE BUT SHOULD AVOID OFFERING AN END-ON TARGET. SHIPS MUST BE PREPARED TO CHANGE FROM DELAY TO NON-DELAY FUZES ACCORDING TO TARGET.

7. PRINCE OF WALES AND REPULSE ARE EACH TO HAVE ONE AIRCRAFT FUELLED AND READY TO FLY OFF IF REQUIRED. IF FLOWN OFF, AIRCRAFT MUST RETURN TO LAND BASE. KOTA BHARU AERODROME IS UNDERSTOOD TO BE OUT OF ACTION.

8. TENEDOS WILL BE DETACHED BEFORE DARK TO RETURN INDEPENDENTLY TO SINGAPORE.

9. REMAINING DESTROYERS MAY BE DESPATCHED DURING THE NIGHT 9TH/10TH SHOULD ENEMY INFORMATION REQUIRE A HIGH SPEED OF AD-VANCE. IN SUCH CASE THESE DESTROYERS ARE TO RETIRE TOWARDS ANAMBA ISLANDS AT 10 KNOTS UNTIL A RENDEZVOUS IS ORDERED BY W/T.

TO PRINCE OF WALES AND REPULSE   FROM C IN C E.F.

INFORM SHIPS COMPANIES AS FOLLOWS: BEGINS

THE ENEMY HAS MADE SEVERAL LANDINGS ON THE NORTH COAST OF MALAYA AND HAS MADE LOCAL PROGRESS. OUR ARMY IS NOT LARGE AND IS HARD PRESSED IN PLACES. OUR AIR FORCE HAS HAD TO DESTROY AND ABANDON ONE OR MORE AERODROMES. MEANWHILE FAT TRANSPORTS LIE OFF THE COAST. THIS IS OUR OPPORTUNITY

BEFORE THE ENEMY CAN ESTABLISH HIMSELF. WE HAVE MADE A WIDE CIRCUIT TO AVOID AIR RECONNAISSANCE AND HOPE TO SURPRISE THE ENEMY SHORTLY AFTER SUNRISE TOMORROW WEDNESDAY. WE MAY HAVE THE LUCK TO TRY OUR METAL AGAINST THE OLD JAPANESE BATTLE CRUISER KONGO OR AGAINST SOME JAPANESE CRUISERS AND DESTROYERS WHICH ARE REPORTED IN THE GULF OF SIAM. WE ARE SURE TO GET SOME USEFUL PRACTICE WITH THE H.A. ARMAMENT.

WHATEVER WE MEET I WANT TO FINISH QUICKLY AND SO GET WELL CLEAR TO THE EASTWARD BEFORE THE JAPANESE CAN MASS TOO FORMIDABLE A SCALE OF ATTACK AGAINST US. SO SHOOT TO SINK. ENDS.

TO REPULSE AND PRINCE OF WALES   FROM C IN C E.F.

FROM DAWN ACTION STATIONS AND THROUGH DAYLIGHT TOMORROW WEDNESDAY ALL RANKS AND RATINGS ARE TO WEAR CLOTHING SUCH AS OVERALLS OR SUITS WHICH KEEP ARMS AND LEGS COVERED AGAINST RISK OF BURNS FROM FLASH.

TO REPULSE, ELECTRA, VAMPIRE,
PRINCE OF WALES, EXPRESS, TENEDOS.
FROM C IN C E.F.

COURSE WILL BE ALTERED TO 320 DEGREES AT 18.00 BY SIGNAL. COURSE IS TO BE ALTERED TO 280 DEGREES AT 19.30 AND SPEED INCREASED TO 24 KNOTS WITHOUT SIGNAL. AT 22.00 DESTROYERS ARE TO PART COMPANY WITHOUT SIGNAL AND PROCEED TO SOUTHEASTWARD SUBSEQUENTLY ADJUSTING COURSE AND SPEED SO AS TO R/V AT POINT C AT 16.00/10 UNLESS OTHERWISE ORDERED*

* Point C was near the Anamba Islands.

TO REPULSE, PRINCE OF WALES   FROM C IN C
E.F.

UNLESS FURTHER INFORMATION IS RECEIVED,
INTEND TO MAKE SINGORA AT 07.45 AND SUBSE-
QUENTLY WORK TO EASTWARDS ALONG COAST. I
HAVE KEPT TO EASTWARDS SO AS TO TRY AND
REMAIN UNLOCATED TODAY WHICH IS THE MOST
IMPORTANT THING OF ALL.

Not only Captain Tennant, but every man on the six
ships of Force Z, now knew what was in the mind of their
commander. The five signals require little amplification;
there is not much to be read between the lines on this
occasion. The fourth signal, ordering the destroyers to
part company after dark, shows that Admiral Phillips had
finally decided that it would be better to make the final
attack without destroyers. A memorandum at the Public
Record Office later written by Captain L. H. Bell, a senior
member of Admiral Phillips's staff, shows the reasoning
behind that decision.

The Admiral's plan had been to detach the destroyers at midnight
9/10th and make a high-speed descent on Singora with the less vulnerable *Prince of Wales* and *Repulse* only. He considered the destroyers
would be very vulnerable to air attack; with the exception of *Electra*
they were not fully worked up and their operational [fuel] endurance
was a perpetual anxiety. The Admiral relied on the speed and surprise of the battleships to avoid damage to these ships sufficient to
slow them down, believing that Japanese aircraft would not be carrying anti-ship bombs and torpedoes and that the Force, on retirement,
would only have to deal with hastily organized long-range bombers
from bases in Indo-China.*

The low cloud and bad visibility had persisted through
the afternoon, but at about 16.45, less than two hours
before sunset, the cloud and misty conditions disappeared

* Public Record Office ADM 199/1149.

and were replaced by a brilliantly clear tropical evening. While this new development made the British apprehensive about the possibility of their being spotted, it did not alter the factual balance of the operation. The Japanese knew that the British were in the area from I.65's signals and had by now mounted their big search operation. Force Z was being hunted, but did not yet know it.

A more important development occurred about one hour later when *Prince of Wales*'s radar screen picked up the traces of three aircraft. The British hoped that these were friendly, but when the first aircraft was sighted visually, low down on the horizon, it was seen to be a small single-engined seaplane. The three aircraft were all Japanese Aichi E13A seaplanes (codenamed 'Jakes' by the Allies), which had been catapulted off from the Japanese cruisers to follow up I.65's sighting report. The seaplanes kept well out of range of the British guns and calmly plotted the speed and course of the British ships. It was now that a standing patrol of R.A.F. or Fleet Air Arm fighters could have been useful, either by shooting down the Japanese shadowers before they could get off their reports, or at least by driving them away so that Force Z could make a change of course unobserved. But the only friendly aircraft seen that evening was one Catalina flying boat.

Now the balance of knowledge really had changed. The Japanese had gained a further confirmation of the presence of the British ships and an up-to-date position, but, more importantly, the British now knew that their presence was no longer a secret. The one remaining condition of Admiral Phillips for the continuation of his operation appeared to have gone.

The sun set a few minutes after 6 p.m. The gathering darkness, coming so soon after the sighting of the enemy planes, brought a sense of foreboding. What lay beyond the horizon? What strength could the Japanese gather around the small force of British ships in the darkness?

Two men, an officer aboard *Prince of Wales* and a rating aboard *Repulse*, describe their feelings at this time.

We stood on the upper deck and watched the Jap float-plane in the now fading light. Our 5·25-in. guns traversed silently and menacingly, but the range was too great and, alas, we had no fighter aircraft available. We could well imagine the excitement, the conjectures, and of course the preparations the Japanese airman's radio messages would arouse at his base. And we cursed the fact that sheer chance had revealed us in that short, clear period before darkness fell.

We were to be at our action stations all night then, and I wandered into the wardroom for supper, by now a bleak, comfortless wardroom, with pictures, books and trophies taken down and all movable objects firmly lashed, in the usual preparations for impending action. There was a cold, uninteresting help-yourself supper, the stewards and attendants being already employed on their various jobs in gun turrets, ammunition hoists and shell rooms.

I didn't feel hungry. But I thought what a curse a vivid imagination could be and wished we could hurry up and get on with it. Everyone seemed rather quiet. I went down to my cabin, put on some warm clothing and stuffed some chocolate, a torch, a hypodermic syringe and a packet of tie-on casualty labels into my pockets, adjusted my uninflated lifebelt round my waist, and went out, taking a last look at my cabin with all its personal belongings and wondering vaguely, 'What the hell will you look like this time tomorrow?' (Surgeon Lieutenant-Commander E. D. Caldwell)

I remember discussing the likely battle with the Master Gunner, who had joined *Repulse* the same day as myself, a quiet, cool, appraisal in which he in as many words stated that 'with surprise on our side we could give a good account of ourselves', meaning *Repulse* mainly as *Prince of Wales* even then was regarded as not fully worked up, but it was unlikely we would get back to base. This was just 'matter-of-fact' discussion but prompted me for the first time in thousands of miles of U-boat waters to prepare for a likely sinking, i.e. I wore my small inflatable lifebelt *constantly* and waterproofed my pound notes in the prescribed sick-bay manner [in a condom] and decided which would be the abandon route or alternative. (Sick Berth Attendant W. Bridgewater)

Half an hour after sunset, the destroyer *Tenedos* swung out from her position in the screen and turned back south.

The old ship had performed a useful function in helping to escort the two capital ships for twenty-four hours and across 420 miles of sea, but her fuel capacity was so limited that she would become a liability in the event of high-speed work, and so Admiral Phillips ordered her to make her own way back to Singapore. Phillips had passed a signal to *Tenedos* which the destroyer was to transmit to Singapore at 08.00 on the following day asking Rear-Admiral Palliser to arrange for as many destroyers as possible, including the American destroyers expected at Singapore, to come out and meet *Prince of Wales* and *Repulse* at a point north of the Anamba Islands at dawn of the 11th. The added destroyer protection would be required to escort the two capital ships past any Japanese submarines that might be stationed in the approaches to Singapore. The detachment of *Tenedos* at this time and with this signal reveals that, despite the recent appearance of the Japanese aircraft, Admiral Phillips had still made no decision to abandon the operation.

Lieutenant Richard Dyer, captain of *Tenedos*, watched Force Z disappear into the darkness. He little suspected that his own ship would be the first to see action.

At 18.50, a further half-hour after *Tenedos* left, the pre-arranged course change was made and the five ships turned north-west, course 320 degrees, and the speed was worked up to 26 knots. Force Z was now heading towards the invasion beaches and into the very heart of enemy-dominated waters, and there was no sign from the flagship that the operation would not still go ahead as planned, despite their sighting by Japanese aircraft. But within only minutes of the course change, an incident occurred that Admiral Phillips would have to take into consideration. The lookouts on *Electra* sighted a flare estimated to be five miles ahead; the light seemed to hover for a few moments just above the surface of the sea and then it died out. The flagship ordered all ships to make an emergency turn to port in order to pass well clear of the flare's position.

Even while Admiral Phillips was pondering the significance of this new development, another signal arrived from Rear-Admiral Palliser.

TO C IN C E.F.   FROM C.O.S.

MOST IMMEDIATE

ONE BATTLESHIP, 'M' CLASS CRUISER, 11 DESTROY-
ERS AND A NUMBER OF TRANSPORTS REPORTED
CLOSE TO COAST BETWEEN KOTA BHARU AND
PERHENTIAN ISLAND BY AIR RECONNAISSANCE
AFTERNOON.

This was the long-awaited signal, giving what Phillips hoped was the latest news about the Japanese landing areas. He had always believed that the Singora area in Siam was the scene of the most important Japanese landing; this signal did not mention Singora, but indicated that a large force was now supporting the landing at Kota Bharu; Perhentian Island was a few miles south of Kota Bahru. A further signal, fifteen minutes later, corrected the time of the air reconnaissance and stated that the Japanese ships had been seen at 10.30 that morning. Kota Bharu was actually 130 sea miles nearer to Singapore than Singora, and a diversion to this target would give the British ships a far less hazardous run when daylight came. What Admiral Phillips did not know was that, since the air reconnaissance at Kota Bharu that morning, the Japanese landing there had been all but completed and most of the ships involved were either on their way back to Indo-China or at that very moment hunting Force Z itself.

It was as well for their peace of mind that the British were unaware of the intense Japanese activity all around and above them. On the other hand, the Japanese had taken the most outrageous risks in launching their ships and aircraft into this hastily prepared and uncoordinated hunt. But, just as the main aim of the British had been to get among the transport shipping supporting the landings, so the main Japanese aim was to protect their landings whatever the risks involved.

It was the seaplane from *Kinu*, the cruiser acting as a submarine flagship, which had got off the first sighting report well before dusk.

FOUND 2 ENEMY BATTLESHIPS. POSITION WSM. COURSE 340 DEGREES. 13 KNOTS. 3 ESCORTING DESTROYERS.

This report surprised Vice-Admiral Ozawa; he did not know that *Kinu*'s captain had sent his seaplane to join in the search. It was as well for the Japanese that he did so since the search plan for the seaplanes of the five other cruisers was spread like a fan to the west of Force Z's true position and they would most probably not have found Force Z before dark. The navigation of the submarine I.65 had been in error and she had been broadcasting sightings at incorrect positions.

The report of *Kinu*'s seaplane was quickly followed by two more, from *Suzuya*'s and then *Kumano*'s aircraft, although the last report contained an error in estimating the British ships' course as 50 degrees and counting the destroyers in the escort as five. (There were still four; these sightings were before *Tenedos* left.) This successful seaplane search had been costly for the Japanese. *Kumano*'s plane was lost; *Yura*'s hit a mountain on Procondor Island and was seriously damaged; and *Sazuya*'s forcelanded on the sea later and the destroyer *Hamakaze* had to be detached to rescue it.

Despite the various errors in the seaplane reports, Vice-Admiral Ozawa had been able to plot the northerly progress of the British ships before the British turned west after dark. Using their radios freely in the attempt to draw the British into battle, Ozawa's cruiser and destroyer force turned north-east to intercept them. When Admiral Phillips did make his turn to the west after dark, Ozawa's ships were only a few miles away and now directly in the path of Force Z.

Meanwhile, the land-based Mitsubishis from Saigon continued their search after dark. It was a dangerous task because it was now completely dark with four hours to go to moonrise. One of the reconnaissance planes met with an accident – of which no details are available – and this dislocated the search plan. But another reconnaissance aircraft, piloted by Lieutenant Takeda, flying just above the surface of the sea, suddenly flew over two bright lanes of white foam – the wakes of large ships! Takeda banked and flew carefully up the wakes and soon found the two black shadows of what he took to be British ships. He was not spotted and climbed away to get off a sighting report.

The fifty-three torpedo- and bomb-carrying aircraft of the main attacking force had by now reached the area. Lieutenant Sadao Takai of the Genzan Corps was again one of the pilots.

The sun had dropped below the horizon. Visibility was very poor, and we were flying in three-plane formation.

Unfortunately, there was still a serious problem to be solved. We had not decided, when the operation began, on any definite measures for differentiating between the enemy vessels and our own warships during close-range sea battles, when such identification can be extremely difficult. We did not know the definite location of the enemy warships; furthermore, we had no information as to the location of our own ships this night. How were we to distinguish one from another?

Not having received any training on this matter, and not having had time to discuss warship identification before we took off, our air and sea forces were rushing into the battle blindly. It seemed as if we might be caught in our own traps!

The clouds seemed to stretch endlessly over the ocean. We could not emerge from them, and the task of observing the ocean surface was becoming increasingly difficult. We could not fly much higher than 1,000 feet. Under such conditions our chances for discovering the enemy fleet were doubtful unless we happened to fly directly over the British ships, or crossed their wakes.

However, the situation was not hopeless. We had many planes searching the ocean and any one of them might sight the enemy forces. There was also the chance that we might discover the enemy

TELEPHONE: BOSTON
(STD Code 0205) 364555

MARTIN MIDDLEBROOK,
48 LINDEN WAY,
BOSTON, LINCS. PE21 9DS
GREAT BRITAIN.

Jane,

You are honoured. Lincoln only ordered three copies for their favoured members of the Gallipoli party! Mary is going as well — no travel insurance this time!

With Compliments

best wishes, MK

inadvertently in the event that he sighted our planes and fired upon them. When one flies in almost total darkness one feels that the enemy might appear suddenly and without warning before one's eyes.

Farther and farther we flew southward in search of the enemy fleet.

A radio report from one of our searching bombers brought jubilation to our hearts. The anxiously sought enemy vessels had been sighted!

The radio report continued: 'We have dropped a flare.'

Vice-Admiral Ozawa promptly received a great fright. It was his flagship, the cruiser *Chokai*, that was being illuminated by the flare and on to which Lieutenant Takeda was directing the other Japanese aircraft. This was also the flare seen by *Electra* which caused Admiral Phillips to sheer off to the south. Admiral Ozawa's reaction was to turn away to the north, and at the same time to send a frantic signal to Saigon:

THERE ARE THREE ATTACKING PLANES ABOVE CHOKAI. IT IS CHOKAI UNDER THE FLARE.

At Saigon, Rear-Admiral Matsunaga read this signal and realized that his hastily mounted intervention in the night hunt had to be brought to an end. He ordered the air search to be discontinued.

It was some time before all the aircraft received this order, but no more sightings took place and no harm was done. The aircraft now had to wait until moonrise, two and a half hours later, before they could land, but they all did so safely, their crews frustrated and tired. The naval commanders too had been badly shaken by the incident. Vice-Admiral Ozawa decided it would be more prudent to withdraw at least until the moon rose, but Vice-Admiral Kondo, the overall commander, who was still well to the north with the battleships *Kongo* and *Haruna*, now stepped in and imposed his will on these confused activities. Kondo sent out orders that all Japanese forces were to prepare for the encounter which he now expected would take place immediately after dawn of the following day, the

10th. The Japanese Official History contains an interesting summary of Admiral Kondo's thoughts at that time.

The British warships' guns were judged to be far superior to ours but we were far superior in supporting units. In other words, greater fire power for them and greater torpedo and air power for us. But much difficulty was expected for our destroyer torpedo attacks because of the great speed of the British ships and they were also believed to be equipped with radar.

So, in a sea battle in bad visibility and rain, our side would be at a great disadvantage. Even in our Navy at that time not everyone believed that air attack was the best method of effectively sinking a large battleship; in fact such men were in a minority. In addition, this battleship was the *Prince of Wales*, the so-called unsinkable battleship. So we prepared with much determination for the battle next morning.*

The intervening hours would enable Admiral Kondo with his two battleships to steam nearer to the expected battle area, some of his destroyers to refuel from tankers, and the air units to be refuelled for further operations — but this time by daylight with much less danger of attacking their own ships.

Lieutenant Takeda's flare and then Admiral Kondo's new plans had finally ruled out all chance of a night encounter. Neither side realized how close they had been to what could well have been one of the decisive sea battles of the war. When the flare dropped and caused both sides to sheer away, there had been only five miles between Force Z and the Japanese cruiser force; indeed, it is surprising that *Chokai* had not been picked up on *Prince of Wales's* radar, which had a theoretical range of up to twenty-five miles. If there had been no flare and the two sides had met, the result of the battle can only be conjecture. The British had the heavy 14-in. and 15-in. guns; the best the Japanese cruisers had were 8-in. Moreover, the British gunnery could be radar-controlled in darkness, and although this type of fighting was still in its infancy, the use of radar

* Japanese Official History, p. 437.

generally would have been an immense advantage to the British in a night action.

What could have been the possible outcome of such a battle between a British battleship, battle cruiser and three destroyers and six Japanese cruisers with their destroyer escorts? If the British guns could have got to work at close range, they might have blown the Japanese ships out of the water. If the Japanese torpedoes had found their marks, the British ships might well have been crippled, or at least slowed down for the morning. And what might the Japanese aircraft have achieved in a confusing night action? If they had carried out torpedo attacks that night, one effect might have been crucial. There were only enough aerial torpedoes in this theatre of war for just one torpedo to each aircraft. Every torpedo launched would have been one less for future use, and if they had been dropped wholesale, and had failed to score hits on the British ships in the darkness, then it really could have changed the course of future events.

But there was no battle. *Chokai* and the other Japanese cruisers continued on their northerly course. Admiral Phillips was soon to make a further and much more significant course change.

When Force Z turned to port to avoid the area where the flare had been seen, everyone on the British ships was expecting that the original course would eventually be resumed. But during these few minutes Admiral Sir Tom Phillips took what was probably the most important and possibly the most difficult decision of his life. There was no lack of courage in him, or of willingness to fight, and there was certainly much of the old naval tradition that an admiral would never go far wrong if he laid his ships alongside those of his enemy. But a modern admiral needed more than these traditional qualities. With Britain's naval strength stretched so thin, with the only sizeable ships in this theatre of war under his hand, Tom Phillips needed to show discretion as well as valour.

It was really quite simple. Constant fighter cover he knew he could not have. Surprise he knew he no longer possessed. Although he did not know how close around him were the Japanese ships and aircraft, he certainly knew that they would all be there in the morning. Japanese warships he could gladly fight, and the aircraft too if necessary, but there was one other factor. Phillips knew that any prudent enemy admiral would by now have scattered the merchant ships, that the Japanese would have cleared the waters off Singora and Kota Bharu. Even if *Prince of Wales* and *Repulse* did fight their way through, Phillips knew that there would be no targets for their big guns in the morning. A risk incurred for a great prize was certainly acceptable, but the possible loss of two ships for nothing was not. The various factors must have been tossed about in Tom Phillips's mind, but the trained mind of a high-ranking professional naval officer could only lead him to one conclusion. There was no longer any chance of success. This operation must now be called off – and quickly. They had already lost nearly two valuable hours of darkness, hours in which his ships could have been speeding back to the comparative safety of Singapore to fight another day.

Admiral Phillips had actually been thinking of taking this course of action ever since the Japanese seaplanes spotted Force Z late that afternoon, and had told his staff that he would turn back for Singapore at midnight unless there was any change in the situation. It was a bitter moment for the British admiral. In a few hours he might have been making a glorious name for himself; now he would be known as an admiral who brought his fleet home after deliberately avoiding action with the enemy. The decision also marked the final failure of twenty years of British naval policy for the Far East, but as taken by Tom Phillips it showed a great deal of moral courage. The next twenty-four hours would tell whether it had been delayed too long.

.   .   .   .   .

The original course was never resumed. At 20.05 a reduction in speed to 20 knots was ordered, and fifteen minutes later a new course given that would take Force Z back to Singapore via the Anamba Islands. At 20.55 a blue night-signalling lamp blinked out this message to *Repulse*:

I HAVE MOST REGRETFULLY CANCELLED THE OPERATION BECAUSE, HAVING BEEN LOCATED BY AIRCRAFT, SURPRISE WAS LOST AND OUR TARGET WOULD BE ALMOST CERTAIN TO BE GONE BY THE MORNING AND THE ENEMY FULLY PREPARED FOR US.

Captain Bell, the officer on Admiral Phillips's staff who later filed a memorandum on the operation, stated that this signal brought 'a spontaneous signal from *Repulse* which cheered the Admiral as it showed that the Captain of *Repulse* appreciated the difficulty of the decision and agreed with it'.

8

Kuantan

The five ships of Force Z steamed on to the south, away from the scene of a battle that might have been. The moon crept above the horizon to improve visibility, but there was nothing to be seen by the British lookouts; there were no Japanese eyes to witness the British withdrawal. Some of the 3,000 or more men on the British ships were asleep, but most were at or near their Action Stations and had ample opportunity to digest the implication of the recent course change and the news that they were returning to Singapore. It is not possible to generalize on the sailors' reactions to this latest change in their prospects; a feeling of disappointment by many who had nerved themselves to face action was probably balanced by the more basic human reaction of relief that this particular battle was not now to be fought.

It was now almost thirty hours since Rear-Admiral Palliser at Singapore had last seen his chief. Palliser was keeping in touch as best he could with all developments of the two-day-old war, and was keeping Force Z informed by signal of those events which he thought would be of interest to Admiral Phillips. Palliser knew that Phillips would not break radio silence until it became compelling to do so, and he had to try and imagine what decisions Phillips would be making on receipt of each of his signals – a mental exercise that became progressively more difficult as the hours passed and the number of dispatched signals piled up. Palliser must have been aware of the difficult choices that had faced his superior that evening, and at 21.45 he sent a further signal.

1. ONLY SIGNIFICANCE OF ENEMY REPORT IS CONTAINED IN MY 11.26Z 9TH. ENEMY APPAR-

ENTLY CONTINUING LANDING IN KOTA BHARU
AREA WHICH SHOULD BE FRUITFUL AS WELL AS
SINGORA.

2. ON THE OTHER HAND ENEMY BOMBERS ON
SOUTH INDO CHINA AERODROMES ARE IN FORCE
AND UNDISTURBED. THEY COULD ATTACK YOU
FIVE HOURS AFTER SIGHTING AND MUCH DEPENDS
ON WHETHER YOU HAVE BEEN SEEN TODAY. TWO
CARRIERS MAY BE IN SAIGON AREA.

3. MILITARY SITUATION AT KOTA BHARU APPEARS
DIFFICULT. AERODROME IS IN ENEMY HANDS.

4. ALL OUR NORTHERN AERODROMES ARE BECOM-
ING UNTENABLE DUE TO ENEMY AIR ACTION. C IN C
FAR EAST HINTS HE IS CONSIDERING CONCEN-
TRATING ALL AIR EFFORTS ON DEFENCE OF
SINGAPORE AREA.

5. EXTREMELY DIFFICULT TO GIVE YOU CLEARER
PICTURE BECAUSE AIR RECONNAISSANCE COM-
MUNICATIONS ARE SO SLOW DUE PARTLY TO
DAMAGE TO AERODROMES.

There is more here than a gentle hint of restraint by
Palliser. He was pointing the finger at Kota Bharu, much
nearer than Singora, as a possible target for Force Z, and
then spelling out in some detail the dangers from Japanese
aircraft and the deteriorating position of the R.A.F. The
unwitting errors in this signal were that there were no
Japanese aircraft carriers at Saigon, only comparatively
harmless seaplane tenders, and that the Japanese had now
completed their main landing at Kota Bharu. In fact all
the information was now irrelevant since Admiral Phillips
had already called off the main operation and Force Z was
steaming south. The signal is of interest, however, in that
it reveals that Palliser was well in step with his chief by
sending this information within two hours of the time that
Phillips had been faced with the important decision of
whether or not to carry on with the operation. It is also

of interest in that it seems to indicate that Palliser was only too well aware of the potential danger from Japanese aircraft.

The all-important factor of how much in tune with each other's thoughts were Admiral at sea and Chief of Staff ashore was soon to be put to a further test as Palliser now had a new, and startling, item of information to send.

IMMEDIATE

ENEMY REPORTED LANDING KUANTAN. LATITUDE 03.50 NORTH.

Kuantan was a town on the east coast of Malaya, exactly half-way between Kota Bharu and Singapore. There was there a small harbour, an important R.A.F. airfield, and several roads running not only north and south along the coast but also inland, right across the peninsula. A successful landing by the Japanese at Kuantan could cut off the British forces in northern Malaya and bring the Japanese to within 180 miles of Singapore.

The Kuantan signal was received in *Prince of Wales* just before midnight, and tired as he must have been, Admiral Phillips realized at once the implications of this latest development. It is easy to deduce Phillips's reaction. Kuantan was not far from Force Z's return route and the British ships could easily appear off Kuantan early the next morning. The Japanese, as far as Phillips knew, had last spotted Force Z well to the north, still steaming north and presumably about to make a sortie into the Gulf of Siam. The Japanese could have no means, on the intelligence they held at that moment, of expecting the British ships to appear off Kuantan in five hours' time. This assessment by Phillips was perfectly justified. Moreover, Kuantan was four hundred miles from the Japanese airfields in Indo-China, which Phillips might have reckoned was a safe distance from Japanese torpedo bombers at Saigon, and certainly a safe one from the two Japanese aircraft carriers that Palliser believed to be off Saigon.

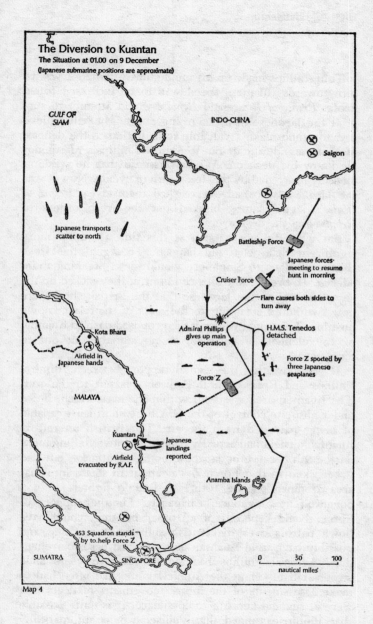

The Diversion to Kuantan
The Situation at 01.00 on 9 December
(Japanese submarine positions are approximate)

GULF OF
SIAM

INDO-CHINA

⊗ Saigon

⊗

Japanese transports
scatter to north

Battleship Force

Japanese forces
meeting to resume
hunt in morning

Cruiser Force

Flare causes both sides to
turn away

Admiral Phillips
gives up main
operation

H.M.S. Tenedos
detached

● Kota Bharu

⊗
Airfield in
Japanese hands

Force Z spotted by
three Japanese
seaplanes

Force Z

MALAYA

Kuantan
⊗
Airfield
evacuated by R.A.F.

Japanese
landings
reported

Anamba Islands

⊗

453 Squadron stands
by to help Force Z

SUMATRA

SINGAPORE

0   50   100
nautical miles

Map 4

Tom Phillips made up his mind quickly. Force Z was to turn towards Kuantan, speed was to be increased to 25 knots. *Prince of Wales* and *Repulse* would attempt to surprise the Japanese in the morning and might still achieve a victory and make a valuable contribution to the defence of Malaya and Singapore. We know Phillips's reasoning, we know his decision. We can assume that he was immensely heartened by this fresh turn of events. Now it was the Japanese who had overreached themselves. *Prince of Wales*'s signal lamps blinked out the fresh orders to *Repulse* and the destroyers.

But what did not happen at this time is rather more significant than what did happen. To signal this fresh change of plans to Singapore would mean breaking radio silence. To break radio silence might, if they picked up the signal, reveal to the Japanese that the British ships were now two hours steaming to the *south* of their last known position. This could well rob the proposed dash to Kuantan of any element of surprise, so no signal went out to Singapore.

It was now that the mental rapport between Admiral Phillips and Rear-Admiral Palliser was put to the test. The Kuantan area was well within the area which, if not under absolute control of the R.A.F., was at least capable of being patrolled from the air. The British aircraft at Kuantan airfield had actually been withdrawn to Singapore on the 9th because of Japanese bombing attacks, but had it been known that Force Z was about to steam into that area at dawn on the 10th, the Buffalo fighters of 453 Squadron at Singapore, earmarked for the support of Force Z and kept out of all other fighting, could have flown patrols over the British ships next morning and possibly have used Kuantan as a forward base for refuelling. Admiral Phillips had served for two years as a senior staff officer at the Admiralty and had often had to make assessments of the future movements of fleets that were at sea and keeping radio silence. It is quite possible that Phillips assumed that Palliser would automatically arrange for the Buffaloes to be patrolling off Kuantan next morning. It is not known whether Palliser did consider this, but certainly nothing was done about it. R.A.F. Headquarters at Singapore had no idea at all of where Force Z was, and the Buffaloes remained on the ground at Singapore next morning.

There is one more factor that may have been at work. When at the Admiralty, Phillips had often had a hand in directing the operations of ships at sea; the Admiralty liked to have centralized control of such operations. Although London was half a world away, Phillips was well aware that the Operations Room at the Admiralty would be monitoring all Pallisers' signals and following this operation closely. If Phillips now signalled his future intentions to Palliser at Singapore, the Admiralty also would get to know of them. It can only be conjecture that Tom Phillips wanted to keep control of this operation himself, and by making sure that the Japanese did not know where Force Z was bound, was also ensuring that the Admiralty did not know and were less likely thereby to interfere in his decisions. But the R.A.F. were also prevented from knowing the movements of Force Z.

When the Japanese had harnessed all their forces to hunt down the British ships the previous evening, the submarines in the patrol lines farther south had been ordered to move north, to spread out and keep their eyes open for the British ships. Mindful, no doubt, of the two-hour delay in receiving I.65's sighting report the previous afternoon, the Japanese had also ordered a new and much tighter signal procedure.

One of these submarines was I.58, captained by Lieutenant-Commander Sohichi Kitamura. The Japanese Official History says that I.58 sighted the British as early as 23.52 (Singapore Time), which was while Force Z was on a southerly course after Admiral Phillips had given up the idea of raiding the Japanese invasion beaches to the north but before the course was altered to the south-west towards Kuantan. I.58 had been on the surface when her lookouts spotted the dark shadows of two large ships only 600 metres away. Kitamura dived immediately, examined the ships through his periscope and correctly identified them as the British ships he was searching for, not heading north, as he had expected, but south. He immediately prepared to carry out a submerged torpedo attack on the leading ship, *Prince of Wales*, which was coming into an ideal target position. But I.58 was an old submarine; she had been launched in 1925 and was now one of the veterans among Japanese submarines on active service. To the frustration of her crew, one of the torpedo-tube hatches jammed and the British battleship passed out of range. *Repulse* also steamed by while the Japanese were struggling with the faulty hatch, and by the time the trouble was cleared, *Repulse* was no more than a stern target drawing rapidly away. Five torpedoes were fired; all missed. Neither the radar of the British capital ships nor the Asdic sets of the destroyers had detected the submarine.

Lieutenant-Commander Kitamura had got a sighting report off before making the torpedo attack, but this first report was only picked up by a ship of the Japanese 3rd Destroyer Division and was either not forwarded to a higher command or not picked up by that command until much later. Kitamura continued to shadow on the surface and sent out three more signals.

OUR POSITION FU.MO.RO.45. HAVE LAUNCHED 5 TORPEDOES AT REPULSE BUT MISSED. ENEMY COURSE 180 DEGREES, SPEED 22 KNOTS. 03.41. [02.11 Singapore Time]

ENEMY FLEET NOW STEAMING 240 DEGREES, EMITTING MUCH BLACK SMOKE WHICH WE ARE FOLLOWING. 04.25. [02.55]

WE HAVE LOST SIGHT OF THE ENEMY. 06.15. [04.45]

The first and last of these three signals were received safely by the relevant naval and air headquarters, but not the vital second one which would have told the Japanese that the British had changed course to the south-west. Again, that signal was picked up by the 3rd Destroyer Division, but again not forwarded properly up the Japanese chain of command.

I.58 had done a fine job in hanging on despite her age for nearly five hours to a battle fleet steaming at 25 knots.* The Japanese commanders now knew that the British had given up their foray to the north and were returning, but again because of their faulty signal procedures, did not appreciate that the British ships were steaming south-west towards the Malayan coast and not due south to Singapore.

Completely unaware of I.58's activities, Force Z steamed through the early hours of 10 December in the direction of Kuantan. The crews were at second-degree readiness the whole time – a period of tension, lassitude and the low spirits often found in those last hours before dawn. For some it was a time for routine work. Cook J. H. Larthwell came on duty in *Repulse* at 02.00 and baked 800 pounds of bread in the next four hours. 'I reckoned I was the last man to bake bread in the *Repulse*.'

Yet another signal was relayed to *Prince of Wales*'s signal office, this time from the Admiralty in London.

PERSONAL FROM FIRST SEA LORD

AS TORPEDO AIRCRAFT ATTACK ON SHIPS AT ANCHOR IN JOHORE STRAIT CANNOT BE RULED OUT, I AM SURE YOU HAVE IN MIND M/LD. 02033/ 41, DATED 22 APRIL 1941, PARAGRAPH 18-(14), WHICH YOU TOOK SO MUCH INTEREST IN.

---

* I.58 was renumbered I.158 in 1942 and relegated to the role of training submarine the same year. In the last months of the war she was, like I.65(I.165), adapted to carrying Kaiten midget submarines and returned to active service. She was surrendered to the U.S. Navy at the end of the war and later scuttled.

Did Tom Phillips smile when he read this signal? Could he imagine Sir Dudley Pound in London, nervous, not about the possibility of *Prince of Wales* and *Repulse* being caught at sea by Japanese aircraft, but at the chance of them being attacked while at anchor as the Italian battleships had been caught by the Fleet Air Arm at Taranto – the incident which probably inspired the document referred to in this signal? The staff officer who took this signal to Admiral Phillips remembers that both he and the admiral could not understand the relevance of this signal and that Phillips said something about 'the first Sea Lord going off at half-cock'. This was an important signal, however, because it *might* have meant that the Admiralty were in possession of intelligence information that the Japanese aircraft in Indo-China had a torpedo-carrying capability. If this was so, then it was a tragedy that the Admiralty did not spell out the danger more clearly. No one on board *Prince of Wales* paid any further attention to the signal.

The receipt of this signal was the only incident before dawn.

An early breakfast had been served on the British warships an hour before dawn, and there was a noticeable heightening of tension. 'We had visions of surprising a large number of Jap transports and warships at dawn, sinking the lot and beating a hasty retreat south.' But, again, for many men it was just a time of normal routine. A group of communication ratings on watch in *Prince of Wales* had tested all their lines and then settled down to share out some private delicacies that one man had brought on watch. Lieutenant-Commander Hancock, the Fleet Wireless Officer, suggested that a fund be started for such refreshments to be purchased on a regular basis, and every man gave a shilling to start the kitty.

Full Action Stations were manned just before dawn, which broke at about 05.00. It was cool, and the light gradually spread from the horizon behind the ships to bring forth a calm day with excellent visibility. To everyone's relief the lookouts could see nothing in any direction. Force Z was still some sixty miles from Kuantan and the coast not yet in sight. The sun climbed higher and began to warm the gun crews and the lookouts in their exposed positions. There was every promise of a hot day to come.

At 05.15 four dots were spotted on the horizon to the north; they were at first judged to be a cruiser and three destroyers, and, if so, could only be Japanese. Admiral Phillips ordered his force to turn towards this sighting, but within minutes the dots were identified as a large tug or small steamer towing three barges – Japanese invasion barges perhaps? Phillips spent only the shortest time coming to his next decision. If these were Japanese they were not at that stage worth the attention of the British ships; more important targets were probably just over the horizon in the direction of Kuantan. The original course was resumed.

Soon after 06.30 there was a further ripple of excitement and some apprehension when *Repulse*'s lookouts spotted an aircraft low on the horizon, apparently shadowing the British ships. The aircraft could not be identified, but remained at the same distance for perhaps half an hour – reports vary – before disappearing. The implications were enormous. If the aircraft was Japanese and had reported to its base, as it was reasonable to assume, then the enemy once more knew the exact location and course of the British ships. But no action of any kind was taken by Admiral Phillips. Radio silence was still maintained and no R.A.F. air cover was requested.

After the strange aeroplane had departed, the Walrus amphibian aircraft aboard *Prince of Wales* was hauled on to its catapult and prepared for flight. Its Fleet Air Arm pilot, Lieutenant C. R. Bateman, received his orders – fly to Kuantan and inspect the beaches and harbour, report back to *Prince of Wales*, then fly to Singapore or a friendly airfield to land. At 07.18 the Walrus was catapulted off. Bateman and his crew did not take long to fly to Kuantan, but they could see no Japanese ships and soon reported back to *Prince of Wales*. The Walrus then flew away and is believed to have landed in a minefield near Singapore; the crew were picked up by a launch, but the Walrus was abandoned.

Forty minutes later Force Z was itself within sight of land, but again nothing out of the ordinary could be seen; there was certainly no obvious warlike activity. *Prince of Wales* and *Repulse* could not approach too close to the shore, and turned to steam parallel to the coast at 15 knots. Despite the report of the Walrus, Admiral Phillips decided that he wanted a closer examination of the shore and, in particular, of Kuantan's small harbour. This could be seen from *Prince of Wales* only as a small break in the dense trees of the mainland. The destroyer *Express* was ordered to steam well in to reconnoitre.

As *Express* creamed her way across the blue water towards the land there were hundreds of pairs of eyes peering intently at the shore. One man with binoculars could see 'a nebulous stretch of tropical coastline, nothing but sand, surf and tropical vegetation', and another, 'a solitary motor cyclist scampering along the road between beach and jungle'.

Express was away just an hour.

We sailed into the shore and took a good look around. Could we see Japanese landing craft on the beaches? All I could see was dead vegetation and not a movement of life – not even Dorothy Lamour. (Able Seaman J. M. Farrington)

Another *Express* man says that he saw 'just one solitary white man waving'. Lieutenant-Commander Cartwright finished his search, set course back to the open sea and signalled *Prince of Wales* that all he had found was 'complete peace'. One version of the signal quotes it as being:

ALL IS AS QUIET AS A WET SUNDAY AFTERNOON.

Many men aboard the ships waiting for *Express* were unhappy at this prolonged examination; the destroyer had

done no more than confirm what the Walrus had already
found.

The longer we were hanging about there the less I liked it. There was
absolutely nothing, ashore or at sea, to arouse a scrap of suspicion –
except this very fact itself! Despite frequent changes of course, our
reduced speed made us feel like sitting ducks and I felt that, having
been sighted once, we should have been making straight back to
Singapore. (Ordinary Seaman D. F. Wilson, H.M.S. *Prince of Wales*)

So here we were, those two great ships with mighty little surface
screen and no air cover, nonchalantly meandering about off that
empty coast, executing such ponderous peacetime manoeuvres as
'Turn 135 degrees to starboard in succession' – sitting targets for submarine or air attack for which we were not prepared. Even to the
likes of me it seemed extraordinary that we were wandering about
the sea so lackadaisically in such circumstances. (Lieutenant J. O. C.
Hayes, H.M.S. *Repulse*)

But, despite the fact that they might have been reported
by the aircraft seen three hours earlier or the possibility
that Japanese submarines were in the area, Force Z did
not immediately resume its voyage to the south. It was
Captain Tennant of *Repulse*, with two suggestions signalled to the flagship, who prompted a further diversion.
The first signal, an eminently practical one, was that
Repulse should now catapult off one of her two Walrus aircraft to fly an anti-submarine patrol around Force Z.
Admiral Phillips agreed and the Walrus was soon off.
Tennant's second suggestion was that the small ship and
three barges seen earlier should be investigated more
closely before Force Z finally left the area. Again Admiral
Phillips agreed, and the five British ships, instead of turning south-east for the Anamba Islands and the comparative
safety of Singapore, took a course of 080 degrees, slightly
north of due east. A battleship, a battle cruiser and three
destroyers were setting out to examine one small ship and
three barges – on the face of it a ludicrous risk to take on
an errand that one destroyer could have performed, but
clear evidence of two assumptions that must have been in

Admiral Phillips's mind at that time: that the barges, if Japanese, might be the forerunners of a larger Japanese force which his big guns could then smash; and that, at this range from Indo-China, there was little danger to Force Z from Japanese aircraft.

After Force Z had been steaming away from the coast for thirty minutes, the complacency of the second assumption was badly shaken by a signal received at 10.05. The destroyer *Tenedos*, which had detached from Force Z when short of fuel the previous evening, had rounded the Anamba Islands early that morning and signalled to Rear-Admiral Palliser at Singapore the now partly out-of-date information that the earliest time that Force Z could reach the approaches to Singapore would be dawn of the following day. Now *Tenedos* was signalling that she was being bombed by Japanese aircraft at a position 140 miles south-east of Force Z's present position. The implications of this report were that Japanese aircraft were about, and, furthermore, at a range considerably farther from Indo-China than Force Z. If the Japanese could reach *Tenedos*, they could easily reach Force Z.

Within minutes of this news being received, a lookout sighted an approaching aircraft.

Before leaving the subject of Kuantan for good, some explanation of the reported landings should be given. The Kuantan area was defended by the understrength 22nd Indian Brigade with two infantry battalions, the 5/11th Sikhs and the 2/18th Royal Garhwal Rifles, supported by a few guns. The brigade commander was Brigadier G. W. A. Painter. The Indian units had never seen action before. Their main purpose was to guard Kuantan airfield, which had been the base of three squadrons of aircraft until these had been badly bombed and machine-gunned the previous day, the 9th, and the remnants of the squadrons withdrawn to Singapore before nightfall.

At 19.00 that evening an observation post manned by the Garhwal Rifles had reported seeing several small ships and lighters towing barges approaching the coast, and three hours later firing had broken out, directed on to what the Indians believed to be a Japanese landing craft. This was the foundation for the report sent by Rear-Admiral Palliser to Force Z regarding the 'Japanese landing at Kuantan'. Firing continued spasmodically during the night, but there was no firm evidence that any fire had come from the sea. When dawn broke the 'landing craft' had disappeared and no Japanese troops were to be found. The somewhat shamefaced Indians claimed that they had beaten off a small Japanese reconnaissance party. Four days later several small boats were found some miles to the south; some of these were bullet-riddled, and one contained Japanese rifles, a Japanese postcard and some items of Japanese uniforms.

It is possible that these small boats had been put ashore by the trawler – which was Japanese – seen that morning by Force Z, and that it was an attempt to create diversions at various points on the east coast of Malaya. If this is so, then the ruse brought the Japanese rewards out of all proportion to the effort involved, since it was this that caused Force Z to come to Kuantan that morning.

The Japanese trawler and the boats she was towing will be met again later. The little town of Kuantan did not feature again in the Malayan campaign until Japanese troops from the north advanced upon it two weeks later.*

The vital piece of information received by the Japanese commanders during the night was the sighting report by submarine I.58 saying that the British ships had reversed course and were apparently returning at speed to Singapore. This signal had been received by Vice-Admiral Kondo at 02.11, but he had never received I.58's subsequent signal about the British diversion south-west

* The recreation ground at Kuantan was the setting used by the novelist Nevil Shute for the crucifixion by Japanese soldiers of the Australian Joe Harman in his fictional work *A Town Like Alice*.

towards Kuantan. When he had received I.58's first report, Admiral Kondo immediately ordered his cruisers and two battleships to give chase, and these set off to the south at 24 knots; Vice-Admiral Ozawa's cruiser force was much the nearer to the British, but despite an increase in speed after dawn to 28 knots, Kondo soon realized that the Japanese ships would never catch the British before they reached the safety of Singapore. Moreover, he had no intention of risking his surface vessels so close to the British airfields. Only half an hour after ordering the 28 knots, Kondo ordered that the chase be abandoned and his ships turned back north. Had Kondo known that the British were at that time dallying off Kuantan, he might well have pressed on and the naval engagement that had so nearly taken place the previous night might well have occurred after all. But, as it turned out, the hunting of the British ships was now to be left in the hands of the submarines and the aircraft based in Indo-China.

The supposedly Japanese reconnaissance aircraft seen by the British soon after dawn had not sent a sighting report, or, if it did, the report did not find its way through to Admiral Kondo. In fact it is not certain that the aircraft was Japanese, though it could well have been an army aircraft flying from the newly captured Kota Bharu airfield. If it had been Japanese, then the failure to get a sighting report through to the naval command was to be the cause of much trouble and anxiety to the Japanese later that morning.

From the Japanese viewpoint, this operation to track down and bring to battle the small, fast fleet of British ships was entering the final phase, and it was becoming very much a catch-as-catch-can type of operation. The surface warships, which had been so close to engaging the British the previous night, were now out of the reckoning; the submarines had performed some useful spotting duty but had failed to slow down the British and were now well scattered. Any future success the submarines might gain would be the product of random fortune and not of careful planning. The last Japanese hope now lay with the land-based naval air units far to the north on the airfields around Saigon. The aeroplane, regarded in a lowly light by several of the naval commanders on each side, was now to have the chance to show that it had the speed, range, flexibility and hitting power to succeed where the Japanese warships had failed.

Despite the fact that his aircrews were desperately tired and had only landed in the early hours from their last flight, Rear-Admiral Matsunaga realized that the next few hours were crucial. He gave orders for every available Mitsubishi bomber of his three air corps to be refuelled and prepared for take-off soon after dawn. Out of his total strength of ninety-nine bombers, Matsunaga found that ninety-four were fit for operations. This figure represents a very high rate of serviceability after the continuous operations of recent days and says much for the robust construction of the Mitsubishis and the skill of their ground crews.

For the coming day's operations, Matsunaga's initial plan had been to allocate his available aircraft in the following roles:

17 aircraft to reconnaissance flights
17 aircraft as high-level bombers
60 aircraft as torpedo bombers

The reconnaissance aircraft were to have full fuel loads, and the only bombs they carried were two small 50-kg. ones; they were to take off first, spread out in a huge fan and search the area in which the British ships were believed to be steaming to Singapore. The attack aircraft were to follow later, and because of their heavy bomb or torpedo loads, would be forced to fly with a reduced fuel load. Their endurance, particularly that of the torpedo-carrying aircraft, would be strictly limited, but the captured airfield at Kota Bharu would be available to them in an emergency. Much would depend on the ability of the reconnaissance aircraft to find the British quickly, and then to guide in the attack aircraft. When the attacks did start it was intended

that the high-level bombers would smash up the upperworks of the British ships and cause casualties to their gun
crews. There were no armour-piercing bombs available –
they had all been allocated to the Pearl Harbor attack;
there were not even the ordinary 800-kg. bombs that the
Mitsubishis could carry and Matsunaga's men would have
to manage with 500-kg. bombs, one per aircraft, or, in
some cases, two 250-kg. bombs. The real punch was
expected to be in the force of torpedo aircraft. Much has
been written about the surprise among the Allies in 1941
over the effectiveness of some of the Japanese naval torpedoes, but those to be carried by the Mitsubishis that day
were the relatively humble Modified Type 91, some being
the Model 1 with a 149.5-kg. (330-lb.) warhead, and
others the Model 2 with a warhead weighing 204 kg.
(450 lb.). While the aircrews snatched a few hours' sleep,
the ground personnel worked hard to refuel and arm the
Nells and Bettys.

Just before take-off, however, Matsunaga changed his
mind about the allocation of aircraft and decided that he
needed more high-level bombers. Eight aircraft were
withdrawn from the reconnaissance force, and nine from
the torpedo force. The weakening of these two in favour
of the bombers was almost to prove a mistake.

The final line-up was as follows:

RECONNAISSANCE FORCE

9 Mitsubishi Type 96 G3M2 (Nell) aircraft of the Genzan Air Corps.
Take-off from Saigon airfield at 05.00 (Singapore Time).

GENZAN AIR CORPS ATTACK GROUP

Commander: Lieutenant-Commander Nakanishi
Aircraft Type: Mitsubishi Type 96 G3M2 (Nell)

Squadron	Leader	No. of aircraft	Role
1st	Lieutenant Ishihara	9	Torpedo attack
2nd	Lieutenant Takai	8	Torpedo attack
3rd	Lieutenant Nikaido	9	Bombing

Take-offs from Saigon airfield soon after 06.25.

KANOYA AIR CORPS ATTACK GROUP

Commander: Lieutenant-Commander Miyauchi

Aircraft Type: Mitsubishi Navy Type 1 G4M1 (Betty)

Squadron	Leader	No. of aircraft	Role
1st	Lieutenant Nabeta	9	Torpedo attack
2nd	Lieutenant Higashimori	8	Torpedo attack
3rd	Lieutenant Iki	9	Torpedo attack

Take-offs from Tu Duam airfield soon after 06.44.

MIHORO AIR CORPS ATTACK GROUP

Commander: none designated

Aircraft Type: Mitsubishi Type 96 G3M2 (Nell)

Squadron	Leader	No. of aircraft	Role
1st	Lieutenant Shirai	8	Bombing
2nd	Lieutenant Takeda	8	Bombing
3rd	Lieutenant Ohira	9	Bombing
4th	Lieutenant Takahashi	8	Torpedo attack

Take-offs from Tu Duam airfield between 06.50 and 08.00.

Total: 9 reconnaissance aircraft
       34 bombing aircraft
       51 torpedo aircraft

The Japanese airmen were woken and wearily took themselves to the briefing rooms where they were addressed by as many as five officers; it is recorded that the younger airmen became quite bored with the lengthy instructions, never realizing that this day they would make history. Captain Kosei Maeda, the commanding officer of the Genzan Air Corps, asked Rear-Admiral Matsunaga for permission to fly as a passenger in one of the high-level bombers, and was allowed to do so. There was speculation over how far south the British ships might have reached, and much anxiety, especially among the crews of the torpedo aircraft, that the British might even have reached Singapore itself and that the torpedo bombers might have to carry out a hazardous low-level attack over the defended harbour.

The crews picked up their flight rations of *Ohagi* – rice cakes coated with tasty bean paste – and thick sweet coffee in flasks. At 06.25 the first attack aircraft, piloted by Lieutenant Ishihara, took off from Saigon; the reconnaissance aircraft had left an hour and a half earlier. On this occasion there was no crowd of army officers to wave the Mitsubishis on their way, only the loyal ground personnel. It was 08.00 before the last attack aircraft took off; these were the nine Nells of Lieutenant Ohira's squadron from Tu Duam. They had been delayed by the decision to change the squadron's loads from torpedoes to bombs.

The Japanese airmen were pleased to find that the weather was fine; they flew straight out to sea on a course slightly west of south that would take them right to the approaches of Singapore Naval Base. The Nells and Bettys flew in formations of eights or nines, and climbed steadily until they reached 10,000 feet. The visibility was excellent with only small patches of low cloud. The Mitsubishis flew steadily south at the most economical speed and engine settings their pilots could manage. It was up to the nine reconnaissance aircraft to find the enemy; these attack aircraft could only cruise on and hope the sighting came before too much fuel was consumed.

There was no radio silence for the Japanese airmen; the reconnaissance planes were reporting back regularly on their progress and on the weather encountered, but the hours passed with no reports of battleships sighted, only a submarine believed to be British (it was not). Saigon ordered the reconnaissance planes to try farther south. Lieutenant Takai was leading one of the Genzan torpedo squadrons:

What is the matter with our reconnaissance planes? Still no sign of the enemy. In spite of the good weather and clear visibility, is it possible the reconnaissance planes still cannot find the British warships? By now our planes should be more than five hundred nautical miles from Saigon. Lieutenant-Commander Nakanishi, flying just ahead of my bomber, must also be growing very impatient.

We have passed the danger line of four hundred nautical miles from Saigon. Still no report on the enemy ships. It is as though we were enveloped in complete darkness. The pilots are becoming more and more anxious about their remaining fuel. We measured the rate of fuel consumption as carefully as possible and reduced it to the lowest possible level. It was not the best way to treat the engines, but we had little choice. Perhaps because of our severe mixture control, one of my bombers developed engine trouble and was forced to leave the formation and return to base. I could not send even one plane as escort. Including my own, the number of aircraft in my squadron was reduced to seven.

It was at this stage that I.58's last signal, reporting that the British had turned towards Kuantan, or a report from the mystery plane which had been sighted by the British soon after dawn, would have been most useful to the Japanese, but the area off Kuantan where the British now were was not in the path of the outward flight of any of the nine Japanese reconnaissance aircraft.

The fourth plane in the search pattern had reached the southern limit of its search area, near the island of Tioman, turned east and flown a short leg before turning north for the return flight. At 09.43 it spotted a small ship below and correctly identified it as a British destroyer. The Japanese pilot made a careful approach and released his two 50-kg. bombs. They missed. He reported the sighting to Saigon and continued his flight north, still searching for the main force of British ships.

Flying down from the north and passing the reconnaissance plane on the opposite course were the three attack squadrons of the Genzan Air Corps, twenty-five aircraft strong. Lieutenant Takai again:

At 10.15 we sighted a small vessel off to our left. The sea was absolutely calm. The ship appeared to be a cargo vessel of about five or six hundred tons. Singapore was near. Since it was possible that other enemy vessels might be in the vicinity, I ordered my men to stay alert. No other object could be seen; this was unusual.

Keeping a sharp lookout above and behind us for enemy planes, we tightened all formations and maintained our flight due south.

Without warning the entire 3rd Squadron dropped out of the mass formation and flew toward the small cargo vessel. Soon they circled over the ship. I could not understand what the squadron leader could possibly be doing.

The enemy vessel suddenly changed its course, and no sooner had it begun its twisting evasive action than a salvo of bombs fell more than seven hundred feet away from the ship without inflicting any damage! What was wrong with the 3rd Squadron leader? Nine 500-kilogram bombs were lost, dissipated without results, after all the trouble of carrying them for such a long time!

Lieutenant Nikaido's 3rd Squadron was the one in which Captain Maeda, the commanding officer of the Genzan Air Corps, was flying as a passenger. It is not known whether Maeda had given the order to attack or not. The nine Mitsubishis that had bombed turned for home. They were now out of the reckoning.

The 'cargo vessel' of Lieutenant Takai's account that had just been bombed was really the destroyer *Tenedos* on her way back to Singapore. She had had an exciting morning. Her Asdic had earlier detected what was believed to be a submerged submarine, and Lieutenant Dyer had ordered two depth-charge attacks on the contact. As the object remained in the same place throughout the attacks, Dyer came to the conclusion that it had not been a submarine after all and continued his voyage. He was correct; no Japanese submarine reported being attacked at this time.

Then the Japanese aircraft attacked, and so well did Dyer handle his ship that the Japanese formation had had to make three passes over the twisting destroyer before deciding to release their bombs all in one salvo. Lieutenant Dyer writes:

The bombing of *Tenedos* was my first real experience of heavy aircraft attack at sea and, I believe, I found this particular incident exciting rather than frightening. It was my first command and she handled like a dream and the Almighty was with us.

The Japanese had been flying too high for *Tenedos*'s guns to open fire and the bombs had fallen over a hundred yards out to the port side. One of *Tenedos*'s sailors had been hit in the thigh by a bomb splinter but he was the only casualty.

Tenedos broadcast four signals giving full details of the attack and of the larger formation of Japanese aircraft – the remainder of the Genzan Air Corps – that had been seen. These signals were received by Force Z, but apparently not in Singapore, only 120 miles away, for no British fighters were sent out after the Japanese. *Tenedos* increased speed so that she could land her wounded seaman more quickly at Singapore.

One by one the remaining eight Japanese reconnaissance planes were reaching the southern legs of their search patterns and turning back towards home, each taking a slightly different return route so as to cover as much ocean as possible. Of the three attack formations, the Genzan and Kanoya aircraft had by now flown down to a position level with Singapore; their crews could quite clearly see the Malayan mountains to the west, and even the Dutch island of Sumatra farther south. They would soon be at the 'point of no return' and would shortly have to abandon the operation and turn about. The Mihoro squadrons, which had taken off later, were farther to the north.

It was the crew of Midshipman Masame Hoashi, in the third plane out from the Malayan coast in the search pattern, who finally made the vital discovery. After reaching the limit of his outward flight near the Malayan coast, Hoashi had turned north-west to fly farther up the coast before turning back for Saigon. At 10.15 his crew spotted ships below and out went three radio signals:

ENEMY FLEET SPOTTED AT LAT. 4N. LONG. 103.55E. COURSE 60 DEGREES.

ENEMY FORCE CHANGED COURSE TO 30 DEGREES.

ENEMY FORCE ESCORTED BY 3 DESTROYERS. ORDER OF FORMATION IS KING-TYPE BATTLESHIP, REPULSE.

Yet again the Japanese signals system failed to function properly. Hoashi's reports were received clearly at Saigon and Tu Duam airfields, but it soon became obvious to the operations officers there that many of the attack planes had not picked up Hoashi's signals or could not understand them. Hoashi was ordered to abandon the use of codes and to broadcast his reports in plain language. He was also ordered to emit a continuous signal on long-wave on to which the direction-finders of the attack planes could home. These measures met with some success, but because of the initial delays, the seventy-six remaining aircraft of the Japanese attack force would only arrive in the sighting area in dribs and drabs over a period of an hour and a half, and all would be short of fuel. There would be no opportunity for them to execute the carefully planned and coordinated combination of high-level bombing and low-level torpedo attacks.

Lieutenant Yoshimi Shirai's squadron of the Mihoro Air Corps, with eight high-level bombers, was first on the scene forty minutes after Hoashi had first spotted the British ships.

When the Japanese reconnaissance plane was first seen by the British ships, Force Z had been steering a course of 080 degrees towards the position of the small ships seen earlier. This course was altered at once to 095 degrees, and soon afterwards to a south-easterly course. This last change was not a move to escape the shadower, which would have been impossible, but to investigate a small ship just sighted. This turned out to be a British merchant ship, the S.S. *Haldis*. The *Haldis* was on the run from her home port of Hong Kong and was hoping to make the safety of Singapore. Her crew were about to have a grandstand view.

The crews of the British warships had been stood down from Action Stations after leaving Kuantan, and many men had been given a second, cooked, breakfast. Some of the off-duty men had then been able to rest or take a stroll along the deck, chatting in the warm sunshine, although several remember that the usual high spirits were absent on this occasion; there seemed to be 'an unusual quietness, a sense of foreboding'. This was especially true when the Japanese reconnaissance plane was spotted high in the sky to the south.

Twenty-five minutes after the plane had been sighted the echoes of a formation of aircraft were picked up by radar. A general order was issued at once by the flagship: 'ASSUME FIRST DEGREE ANTI-AIRCRAFT READI-NESS'. On the bridge of *Prince of Wales*, sixteen-year-old Bugler Squires of the Royal Marines was ordered by Captain Leach to blow the call for 'Action Stations. Repel Aircraft' over the ship's Tannoy, and soon the men of Force Z were rushing to the stations they would man against aircraft attack – a drill they had all performed dozens of times in the past.

The call to Action Stations came just as the issuing of the rum ration was starting. This happy event was immediately suspended, the rum barrels were locked up and the keys removed. Only a few men had managed to receive their rum issue, among them Leading Torpedo Operator 'Scouse' Holehouse in *Prince of Wales*: 'I was always a bit of a fiddler. I managed to get two tots that morning and felt like meeting Tojo all on my own.'

Also in *Prince of Wales*, Marine John Wignall was taking a shower when he heard the call to Action Stations.

I was rather surprised and hesitated at first, not really focusing on what was happening, and by the time I had gathered my things together Damage Control were in operation, closing all watertight doors including the deck hatch leading down to the bathroom I was using. I heard the cleats being fastened on the outside and by the time I had dashed up the ladder I realized that I was well and truly locked in. I hammered on the hatch with my shoe in desperation, and fortunately someone running by heard me and let me out or I would have been there to this day.

Leading Seaman Basil Elsmore in *Prince of Wales* also remembers:

10.45, 10 December 1941. Kuantan, East Malaya, the bugler sounds 'Action Stations, Aircraft'. 'Bomber overhead. Bomber overhead,' the bugle seems to say. Quickly the calls come to the Transmitting Station (Gun Control), 'So-and-so station closed up and cleared away.' In perhaps two minutes at the most this great, floating home-cum-gun-platform was ready.

Was 'Jeff' Jefferies, in the Ring Main Breaker Space, right when he said, 'Cheerio Bas. Watch your step. Take care'? The hatch closed. Did you know, Jeff? Did you survive, Jeff?

It was just after 11.00 hours when the eight Mitsubishis were spotted approaching from ahead, high up and glistening in the sun. The Japanese planes were soon close enough for the control officers of the high-angle guns in *Prince of Wales* and *Repulse* to start their 'plot'. 'Enemy aircraft in sight. Range 16,500 yards. Height 10,000 feet. Speed 200. Commence. Commence. Commence.'

But no signal of any kind had gone out from the flagship to Singapore. That radio silence, so important in the mind of Admiral Phillips, was still being observed.

9

The First Round

The late take-off by some of the Japanese aircraft from their airfields, the long flight over the featureless ocean waiting for news of the British ships, then the false alarm caused by *Tenedos* – all these factors had tended to scatter the Japanese squadrons. Even when Midshipman Hoashi had found the British ships, the hit-or-miss nature of the Japanese communications system brought their attack aircraft to the scene, not in any carefully planned and co-ordinated manner, but in the most haphazard of ways. Many of the Japanese aircraft were running low on fuel, and all their crews were physically weary after so much flying during recent days and nights. The British sailors were also tired after long hours at Action Stations, particularly those men whose duties had kept them below decks in the inadequately ventilated *Prince of Wales*. But all these men – Japanese and British – were young and fit; fatigue or morale would not decide the outcome of the coming encounter, nor even courage. Equipment, skill and training would make more impact, but the elements in this coming battle were, with one exception, all long-established ones: armoured capital ships, destroyers and aircraft, guns and machine-guns, shells, bombs and torpedoes. The only new factor was radar, and radar was to play virtually no part on this clear, sunny day.

What was at issue, and what would decide the outcome, was a theory, a philosophy: could capital ships at sea survive in the face of determined air attack? As has already been indicated, the testing in action of certain theories had been surprisingly long delayed, but the day of reckoning had now arrived. Surprisingly, perhaps, it was to turn out to be a very straightforward and uncomplicated action.

· · ·

The first Japanese formation to approach Force Z was Lieutenant Yoshimi Shirai's squadron of eight Nell bombers of the Mihoro Air Corps. The squadron had been last but one to take off from the airfield at Tu Duam, and had still been well to the north when it picked up the sighting signals. It was probably the first squadron to pick up the signals, and this was why Shirai's planes came on to the scene before other squadrons who had been much nearer at the moment of sighting. Shirai had then led his squadron well behind the ships in order to make his bombing run from a more southerly direction and from out of the sun. These aircraft were the only ones of the Japanese bomber attack squadrons that were each carrying two 250-kg. bombs instead of one 500-kg. bomb. The formation consisted of only eight aircraft because one was unserviceable. Most of the reports of the British ships record that nine bombers took part in this first attack; only the destroyers *Express* and *Electra* reported the correct number. Lieutenant Shirai decided to attack the second of the British capital ships, possibly because he recognized it as *Repulse* whose main deck was known to be more thinly armoured than that of *Prince of Wales*. Settling into the tight formation they had used so often in practice, the Japanese started their bomb run.

The British ships had been following the Japanese formation both by radar and visually for some time. It is probable that *Repulse* saw the aircraft first when Shirai's squadron passed behind Force Z before coming into attack.

I had gone to B gundeck with the other watchkeeping fraternity for a smoke and a yarn. While we were up there an able seaman called our attention to the yardarm which was flying the signal 'A' with three digits which meant, and at this distance in time I'll swear to it, 'Aircraft presumed to be hostile, sighted on bearing (3 figures).' It struck me as odd that the person in our group who saw the signal was the one non-communicator present – and the one who could have pleaded ignorance of its significance. Almost immediately we turned and saw a large group of aircraft approaching and I did not stop to ask their business.

When I reached my Action Station – the Transmitting Room was traditionally well below the waterline for safety reasons – guns were firing, klaxons sounding, and I thought this was great. Action at last! (Boy Telegraphist W. C. Tinkler, H.M.S. *Repulse*)

On sighting the enemy, both big ships had hoisted the White Ensign – the traditional battle ensign – to fore and main masts, and more signal flags were soon flying, this time from *Prince of Wales*. The signal was 'BT3'; this was an order from Admiral Phillips to Force Z: 'SHIPS TURN TOGETHER 30 DEGREES TO STARBOARD'. The two great ships and the three destroyers started their turns towards the approaching enemy. Here was the old Navy in action, but it was not the old Navy's methods of manoeuvring battle squadrons by flag signal that was needed that morning.

The final approach by the Japanese from the south had placed *Prince of Wales* closer than *Repulse* to the enemy. Before the BT3 signal began to take effect, the Japanese bombers had been approaching *Prince of Wales* from the starboard bow; the four 5·25-in. turrets on her starboard side could all train on the approaching enemy. These were the sophisticated high-angle, dual-purpose guns of such high reputation and on which the hopes of the men in Force Z to defend them from aircraft attack mainly rested. It was a young R.N.V.R. officer, Lieutenant E. J. Kempson, the Starboard Forward High-Angle Control Officer, who started the action by reporting the first information about the approaching formation to the High-Angle Plotting Table situated below decks: 'Range 16,500 yards. Height 10,000 feet. Speed 200. Commence. Commence. Commence.'

This information was fed into the calculators of the Plotting Table and a constant stream of fuze setting calculations was soon being produced for the 5·25-in. turrets. When Lieutenant Kempson judged that his rangefinder was getting a really reliable range at about 12,000 yards,

Kempson ordered fire to be opened. The gunners in the turrets set the latest fuze settings and, as each gun was loaded, a lamp came on in Kempson's control position to indicate it was ready to fire. When all his lamps were lit, a hooter blew, Kempson pressed a button and all guns fired automatically at the precise moment that the fuze setting calculation was valid. More information was meanwhile being fed to the Plotting Station, fresh fuze-settings came back to the turrets and the eight starboard guns settled down to fire steady salvoes. Years of training were being put into practice.

Repulse's older and less numerous 4-in. guns were soon in action too, opening fire at about 11,000 yards. Initially only one gun would bear, but after it had fired four rounds a second gun also came into action. Sub-Lieutenant G. H. Peters, *Repulse*'s Forward High-Angle Control Officer, has recorded the effects of his fire. He saw immediately that his bursts were well to the right of the approaching Japanese aircraft, but though he kept correcting to the left, his shells continued to explode to the right of the Japanese. The same thing was probably happening to *Prince of Wales*'s fire. It was not that the Japanese aircraft were taking any evasive action; they continued to fly a straight course towards *Repulse*. What was happening was that both ships were swinging right in answer to the BT 3 signal and the Control Officers' corrections to the left were thus being counteracted. This turn soon caused all the guns on the starboard side of both ships to cease firing as the superstructure of their ships masked their line of fire.

When *Prince of Wales*'s 5·25-in. guns first opened up, they were the first naval guns that Admiral Phillips had heard fired in anger at sea since 1915. He soon realized that he had made a mistake in ordering the turn and countermanded it. More signals flags were hoisted: '5BT': 'SHIPS TURN TOGETHER 50 DEGREES TO PORT.' But a big ship cannot reverse course quickly, and *Prince of Wales* and *Repulse* continued to swing right, so much so their port-side guns were able to come into action and fire a few rounds. But then the turn to port started taking effect; the port-side guns had to cease fire; no guns fired for a few moments and finally the starboard-side guns came into action again. By now, of course, the Japanese had completed their approach and were about to bomb. Those officers in the British ships who had been in action against aircraft before were much disheartened by Admiral Phillips's handling of the situation. The correct action would have been to allow each ship freedom of action and so make best use of their anti-aircraft armament. These cumbersome fleet manoeuvres by flag signal had robbed the gunnery officers of the opportunity to settle down to the long 'run' of firing that would have enabled corrections to be steadily applied and more effective fire brought to bear. The unswerving approach of the compact formation of Japanese aircraft at a constant speed and height was really a gunner's dream. Admiral Phillips had made a fiasco out of his first handling of ships in action, but he was the first to acknowledge it and he gave orders that in future attacks captains were to have freedom of manoeuvre.

The Japanese bombers flew almost directly over the *Prince of Wales*. It was a terrifying few seconds for those above deck who were not engaged on some duty. They could only stand with a feeling of absolute helplessness and wait for the worst. But the bombs did not fall on *Prince of Wales*; *Repulse* was the target. The Japanese aircraft were just low enough for the bombs to be seen leaving their bomb bays.It was the bomb-aimer of Lieutenant Shirai's aircraft who chose the moment of release, and the remaining aircraft dropped their bombs with his.

Men on all the British ships watched in fascination as the salvo of bombs fell through the air. There is no evidence that Captain Tennant tried to avoid the bombs; he probably felt that a ship as big as *Repulse* could do little to avoid such a salvo in the few seconds available. The men aboard *Prince of Wales* and the destroyers watched the huge fountains of water, first one on the starboard side of *Repulse*, then several more on the port side; but there were no stabs of fire to indicate direct hits. As *Repulse* emerged from the spray, however, a small plume of smoke was seen coming from her upper deck near the aircraft hangar on the starboard side.

Each of Shirai's aircraft had only dropped one of its two bombs. Shirai intended to come round and bomb again later so that he could cause the maximum confusion among the British ships. Just one of the eight bombs had struck *Repulse*. It had cut through both the roof and the floor of the hangar and then the Marines' mess deck without exploding while leaving neat holes fifteen inches in diameter. The bomb finally burst on the armoured deck. If it had been an armour-piercing bomb, or one of the 500-kg. bombs that the other Japanese aircraft were carrying, it might well have burst through the one inch of steel plating which was all that was protecting the lightly armoured battle cruiser at this point and have exploded inside one of the boiler rooms. But this did not happen and the bomb caused no serious structural damage. The explosion had been so slight that, when the flagship asked for details, Captain Tennant's initial report was that his ship had only been damaged by a near miss. *Repulse* had been fortunate; her speed was unaffected and she steamed on with just the curl of smoke to show she had been hit.

When they released their bombs, the Japanese planes were seen to surge upwards like a flock of birds, and then to fly steadily away to the north. The high-angle guns of both ships and of the destroyers continued to fire for a few moments, but then stopped to conserve ammunition. *Prince of Wales*'s single Bofors guns, mounted on the quarterdeck and manned by Royal Marines, had opened fire and even her pom-poms had let off a few defiant rounds when the Japanese had been directly overhead though still out of the pom-poms' range. The 5·25-in. guns of *Prince of Wales* had fired 108 rounds and the 4-in. guns of *Repulse* thirty-six rounds. The British gunners were probably disappointed at failing to shoot down any of the

Japanese, but they had actually done quite well. No less than five of Lieutenant Shirai's eight aircraft had been hit by the fire, two so seriously that they left the scene of action and flew straight back to their airfield.

It is not possible to be precise about the effects of *Repulse*'s bomb hit. The official documents are not comprehensive and private accounts are sometimes contradictory. It is certain that small fires were started on the catapult deck, in the Marines' mess deck and in a near-by fan casing. Two men were trapped in the wrecked Torpedo Office and the Engineer's Office. A dynamo room was damaged and reported to be flooding, probably from the water of a fire party's hoses. Commander Dendy, in command of Damage Control, detailed five damage control parties and one shipwright's party to attend to the fires and the damage. *Repulse*'s remaining Walrus aircraft was a hazard. The blast of the bomb had knocked it half off its catapult trolley and its tanks were leaking petrol over the deck. The Walrus was hooked on to a crane and swung out over the side, and a Fleet Air Arm pilot, Sub-Lieutenant 'Ginger' Holden, a New Zealander, climbed out along the arm of the crane and released the Walrus, which was thus dumped into the sea.

Several men had been injured by blast and at least one was killed outright. The worst suffering came from the fracture of several steam pipes in the boiler room below the armoured deck; these were caused either by the shock wave from the bomb burst above the boiler room or by the resulting distortion of the framework supporting the pipes. Some stokers were terribly scalded and found great difficulty in getting out to reach medical attention. It was several minutes before the crew of a 4-in. gun detailed to help with the damage were able to get the burned stokers up on deck.

During the lull, to our amazement, some of the stokers had managed to climb up through the uptakes or ventilation system and were screaming for us to let them out. These uptakes were covered with heavy wire netting and I remember them trying to tear the wire away with their bare hands. They were like monkeys in a cage. Ginger Wilkinson soon took the initiative and we found a rope and weaved it through the wire and the twelve of us ripped the wire away and helped these poor fellows out. It was only then did we realize that they were naked and all badly burnt and screaming in agony. It was a horrible sight; they had been burnt by steam from broken steam pipes down below in the boiler room. We did our best to make them comfortable on the deck until the first-aid 'tiffys' arrived and took them down to the Sick Bay. (Able Seaman S. C. Baxter)

So ended the first attack. The Japanese had pressed it home in the most resolute fashion and had dropped their bombs with great accuracy. So much for the myth that the Japanese would be incompetent and ill-equipped adversaries, even though the small 250-kg. bomb that had hit *Repulse* had not caused any serious damage. Her guns and gun crews were all intact to face future attacks and her damage control parties would all be finished work and available for future demands before they were needed again. Despite the partial loss of steam pressure from one boiler room and the injuries to some of her stokers, *Repulse*'s steaming performance was hardly affected. The British ships had not been well handled by their admiral, but he had been taught a valuable lesson and had not had to pay too dearly for the learning of it.

This first encounter had lasted just twenty minutes from first to last sight of Lieutenant Shirai's formation. But while it had ended inconclusively, it was no more than a curtain-raiser. Besides the six remaining aircraft of Lieutenant Shirai's squadron there were seventeen more high-level bombers and no less than fifty torpedo bombers still looking for the British ships.

There was a small breathing space after the bomb attack and Force Z was able to steam a few miles nearer to its base at Singapore. Within ten minutes, however, *Prince of Wales*'s radar had picked up an even larger force of aircraft approaching, not from the north, as might have been expected, but from the south-east. There may have been momentary hopes that these were friendly fighters looking for the British ships but any such hopes were soon dashed when two separate formations of twin-engined aircraft similar to those that had just bombed *Repulse* were seen flying at about 10,000 feet. The time was 11.38.

These aircraft were more Nells, but this time from the three Genzan squadrons that had flown together to a position so far south as to have been level with Singapore. The high-level bomber squadron of the Genzan Corps that had wasted its bombs on the destroyer *Tenedos* was now on its way home. The two remaining squadrons were both armed with torpedos – the Modified Type 91 Model 1 with the 149·5-kg. (330-lb.) warhead – so there would be no chance for the Genzan Corps to carry out the combined high-level bomb and low-level torpedo attack it had often rehearsed. The first of the Genzan squadrons was commanded by Lieutenant Kaoru Ishihara and was at the full strength of nine aircraft. On board one of Ishihara's planes, possibly in Ishihara's, was Lieutenant-Commander Niichi Nakanishi, the commander of the Genzan Corps who would coordinate the attack of the two squadrons. The second squadron was led by Lieutenant Sadao Takai, but it had started out with only eight aircraft, and one of these had been forced to turn back with mechanical trouble.

When Midshipman Hoashi had first transmitted the report placing the British ships just off the Malayan coast, one of the torpedo-bomber crews had radioed back to the airfield at Saigon asking to be told the depth of the water in the area where the British ships had been located. The reason for his request was that, if the water was less than a certain depth, the torpedo attack would have to be carried out at a lower level and at a slower speed than normal, otherwise a torpedo could strike the sea bottom and explode when it first entered the water and before it had settled to its running depth of six metres (about twenty feet). The Japanese Operations Officer at Saigon was surprised that the airmen should have paid attention to such a detail at this exciting time and was immensely heartened by the signal.

Lieutenant Sadao Takai recorded his emotions as his squadron was on its approach flight to the British ships.

In spite of repeated warnings to the crew members not to relax for a moment their vigilance to the rear and above our aircraft, everybody was straining to look ahead of our bomber to sight the enemy fleet. Everybody wanted the honour of being the first to see the British warships.

It was just past 1 p.m. [11.30 Singapore Time]. Low clouds were filling the sky ahead of us. Fully five hours had passed since we left Saigon that morning. The enemy fleet should become visible any moment. I became nervous and shaky and could not dismiss the sensation. I had the strongest urge to urinate. It was exactly like the sensation one feels before entering a contest in an athletic meeting.

At exactly 1.03 p.m. a black spot directly beneath the cloud ahead of us was sighted. It appeared to be the enemy vessels, about twenty-five miles away. Yes – it was the enemy! Soon we could distinguish the ships. The fleet was composed of two battleships, escorted by three destroyers, and one small merchant vessel. The battleships were the long-awaited *Prince of Wales* and the *Repulse*!

The 1st Squadron picked up speed and moved ahead of my squadron. Lieutenant-Commander Nakanishi ordered, 'Form assault formation!' A little later, 'Go in!'

The enemy fleet was now about eight miles away. We were still flying at 2,500 metres and were in the ideal position to attack. As we had planned, Nakanishi's bomber increased its speed and began to drop toward the enemy fleet. He was headed to the right and a little ahead of the warships. Trying to maintain the same distance and not be left behind, the bombers of my squadron also increased their speed as I started a gradual dive. I headed toward the left flank of the enemy formation. It was a standard practice among us for the 1st Squadron to attack the largest vessel, and the 2nd Squadron the next largest.

All crew members searched the sky vigilantly for the enemy fighters which we expected would be diving in to attack us at any moment. Much to our surprise not a single enemy plane was in sight. This was all the more amazing since the scene of battle was well within the fighting range of the British fighters; less than 100 nautical miles from both Singapore and Kuantan.

The small merchant ship seen by Lieutenant Takai and

thought by him to be part of the British fleet was the *Haldis*, now steaming hard to get away from this battle of which she had no wish to be a part. Takai is a little in error over his distances; Kuantan was only seventy nautical miles away, but the distance to Singapore was 150 miles.

The two Japanese squadrons separated while well out of the range of the British guns and manoeuvred themselves so as to approach the British force from different directions. The intention was to make simultaneous attacks on *Prince of Wales* and *Repulse* in a pincer-like movement to split the British gunfire, but for reasons which will be explained later, the attack of Lieutenant Takai's squadron on *Repulse* was a little late. We can thus leave his seven aircraft on one side for the moment and concentrate on those about to attack *Prince of Wales*.

· The men on the British ships watched as this formation flew up from the south-east and then across the bows of their ships though still well out of range. The Japanese could be seen steadily losing height and at the same time forming themselves into a line-astern formation. Admiral Phillips was sitting in his own chair on *Prince of Wales*'s compass platform; Captain Leach and several other officers were stood near by – all were watching the Japanese aircraft. Admiral Phillips had already ordered Force Z to work up to 25 knots to present a more difficult target in this next attack, and all captains now had freedom to handle their ships independently. Phillips was observed to be 'very composed, very calm'. Lieutenant-Commander R. F. Harland, *Prince of Wales*'s torpedo specialist officer, remarked, 'I think they're going to do a torpedo attack.' Harland cannot be sure of the exact wording of Phillips's reply, but believes it to have been, 'No they're not. There are no torpedo aircraft about.'

The Japanese squadron continued to lose height, however, flew into some low cloud and then reappeared off *Prince of Wales*'s port bow. The deployment was completed when the line turned in three neat turns, three aircraft to each turn, to face *Prince of Wales*. Despite Admiral Phillips's belief, nine torpedo bombers, in a huge extended arc, were now flying steadily towards his flagship.

The Japanese planes now presented a good, no-deflection, target for the eight 5·25-in. guns on *Prince of Wales's* port side. These guns were controlled in two groups. Sub-Lieutenant G. H. Hopkinson was in charge of the after group, and post-action report shows that the Japanese aircraft were soon within range and he had commenced his 'run' of information to the plotting table; but 'permission to open fire from the Air Defence Position was so slow in being passed that I had to request it. Not till then was it given. Fire could have been opened earlier but for this.'* All eight 5·25-in. guns eventually opened fire with a crash and settled down to fire salvoes at the approaching Japanese. They were soon joined by the single Bofors gun on the quarterdeck, manned by the Royal Marines, then four sets of eight-barrelled pom-poms steadily pumping out their 2-pounder shells, and, finally, the Oerlikons and machine-guns.

The guns were all firing well, but no planes were seen to be hit during the first phase of the Japanese approach. On *Prince of Wales's* bridge, Captain Leach had the classic problem of how to manoeuvre his ship. On this occasion, this meant deciding at what point to turn to meet the Japanese attack so that the torpedo tracks could be combed. To turn before the torpedo bombers had committed themselves to dropping would be too soon and would also spoil the aim of his gunners. To turn too late might leave *Prince of Wales* as an easy broadside-on target for the Japanese torpedoes. It was a problem to which every Royal Navy captain gave much thought; now Captain Leach had to make the decision. When he decided the correct moment had arrived he ordered the helm 'hard-

---

* These reports continue to come from Public Record Office ADM 199/1149 unless otherwise stated.

a-port'. The great ship, steaming at 25 knots, started to come round. The next three minutes would show whether Captain Leach had chosen wisely.

Many of the British were amazed at the approach of the Japanese aircraft. The standard British naval torpedo bomber, the Swordfish, was a slow, lumbering aircraft whose torpedo approach had to be made at a speed of less than 100 miles per hour and at a height of only fifty feet, and, in their training, the British gunners had become used to this low and slow approach. It is obvious that the British did not believe that the Japanese had anything better than the Swordfish, and there was much surprise when these modern, two-engined aircraft commenced their approach at a far greater speed and at a greater height than anything expected. The Japanese Official History records that their planes carried out this attack at 150 knots (180 miles per hour), while the average torpedo release height was 33 metres (108 feet). Many men on the *Prince of Wales* believed that they were facing a low-level bomber attack rather than a torpedo attack.

The Japanese pilots released their torpedoes at distances varying between 1,500 metres (1,640 yards) and 600 metres (656 yards) from *Prince of Wales*. The destroyer *Express* was in the line of approach and may have been responsible for causing some of the Japanese to drop their torpedoes too early. Lieutenant-Commander Cartwright recorded that one torpedo exploded near his ship on first hitting the water, and this may be correct, though none hit *Express*. The turn ordered by Captain Leach caused the Japanese planes nearest *Prince of Wales*'s bow to lose its aim and this aircraft banked away and made for *Repulse* (its torpedo missing *Repulse*) while the other planes' torpedoes ran on towards *Prince of Wales*, set to run at a depth of 6 metres (nearly 20 feet) and a speed of 25 knots. The white lines of bubbles from the compressed air expelled by the torpedoes could clearly be seen on the surface, but the actual position of each torpedo was well ahead of its visible tracks. The torpedo dropped by the

most daring of the Japanese pilots would take just over
two minutes to reach its target.

The Japanese planes were too large and too fast, and
their turning circle too great, for them to pull away quickly
to safety, and to climb too soon would slow them down and
expose their soft underbellies to British gunfire. The pilots
now swept even lower, some of them straight at the
Prince of Wales, machine-gunning as they came. The
British gunfire rose to a crescendo. After firing twelve
salvoes, the $5·25$-in. guns had given up the controlled fire
at individual planes and had gone over to 'barrage fire' in
which shells were fired to explode in a wall ahead of the
approaching aircraft in an attempt to make them drop their
torpedoes too early. It is easy to use dramatic phrases like
'curtain of fire' and 'wall of death', but the Japanese seemed
to fly straight through the $5·25$s' barrage and the increasing fire of the close-range guns apparently unharmed.
Certainly they were not deterred from dropping their
torpedoes within range. Whether it was the unexpected
height and speed of the Japanese approach or the wheel
to port that *Prince of Wales* was now making, but this
battleship was certainly not fighting off this aircraft
attack.

A further difficulty was that many of the pom-poms were
having problems with their ammunition; their small shells
were becoming separated from their cartridges while being
fed into the quick-firing weapons and were jamming the
barrels. There were frequent stoppages; one of *Prince of
Wales*'s pom-poms suffered twelve such failures, another
suffered eight. This was particularly unfortunate because
the low-flying Japanese aircraft were ideal targets for
pom-poms. The weapon mounted on top of B Turret
jammed just as one of the Japanese aircraft swept low over
Prince of Wales's bow, and the officer in charge, Lieutenant
Ian Forbes, later claimed that 'this could have been shot
down with ease'.

Several men describe their experiences during that
attack. Ordinary Seaman W. E. England was acting as a

lookout for the Lewis gun manned by the boxer Johnny King:

I focused my glasses at about 090 degrees to port and there, like dots on the horizon, I could see a formation of about ten planes skimming low on the water towards us. I had, of course, seen this low type of V formation before and awaited with excitement the massacre of this echelon monster that would frighten the life out of lesser mortals. But, no, not us; let them get nearer, catch them on the upsweep. A deafening crescendo of noise erupted into the heavens. Eight 5·25s fired simultaneously. I watched the shells burst – but not a plane was hit. To me they seemed *well* off target. The planes came on remorselessly as all the pom-poms, machine-guns and the Bofors gun opened up. All hell seemed to be let loose at once but nothing seemed to stop them and, as they passed over the masts, I could see the faces and goggles of the Japanese pilots looking down at us. Johnny King with his machine-gun might as well have had a pea-shooter for all the effect that he had on the oncoming horde.

Ordinary Seaman Derek Wilson recollects:

I was at the very top of the after superstructure, just between the two after 5·25 Control Positions on a circular platform about ten feet across. We had two old Lewis machine-guns mounted on tripods but mine was out of action so I had to act as an anti-aircraft lookout.

The torpedo planes approached at a lower level than those that had attacked *Repulse* and in looser formation. Our guns were deafening as they passed over. In this bewildering racket there can be few whose ears were more exposed to these detonations. Most other high positions had some protection from sound blast up to neck height. I recollect that one of my colleagues jumped on me to duck me as our own machine-gun, following its target, was swinging round towards me. At point-blank range, I just could not hear it above the racket.

I remember a feeling of relief as these planes passed over without bombing.

Yeoman of Signals E. A. Randall was on the Signal Bridge when it caught a burst of Japanese machine-gun fire.

I saw one of the bridge lookouts fall with four bullet holes in a pattern round his stomach and one of my signalmen also went down. His face, what was left of it, was just dripping blood, causing me to vomit.

But the Japanese did not get away entirely without loss.

One Nell was seen to lose height and to crash into the sea on the starboard side of *Prince of Wales*. Many accounts say that two Japanese planes were shot down in this attack, but it was not so.*

The aircraft that did crash was piloted by Petty Officer Katsujiro Kawada and there were no survivors. The Japanese Official History claims that Kawada's plane was hit soon after releasing its torpedo, and the pilot, realizing he was going to crash, attempted a suicide attack on *Prince of Wales* but never made it. Three of the remaining eight Nells were damaged by *Prince of Wales*'s gunfire, but none seriously.

Prince of Wales did not escape this attack unscathed. It had taken the Japanese aircraft about twenty-five seconds to reach the battleship after releasing their torpedoes; the torpedoes would take about one and a half minutes longer to reach or pass the ship. Captain Aylwin of the Royal Marines was with the pom-pom on the top of Y Turret, the 14-in. turret at the rear of the ship, where his men were in action.

We awaited the approach of nine torpedoes with baited breath, knowing that the Captain on the bridge would be doing his best by alterations of course to avoid all. Suddenly there was the most terrific jolt accompanied by a loud explosion immediately where I was standing on the port side. A vast column of water and smoke shot up into the air to a height of about 200 feet, drenching the quarterdeck, and a vast shudder shook the ship. At least one torpedo had hit us. The jolt received was just as though the ship had encountered a rock below the surface and, though hitting it, the ship's momentum was sufficient to clear it. When the smoke and spray had dispersed it was evident that the ship had taken on a 10-degree list to port and speed was considerably reduced.

Many other men remember this explosion. 'It was as if the ship had collided with a very solid object coupled

---

* The Compass Platform Narrative of *Prince of Wales* which was kept throughout the action is one report that erroneously records two planes shot down. The narrative is given in Appendix One.

with a leap in the air.' 'The ship appeared to be on springs; it lifted into the air and settled down again.' 'She seemed to bounce three or four times and then steadied herself.' 'There was a great thump and the ship's structure whipped violently like a springboard.'

Immediately after the explosion every man aboard *Prince of Wales* felt a most unnatural vibration running through the ship, 'like a boy running a stick along a stretch of corrugated iron, although much magnified'. This horrible sensation lasted perhaps thirty seconds and then ceased. In that half-minute, the ship had lost much speed and had taken on a violent list to port; there was also a distinct settling by the stern. Instruments soon recorded that the speed had dropped from 25 to 15 knots, that the list was an amazing 11½ degrees (some reports say 13 degrees) and that the stern had settled so much that the deck was only two feet above sea level instead of the normal twenty-four feet! Almost immediately it was clear that there were further dire after-effects of the explosion. Men in many parts of the ship found that their electrical supply had failed – there were no communications in these places, no lights, no power for many of the guns, no forced ventilation below decks.

So the first part of the first torpedo attack ended. The time between the first sighting of the two squadrons of Japanese torpedo bombers and the explosion in *Prince of Wales* had been a mere six minutes, but it has been worthwhile describing those minutes in detail since what happened during them is of much significance. On the Compass Platform of *Prince of Wales*, Admiral Phillips and Captain Leach were observed to say little over the effects of the torpedo hit, both appearing 'somewhat stunned'. This is not surprising when they must have known that their ship had taken in a massive tonnage of water and that severe damage had been done to at least one propeller shaft – for that, they knew, must be what the strange vibration had been. Reports would soon reach them moreover that most of their anti-aircraft guns were now without power.

What was reputed to be one of the most efficient fighting ships in the world had been crippled by a cylinder of steel and 330 pounds of explosive. The men on the bridge of *Prince of Wales* could now see another formation of Japanese torpedo bombers preparing to attack *Repulse*; they had no means of knowing that there were a further thirty-four torpedo bombers and twenty-three high-level bombers still in the area.

Prince of Wales will be left in her pitiful state and the fortunes of *Repulse* chronicled in the attack she was now about to face.

Repulse had witnessed the whole course of the torpedo attack on *Prince of Wales*. Captain Tennant, now that he had permission to manoeuvre freely, had drawn well away to starboard and *Repulse* was now perhaps a mile south of the flagship. (No accurate records of the relative courses and positions of the two ships exist and these details are based on estimates rather than reliable documents.) The initial deployment of the two formations of Japanese torpedo planes had been watched carefully, one *Repulse* officer remarking that 'they seemed to circle our ships like Red Indians about to attack wagons'; but it could be seen that the second Japanese squadron would not attack at exactly the same time as the first. The reason for the second squadron's delay may be found in the account of Lieutenant Sadao Takai who was piloting the formation's leading aircraft.

Coordinating my movements with those of the 1st Squadron, I led my squadron to the attack so that the enemy ships would be torpedoed from both flanks. The 1st Squadron was circling about four miles to the left and forward of the enemy ships and was about ready to begin its torpedo run. Anti-aircraft shells were exploding all around the circling bombers. The planes could be seen between the flashing patches of white smoke as the shells exploded.

Not a single anti-aircraft shell exploded near my squadron. Perhaps the clouds hid us from the enemy gunners. . . .

1. Winston Churchill and Admiral Sir Tom Phillips – two of the central figures in the *Prince of Wales* and *Repulse* story. This photograph was taken in February 1940, when Churchill was First Lord of the Admiralty and Phillips was Vice-Chief of the Naval Staff.

2. H.M.S. *Repulse*. This photograph, taken at Portsmouth in May 1939, shows the elegant lines of the First World War battle cruiser. She had just been specially fitted out to take King George VI and Queen Elizabeth on the Royal Tour of Canada. The masts of Nelson's *Victory* can be seen beyond *Repulse's* two forward 15-in. turrets.

3 and 4. The launching of H.M.S. *Prince of Wales* at Birkenhead, May 1939. The lower photograph shows the recesses in her hull side that will be covered with the 15-in. side-armour meant to protect her engine and boiler rooms and her magazine from shell fire. The force of any torpedoes striking below this armour plating was intended to be absorbed by a double system of watertight compartments.

The 20 feet of black-painted hull still above the waterline represents the extent to which the battleship will settle when fitted out with armour plating, gun turrets and the remainder of her superstructure and stores.

5. *Repulse* in wartime camouflage. On this occasion she is forming part of the escort of WS.11, a valuable troopship and trade convoy, sailing around the Cape of Good Hope to Suez. It was after this convoy that *Repulse* joined *Prince of Wales* to form the nucleus of the new Eastern Fleet.

6. This photograph, taken from *Repulse* on the same convoy, shows one of *Repulse*'s 4-in. anti-aircraft guns. Eight of these old, hand-operated guns in exposed, unprotected positions, like the one shown here, comprised the ship's main anti-aircraft defence.

7. 'X' Engine Room of *Prince of Wales*. Rear, the Senior Engineer, Lieutenant-Commander (E) Lockley, monitoring the repeater gauges from all four engine and boiler rooms. Right foreground, Engine Room Artificer Chesworth at the throttle, controlling the speed of 'X' propellor shaft; watching him, Lieutenant (E) Pybus, who left *Prince of Wales* before the ship sailed to the Far East. Left, an unidentified petty officer writing up the Engine Room Register.

8. *Prince of Wales* docks at Cape Town on her way to Singapore. This photograph shows the camouflage pattern and the thick armour side-plating. The wartime censor has blotted out the radar aerials.

9. Admiral Sir Tom Phillips and his Chief of Staff, Rear-Admiral A.F.E. Palliser, wait on the quayside at the Singapore Naval Base for the arrival of *Repulse* and *Prince of Wales*.

10. *Prince of Wales* reaches Singapore, her hull paint showing signs of the long voyage from Britain. The censor has not obliterated the radar aerials, but the picture was probably not published. The Fiji Class cruiser at the quay is H.M.S. *Mauritius*, under repair for engine defects, and alongside *Mauritius* is the yacht used by the Commander-in-Chief, Far East. The land in the background is Johore on the mainland of Malaya.

11 and 12. *Prince of Wales* (upper) and *Repulse* (lower). These sombre photographs show the two capital ships of Force Z in the Johore Strait just after sailing from the Naval Base to seek out the Japanese invasion forces. The top flag on the mainmast of *Prince of Wales* is the Red Cross of St George, the flag of a full admiral.

13, 14, 15 and 16. The destroyer escorts of Force Z.
H.M.S. *Tenedos* (H04), H.M.S. *Express* (H61), H.M.S. *Electra* (H27), H.M.A.S. *Vampire* (D68). All these are pre-war photographs.

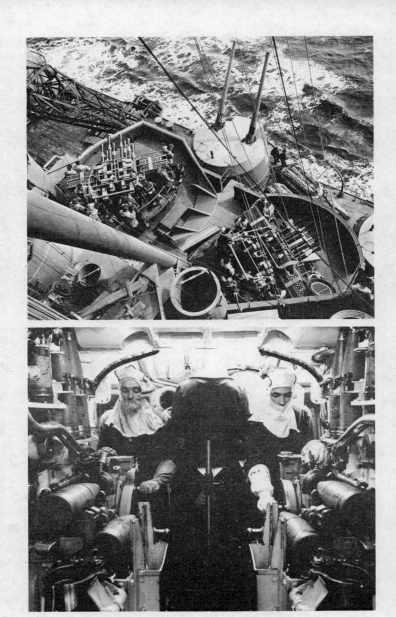

17. Gun drill (1). This photograph, taken from the port wing of *Prince of Wales*'s bridge, gives a good view of two of the ship's six sets of multiple 2-pounder 'pom-poms', sometimes called 'Chicago pianos'. Also in view is P2 5.25-in. gun turret with its guns in the 'high-angle' anti-aircraft position. These guns could also operate in the 'low-angle' role against surface targets.

18. Gun drill (2). The interior of a 5.25-in. turret's gunhouse, believed to be in *Prince of Wales*. This photograph was taken from the rear of the turret. The two men facing the camera are the ratings who set the fuses on the shells coming up from below. The third man is the 'Turret Trainer'. Not visible are the Turret Captain – a Petty Officer or a Royal Marine Sergeant – and the remaining five members of the gunhouse crew.

19. Japanese submarine I.65 (later I.165), the first Japanese naval or air unit to sight Force Z at sea. This photograph was taken at sea off Hiroshima in 1932, soon after I.65 was built.

20. Japanese naval air crews run to their Mitsubishi G3M2 ('Nell') bombers. It is not known where or when this photograph was taken, but it was with this type of aircraft that the Genzan and Mihoro Air Corps were equipped.

21. A 'Nell' in flight.

22. A formation of Mitsubishi G4M1 ('Betty') bombers in the type of loose formation in which the Kanoya Air Corps would have flown while searching for Force Z.

23. The opening of the Japanese attack on Force Z. A salvo of bombs has just exploded around *Repulse*, and one hit – the dark smoke – has been scored. The white smoke is funnel smoke. The wake of *Prince of Wales* (top of picture) shows the rapid course changes ordered by Admiral Phillips during this first attack.

24. The heavily listing *Prince of Wales* seen from the bridge of the destroyer *Express* in a photograph taken by Sub-Lieutenant P.F.C. Satow. The 5.25-in. turret visible is S3. The plate seen below the glass screen of *Express's* bridge contains the half-eaten sandwiches of Lieutenant-Commander Cartwright's lunch.

25. *Prince of Wales* survivors trying to get across to *Express* just before the
increasing heel of the battleship forced the destroyer away.
26. 'That magnificent but awful picture.' This dramatic photograph of the
German battleship *Blucher* sinking at the Battle of the Dogger Bank in
January 1915 is often mentioned by survivors of *Repulse* and *Prince of Wales*
as being similar to the scene when their own ships heeled over before
sinking. *Blucher* was less than half the tonnage of *Repulse* or *Prince of Wales*.
Only one-fifth of the German sailors survived the cold waters of the North
Sea in mid-winter.
27. The Brewster Buffalo fighter aircraft of the Australian 453 Squadron
drawn up for review.
28. 453 Squadron in the air over Malaya accompanied by one Bristol
Blenheim. The censor has obliterated the squadron identification letters.

The future of peoples is not decided by organised demonstrations of emotion, but by the hard facts of life. Future allegiances in the Pacific were settled in 1941 when the British battleships REPULSE and PRINCE OF WALES were sunk off Malay peninsula.—

U.S. CANDID FRIEND

AMERICAN SENSE OF RESPONSIBILITY

HURRY 'TONIA, OR YOU'LL LOSE 'EM

29 and 30. Lucky survivors of the sinkings. These are probably *Repulse* men on board the destroyer *Electra*.

31. Captain W. Tennant and Canon J. S. Bezzant, captain and chaplain of *Repulse*, sitting on depth charges in the stern of the Australian destroyer *Vampire* after their rescue.

32. The political effects of the sinkings still being quoted in one of David Low's famous political cartoons thirteen years later. 'Tonia' is the British Foreign Secretary, Anthony Eden, and the 'nanny' who is making off with Australia and New Zealand is the United States Secretary of State, John Foster Dulles. The occasion is a conference at Geneva in April 1954 at which the future of Indo-China and other Far East problems were to be discussed.

33. The White Ensign secured to the port inner propellor shaft of the wreck of *Repulse* ninety feet below the surface of the South China Sea.

34. The Memorial to the Missing on The Hoe at Plymouth. The names of the men lost in *Repulse* and *Prince of Wales* are recorded on this memorial, both ships having been manned from the near-by Devonport Naval Barracks.

A long, narrow plume of white smoke drifted upward from the second battleship. Later I discovered that this was due to a direct hit scored by the high-level bombers of the Mihoro Air Corps which had made the first attack.

There was no doubt that it was a battleship. However, when I studied carefully the details of the vessel, it resembled – it even appeared to be – our battleship *Kongo*! We were completely unaware of the whereabouts of our own surface forces in this area; it was not impossible that it was actually the *Kongo* below us. The narrow escape of the *Chokai* from our bombers last night was still fresh in my memory, and my blood ran cold at the thought that we might be attacking our own vessels.

However, the 1st Squadron bombers were plunging into the attack, one after the other, and the enemy gunners (if it really was the enemy!) were filling the sky with bursting anti-aircraft shells.

I was still undecided about attacking. I called our observer and inquired as to the identity of the ship below us stating that it greatly resembled the *Kongo*. I was shocked to hear the observer reply, 'It looks like our *Kongo* to me, too.'

It was a terrible situation to be in. I could not decide whether or not the vessel was a British battleship or actually the *Kongo*. I had been on the *Kongo* three years ago, and was trying to remember details of the battleship. To confess, I had not studied to any extent the details of British warships, but had concentrated instead on American vessels. My knowledge of the British vessels was very meagre. . . .

The clouds were increasing steadily, and visibility was already reduced. It would be to our disadvantage to attack from the sterns of the enemy ships. Boldly the formation circled out from the protection of the clouds, and checked once again the position of our targets. We were able to get a very good look at the battleship.

I was greatly relieved. I was sure of it – the vessel below was not the *Kongo*.

It may be that the Takai Squadron's failure to come in at exactly the same time as the Ishihara Squadron was due to the fear that the ships below were Japanese, but it is also possible that, on this occasion, Lieutenant Takai just did not manage to achieve the simultaneous attack that he had practised so often with the other Genzan squadrons. Whatever the cause, there was a delay of about twelve minutes before his seven Nells were running in to attack *Repulse*. Captain Tennant prepared to turn his ship, this time to starboard, to meet the attack. Lieutenant Takai resumes his description.

I was nervous and upset and starting to shake from the excitement of the moment. . . . The *Repulse* had already started evasive action and was making a hard turn to the right. The target angle was becoming smaller and smaller as the bow of the vessel swung gradually in my direction, making it difficult for me to release a torpedo against the ship. It was expected that the lead torpedo-bomber would be compelled to attack from the most unfavourable position. This was anticipated; and it enabled the other planes following me to torpedo the target under the best of conditions.

The air was filled with white smoke, bursting shells, and the tracers of anti-aircraft guns and machine-guns. As if pushed down by the fierce barrage thrown up by the enemy, I descended to just above the water's surface. The airspeed indicator registered more than two hundred knots. I do not remember at all how I was flying the aircraft, how I was aiming, and what distance we were from the ship when I dropped the torpedo. In the excitement of the attack I pulled back on the torpedo release. I acted almost subconsciously, my long months of daily training taking over my actions.

Repulse's anti-aircraft armament opened up but no one had ever claimed that *Repulse* was a well-provided ship when it came to dealing with aircraft attack. *Repulse* had almost as many anti-aircraft guns on her decks as had *Prince of Wales*, but some of *Repulse*'s guns could not elevate to high level and others could not depress sufficiently to engage low-flying aircraft. All these old guns had either old-fashioned control systems or none at all, and many were not even power-operated but had to be trained by hand. It is probable that Captain Tennant put his main hope in the avoidance of the torpedoes by vigorous ship handling rather than in his anti-aircraft armament.

As the Japanese flew in those 4-in. guns that could bear opened fire and were soon joined by the close-range weapons. These, too, had their troubles, however; the best-placed pom-pom immediately had stoppages in six of

its eight barrels because of separated cartridges – the
same complaint suffered by *Prince of Wales*'s pom-poms.
The only other pom-pom's electrical motor had been
damaged by the earlier bomb hit and the changeover to
manual operation had not yet been implemented. The result
of all these problems was that *Repulse* was able to put up
only the weakest of barrages.

The *Repulse* had been due for a refit and much better A.A. armament –
six 4-in. hand-worked A.A. guns for a ship of that size! Some attacks
were too low for these so we opened up with our triple 4-in. mount-
ings – a surface-ship armament – without fused shells. They made a
lot of noise and flashes; might have frightened some pilots but not
the Japanese. Some took no avoiding action at all, flew over us and
waved, aluminium shining in the dazzling sun and the Rising Sun
painted on their rudders. Ye gods, and we couldn't shoot them down.
Our Oerlikon guns were going right through their fuselages. (Petty
Officer A. T. Skedgell)

A small mystery should be mentioned at this point. The
Japanese Official History covers in some detail the
separate attacks of each squadron of Japanese aircraft, and
the attack of all of these, except one, fit in with British
descriptions of events. The exception is a torpedo attack
by eight Mitsubishi Nells of Lieutenant Takahashi's
squadron of the Mihoro Air Corps which is supposed to
have attacked *Repulse* within a few minutes of Lieutenant
Takai's squadron. It is possible that in the confusion and
stress of the attacks no one on the British ships noticed the
arrival of Takahashi's squadron, and it may be that one of
the squadrons, or perhaps some planes from each squadron,
did not press home their attack but released their torpedoes
from extreme ranges. As the planes of Lieutenant Takahashi's squadron were not hit by any anti-aircraft fire, it
may be that their torpedoes were dropped from more
distant positions at the same time as Lieutenant Takai was
attacking. If this is the case, then fifteen Mitsubishis in all
were aiming torpedoes at *Repulse*.

Once more the white lanes of torpedo tracks could be
clearly seen marking the surface of the calm blue sea.

Once again, also, some of the Japanese pilots flew on close to the British ship and their gunners opened fire with machine-guns. Aircraft flew down both sides of *Repulse* and the exposed positions on the battle cruiser's decks and superstructure suffered far more severely than had *Prince of Wales* a few minutes earlier.

When we heard machine-gun bullets being sprayed along the upper deck by the Japanese torpedo bombers, my God, did we move! As one man we all rushed for cover in the well-hole of the 4-in. gun underneath the breech block. We heard the bullets ricocheting off the gun shield but we were lucky as no one was hurt. After the firing had stopped we had a look to see what had happened. It was a good job we had that steel plate round our gun and we were behind it, otherwise we would all have been killed. One of our big launches immediately behind our gun was riddled with bullet holes and we just couldn't believe how lucky we had been. (Able Seaman S. C. Baxter)

Another gun position was not so fortunate and a Royal Marine had 'half his head blown away' by a bullet which entered the turret through a small gap. His comrades took the body outside and laid him down in a quiet corner, and a sailor from a near-by ammunition party placed a heap of cotton waste over his face. This Royal Marine was only one of many gunners killed or wounded by the machine-gun fire. Others to suffer were a party of men keeping one of the anti-aircraft guns supplied with ammunition by carrying shells up from the deck below: there were no sophisticated mechanical hoists direct to this old weapon and several of the ammunition party were killed.

It was now, with the Japanese torpedoes approaching, that Captain Tennant's judgement in shiphandling was of the utmost importance. The man who was at the wheel in the armoured conning tower just below *Repulse*'s bridge was Leading Seaman John Robson.

The conning tower rapidly filled with officers and ratings. I was not relieved at the wheel and the P.O. Quartermaster stood by the bridge voicepipe passing wheel orders to me as we took avoiding turns. The noise was terrific when the guns fired. I always remember the

P.O. Quartermaster only a foot from me shouting the wheel orders to me – his face red with the effort to be heard above the noise all around us.

I thought about the Engineer Commander's orders given a long time ago, about going easy on wheel movements, as the steering mechanism engines were long past their best, but the Captain was giving alternate wheel orders against the torpedoes approaching us as though we were a destroyer. The whole ship shuddered with the effect of twisting to port and starboard.

Many observers have praised the skill displayed by Captain Tennant on this occasion. He had managed to dodge the 'overs' from the attack on *Prince of Wales* and now he managed to avoid every one of the torpedoes dropped by these two Japanese squadrons. Captain Tennant later submitted his own, somewhat modest report.

The second attack was shared by *Prince of Wales* and *Repulse* and was made by torpedo-bomber aircraft. I am not prepared to say how many machines took part in this attack but, on its conclusion, I have the impression that we had succeeded in combing the tracks of a large number of torpedoes, possibly as many as twelve. We were steaming at 25 knots at the time. I maintained a steady course until the aircraft appeared to be committed to the attack, when the wheel was put over and the attacks providentially combed. I would like to record the valuable work done by all bridge personnel at this time in calmly pointing out approaching torpedo-bombing aircraft which largely contributed to our good fortune in dodging all these torpedoes.

These torpedoes were not the only hazard survived by *Repulse* at this time because a small formation of high-level bombers had flown over her at 12,000 feet and carried out a bombing attack at the very moment when the torpedo bombers were making their attacks. These six aircraft involved were from Lieutenant Shirai's squadron that had already made one attack on *Repulse*. This was the only squadron to have been carrying two bombs for each aircraft, and Shirai had brought the six aircraft that remained after two had flown home with serious damage from the first attack to achieve a perfect coordination with the low-level torpedo attacks. The six 250-kg. bombs failed to hit

Repulse, but they did fall in a tight group around the battle cruiser and it was a good example of precision bombing.

Lieutenant Takai's personal account does not mention the bombing attack, and he was probably never aware of it. After his gunners had machine-gunned *Repulse*'s deck, he sheered away from *Prince of Wales*, which loomed ahead of him and from which one or two guns opened fire on him briefly, but was able to climb away to safety. He then saw the spray of Lieutenant Shirai's bombs and presumed it was caused by torpedo hits scored by his squadron. He relaxed.

Suddenly my observer came stumbling forward through the narrow passageway, crying 'Sir! Sir! A terrible thing has happened!' When I looked at him in surprise, he shouted, 'The torpedo failed to release!'

I felt as though cold water had been dashed over my head and entire body. We were still carrying the torpedo! I forced myself to be calm and reversed our course at once. I passed on my new orders to the men. 'We will go in again at once.'

I began to lower our altitude as we flew through the clouds. The second torpedo run on the battleship would be very dangerous; the enemy gunners were fully alert and would be waiting for us. I did not like the idea of flying once again through a storm of anti-aircraft fire which would be even worse than before.

We dropped below cloud level. We were on the side of the enemy battleship, which was just swinging into a wide turn. Our luck was good – no better chance would come!

I pushed the throttles forward to reach maximum speed and flew just above the water. This time I yanked hard on the torpedo release. Over the thudding impact of bullets and shrapnel smashing into the aircraft, I felt the strong shock through the bomber as the torpedo dropped free and plummeted into the water. It was inexcusable that we did not notice the absence of this shock during the first torpedo run.

Repulse's lookouts saw Lieutenant Takai's aircraft coming in again, and at least one pom-pom and several smaller weapons opened fire on him but without causing serious damage. Takai too was unlucky. His torpedo missed. Another plane in his squadron had even more trouble with its torpedo release mechanism and the torpedo never did drop. Four planes from this squadron suffered slight damage from anti-aircraft fire.

The time that had elapsed between the first sighting of the torpedo bombers and the departure of Lieutenant Takai was approximately twenty-two minutes. The Japanese claimed no less than seven torpedo hits on *Repulse* – four of them by the squadron of Lieutenant Takahashi, whose attack cannot be pinned down in British accounts. In fact, only *Prince of Wales* had been hit. Twenty-five torpedo bombers and eight high-level bombers had now completed their attacks at a cost of one aircraft shot down, two seriously damaged and ten slightly damaged. It was now forty-seven minutes since the first attack on the ships had occurred and the British were still far from being out of danger. Twenty-six further torpedo bombers and seventeen high-level bombers remained to be reckoned with, although none of these had yet found the British ships and all would soon be running low on fuel.

   But this first phase of hectic action was now to be followed by a lull.

10

The Lull

It was almost exactly noon when Lieutenant Takai turned from his second torpedo run and flew away, pursued by the few last rounds of *Repulse*'s anti-aircraft fire. Then it became uncannily quiet and the crews of the British ships were able to recover their breath. *Prince of Wales* wallowed sluggishly along at her reduced speed, and *Repulse*, possibly three miles away, emerged from the smoke of her own gunfire and from the hectic twisting and wheeling that had evaded so many torpedoes. The weather had now become very hot, and although the patchy low cloud was gradually extending, it was neither low enough nor thick enough to give any protection to the British ships. The sea continued to be as calm as the open sea ever could be.

The lull enabled both ships to survey their damage and the state of their anti-aircraft armament. Gunnery officers hurried across decks that a few minutes before had been swept by machine-gun bullets and visited their gun positions, calling for specialist ordnance or electrical ratings to repair damage and the many defects. Casualties among gun crews were replaced. Great heaps of empty cartridges were cleared from around the guns and dumped overboard.

Large numbers of spare men were detailed to form extra ammunition parties for those gun positions where the power hoists had failed, or where the normal supply route had been affected by damage and a makeshift alternative had now to be found. The pom-poms and Oerlikons in particular had consumed large quantities of ammunition and had to be resupplied. It was a laborious task, manhandling the cases of ammunition for the smaller guns or the heavy, greasy shells for the larger guns from magazines deep down in the ships up through several deck levels to the gun positions. At least one party had to improvise their supply by hauling individual boxes up a long plank by ropes, and as many as four parties of men might be required to keep one chain of supply going. Everyone knew it was a vital task and worked with a will though it was exhaustingly hot work in the lower decks.

The following report by Sub-Lieutenant G. H. Peters, who was in charge of *Repulse*'s forward group of 4-in. high-angle guns, is maybe typical of the decisions being taken; once this type of battle had opened, much depended on such young officers.

My impression is that there was an appreciable interval now, during which time the T.S. reported that circuits had failed at two of the 4-inch guns (which I don't know). I told the captains of these two guns that if an attack developed again before a Leading Torpedo Operator had fixed them up they were to do the best they could on local control at anything directly menacing the ship. I passed down to the T.S. to get hold of all available ammunition.

I reviewed the ammunition situation and, bearing in mind previous orders on the conservation of ammunition, decided that it was all or nothing as, if we did get away, fighter protection might have reached us by then. I therefore decided that I should from now on develop maximum rate of fire on all aircraft in range.

In the interior compartments of both ships there was also much activity. The main medical parties were stationed well below the armoured deck and had only sent small emergency parties out on specific calls for help while the ships had been in action. Now, with this lull, they were able to open the armoured hatches that protected them and take in more casualties or to send out larger parties under surgeons to establish new aid posts near the scenes of major damage. *

The Damage Control officers in *Prince of Wales* found

---

* Surgeon-Lieutenant S. C. Hamilton, one of *Repulse*'s doctors, wrote up a full report after the action of the first-aid arrangements in his ship and the way these worked during the action. This report is reproduced in full in Appendix Two.

their ship to be in a state that they would never have believed possible. The column of water seen to be thrown up by the explosion on the port side was at a part of the ship well covered by a new system of protection against underwater attack known as the 'liquid sandwich'. In this, a strengthened inner hull around the ship's vitals was itself surrounded by an inner air space; then with a belt of tanks always kept filled with either fuel oil or water; and finally with an outer belt of air-filled compartments.

Research had shown that a torpedo or mine explosion should dissipate its force in these three belts, that the resulting flooding should be very limited and the inner hull should remain intact. A torpedo hit near Y Turret should have been followed by only a slight list, a little flooding of the outer compartments and certainly not by any of the flooding of inner compartments now clearly taking place. The exact cause of this horrifying state of affairs on *Prince of Wales* has since been the subject of much learned investigation and speculation, and while there is no full agreement on the finer points, there is a general consensus about the broad reasons for the extensive damage. Before describing the full details of the damage and its effect upon *Prince of Wales*'s capacity as a fighting unit, it would be useful to look carefully at the probable cause.

Many observers have told of the huge column of water thrown up, presumably by a torpedo explosion, on the port side of *Prince of Wales* at a point roughly level with the mainmast. There is also the evidence of the peculiar lifting sensation of an explosion followed by the tremendous vibration. Finally, from a post-war investigation, it is known that there is a hole twelve feet in diameter with jagged edges bent inwards near *Prince of Wales*'s stern on the port side and close to where the port-outer propeller shaft leaves the hull, *even though no column of water was ever seen at this point.*

It is clear that the hole near the propeller shaft must have been caused by a direct hit from one Japanese torpedo. The absence of a column of water at this point is probably

Prince of Wales in First Torpedo Attack

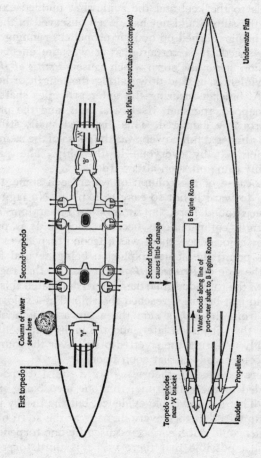

Deck Plan (superstructure not complete)

First torpedo

Second torpedo

Column of water seen here

'A'

'B'

'Y'

Underwater Plan

Second torpedo causes little damage

B Engine Room

Water floods along line of port-outer shaft to B Engine Room

Torpedo explodes near 'A' bracket

Propellers

Rudder

Diagram 1

explained by the fact that the ship's side here slopes steeply inwards to the keel and the somewhat muffled explosion under the ship would not have been observed in the white water being churned up by four propellers running almost at full speed. It is certain that it was the effect of this explosion under the stern which caused *Prince of Wales* to whip violently up and down along the length of her hull. The 'A' bracket securing the outer propeller shaft to the hull snapped, the shaft itself was bent, and the propeller was probably damaged. This distorted shaft, still being driven almost at full power, was the cause of the tremendous vibration felt by everyone in the ship. The propeller probably came off soon afterwards.

The cause of the column of water seen some 140 feet farther forward is not so easy to explain. No jagged hole has been found here, but it is known that four near-by watertight compartments became flooded. It is probable that, by coincidence, there was a second torpedo explosion at this point, the actual explosion being several feet out from the side of *Prince of Wales*. It may be that the shock-wave of the torpedo hit farther astern detonated this second torpedo just before it reached the ship. The explosion just away from the ship's side threw up a column of water higher than any seen later, and the underwater effect was probably to spring the rivetted plates over the four water-tight compartments that soon flooded.

There are even theories that a third torpedo was exploded at the same time, this one also being near the stern. There is no visible evidence, but the theory is based on estimates that the severe damage at the stern of *Prince of Wales* could not have been caused by one torpedo alone. It is just possible that there was this third torpedo, but for present purposes we must assume that there was only the direct hit at the stern and the explosion of a second torpedo near the hull farther forward.

What was of more importance to the men in *Prince of Wales* were the effects of the torpedo blasts. The first was seen in B Engine Room which was at the forward end of the 240-foot shaft that had been distorted by the explosion. Lieutenant Dick Wildish was in charge here.

All the main machinery set had an appalling, thumping-vibration and great clouds of muck, smoke, cordite fumes and dust poured out from the ventilation trunking. It was clear that the shaft had suffered serious damage and I gave orders for it to be stopped. This took some doing at 25 knots. I did this on my own authority. There was no time to consult. Once stopped, the vibration stopped. Then, and as my boiler room was still intact, and with thoughts of trying to maintain ship's speed during the attack, I decided to try running up the shaft again. As we reduced the 'astern' steam holding the shaft stopped, it started revolving again (I suppose indicating that the propeller was still there). However, as we started it going again, a rating reported that water was entering at the after end of the engine room. He was dead right. It was pouring through the flexible watertight shaft gland in the bulkhead. I rather think that we tried to tighten up on this but it was hopeless.

So we started all pumps on bilge suction – including putting the main circulator pump on bilge, instead of sea, suction. It soon became clear that the pumps could not control the flooding so we prepared to évacuate. There were certain steps to be taken to enable machinery to run on for as long as possible under flooded conditions. These concerned stopping sea-water entering the lubricating oil and boiler- feed water systems. Clearly, as my boiler room was still intact, it would help if my machinery could run on during the attack.

By the time we had done this, water was up around the control platform and rising fast. I gave the order to evacuate. As I followed the rest up, my Unit E.R.A. just ahead of me, the water swirled up in oily confusion just behind us. I have once since experienced a flooded machinery space and it is a horrifying, terrifying sight

Lieutenant Wildish's B Engine Room was not the only one in trouble. There were three other engine rooms – A, X, Y – each with its own boiler room. Each of the engine rooms was also connected to an 'action machinery room' where huge dynamos converted steam power to the electricity which was the source of power for the gun turrets, the ammunition hoists and the multitude of other pieces of equipment that enabled a warship to live and fight. In this area also were two reserve 'diesel dynamo rooms' and the harbour machinery room, which also provided electrical power. These vital compartments, deep in the heart of the ship, were well protected by steel armour and the 'liquid sandwich', and were normally considered safe from danger. Yet, not only was B Engine Room flooded, but Y Boiler Room, Y Action Machinery Room and one of the diesel dynamo rooms were also flooding fast; the harbour machinery room was flooding more slowly and Y Engine Room was losing its steam pressure: its turbines were shaking violently and a fractured oil pipe was robbing the turbines of lubrication. The engines in this room were quickly shut down. Thus, within a few minutes of first being hit, one of the world's most powerful and advanced battleships had lost half its primary power, and three of the seven machinery rooms that supplied electricity for the guns and the rest of the ship were also out of action. In addition, three out of the eight 5·25-in. magazines and a multitude of small compartments were also flooding.

This flooding was all the result of damage caused by the port-outer shaft during the few seconds when it ran amuck and before Lieutenant Wildish was able to stop it. The violent vibration of the 240-foot shaft had opened up bulkheads and smashed oil and fuel pipes right along its length. The passage in which the shaft was housed was a long corridor, the rear eighty feet of which was 'wide enough for three men to walk down side by side'. The stern torpedo explosion had torn open the rear end of this shaft passage and a tremendous rush of water along it was flooding the damaged compartments above, below and on both sides. The second torpedo explosion farther forward had flooded four watertight compartments, but the weight of water in these was almost as nothing compared to the vast quantity that had entered at the stern. Two levels of the ship, the hold and the lower platform, were flooded on the port side for a length of 270 feet, and, above these, water was forcing its way upwards through damaged ventilation trunks as high as the compartments on the middle deck.

Prince of Wales—Extent of initial horizontal flooding in hold level. (Based on survivors' reports to Buckhill Committee)

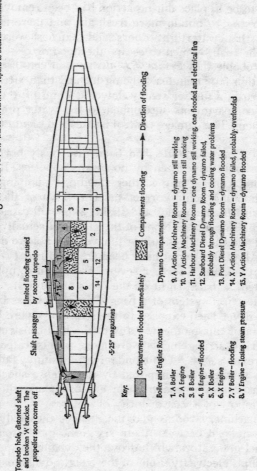

Torpedo hole, distorted shaft and broken 'A' bracket. The propeller soon comes off

Limited flooding caused by second torpedo

Shaft passage

5·25" magazines

Key:

▨ Compartments flooded immediately   ▨ Compartments flooding   ⟶ Direction of flooding

▨ Dynamo Compartments

Boiler and Engine Rooms
1. A Boiler
2. A Engine
3. B Boiler
4. B Engine – flooded
5. X Boiler
6. X Engine
7. Y Boiler – flooding
8. Y Engine – losing steam pressure

9. A Action Machinery Room – dynamo still working
10. B Action Machinery Room – dynamo still working
11. Harbour Machinery Room – one dynamo still working, one flooded and electrical fire
12. Starboard Diesel Dynamo Room – dynamo failed, probably through flooding and cooling water problems
13. Port Diesel Dynamo Room – dynamo flooded
14. X Action Machinery Room – dynamo failed, probably overloaded
15. Y Action Machinery Room – dynamo flooded

Diagram 2

One of the worst upward escapes of water was found to be at places where circular discs in the trunking that were intended to be in place during action had been removed by seamen trying to obtain more fresh air, and there is also evidence that watertight doors and hatches were left open in the rush by men to escape the flooding.

It is probable that *Prince of Wales* took in 2,400 tons of water within four minutes of being hit and that, after this first big rush, a further steady flow was entering the ship as more compartments succumbed to the water pressure around them. The damage control parties had plenty to do.

Although *Prince of Wales* had been grievously hurt, the position should have been by no means hopeless. Repair work could contain any further flooding; pumping and counter-flooding could correct the list. Two of the four boilers with their engines and shafts were still capable of driving the ship along. None of the guns had actually been damaged and the ship should still have been able to defend herself. All of this might have been achieved had *Prince of Wales* not suffered a further severe, and again completely unexpected, setback, right on the heels of the first.

The electrical system of a King George V Class battleship had never been exposed to the stress of severe battle damage until this moment. As with the hull construction, the electrical arrangements were more sophisticated than in any previous ship. * Unfortunately, they simply failed to stand up to the strain imposed by the intense shock and vibration caused by the torpedo explosion and the subsequent inflow of a vast quantity of water.

The machinery rooms and the reserve diesel dynamo rooms contained between them six turbo-generators and two diesel generators which drove the dynamos supplying all the ship's electricity. Four of these eight dynamos failed immediately when the compartments in which they were situated flooded and a fifth dynamo went soon afterwards

* The electrical system was 220 volts on D.C.

for reasons which are not known because the two men tending it did not survive. * The four dynamos supplying the rear half of *Prince of Wales* were among those that had failed. In theory, it should have been possible to transfer power from the three remaining dynamos by means of ring-main breakers, but this was never satisfactorily done; such a major failure at one stroke had never been visualized and the design of the electrical system failed to cope with this emergency.

Prince of Wales's damage control organization never managed to overcome the electrical failure, and except for the battery-powered emergency lighting which functioned where the shock of the torpedo explosion had not ruined it and the occasional temporary supply brought in by emergency leads, no significant amount of electricity ever again reached the rear half of the ship. A warship lives on electricity and exactly half of *Prince of Wales* was dead.

These are some of the after-effects of the electrical failure:

Pumps

Prince of Wales had fourteen 350-tons-an-hour pumps and four bigger 1,000-tons-an-hour emergency bilge pumps – a total pumping capacity of 8,900 tons per hour – but every pump in the rear half of the ship was without power and could not operate.† Some pumping was attempted in the flooded midship sections, but no progress was made against the volume of water entering at the stern.

* The five dynamos that failed were No. 4 Turbo Dynamo in the harbour machinery room, port side; No. 5 Diesel Dynamo in the starboard diesel room; No. 6 Diesel Dynamo in the port diesel dynamo room; and Nos. 7 and 8 Turbo Dynamos in X and Y Action Machinery Rooms respectively.

† The pumps that failed were Nos. 9, 10, 11, 12, 13 and 14 Salvage Pumps, X and Y Emergency Bilge Pumps and Y Fire and Bilge Pump.

Counter-Flooding

One of *Prince of Wales*'s greatest needs was a level or almost level platform so that the guns could be trained. With the 11½ degree list at that time, not one of the eight power-operated 5·25-in. gun turrets could be trained. Captain Leach immediately ordered compartments in the starboard side of the ship to be flooded to correct the list and some counter-flooding was possible in the forward and midship compartments on the starboard side. The list was thus reduced to 10 degrees, but there was so much water in the port side of the ship that no further improvement was possible.

Communications

There was no telephone communication at all with the after part of the ship. Messages had to be passed by hand and much effort and time was wasted. Details of the damage in the rear half of the ship were thus slow to arrive at the damage control centre and repair parties were often working on less serious tasks when more urgent ones were left unattended. One example of this occurred when electrical repair parties were dragging emergency cables to individual 5·25-in. turrets while hardly any effort was being made to correct the more fundamental ring-main faults which were preventing power being supplied to the entire rear half of the ship.

Ventilation and lighting

There was no powered ventilation and only emergency lighting in all the compartments below deck in the after half of the ship. This was particularly serious for the repair parties, who rapidly became exhausted and therefore less effective, and for the men manning X Boiler Room and Engine Room and A Engine Room. These were in perfect running order, but became so hot that men collapsed with the heat or had to be relieved every few minutes – temperatures as high as 150°F (66°C) were recorded. The relief method did not last long and these compartments had to be left with machinery unattended, except for the occasional visit of an engineering officer or senior rating. Even this system failed eventually since the men who made these short visits had to have fifteen minutes' recovery time in the open air after each visit.

Another place affected by the lighting and ventilation problems was the after medical station which was forced out of its safe place below deck to the ship's chapel on the next deck up, but the many wounded and semi-suffocated men here soon overflowed on to the next deck above and had to be placed in a space known as the Cinema Flat. This was later to have tragic consequences.

Steering

Although the rudder may not itself have been damaged by the stern torpedo explosion, both the steering motors immediately went dead following the electrical failure. After several messages had been passed by hand between the main and the after steering positions, an attempt was made to change over to emergency steam-operated steering, though this was probably never achieved.

Anti-aircraft armament

The four 5·25-in. turrets in the after half of the ship – P3, P4, S3 and S4 – were all without power and were too big and heavy to be trained manually. Two of the four forward turrets suffered temporary failures, but even while these were soon rectified, the list of the ship was so steep that none of the four forward turrets could swing its gun from side to side although all the weapons could be elevated. Some of the pom-poms suffered temporary power failures, but these mostly remained in action, though continually plagued with stoppages as a result of their faulty ammunition belts.

Such was the plight that poor *Prince of Wales* found herself in during the lull in the action: not sinking, not completely out of commission, and not in a completely hopeless position, but certainly a cripple at this stage. At 12.10 the two black balls which told the other ships of Force Z that *Prince of Wales* was 'NOT UNDER CONTROL' were hoisted. The Japanese pilot who had put his torpedo into the battleship's port-outer propeller shaft while that shaft was revolving at 204 revolutions per minute had set off a chain reaction that had brought this great ship to her knees. It is unlikely that a hit at any other part of the ship could have had such serious consequences.

In some of those parts of *Prince of Wales* not directly affected by the damage and flooding, there was now an air of unreality and aimlessness. One man says that, 'There seemed to be lots of people with nothing to do and nowhere to go; many laid down and seemed to sleep on mess tables and stools.' It is probably an exaggeration to say that the organization of the ship was breaking down, but it was certainly under a great strain and it was at this time that the lack of a proper working-up period was felt. Telegraphist C. V. House is a good observer of the scene in the forward part of the ship below decks. He had been fallen out from duty and, with several other spare men, was shut in a mess deck. He had felt the torpedo explosion.

For a few moments my brain worked fast – would there be an internal explosion? Shut in a steel box below the water-line, was I going to be drowned like a rat? Seconds ticked away, and then I noticed the chap still sitting on his haunches in the gangway and as white as a ghost. I went over and spoke to him asking if there was anything I could do. I tried to chat but it didn't seem to ease the position at all.

I asked him if he thought there was any possibility of our getting out of the mess deck on to the upper deck, but he said, 'No. Not an earthly!' By then the ship had begun to list, not the usual kind of roll that I had always been used to, but a gradual tilt one way, steadily increasing, until the ship was canting at an alarming angle. I remember seeing a streak of red running across the deck and following it up found it to be beetroot juice which had spilled from one of the mess shelves. Seeing there was nothing to be done but to sit and wait events, I entered one of the messes and sat down, looking at the pictures in an American magazine, *Life*.

It was about this time that a bunch of engineer officers made their way into the mess deck in order to open up various valves and flood several starboard compartments – bathrooms and such like – in an effort to correct the list and trim the ship off. The first arrivals had no spanner with which to turn the wheels, or the knowledge (apparently) of which wheels to turn. The arrival of a warrant engineer who knew his job saved them from ridicule and the flooding commenced. It definitely stopped the listing, and after a while the ship appeared to level up a little, although she never came back to an even keel. It was about then that I noticed the Leading Tel. previously mentioned had left the mess-deck; apparently he managed to slide out as the flooding party came in. By now it was dinner time, but as the cooks had all been busy as 'repair parties' or 'first aid parties' there was no possibility of getting anything to eat.

There were men in *Prince of Wales* who were beginning to think that the ship might not survive.

I think I realized the ship was going to sink very early on because the list we had taken on showed we were badly crippled and the torpedo bombers could easily run a shuttle service until we were finished, even if it took days. Naturally there was a sensation of astonishment that our tremendous ship was knuckling under so easily and apprehension at what was going to happen to me personally. However, there was no time to sit and think it all out! (Sub-Lieutenant G. A. G. Brooke)

Many others were not so pessimistic and there was excited anticipation by some that *Prince of Wales* might be 'going to Aussie for repairs'.

If *Prince of Wales* contained men who were full of gloom, *Repulse* did not. This great-hearted ship had performed well and her crew knew it. There was immense pride in the ship-handling qualities of Captain Tennant, and there was much excited talk of how many torpedoes had so far been dodged – 'nineteen' is the figure quoted by *Repulse* men. Those men above decks on *Repulse* were shocked to see the state of *Prince of Wales* and many have recorded their disappointment in the performance of this new battleship with its high reputation. *Repulse* knew that its own anti-aircraft armament was primitive and weak, but great things had been expected of the modern high-angle anti-aircraft armament of *Prince of Wales*.

During the lull, *Repulse* completed most of the immediate repair work connected with her one bomb hit, though a small fire persisted and some men remained trapped in a compartment below the catapult deck. The medical work was well in hand, as was the repair of gun faults and the restocking of anti-aircraft ammunition. On her flag bridge, three passengers had had a grandstand view of this aircraft *versus* warship engagement. The *Daily Express* reporter, O'Dowd Gallagher, and the American, Cecil Brown of the Columbia Broadcasting System, were making notes of the action, and Lieutenant Horace Abrahams, the naval photographer, had taken many priceless photographs.

Repulse had emerged from the first phase of the battle almost unscathed. All her engines and armament were in working order and her crew's morale was high. Captain Tennant turned his ship towards *Prince of Wales*, still about three miles away, to see how he could help the flag-ship. But *Repulse*'s lamp signals asking about *Prince of Wales*'s damage and whether her wireless was out of action brought no reply. It was as though the flagship was too preoccupied with her grievous condition to have time to answer solicitous inquirers.

Captain Tennant had asked his signal office what signals *Prince of Wales* had sent to Singapore during the recent attacks and was astonished to be told that the flagship had still not transmitted. Tennant decided he must now send a signal, and at 11.58 what was the first message to be sent by Force Z since it had left Singapore two days earlier was tapped out from *Repulse*.

FROM REPULSE   TO ANY BRITISH MAN OF WAR
ENEMY AIRCRAFT BOMBING. MY POSITION
134 N Y T W22 x O9.

Prince of Wales's wireless aerials had been partially

affected by the shock of the torpedo explosion, but it is certain that her ability to send signals had not been affected. Petty Officer Telegraphist Arthur Best was the senior of the ratings in charge of the two transmitting rooms inside the armoured citadel, and he states that 'up till a few minutes before she sank, H.M.S. *Prince of Wales* was capable of sending any form of wireless message over any distance'. It is an important point because the impression is sometimes created that Admiral Phillips had not been able to send this initial emergency signal as *Prince of Wales's* transmitter was out of action. The truth is simply that Captain Tennant had taken matters into his own hands and had got this first vital signal away without receiving permission from the flagship. The view in *Repulse* over the long delay in sending the first signal was that 'had Captain Tennant been in command of the force, as he invariably had been in command of much larger forces for the last two years, the story might have been different'.

It took six minutes for the Naval Signal Station at Kranji on Singapore Island to decode and process the signal. It was the first news received in Singapore of Force Z since the signal from *Tenedos*, earlier that morning, which had stated that the British ships were returning directly to Singapore. It was the first indication that there had been a diversion to Kuantan or that Japanese aircraft were attacking, although Force Z had first been shadowed by Midshipman Hoashi's aircraft nearly two hours earlier.

It took a further fifteen minutes for the signal to reach the operations room in Air Headquarters at Sime Road. An immediate order was sent to Sembawang airfield, where the Australians of 453 Squadron had been standing by for two days to help, and their eleven serviceable Brewster Buffaloes had all taken off within five minutes. The formation was led by Flight Lieutenant Tim Vigors, an Irishman and an ex-Battle of Britain pilot in temporary command of the squadron. But it was 150 nautical miles, one hour's flying time, to the area off Kuantan where Force Z was in trouble. The R.A.F., who had kept a scarce fighter squadron out of the fighting to help the Navy, were very annoyed at not being kept informed of Force Z's progress and at not being called upon to help earlier. Yet had it not been for Captain Tennant's breaking of Force Z's self-imposed radio silence, the Buffaloes would still not have taken off even by this late stage.

The contest so far had been almost exclusively between the Japanese attack planes and the two capital ships. The closest of several less fully engaged participants were the three destroyers. These were keeping a sharp watch by Asdic for submarines, but the Japanese submarines had not managed to reach the scene of this action. The destroyers had tried hard to help defend the bigger ships and had opened up with every gun which could engage aircraft.

Express had been in the direct line of the first wave of torpedo bombers attacking *Prince of Wales*, and her log shows she believed that three torpedoes had been deliberately aimed at her, one of them seeming to pass directly under the destroyer but evidently not running shallow enough to strike. The Mitsubishi had then flown straight over *Express*, machine-gunning as she went but causing no casualties. Stoker Robert Burnett had been helping to keep one of the 4·7-in. guns on *Express* supplied with ammunition.

I had to stand on a table maybe one yard square. There was a pole at one corner fastened to the deck; it had a belt on the pole fastened to my waist to keep me from falling off if the ship lurched. While another stoker and I were handing shells and cordite from the hoist to the gun, there was a big Australian seaman lying on the deck screaming. I wondered at times where the biggest danger was coming from – him or the bombers. Anyhow, our doctor came up and gave him a needle that quietened him down. Funny thing about that Aussie, before there were any signs of action he walked round the upper deck with a large sheath-knife in his belt saying what he was going to do with the Japs if we clued up with them.

I kept on handing shells and cordite up, wringing with sweat, till I heard a voice shout, 'Are you going to send some bloody H.E.

shells up here?' I looked up and saw Gunner Petty Officer Appleby. I told him I was giving what was handed to me. He then replied, 'They are bloody star shells.' I found out that they were the only shells we had left.

Surgeon-Lieutenant T. E. Barwell also remembers the Australian seaman as well as another incident.

The only casualty *Express* had was an acute 'shell-shock'. He was a giant of a man we had embarked on the way out and was obviously mentally unfit to be at sea. We had sent him ashore on arrival at Singapore but he had been returned to us. When the Japs came over he became quite helpless with fright and I was called to see what I could do as he was standing in the way with a 4·7-in. shell in his arms simply quaking with fright. We managed to get him down below, where I gave him an injection of a half-grain of morphine to keep him quiet.

There was one amusing episode. When we first arrived in Singapore the captain, Lieutenant-Commander Jack Cartwright, sent his servant Clingham ashore to buy him a papya, or 'pawpaw' as Clingham called it as he came from St Helena and that was the South African name I think. He took it into Cartwright next day at breakfast time, but was told to take it away and bring it back when it was ripe. In the middle of the action, amidst all the gunfire, Clingham arrived on the bridge with the pawpaw, saluted, and said, 'Captain, sir. Your pawpaw's ripe. Will you have it now, sir?'

Electra and the Australian ship *Vampire* had also been firing on the Japanese aircraft with all they had, and had been machine-gunned in return; *Vampire* claimed to have damaged at least two enemy planes. During the lull, both of these ships were ordered to search in the wake of *Prince of Wales* for men believed to have been blown overboard by the shock of the torpedo explosion, but nobody was found and it may be that the 'man overboard' scare resulted from a mistaken report in *Prince of Wales*, though several witnesses say this did happen.

A less involved observer of the battle was *Repulse*'s Walrus aircraft which had been flying an anti-submarine patrol around Force Z when the action opened. The petty officer who was piloting the Walrus – his name is not recorded – continued to circle the area throughout the entire action. The Walrus was seen by many of the Japanese pilots, but was completely ignored by all of them and the slow, lightly armed Walrus could do nothing to attack the faster Japanese aircraft. *Repulse* never got the chance to take her aircraft back again, and the Walrus eventually flew off towards Singapore, but ran out of petrol on the way and landed on sea. A friendly Catalina found her and dropped food and water, and the destroyer *Stronghold* eventually towed the Walrus into Singapore.

The crew of another aircraft witnessed the action, or most of it. This was Midshipman Hoashi's aircraft which had first spotted the British ships. Back in Saigon, Vice-Admiral Matsunaga ordered Hoashi to maintain contact until 13.30 and sent off another plane to relieve Hoashi at that time. It was now essential for the Japanese to keep in touch with the British until the conclusion of the action, whenever that might be. It was their greatest good fortune that no British fighters had yet appeared to drive away the shadower. The Japanese were operating at about 450 nautical miles from their main base; the British were 150 miles from their Singapore airfields and only sixty miles from Kuantan, where there was a military airfield built specifically for the defence of Malaya!

Just before the present lull, Hoashi had left the scene of action and flown to Kuantan airfield where he dropped his two 50-kg. bombs. This small contribution was to deter any British aircraft that might have been there from taking off, but the initiative was wasted. Kuantan airfield was empty. The Japanese pilot returned to the British ships after an hour's absence and resumed his watching and reporting.

There was a final spectator. The old steamer *Haldis* had been near enough to see all these bombing attacks and her log records the main events as seen from her bridge. It identifies the two big British ships by name, but the destroyers only by the pennant numbers painted on their fo'c'sle sides. The master of the *Haldis*, Captain A. Hall,

got the two big ships mixed up after the air attacks
started, however, and each is recorded as being the
recipient of the other's attacks. Captain Hall, declining to
become involved in this dangerous-looking action, had
pushed on as fast as he could and *Haldis* soon disappeared
from the scene.

11

The Final Round

Any hopes that the men in the British ships may have had that they had seen the last of the Japanese aircraft, or that help in the form of friendly aircraft might arrive before the next Japanese attack, were soon dashed. At 12.20 hours, after the lull had lasted just twenty minutes, look-outs on all the British ships saw a large formation of aircraft to the east. These aircraft soon lost height and split into two formations as though preparing to make further torpedo attacks.

Prince of Wales and *Repulse* were still about two miles apart. *Prince of Wales* could just manage 15 knots on her starboard engines, but could not steer and still had a huge list to port. *Repulse* was in fine form and had been coming across to see if the flagship could be helped in any way when the Japanese aircraft were sighted. It was exactly at this moment that the flight of Buffalo fighters was taking off from Sembawang airfield 150 miles away.

The aircraft seen approaching were the entire strength of the Kanoya Air Corps: twenty-six Mitsubishi Bettys led by Lieutenant-Commander Shichizo Miyauchi. The Kanoya aircraft were all carrying the heavier Model 2 torpedo with the 204-kg. (450-lb.) warhead. These were the aircraft which had been detached at the last moment from the Philippines operation and diverted to Indo-China at the time when the Japanese learnt of the arrival at Singapore of *Prince of Wales* and *Repulse*. The Kanoya crews had actually been flying back to Indo-China from well to the south when they somewhat belatedly picked up Midship-man Hoashi's signals. They had immediately turned west, but had at first been unable to find the British ships below the thickening cloud cover and had been on the verge of abandoning the search because of low fuel tanks.

Then a solitary aircraft, flying at a lower level, was seen through a gap in the cloud. Lieutenant-Commander Miyauchi turned towards it. It was *Repulse*'s Walrus, still on her anti-submarine patrol. Soon, three destroyers and finally the two bigger ships came into sight.

There were three Kanoya squadrons, commanded by Lieutenants Nabeta, Higashimori and Iki, with Lieutenant-Commander Miyauchi flying in one of Lieutenant Nabeta's aircraft. Miyauchi could not take too long preparing for the attack of his air corps because of the fuel position, and it is possible that the attack which developed was not the result of specific orders from Miyauchi but an 'every man for himself' affair. The Kanoya aircraft quickly split themselves into two groups. The first contained the seventeen aircraft of Lieutenant Nabeta's and Lieutenant Higashimori's squadrons and made as if to approach *Prince of Wales*, though some of them were intending to turn away at the last minute and attack *Repulse*. The third squadron, Lieutenant Iki's with nine aircraft, was farther away. Most British reports record the approach of the two formations, but there were so many aircraft approaching, and changing courses as they did so, that the British observers, used by now to seeing flights of eight or nine Japanese aircraft at a time, mostly recorded two groups of nine aircraft making this attack, not realizing that an extra squadron was present. No one recorded that these Bettys were a different type of aircraft from all those that had attacked before.

The attacks on *Prince of Wales* would develop just two minutes before those on *Repulse*, so it is the attack on the flagship that must come first in our narrative.

The hurried and somewhat ragged development of the Kanoya aircraft did not give *Prince of Wales* much time to prepare for action, though there was little she could have done in any case. The remaining engines were worked up from 204 to 220 revolutions to push along the sluggish, waterlogged cripple a little faster, and the gunners once

more stood by ready to open fire, but only two of the
four 5·25-in. turrets on the starboard side, from which the
Japanese attack appeared to be coming, were still work-
able, and the close-range weapons were not in much better
shape. Ordinary Seaman Derek Wilson was a lookout on
Prince of Wales and compares this attack with the earlier
neat, line-abreast approach of the earlier torpedo assault
on his ship.

The attacking policy of the Japanese seemed to change to individual
but simultaneous approaches from many different angles. As *we* were
not in a position to manoeuvre, this may have been adopted to confuse our central gunnery control. I was surprised how quickly these
attacks developed and later formed the impression that there might
have been a slight haze at this time, but this impression might have
been caused by the confusing manner of approach.

The few guns aboard *Prince of Wales* that could do so
opened fire. The four 5·25s of S1 and S2 turrets did their
best, but the angle of the deck prevented any of them from
depressing below 5 degrees of elevation and they could
not hit the low-flying Japanese aircraft. S3 and S4 turrets
were without power, and although their crews had sweated
to drag the turrets round by rope or chain to bear on the
approaching targets, they never opened fire. Several of
the pom-poms were also without power, and others soon
jammed again with the old ammunition faults. *Prince of
Wales* was in such a poor state that she was virtually
incapable of defending herself and it is not surprising that
no Japanese aircraft was shot down in this attack.

The first six Mitsubishis came in at differing heights
and from different angles, but all were aiming at the starboard side of *Prince of Wales*. Some of the Japanese pilots
came right in to 500 metres (under 550 yards), almost
point-blank range for torpedo dropping, before releasing
and starting to break away. So close did the Japanese
release their torpedoes that one Lewis gun on *Prince of
Wales*, manned by Petty Officer Coles, fired at a torpedo
when it was released in a vain attempt to detonate it

before it entered the water. Once again some of the Japanese pilots had to fly almost over the battleship, but on this occasion there was no machine-gunning. As the attackers flew away, the tracks of several torpedoes approaching *Prince of Wales* could be clearly seen. There was nothing Captain Leach could do; the steering gear of his ship was completely useless. Hundreds of men held their breath and waited for the worst.

The torpedoes could hardly miss. British reports are again confusing, but it seems that the first hit was well forward, near the stem of the ship, and that the explosion at this narrow point blew a hole clean through the ship and out on the port side. The second hit was just forward of the bridge and produced a huge tower of water and what appeared to be oil from a ruptured fuel tank. A third torpedo attack struck farther aft, alongside the rear 14-in. gun turret, and this again threw much water up into the air to descend on the deck and soak every man near by. (One sailor is believed to have been washed overboard by this deluge.) A fourth torpedo struck just forward of the stern, bending the outer propeller shaft inwards and jamming it between the inner shaft and the hull. The turbines in A Engine Room stopped dead. The whole effect of these four successive explosions on the starboard side of the ship was 'quite stupendous, the ship appeared to jump sideways several inches, rather in the manner of an earth tremor'.

There is no need here for a long technical description of the damage and after-effects. The earlier counter-flooding of many of the watertight compartments in this side of the ship now aggravated the damage of the latest hits. The effect of an explosion against a water-filled compartment was more extensive than that against an air-filled one and the consequent damage done by these explosions had therefore extended much farther into the ship. Certainly many of the fuel tanks were pierced so that not only water but thick diesel oil was also entering the ship. It has been estimated that *Prince of Wales* had, with the earlier flooding, now taken in almost 18,000 tons of water. Apart from this huge amount of flooding, only one of her four engines was now giving power and only two of the eight dynamos were supplying electricity for guns, lights, ventilation and the all-important pumps that could alone save the ship.

There was only one small benefit from these hits: the inrush of water on the starboard side almost entirely corrected the previous list to port. In addition, the explosions had caused no great loss of life; some men had been trapped and drowned in the isolated compartments which were their Action Stations, but they had not been many and there had been no internal explosions. But *Prince of Wales* could now only make 8 knots and was settling still deeper in to the water. The pumps and repair parties were not winning the mariner's age-old battle with the sea.

From the first sighting of the Japanese aircraft to its conclusion, this attack on *Prince of Wales* had taken only five minutes. Only six of the twenty-six Kanoya aircraft had dropped their torpedoes, and it is a measure of how helpless was *Prince of Wales*, and how close-pressed the attack, that four torpedoes out of six had scored hits. The remaining Kanoya crews now turned their attention on the second big British ship.

The attack by the remainder of the Kanoya aircraft on *Repulse* was a confused affair and not easy to describe in any simplified way. Eight Bettys from the leading group of Kanoya aircraft – probably three from Lieutenant Higashi-mori's squadron and five from Lieutenant Nabeta's – turned away almost immediately from that group, joined up with the nine aircraft of Lieutenant Iki's squadron and formed themselves into one loose attacking force approaching *Repulse* from many different angles but most heading for the battle cruiser's starboard side. Captain Tennant had seen the first group of Japanese aircraft flying across his bows making for *Prince of Wales*, and could also see the second group approaching the starboard side of his own ship. Once again he started manoeuvring and turned

Repulse into the attack. *Repulse* was still fully effective, had so far only been hit by the one small bomb thirty minutes earlier and her guns were firing well. Able Seaman S. C. Baxter was on a 4-in. gun on the starboard side boat deck during this attack.

We continued with our rapid fire until we had a misfire. There was a shell in the breech and the firing mechanism which had operated should have fired the shell. The drill here, according to the book, was to go through the misfire drill and, if it still had not fired, to wait half an hour before opening the breech to remove the shell in case of a premature explosion, but that all went by the board under the circumstances. Ginger Wilkinson opened the breech and out popped the shell, which in no uncertain terms was immediately dumped over the side with a sigh of relief from all of us.

Repulse started her turn to starboard, but the eight Japanese planes on that side did not press their attack and released their torpedoes at about 2,280 metres (2,500 yards) out, the Bettys then turning away without any being shot down. But, just at this moment, three of the Japanese aircraft suddenly peeled off from the group that had appeared committed to attacking *Prince of Wales*, quickly switched towards *Repulse*'s port side and dropped their torpedoes. Everyone who saw it said how neatly the feint towards *Prince of Wales* and then the attack on *Repulse*'s exposed side was carried out.

Repulse was now in an impossible position. There was no chance that she could manoeuvre to avoid both salvoes of torpedoes. The Japanese move had been so precisely executed that Captain Tennant could do no more than continue in his attempt to avoid the eight torpedoes dropped earlier. In his post-action report he summarizes the incident:

About three miles away, the Japanese had split up into two formations and I estimated that those on the right would launch their torpedoes first and I started to swing the ship to starboard. The torpedoes were dropped at a distance of 2,500 yards and it seemed obvious that we should be once more successful in combing their tracks. The left-hand formation appeared to be making straight for *Prince of Wales* who was at this time abaft my port beam. When these aircraft were a little before the port beam at a distance of some 2,000 yards, they turned straight at me and fired their torpedoes. It now became obvious that, if these torpedoes were aimed straight, *Repulse* would be most certainly hit as any other alteration of course would have caused me to be hit by the tracks of those torpedoes I was in the process of combing. One torpedo fired from my port side was obviously going to hit the ship and it was possible to watch its tracks for about a minute and a half before this actually took place. The ship was hit amidships, port side. The ship stood this torpedo well and continued to manoeuvre and steamed at about 25 knots.

It is a calm description of a hectic moment. *Repulse*'s guns had been crashing away in a desperate attempt to put off the Japanese aim; she had actually worked up to $27\frac{1}{2}$ knots and Captain Tennant did well to avoid all eight of the torpedoes dropped on the starboard side. His helm orders had again been bellowed down from the bridge to the steering position below, and the old battle cruiser had swerved one way and then the other but had been unable to avoid that one torpedo. The other two torpedoes from the portside attack missed. It was *Repulse*'s first torpedo hit after avoiding at least sixteen aimed directly at her and several more 'overs' from attacks on *Prince of Wales*.

Ordinary Seaman Stanley Dimmack had been in a gunnery control position and had watched the attack.

Suddenly there were more tracks heading straight for us and I knew there could be no avoiding them. As they disappeared under the sheer of the bow, I held my head between my arms and gritted my teeth, expecting one almighty explosion, but much to my surprise the ship hardly shuddered and ploughed steadily on.

Repulse was well protected by her old-fashioned torpedo bulge at the point hit by the torpedo; this was why the explosion had not seriously shaken the whole of the ship. Water poured into the bulge through the torpedo hole and the ship began to list, but Commander Dendy's damage control organization immediately started counter-flooding on the opposite side to compensate and *Repulse* had still not been seriously hurt. The ship had actually come very close to being hit by a second torpedo.

I remember seeing a Japanese torpedo which had hit the ship at such an oblique angle that it had failed to explode. I remember looking over the ship's side from my Action Station and seeing this ominous weapon with its yellow head, gently nosing its way up the ship's side, in and out. Each time it came back in I expected an explosion but it never came. I was told afterwards that it was caught in the paravane chains forward. (Lieutenant R. A. W. Pool)

But *Repulse*'s luck was running out fast. There still remained the third of the Kanoya squadrons, the nine aircraft of Lieutenant Iki. Iki had been intending to attack *Prince of Wales* and had initially led his squadron towards that ship but soon found that he was not well positioned. At the same time, the fountains of water thrown up at the battleship's side told him that the attack of the other Kanoya squadrons on *Prince of Wales* had been successful. Iki decided to change targets and try instead for the *Repulse*. He ordered his formation to split up and take on the battle cruiser from different angles. Six aircraft attempted to work their way round to *Repulse*'s starboard side and Iki led the remaining three straight into the port side. It was probably the most skilfully executed attack of the day.

Less than two minutes had elapsed since the last attack and Lieutenant Iki's flight of three aircraft was on to *Repulse* even while the ship was shaking off the last attack. The three Bettys came right in to about 600 yards (500 metres) before releasing their torpedoes. What developed next was the most dramatic incident of the day. Lieutenant Iki managed to bank quickly and turn away, so close to the British ship was he that he could see sailors on her deck throwing themselves down to avoid the fire of his machine-gunners; his plane was slightly damaged by *Repulse*'s fire. But two other pilots could not turn quickly enough and flew right over *Repulse*'s bows.

It was an important principle of anti-aircraft gunnery that as soon as a torpedo bomber had released its torpedo and ceased to be a danger, fire should be switched from that target to other aircraft that had yet to release their torpedoes. Lieutenant Pool was fire distribution officer at one of *Repulse*'s pom-poms, a lethal weapon at short range.

It became obvious that the Japanese aircraft were firing their torpedoes out of our effective pom-pom range. Almost immediately, another attack developed . . . As the ship's position appeared hopeless, I did not shift target after these aircraft had dropped their torpedoes. As the two aircraft passed by the ship we hit and set on fire both of them and they crashed.

The first of the pom-pom's victims was the aircraft piloted by Petty Officer Satoshi Momoi; it exploded in a spectacular ball of fire leaving only a few fragments of aircraft to splash into the sea and then a huge red circle of burning petrol on the surface. The second aircraft hit was piloted by Petty Officer Ryochi Taue. This caught fire at the rear of its fuselage and gradually lost height with the fire eating its way rapidly up towards the cockpit and wings until the plane hit the sea in a huge cloud of spray. One report says that a Japanese airman from this aircraft was later seen standing on a floating wing and waving for help, but even if this is true, no one had time for a solitary Japanese that morning.

The cheers of *Repulse*'s crew at this double shooting-down were short lived. All three torpedoes dropped by this flight of aircraft exploded against *Repulse*'s port side – one near the engine room, one abreast of her rear 15-in. turret and one nearer the stern. This last hit, believed to be the torpedo dropped by Lieutenant Iki himself, jammed the rudder, and *Repulse*, though able to steam on, could not be steered. Because she had been turning to starboard when Iki's torpedo jammed the rudder, *Repulse* could now steam only in a wide circle.

These three hits were soon followed by a further blow. The six other aircraft of Lieutenant Iki's squadron had earlier launched their torpedoes from more distant firing positions and one of these now arrived and scored a hit, this time on the starboard alongside E Boiler Room.

The old battle cruiser had been grievously injured. Water was pouring into the ship through five holes made by torpedo explosions, and she had not been designed to withstand such severe damage. The list to port increased – 7 degrees, 9 degrees, then 12 degrees. Captain Tennant's report again:

I knew now that she could not survive and at once gave the order for everyone to come on deck and to cast loose Carley floats. It had been learnt that the broadcasting apparatus was still working throughout the ship, with the exception of the compartments down below aft, but word was quickly passed down from Y Turret and the After Control. The decision for a commanding officer to make, 'Cease all work in the ship below', is an exceedingly difficult one, but knowing the ship's construction, I felt very sure that she could not survive four torpedoes.

Captain Tennant obviously did not realize that his ship had been struck by five and not four torpedoes.

One gets the impression that the Kanoya Air Corps was a particularly skilled and audacious unit. Its twenty-six aircraft had scored nine torpedo hits – four on *Prince of Wales* and five on *Repulse*. Two of its aircraft had been shot down, three more seriously damaged (one of which would crash on landing at its airfield) and five more slightly damaged.

The action involving *Repulse* had been compressed into a time far shorter than the description of it takes to read. She had been hit by five torpedoes in four minutes. There is no need to conceal the fact that *Repulse* was about to sink, but the description of her sinking will be left over for the next chapter.

It was just 12.30 when this last devastating series of torpedo attacks died away – one and a half hours after the opening of the action. During those ninety minutes all fifty of the Japanese torpedo bombers had completed their attacks but only eight of the high-level bombers had done so, although six of these had bombed twice. *Repulse* was now sinking and *Prince of Wales* was not in much better shape. It would be forty-five minutes at least before the Australian fighters could arrive. Midshipman Hoashi, in the Japanese shadowing plane, had not yet returned from his bombing of Kuantan airfield. There remained two squadrons of Japanese high-level bombers that had not yet attacked – the Mihoro Air Corps squadrons of Lieutenants Ohira and Takeda with nine and eight Mitsubishi Nells respectively. Each plane was loaded with one 500-kg. bomb.

These two squadrons had recently arrived in the area of action, but just too late to coordinate their attacks with those of the Kanoya torpedo bombers. Lieutenant Ohira's nine aircraft were the first to start their bomb run, and there are two Japanese accounts of what happened next. Their Official History says that Ohira spotted a British ship through a gap in the cloud at 12.33 hours and his squadron dropped their nine bombs on that target but without scoring any hits. But Lieutenant Takai's personal account of the action states that, while running up to bomb, the bomb aimer in Lieutenant Ohira's aircraft accidently pressed his bomb release. His bomb then dropped far too soon and the other eight aircraft all followed suit. Takai states that the bombs of this squadron fell harmlessly in the sea well away from any target. Although Takai was miles away by then, his version is certainly the correct one since several observers on the British ships noted the explosion of these bombs harmlessly on the horizon. Their conclusion was that a damaged Japanese aircraft had jettisoned its bomb load.

The next stage of this dying action now centred around *Prince of Wales*, still unable to steer, just creeping through the water, settling more and more by the stern and with her list to port increasing again despite the four torpedo holes in the starboard side. Large sections of the ship had ceased to function, and there were many men idly waiting for the next development. Some of the more seriously wounded had now been brought on deck and the ship's Carley floats, and some of the smaller ship's boats, were being prepared for launching so as to get the wounded away if *Prince of Wales* should go down. Lookouts and gun crews were still vigilant, but very few of the guns were now capable of being fired.

Repulse could be seen some miles away to the west with two destroyers standing by. The battle cruiser was obviously sinking. One seaman in *Prince of Wales* watched *Repulse* heeling over and thought sadly about the many boy seamen he had once trained with who were now aboard her, though Captain Aylwin of the Royal Marines says 'it was difficult to describe exactly what my feelings were on seeing *Repulse* bottom up. I don't think I was particularly affected in any way. She was sinking and that was that. The enemy could now concentrate all their efforts on *Prince of Wales*.'

It is not possible to state exactly what was happening on *Prince of Wales*'s bridge at this time. No doubt a constant stream of reports was coming from various parts of the ship, but few, if any, of these could have contained cheering news for Admiral Phillips or Captain Leach. Once a flagship had become crippled, as *Prince of Wales* clearly now was, many admirals would have been transferring with their staff to another ship so as to remain mobile and effective. Yet it is obvious that Admiral Phillips was planning no such move; with *Repulse* sinking, he really had nothing much left to command. One can only guess at the emotions being experienced by Tom Phillips at this time. Seldom can a naval officer have experienced such a reversal of fortunes in such a short time, and by means of a type of enemy action that he had considered to be impossible.

The flagship had at last broken its radio silence when, at 12.20, this signal was transmitted.

EMERGENCY

HAVE BEEN STRUCK BY A TORPEDO ON PORT SIDE.

NYTW022R06. 4 TORPEDOES. REPULSE HIT BY 1
TORPEDO. SEND DESTROYERS.

The two amazing aspects of this signal are the delay before
it was sent at all – it was twenty-two minutes after Captain
Tennant in *Repulse* had broken radio silence – and that the
appeal was for destroyers, not aircraft cover. It was a very
revealing signal.

At 12.41 *Prince of Wales*'s lookouts reported two more
dangers. Eight high-level bombers were seen approaching
from ahead, and what was believed to be a submarine
periscope on the starboard quarter was also sighted. The
bombers were real enough – Lieutenant Takeda's squadron had seen *Prince of Wales* and were starting their
bombing run – but the periscope report was almost certainly a false one. *Prince of Wales* opened fire with what
guns were still in action; three of the 5·25-in. turrets fired
well but one of them, P2, soon had to stop firing because of
a bad oil leak in the turret hydraulic gear, and the others,
S1 and S2, were hampered in their firing as the range-taker
had been wounded in his right eye and an estimated height
had to be used. Some of the pom-poms and other close-
range weapons also joined in, though this was more an act
of defiance than anything else as Takeda's bombers were
flying at over 9,000 feet. The helpless *Prince of Wales*
would be an easy target for them. Many men saw the
attack developing and there was time for them to seek some
protection. On the bridge it was Captain Leach who
watched the bombs coming down; he turned to Admiral
Phillips and said the one word 'Now!' Everyone laid flat.

Men in other parts of the ship also remember that
moment.

While I was helping to cut the lashings on the boats, I heard shouts
about more aircraft. I could see them – high this time – approaching
in line abreast from forward, their purpose obvious. 'Why? Oh why?'
We were sinking already! The forward 5·25s and pom-poms opened
fire, but clearly the fire-control calculators were not functioning as
the shell bursts were quite erratic. Each plane detached one large

bomb. In such close formation at least one bomb would hit the ship. It was inevitable that hundreds of men now alive would be dead in a few seconds and for the one time in my life I completely lost my temper, screaming impotent abuse at them. As the bombs got nearer, a group of us dived for cover in a rope store and waited. (Ordinary Seaman D. F. Wilson)

Before the final bombing attack, I remember our pom-pom director was useless so, as we saw bombs leaving the aircraft, we all lay flat on the deck in and around the director. An officer rounded on us royally for our cowardice, and we arose, shamefacedly, to our feet. I wandered through the bridge flat to see a friend of mine on a starboard director, only to find the deck there littered with officers and men also lying prone! Whilst these air attacks were being carried out, everyone on the lower deck was cursing the lack of air support. I am afraid that poor Admiral Tom Phillips was not popular at this stage, as the lower-deck rumour had it that the Admiral had told his peers that we could manage without air cover! I repeat that this was the lower-deck rumour. (Able Seaman R. H. James)

A hand klaxon or warning device sounded from the bridge. I thought 'Lord, not again.' But, looking up into a perfectly cloudless sky, high up, very high, we could just see eight or ten planes with wings tip to tip. As we watched, something that looked like snowflakes (impossible) fell from them. We watched fascinated and then I awoke – Bombs! Falling on us! I shoved the lads into the bos'n's steel cabin and banged the door, then there was a crash like thunder and a tearing of metal. It took a while for my ears and senses to come back to normal, but I suddenly thought that we might be sinking. I unwrapped somebody's legs from around my neck (the cabin was only very small and we had all tried to jam in together). I managed to get the door open and we spilled on to the deck to behold a scene of desolation, with fire and smoke pouring from air vents. The boat deck was all right and we made our way to look into the 'waist' where we found the bombs had missed us by only a few feet but had gone right through the armoured deck of the plane-launching apparatus down into the cinema flat where the wounded had been mustered. (Ordinary Seaman W. E. England)

Lieutenant Takeda's squadron had dropped seven bombs; the release mechanism of the eighth aircraft had failed. It was a well-aimed salvo and one 500-kg. bomb had penetrated the catapult deck on the port side and exploded on the 5-in. thick armoured deck below. The explosion pushed up the catapult deck 'like a small mountain'. Underneath the armoured deck and not far from the position of the explosion was X Boiler Room, the only one still being manned; the flash and fumes of the explosion forced their way through shafts into this boiler room causing more injuries, and this last source of power for the battleship was put out of action. Lieutenant Takeda later claimed two bomb hits, but this was not so, though two further bombs which were near misses on either side of the ship aft probably caused further damage to the hull of *Prince of Wales*. Takeda's squadron flew away, its crews probably not realizing that they had carried out the last action of a historic battle. No less than five of these aircraft had been damaged by *Prince of Wales*'s anti-aircraft fire — a very creditable performance by the turrets that had remained in action.

From a technical point of view the explosion of this one bomb had not caused much damage, but the human effects of it were terrible. It could hardly have burst in a worse place, for the actual explosion took place in the large compartment known as the Cinema Flat, being used at the time as an overflow casualty station and as a rest place for men suffering from heat exhaustion. There were between 200 and 300 men in the Cinema Flat, and the casualties here and in the adjoining corridors were frightful — blast, burns and shrapnel. The area had been reduced to a bloody shambles. Two men who survived describe their experiences.

The next thing was that I seemed to see a terrific flash and a tremendous explosion, with screams being forced out of everyone's throats and a great burning sensation all round and inside my lungs. I must then have become instantly unconscious, for how long I don't know, but the time came when I realized that I could see a faint glimmer of daylight which I made my way towards. (Marine R. B. Wade)

Lieutenant Dick Wildish was one of those who had

become affected by the heat in the engine rooms and had been ordered to the Cinema Flat to recover.

I lay down on the deck alongside the Senior – Lieutenant-Commander (E) R. O. Lockley. There were many people there and the padre was going round with a welcome can of grog – very acceptable. Then the bomb arrived – although I was sure at the time that there were two bombs not one - the structure above us fell in on us – the Senior and I. I turned to look at him and was sure he had been killed. I couldn't move myself for a while but managed to extricate myself from the debris and nauseating shambles and get to the quarterdeck where I met Lieutenant-Commander Terry. He was the Q.D. officer, I recall, and had presumably had to clear out of his Action Station. I told him of the appalling mess below and I thought that Lockley had been killed. I believe that Terry organized a rescue team and was delighted to find out later that the Senior had been found and brought out alive. I was in no great shape myself by then – stone deaf from bomb blast and therefore unable to exercise or hear orders, extensively burned, and with minor shrapnel wounds. Also, I suppose, shocked pretty badly. I remember little constructively after this.

Many men remember an uncanny silence in *Prince of Wales* after the bombing. The guns had ceased firing. The engines had stopped. The huge battleship was settling still deeper by the stern, with water creeping up along the port-side deck from the stern 'as though the tide was coming in'. *Prince of Wales* had sent out another signal asking for 'all available tugs', and then a further signal that was coded up wrongly in the rush so that it never was understood at Singapore what type of help was being requested – perhaps aircraft at last? No mention was made in any of *Prince of Wales*'s signals that *Repulse* had sunk twenty minutes earlier; it was left for the destroyer *Electra* to send out this bad news.

The destroyer *Express* was the only one still in her screening position off *Prince of Wales*'s starboard bow, and even before the last Japanese bombing attack, Lieutenant-Commander F. J. Cartwright had made up his mind that *Prince of Wales* was sinking.

I decided that *Prince of Wales* was in serious trouble and I could already see men jumping off the ship. I decided to go alongside to see if I could be of any assistance. I could see the Japanese bombers approaching and we held off until their attack was over; I didn't want to give them a bigger target. Then, after the bombs had dropped, I circled round and secured alongside *Prince of Wales*'s starboard quarter. As we did so, a signal was flashed down at us from *Prince of Wales*'s bridge – 'WHAT HAVE YOU COME ALONGSIDE FOR?' I told them, 'IT LOOKS AS THOUGH YOU REQUIRE ASSISTANCE.' I don't think they realized how serious the situation was.

Excepting a miracle, nothing could now save this once fine battleship. Captain Leach ordered that the wounded were to be got away, and soon these were being floated off the stern in Carley floats; other wounded were sent across to *Express* on stretchers. Captain Leach had come down from the bridge to the quarterdeck where a large crowd of his men had congregated. He told them that *Prince of Wales* had been badly hit but was still a fighting unit, and he asked for volunteers to stay aboard to try and get the ship back to Singapore. Many men tell of the dignified way in which Captain Leach spoke to them at this sad moment. There were some volunteers, but they all knew that it was hopeless and Captain Leach soon realized he was going to lose his ship. Paymaster-Lieutenant J. G. Baskcomb remembers 'the distinct picture I have in my mind of the little hopeless gesture he made as he turned away and ordered that everyone had better blow up their tubes'.

Captain Leach gave permission for those men not needed to man the guns or other vital services to get across to *Express*, and then he climbed back up to the bridge to rejoin Admiral Phillips. Phillips had not made any appeal to the men; it was not his place to do so. This was no longer an affair of admirals but of a captain and his ship's company. One report says that Admiral Phillips had sent someone below to fetch up his best cap.

At 13.15 the list to port that *Prince of Wales* had experienced since the first torpedo hit an hour and a half earlier suddenly started to increase. The ship was now beyond the help of aircraft, destroyers, tugs or anything else. She was going. Those dread words that every sailor hopes never to hear were soon passed around: 'Abandon Ship!'

12

'Abandon Ship'

When Captain Leach ordered his crew to abandon ship, the rescue work around the site of *Repulse*'s sinking had been in progress for forty minutes with the British destroyer *Electra* and the Australian *Vampire* hard at work picking up survivors. *Prince of Wales*, with *Express* standing by her, would survive for just eight more minutes. The only outside witnesses to the sinkings of these two great ships were the crews of several Japanese aircraft, who had remained as curious observers, and the first of the Brewster Buffalo fighter pilots who arrived just as *Prince of Wales* was disappearing beneath the sea.

The loss of any large ship is a sad and tragic event. When it is the result of a battle, then the actual sinking can come very quickly and the lives of large numbers of men are at risk – risk of being trapped inside a sinking ship, risk of being choked to death by the thousands of tons of diesel oil from ruptured fuel tanks, risk of further hostile action by the enemy, risk of drowning or exposure, and in these tropical waters, the risk of shark attack. Nearly 3,000 *Repulse* and *Prince of Wales* men had to face these many hazards. We will now look at the last moments of both ships, the efforts of their crews to save themselves and the help given by the three destroyers. The fact that *Prince of Wales* sank forty-eight minutes after *Repulse* went down is not important here, and incidents concerning both ships will sometimes be described simultaneously.

The battle cruiser *Repulse* had been a fully effective fighting unit until just before the end. Despite her poor anti-aircraft armament and the early bomb hit, she had played a full part in the battle for well over an hour. Captain Tennant's well-drilled, mainly pre-war crew had kept the old ship in action until the last series of Japanese attacks when five torpedoes had transformed her into a wreck. There was not for *Repulse* the lingering agony of *Prince of Wales*. At 12.23 she had been a fine, live ship. Four minutes later she was foundering.

With his ship heeled over to the port side but still moving ahead at about 6 knots, Captain Tennant announced over the loudspeaker system: 'All hands on deck. Prepare to abandon ship. God be with you.' In compartments all over the ship – in gun positions, plotting positions, damage control parties, signal offices, ammunition magazines and rooms, in what was left of engine and boiler rooms and in all those small places where men had done their duty – officer or senior ratings fell their men out and ordered them to get to the decks. Not one account by anyone who was in *Repulse* says that a single man left his place of duty until ordered to do so. Dozens of men now came pouring up through hatches from below or scrambling down ladders from the upperworks, but still no one went over the side. Captain Tennant's report reads:

When the ship had a 30-degree list to port I looked over the starboard side of the bridge and saw the Commander and two or three hundred men collecting on the starboard side. I never saw the slightest sign of panic or ill discipline. I told them from the bridge how well they had fought the ship and wished them good luck.*

Captain Tennant then ordered: 'Abandon ship.'

There was no delay once this order had been given and the first rush of men was soon away. Every man had, or should have had, an old-fashioned but efficient rubber lifebelt that he had been under orders to wear at all times for the past twenty-four hours. It took only a few seconds to blow these up. There were also a number of Carley floats which could easily be slipped overboard, but the motor boats and whalers could not be launched quickly and it is believed none of these was used.

* British Official History, p. 197.

For most men it was a case of going into the sea over the side, and to have the best chance of saving himself each man now had to do something that was against all natural inclinations. The automatic tendency was to run *down* the sloping deck to the listing port side and then jump or dive into the sea a few feet below. But this would entail the risk of being caught by *Repulse*'s massive superstructure or by the suction that would occur when the ship sank. The safer way was to climb *up* the sloping deck to the starboard side, climb over the guardrails and then face a frightening slide down the side of the ship and into the sea. The huge side of *Repulse* was soon alive with men slipping down on their bottoms. At one spot where many men were leaving there was a huge torpedo hole in the ship's side just beneath the surface of the sea. An alert petty officer still on the deck noticed that several men who jumped into the sea near this spot promptly disappeared as they were sucked into the hole, and he stood by at the danger spot and warned men to keep away from it. It was not long before *Repulse* listed farther to port and the jagged torpedo hole and the huge torpedo bulge appeared above the surface.

Lieutenant Abrahams, the Admiralty photographer, was trying to save his priceless photographs of the recent action.

When the order came to abandon ship, I knew I could not keep afloat because of the weight of camera and metal slides so I placed the camera and unexposed slides in an empty steel lifebelt locker near a pom-pom gun on the main deck – some of the gun's crew were dead – and took the slides containing pictures of the action with me when I went over the side.

There were a few wits – 'See you in Singapore, mate' and 'Now you can draw the dole.' I slipped down the ship's side until I was on the protruding bulge but, as I saw one of these gaping, jagged holes made by a torpedo, I walked further aft on the beam and then went in the sea. As I came to the surface I saw a man jumping from the deck above – he had hobnailed boots on and must have been a Royal Marine. He hit me hard, split my Mae West and closed one eye. I came to the surface minus the camera slides and lost sight of the man

who had hit me amongst hundreds of bobbing heads all black with
fuel oil.

Sergeant H. A. Nunn of the Royal Marines was one of
several men trying to put floatable objects over the side.

In happier times B Gundeck was the Chief P.O.'s smoking space and,
as such, there were large wooden garden-type seats. A seaman and
myself dragged one of these to the guardrail and dropped it over the
side as we thought it might be of assistance to somebody in the
water, but to our consternation it sank like a stone so our effort was
all in vain.

By this time it was time for me to go over the side so I kicked off
my shoes and climbed over the guardrail. It was possible to walk
part-way down the ship's side, but I had to finish the rest of the
journey on my seat, regardless of the rips and tears to my person and
clothing. I had my lifebelt with me but I had no qualms about going
into the water as I was a strong swimmer. I didn't even think of the
possibility that there may be sharks in the vicinity; my only concern
was to try and get away from the ship and the oily patch that was
beginning to spread out over the surface of the water.

Hundreds of men got safely away from *Repulse* in these
few minutes. It was all quite orderly, with no panic, no
pushing, with men waiting their turn to go down the side
'like queueing up for the pictures'. The ship's physical
training instructor found a young marine without a lifebelt,
handed over his own and the two jumped together from
Repulse's bow. A stoker found a young seaman standing on
the torpedo bulge, afraid to enter the water and crying; he
had also lost his lifebelt and had never learned to swim.
The stoker handed over his lifebelt and told the youngster
to jump with him, but when the stoker surfaced the other
had vanished.

The speed of events and the fact that the loudspeakers had
broken down in some parts of the ship resulted in many
compartments below being late to realize that the order
to abandon ship had been given. The men in such compartments, particularly those deep down in the ship, often
had a struggle to escape being trapped. Each level of the

ship was separated from the level above by hatches which
had been closed during the action and now had to be forced
open, often against the list of the ship. The heavy steel
hatches of the main armoured deck, many of which could
only be opened with chains and pulleys, were a particular
hazard. Dozens of men from below only just got out in the
nick of time after frantic climbs up ladders or shafts and
dashes along corridors, sometimes in pitch-dark conditions.
For such men it was literally a race for life.

Leading Supply Assistant Leonard Sandland had been
in a party of men below loading shells on to a conveyor for
one of *Repulse*'s anti-aircraft guns when the torpedoes
struck.

One bloke shouted, 'The conveyor. Look!' For a second we all froze
as we realized that the gun's crew up aloft must have caught a
packet. No one was offloading the shells any more and they were just
going up from us, straight over the top still on the conveyor, and then
crashing down again. Nobby, a leading seaman member of our team,
and myself had a hurried conference, wondering whether the gun's
crew *had* been wiped out, or if the order had been given to abandon
ship. It was obvious that we were in a bad way, though how bad we
had no way of knowing. Nor did we fancy being trapped down there
either.

We wondered what best to do, when suddenly our minds were
made up for us. Another reverberating crash, the ship gave a terrific
shudder, and the vertical wall in front of us was no longer vertical
but was leaning over at an angle of about 30 degrees. That decided
us. We dropped everything and made for the shaft, the top of which
we could just see, leaning over us, and up we went. We had then one
fear, that we might find that the hatch at the top had been clamped
down, but luck was with us, probably only because the lads up top
had also been so busy that they hadn't had time to secure it. Anyway,
we made it to the top, lifted the hatch, and found that the lower deck
into which it emerged had no lighting and we were in total darkness.

I think all our lads had been on the *Repulse* about twelve months
and you get to know a ship inside out in that length of time, which
was just as well. Anyway, in pitch blackness we felt our way round
the bulkhead until we came to the big hatch which we knew would
let us out on to the upper deck, and this one was a real stinker. It was
extremely heavy and was sealed over us because of the heavy list.

We had to exert every last ounce of our combined strength to push it upwards. But we made it, and out we shot into brilliant sunshine.

Able Seaman Tom Barnes had been working at a plotting table in the main transmitting station, feeding information to the anti-aircraft guns.

We'd been hit again, sounded like the other side. Feels like she's turning on her side. Hang on to anything – not a man amongst the team has made a move. Then, over the loud hailer, 'Abandon Ship.' Through B Space, up the steel ladder on to the mess deck, a scramble for the ladder leading to the main deck starboard side, along the P.O.'s mess flat. *Repulse* is listing steeply now; am I going to make it to the upper deck? The door to the P.O.'s mess is hanging open and a glimpse inside shows a deadlight up and a porthole open – in, and scramble through the porthole almost vertically, on to the ship's side and down to the bulge – a jump and that's it. I'm in the sea.

Stoker Mechanic George Avery had been in one of the condenser rooms.

We had heard the various thumps of the torpedoes hitting the ship. Down below we had a big porthole between the two condenser rooms and my best friend, Patrick Sheam from Cork, was down the other condenser room. I looked through the porthole; he waved to me. Then there was a big load of smoke and bits flying around. A torpedo explosion had entered the other condenser room. I sat down and cried.

I noticed the steam dropping back on the evaporators; the more I opened the valves it didn't make any difference to the pressure so I said to the Chief Mech who was in charge, 'I think it's time to leave.' He said, 'Let's wait for orders.' The Tannoy system had broken down and I said it would be too late if it wasn't too late already. There were seven of us down in the compartment. We opened the big hatch from down below to the next flat up and the hatch above us was closed but the small round manhole was open and all we could see was the water rushing through. We climbed through the manhole and the water just pulled us back inboard. I grabbed something on the half-deck and the pressure of the water broke the gold ring on my finger but it saved me being pulled back into the mess deck.

Unfortunately there were many men, like Stoker Avery's friend in the next condenser room, who never made it.

There were the badly wounded, the stunned, the men trapped in the deepest compartments of the ship – the magazines, shell-handling rooms, boiler and engine rooms. There were the men who ran up and down corridors, hammering at bulkheads and armoured hatches until over-taken by the water now rushing through the ship. Some of those on duty in the 15-in. transmitting station were Royal Marine bandsmen who, just before the action started, had been having a cheerful off-duty 'jam session', but now, in contrast, were in extreme danger. Sixteen-year-old Boy Seaman Heydon was among them.

We had counted another two torpedoes before we felt a movement of the ship heeling over. With a look of utter disbelief on the faces of all around me, I waited during a shattering silence and with great con-cern for someone to say something – anything. The next voice to speak, however, was that of the Captain ordering, 'Prepare to abandon ship.' None of us could move because of the unreality of the whole thing until I, as the youngest member of the T.S. crew, was ordered 'out and over the side'. The fact that I was a messenger had taught me all the short cuts around the ship and I scrambled up an escape pipe wide enough to take only one person at a time. Several people were following me by the time I came to the door leading out to B Gun Deck – the door was above me at about 45 degrees. The only way I could reach up to it was to recruit the aid of the one below me, a personal chum of mine, another boy, to give me a push. Unfor-tunately, having done so, he lost his footing and fell back taking about another dozen with him. I still dream of the sight of those people falling, never to make it up again. When I slid into the water from the gun deck I was alone and felt sick at the thought that they had lost their lives to save mine. I still suffer remorse.

At least *Repulse* was spared the massive internal explosions that had completely destroyed three battle cruisers at Jutland and, more recently, the *Hood*, but almost four out of every ten men in *Repulse* died, an unknown but substantial proportion of this loss being crew trapped inside the ship. Perhaps the most tragic cases were those who were trapped in small compartments that retained air but who had no means of escape when water filled the ship. *Repulse* sank in 185 feet of water, and the pressure at that

depth would not have been so great as to bring immediate
death. There are unfortunately no dramatic tales of underwater rescues or miraculous escapes to the surface in the
Repulse story.

The last few men were now escaping from *Repulse*'s deck
as she rolled still farther over to the port side. Commander
R. J. R. Dendy was one of these.

I remember seeing the starboard 4-in. triple mounting on the Flag-
deck break away and go crashing over to the port side. Simultaneously, a great wall of water came up from aft and swept me away.
I remember how light in colour was this wave and I realized I was
not being taken down but swept away from the ship in surface water.
Eventually I came to the surface.

Lieutenant J. O. C. Hayes had made sure that the Con-
fidential Signal Books would go down in the ship's safe
before he set out to save himself.

My movements were then dictated by gravity, like one of those balls
on a bagatelle table which bounces off pins – the funnel, red-hot from
fast steaming, then against the port flag lockers by which time, normally some fifty feet above the waterline, they were almost awash,
and so overboard helplessly and down for what seemed a long time.
When I bobbed up, the great iron structure of the main top, separ-
ating the mainmast from the main topmast, normally some hundred
feet above the waterline, skidded just above my head as the ship
plunged on and down with the screws still turning.

Many men speak of the courage of a young Australian,
Midshipman R. I. Davies, who was last seen strapped to
his Oerlikon gun still firing at a Japanese aircraft and
cursing anyone who got in the way of his sights. He was
never seen again. *

Repulse gave a sudden lurch and now lay on her beam
ends – that is, exactly on her side with masts, funnel and
superstructure at water level. Men who had yet to leave

---

* Robert Ian Davies, aged eighteen, was from Greenwich, New
South Wales. He was awarded a posthumous Mention in Dispatches.

could now stand on the exposed starboard side of the ship, and many compared the scene to the classic photograph of the German armoured cruiser *Blücher* sinking at the Battle of the Dogger Bank in January 1915 which showed a great crowd of German sailors standing on the side of the sinking ship – 'that magnificent but awful photograph'.

Able Seaman D. W. Avery was on *Repulse*'s side.

We made our way on to the starboard bilge, which was now out of the water with the ship lying on her port side. I didn't seem to be able to pluck up enough courage to join the struggling men in the water, so I sat on the bilge and tried to blow up my lifejacket, but it was no good; it had perished with the heat of the tropics and I hadn't a new issue.

As I sat there wondering what to do to save myself, Cecil Brown, an American reporter who had joined the ship at Singapore, came along and sat beside me, took off his boots, put them neatly beside him, stood up, turned to me and said, 'Good luck, pal,' then dived into the water and swam for the nearest destroyer. This, and the fact that the ship was getting lower into the water, made my mind up for me and I dived off. But I didn't seem to be able to come to the surface; I kept going down and down with my eyes open. I could see the light going duller and duller, then I began to panic and struggled madly to get to the surface and my lungs seemed to be bursting. I stopped panicking and kicked to the surface, but it was no good, I was beginning to pass out. I had to breathe so I let out the air in my lungs slowly; this helped but it was no good, I had to take a deep breath. I then realized I was breathing air yet I wasn't at the surface. I had been sucked under with the ship as she was sinking and while I was struggling I must have got caught in an air bubble.

Sick Berth Attendant Walter Bridgewater had been one of the last away from the Forward Medical Station.

One by one the casualties were helped to the door and with hardly a word being exchanged were then assisted, by magazine workers passing up, to get up the first set of wooden ladders. The last two I had to push up myself, and then I remember one of the seamen shouting at me that, 'Abandon Ship had been piped, didn't I know?'

Back to the Sick Bay Action Station for the last patient, but he was in a coma and could not help himself in any way. I will always remember his helpless, pathetic look. By then, the ship, which up till then had seemed quite stable, started to shudder, the deck then was at a tilt and the dressing bins and stands were rolling about and, worse still, the antiseptic liquids had spilled and the deck was wet and very slippery with the yellow acraflavine liquid, etc.

No one had gone by the door all this time and I just could do nothing with the last casualty and when the ship gave quite a shudder I just decided I'd better get out myself and I left the last one propped up in the corner.

Bridgewater then describes his escape up several decks until he reached a porthole.

Just as I was trying to pull and push myself through, the ship listed heavily and I found myself with my right arm jammed into the angle bar on my inside bicep and I was stuck there with the sea thudding down on top of my head and bending my neck nearly to my chest. Two shipmates who must have 'slept in' like myself and who were trying to get out at the same time, were just washed back and out of sight just after reaching the portholes.

I was held rigid in this awkward, arm-held, head-bent position for several minutes and I remember deciding, 'Well you've had it this time, son,' and I prepared to swallow as much water as quickly as possible and get it over with. The last thought I had was quite a selfish one, 'Well, I'll never marry Muriel now,' and I said a quick prayer as the water reached up to my nose.

Then, all of a sudden, I felt my right arm free and I grabbed at the port and was out in a split second, possibly the last to leave the old ship alive.

Walter Bridgewater also received a Mention in Dispatches, for having stayed so long with the wounded, and he did marry his Muriel.

The end came quickly. The roll of the ship continued with the great weight of the upperworks pulling *Repulse* completely over. The stern reared up with the propellers still turning, then disappeared, leaving the bows hanging in the air, glistening in the sun and showing the red-painted hull. It is possible that the stern struck the sea bottom before the bows finally disappeared because *Repulse*'s length was more than three times greater than the sea's depth here. The bows finally disappeared just eleven minutes after *Repulse* had been first hit by torpedoes. There were a few cheers from the men in the water for this much-loved old ship, but most survivors were too busy swimming away for fear of suction, though this danger turned out to be a negligible one, probably because of the shallowness of the water. 'She went down quite peacefully, as though glad it was all over.'

There remained nothing of the battle cruiser *Repulse* but a few great gulps of air and oil fuel coming to the surface.

After *Repulse* had gone down, one man describes the scene as 'bodies and debris everywhere. Most of the crew were covered in black oil and looked like a party of negro jazz-singers with just the whites of their eyes showing.' Those men who could swim or were calm enough to trust to their life-jackets found the water 'warm and relaxing' once they were clear of the oil fuel. There were those who had always believed that they were non-swimmers but now found they could swim after all. Lieutenant Jim Davis of the Royal Marines was swimming away from the *Repulse* when, as he turned to watch her sink, he was overtaken by a burly seaman who was swimming at high speed and shouting. 'Help me. Help me. I can't swim a stroke.' There were soon the usual jokes – 'Just think you're at Blackpool, lads' – and some singing, but officers tried to stop this, warning their men to save energy and avoid swallowing the oil. There was much fear of sharks and desperate moments of panic whenever a swimmer imagined that something had brushed against his legs under the water; some men deliberately swam into the patches of oil to avoid sharks. There are some reports of one or two dead monsters being seen floating at the scene, presumably killed by the recent bomb and torpedo explosions, but the live sharks had all been frightened off by the same explosions, at least for the present.

Repulse carried at least twelve large Carley floats. These were rectangular, doughnut-shaped rings made of

BOARDING PASS

NAME OF PASSENGER
KYLE/J DR
SILV10098812

FROM
INVERNESS   INV

TO
LONDON   LHR

FLIGHT   CLASS DATE   TIME
BA 4149   M 04JUL 1135

GATE	BOARDING TIME	SEAT	SMOKE
G02	1115	02F	XX

PCS WT   UNCKD   BAGGAGE ID NUMBER
0
CPN
              DOCUMENT NUMBER   CK

SM

cork covered by canvas, with an open slatted-floor interior. They were practically unsinkable and capable of carrying a large number of men. The swimmers set out to reach the sanctuary of the Carley floats and these soon became little communities of oil-soaked, sometimes wounded men. There soon came a moment of fear when a formation of Japanese aircraft was seen approaching at sea level. Many men jumped off the Carley floats, fearing they were about to be machine-gunned, but the Mitsubishis roared overhead without firing.

The destroyers *Electra* and *Vampire* came in to start rescuing *Repulse*'s survivors. It is a convenient time to leave this scene and turn to that a few miles to the southeast, where *Prince of Wales* was sinking.

Compared with the sinking of *Repulse*, which had happened within eleven minutes of her first torpedo hit, the men in *Prince of Wales* had plenty of time to prepare for the end of their ship. *Prince of Wales* had been crippled fifty minutes before *Repulse* sank, and she lingered for a further fifty minutes after that.

For some time the Carley floats had been filled with wounded and then floated gently off the flooded stern, the screams of the burned and scalded men when they entered the water being the most ghastly memory of many involved in this work. Then Captain Leach had made his appeal for volunteers to help get *Prince of Wales* back to Singapore, but had given permission to leave the ship to those who were not in a position to help, though there are several reports of unwounded men jumping into the sea before this time.

The 'non-essentials' made their way in large numbers to the destroyer *Express*, now tied up to *Prince of Wales*'s starboard side and with several gangplanks spanning the gap between the two ships. There was some anger among the ratings still needed on board *Prince of Wales* when they saw an officer clad in immaculate 'whites' calmly walking across to *Express*, carrying what appeared to be an attaché case. This sight brought 'hoots of derision', and there were calls of, 'Come back you yellow bastard.' But non-essential personnel had been released by Captain Leach, and this officer may well have been ordered across to *Express* with essential documents.

Preparations to abandon ship were now in full swing. More and more men were forced up from below by the advancing water, and there was soon a large crowd on the diminishing deck. The lashings on the ship's launches and whalers were released so that these would float off when *Prince of Wales* sank; a party of men unroped a stack of timber near the boat deck and started dumping the planks over the side to provide help to men who would have to take to the water later. One man counted each plank as he helped lift it overboard – twenty-four planks one side and the same number the other. Not far away, Ordinary Seaman James Cockburn was in another party of men at work.

I had come up through the armoured hatch, made my way to the upper deck and found myself in the wardroom where some men were forming a chain to pass wardroom furniture out on to the quarterdeck. Anxious to do something, I joined this chain and passed on a number of chairs. I sensed, rather than saw, that the forward end of the wardroom was a gaping hole. I took one chair out on to the quarterdeck, there being no one to pass it to, and found what was happening to the furniture. It was being thrown overboard. This was my first view of sea and sky since we had closed up at Action Stations. Blazing tropical daylight and not a Japanese plane in sight. The ship was still under way, listing to port, and stretching a long way astern was a string of jetsam, including the wardroom furniture.

There remained much uncertainty even after Abandon Ship was finally ordered. Many parts of the ship never received the order and well-disciplined and panic-free compartments continued to function. Some officers or petty officers realized that something was wrong and ordered their men out; some stayed to the end and paid with their lives accordingly. As in *Repulse* there were several examples of men being rescued from below. Stoker Desmond Ulrick was on deck when he passed an open hatch from which the ladder to the compartment below had been destroyed.

Three or four men were hauling on a rope and pulled out a member of the crew. He was pretty far gone but, before collapsing, said there were other men below, trapped behind lockers. I and two or three other men were then lowered back down the hatch by rope to try and find them. The only man I remember finding, however, was a rating sat in the power control room, in front of the telephone switchboard and heel and trim indicators. This must have been his Action Station. He did not appear to know what was going on and seemed very surprised when we told him the ship was sinking and the order was 'Abandon Ship'.

I remember the strangeness of this second. The lights were out, all was black, water could be heard pouring from somewhere and, above all, there was the quietness, like a blacked-out and deserted town. We were pulled up again through the hatch by the rope.

Men who passed by the canteen at this time could help themselves to unlimited cigarettes and chocolate, and the canteen manager was even giving away bundles of English and Singapore banknotes to anyone who had time to stop and put them in pockets or the moneybelts that many sailors wore, though one witness states that 'nobody seemed to bother much'. Chief Petty Officer Hill and his Food Supply Party H.Q. on the middle deck were still preparing an issue of tea and sandwiches when they noticed a sudden lurch of the ship, ran like mad and just had time to escape through some open portholes.

As the list to port steepened, the starboard side of *Prince of Wales* rose farther out of the water and the lower side of the battleship started to come up underneath the *Express* secured alongside. Her captain, Lieutenant-Commander Cartwright, had a delicate decision to make. To remain indefinitely would endanger his own ship, but to leave too soon would stop the flow of wounded and other survivors still coming across. The gangplanks fell into the sea as the gap widened, but men continued to swing across on ropes and the cable that still joined the two ships. Others, more daring, were jumping the gap, but the results of the occasional failure were horrible. As the cable tightened, men on the foc's'le of *Express* tried to release it, but it proved impossible to do so and the cable eventually snapped with a resounding crack. Engine Room Artificer Robert Woodhead was one of the last men to try his luck at leaping across.

I looked over the side and was horrified. The oil was thick on the water, some bodies were floating in it, and some of the other chaps around said there was no chance of living in that stuff. As I said earlier, I had no lifebelt, but on looking around I saw the destroyer alongside just beginning to move off. So I ran along the decks to a clear space to give myself a run at the empty space where the rails had been. Some fellows there shouted to me not to be foolish as the *Express* was already under way and I would be under the screws, but I just ran as fast as I could and jumped out and down.

I know now (have done ever since that day) that there is divine guidance for us. My heels landed on the ropes around the side of the *Express* and I pitched forward on to two chaps who were near, thus breaking my fall. When I recovered from this fright, I looked up at the *Prince of Wales*, which was receding astern very fast, and the first thing I noticed was the group of chaps who had cautioned me not to jump still standing there.

Express was indeed backing away. Lieutenant-Commander Cartwright had been watching the list on *Prince of Wales* increasing and her bilge keel coming up and under *Express*, and was judging the latest moment when he could safely leave the battleship. Able Seaman John Farrington was in the wheelhouse of *Express*.

I watched the confused exodus – men scrambling on any line they could find and the cries of hell as some dropped between the heavy ships, squashed in a surging torrent of sea, oil and blood. *Prince of Wales* lurches badly now and we anxiously await orders. I have one eye on the wheelhouse door and one hand on the telegraph. My opposite number, 'Bungy' Williams, eyes me with a threat, 'Don't move.' Then, 'Full Steam Astern' cracks the order from the bridge, and with a crashing bump we slide off the heaving keel of *Prince of Wales*.

At this point we witness truly a brave sight – Admiral Tom Phillips is leaning over the bridge, chin resting on hands, looking like some gold-braided 'What-Ho', a signalman at his side flashing out hurried messages to our bridge.

Express had very nearly capsized when *Prince of Wales* heeled over, and several survivors on the destroyer's deck were either tipped into the sea, or else they jumped in, thinking that the destroyer was indeed capsizing. But Lieutenant-Commander Cartwright, by what was considered by many onlookers to be a superb piece of ship-handling, had judged the moment nicely. *Express* backed away with no more than a twenty-foot gash in her hull plating. As *Express* pulled away, Cartwright received a calm wave, presumably of approval, from Admiral Phillips.

There were still several hundred men aboard *Prince of Wales*. For a minute or so, they stood in large groups on the foc's'le and on the starboard-side quarterdeck, whence there came a shout from some wag to the departing *Express*, 'Does anyone want a cheap ship?' Then a large-scale evacuation over the starboard side of the ship commenced. Men jumped or swung down on ropes until the list of the ship became so steep that they could slide down on their bottoms – a perilous journey down the forty-five-foot steel side.

I walked or slid down on to the armoured plating which jutted out from the ship's side. From there my intentions were to make my way along to where two ropes secured on the upper deck led down almost to the water. But, as I neared them, I saw about a dozen men scrambling to get a hold on the rope and, one by one, sliding down to the sea. Another lurch of the ship decided me and with scarcely another thought I moved and, in a sitting position, let myself go. The ship was then at an angle of about 45 degrees, the sides thick with oil, so that the speed with which I shot down the ship's side is best left to the imagination. As I started, I remember seeing dozens of heads bobbing about below me but it was too late to call a halt and, at terrific speed, I shot down and by some miracle missed all obstructions. (Telegraphist C. V. House)

A large party of men had found its way to the foc's'le, which was now the highest part of *Prince of Wales*'s deck

clear of the water. Many survivors remember an officer
here, 'a big, red-headed lieutenant', who was keeping
excellent order and controlling the men.* Surgeon
Lieutenant-Commander Dick Caldwell was also there,
tending the last of the wounded who would leave *Prince of
Wales*.

The foc's'le now presented an amazing sight, with hundreds of sailors
standing placidly smoking and chatting on the sloping deck – they
had mostly been driven up from below by the encroaching, rising
water. The guns' crews on the upper deck were still at their posts and
there was nothing for the remainder to do but wait for the ship to
sink. We enlisted several of them into stretcher and first-aid parties
for the wounded. Someone told us there was a man with a broken
leg lying in one of the compartments. We tended him, launched him
and two of his pals in a float into the sea, now lapping all along the
port side of the foc's'le.

Men started climbing over the rails and diving and jumping thirty
or forty feet into the sea below; but 'diving' off the high side of a
sinking ship is a euphemism! I took off my cap and my shoes and
looked carefully round for somewhere to put them – an extraordinary
action which I have read and heard of other people doing. I stood for
a minute in the orderly crowd waiting their chance and heard a sailor
say to his pal, 'Come on, chum. All them explosions'll have frightened
the blinkin' sharks away.'

The ship was heeling over more now, and I climbed over the guardrails and slid down to a projection on the ship's side. I stood there
and looked down on dozens of heads, arms and legs in the water, still
far below. Then I said to myself, 'Please God. Don't let me be
drowned!' – took a deep breath, and dived into the oily water.

The final preparations were made to leave the dying
ship. The gun crews were at last released from duty; one
observer comments particularly on the orderly behaviour
of the Royal Marine gun crew of P1 5·25-in. turret, whose
gun captain, Sergeant Brooks, was seen falling in and
counting off his men, including the magazine party, to

* This officer has been identified as Lieutenant E. J. Kempson,
R.N.V.R., whose father had been Director of Studies at the Royal
Naval College, Dartmouth, before the war. Lieutenant Kempson
survived the sinking, but was drowned in February 1942.

ensure that all were safely up on deck before ordering them to blow up their lifebelts and get over the side. Sergeant Thomas of S1, the other 5·25-in. turret manned by the Marines, had kept his turret in action to the end because it was the only one of the eight 5·25-in. turrets to have functioned properly throughout the action. S1's gun crew escaped, but ten of its working-chamber men were trapped and lost. Lieutenant W. M. Graham dismissed the crews of the close-range guns for which he was responsible, and these also joined the men leaving *Prince of Wales*.

The last few men who would ever get out from below decks did so at this time. One party of telegraphists who tried to reach the upper deck found their way barred by a determined commissioned gunner, who was still trying to pass ammunition by hand up to the now silent anti-aircraft guns. He turned the telegraphists back saying, 'Guns before men'. One or two managed to get past the gunner, but the remainder were never seen again. Leading Telegraphist Bernard Campion had been in the transmitting room.

Astonishing though it may be to recall, there was no mad rushing and the evacuation seemed to be absurdly leisurely considering the circumstances. As we climbed the ladders – with difficulty, as the ship was now almost lying on her port side – I found myself getting a little worried as to whether I would reach the upper deck before she turned right over and I remember playfully flicking the backside of the bloke in front of me – or rather above me – and muttering, 'Get a move on, Jan, for God's sake.' (I didn't know who it was, of course, but 'Jan' was a sort of general label in a West Country ship.)
    Anyhow, when at last I emerged through the port door of the fore superstructure, I was wondering how on earth I was going to get into the water – whether to dive in over the port side or scramble up the deck as best I could and walk down the starboard side – and for a few brief seconds I stood on the side of a mushroom vent, kicking off my shoes and blowing up my lifebelt. Before I could make any further decisions the ship decided for me, as the port guardrails disappeared under the water and I was sucked down for what seemed

ages in a mass of wreckage, with a derrick boom wedged firmly over my thighs and all kinds of loose spars belting me about.

I must confess that I gave up hope of ever surfacing again and hoped it would all be over swiftly. However, my inflated lifebelt served its purpose and what seemed several minutes later I did break surface in a thick mass of brown oil fuel, with a black eye, a broken thigh, and a lot of deep cuts and bruises. Incidentally, when I broke surface everything had been ripped off me except my lifebelt and my right sock!

Prince of Wales heeled right over on her port side, but not as quickly as *Repulse* had done, and several dozen men were able to walk calmly down the huge starboard side of the ship. Lieutenant W. M. Graham was one of those who took this strange walk.

I was able to muster most of my close-range guns' crews over on the starboard side and remember quite clearly walking over the bilge keel, keeping pace with the roll and thinking how clean the ship's bottom looked as I swam away. The last time I had seen the underside of the *Prince of Wales* was when I saw her being launched at Cammell Laird's yard in Birkenhead in 1939!

I should like to place it on record that there was no confusion or panic during the action and, when the time came to abandon ship, it was done quietly and almost as if hands had been piped to bathe! I suppose that many felt, like me, that this just could not be happening to them as it seemed like a bad dream – a long swim brought one back to reality!

There has been much speculation over what happened to Admiral Phillips and those around him. It is known that about ten minutes before *Prince of Wales* capsized he leant over the side of the compass platform, where he had spent the entire action with Captain Leach, and called down to the staff bridge where his immediate Fleet Staff had been working. Phillips dismissed these officers and told them to 'look after yourselves'. Commander H. N. S. Brown, Fleet Gunnery Officer, says that there was no particular expression on the admiral's face or his tone of voice, 'it was more matter of fact than anything else'. Most of these officers were saved. Various survivors saw Admiral Phillips after this. His coxswain has said that Admiral Phillips refused to put on a lifebelt, and that both he and Captain Leach were seen 'silent and impervious to entreaties to abandon ship before it was too late'.

There are several stories that Admiral Phillips, Captain Leach and Captain Simon Beardsworth, the admiral's secretary, were seen walking side-by-side down the ship's side and into the water but this cannot be confirmed. Commander Hilary Norman, Fleet Torpedo Officer, definitely saw Phillips, slumped on a stool and 'in deep despond', at a very late stage and then saw the admiral's body in the sea after *Prince of Wales* sank. Norman thought of swimming to the body and taking off it a signet ring or some other souvenir for the family but then decided that this was a little macabre and gave up the idea. He does not remember whether the body was wearing a lifebelt but presumes from its floating position that it was. Many people agree that there had been plenty of time for Admiral Phillips to save himself if he had wished to do so.

Lieutenant W. M. Graham later found Captain Leach's body, lying face downwards in the water but with a partially filled navy-pattern lifebelt around his chest. Graham and some sailors turned the body over and found the mouth clogged with vomit, the nose full of froth and the face purple; the neck may also have been broken. They tried to tow the body to H.M.S. *Express* but became exhausted, and Lieutenant Graham ordered the attempt to be abandoned. Captain Leach's son does not believe that his father would have deliberately gone down with the ship – he is certain that his father would have regarded that as an unnecessary waste of life – but he feels that, out of loyalty to Admiral Phillips, his father would not have left the compass platform until released. It is probable that this vital permission was given, but too late to save Captain Leach, who was obviously dragged down when *Prince of Wales* sank. Phillips's flag lieutenant, who had once been a university swimming 'half-blue', was later

seen swimming strongly towards *Express*, but he collapsed and died on the destroyer, possibly from heart
failure. Two yeomen of signals, observed at a late stage on
Prince of Wales's bridge, were never seen again.

There are several reports of the courage of Commander
H. F. Lawson who was in command of damage control. He
was attempting to repair *Prince of Wales*'s steering, deep
down in the stern of the ship, but ordered the ratings with
him up to safety and was last seen continuing to work
alone at this impossible task. The ship's padre, the Rev.
W. G. Parker, a New Zealander, was tending badly
wounded men at the bottom of a shaft passage and refused
to come up when the hatch at the top of the passage had to
be closed. He, too, was never seen again. And a Royal
Marine who survived can 'never forget the terrible screaming and shouting coming up the ventilation shafts from the
men trapped down below'. But, with the slower sinking of
Prince of Wales and the help given by *Express* in taking so
many men straight over the side, four out of every five
men on *Prince of Wales* were saved.

The end was near. The slow roll to port continued until
Prince of Wales was lying upside down with her flat bottom
completely exposed.

May I say it is something I will never forget now, for the ship was
completely upside down. I was standing on the bottom – almost
falling into a large torpedo hole – and I could see the propellers
slowly turning. I had the feeling that I was the only one there but I
could still hear screams from inside the torpedo hole and there appeared to be lots of people in the water. As the stern began to disappear, I realized the water would reach me standing there, so I
began to swim for it. (Petty Officer L. V. Leather)*

Several of the last men on the ship's bottom were non-
swimmers, or were determined to leave the ship as late as

* Mr Leather's christian names are Loos Verdun; he is one of the
many First World War children named after battles on the Western
Front.

possible. Leading Stoker Harry Roberts sat with several of these on the ship's bottom, calmly opened a tin of Craven A cigarettes and handed them around. Another stoker, a non-swimmer, walked up towards the bows until overtaken and sucked down by the water and, with no thoughts of surviving, began drinking in sea water to hasten his death. He was caught in an air bubble, brought to the surface and found himself next to a convenient plank of wood. A well-known character, Signalman Cole, was seen calmly standing with his white cap still on his head and, being another non-swimmer, simply stood still, trusting to his lifebelt to save him. Cole disappeared beneath the water, but also came to the surface safely.

Hundreds of men in the water and on *Express* witnessed the end. Leading Seaman Basil Elsmore remembers that 'our ship did not go easily. My last memory picture is of a huge football pitch – the ship's bottom – with all the players and spectators sliding down to one end.' The bows of *Prince of Wales* reared high in the air, the great torpedo hole in her forepeak clearly visible; then there was 'a fantastic noise' to be heard, obviously made by the inside fixtures tearing loose, and the battleship slipped quietly beneath the sea. One officer in the water was seen to salute, to the amazement of a near-by stoker who thought that 'that sort of thing only happened in books'. One survivor says that 'there were plenty of tears', and another remembers it as 'a terrible sight and, for any sailor, not possible to contemplate a worse'.

13

The Rescue

Several of the Japanese aircraft that had made the successful attacks on the British ships had remained in the area. These onlookers were either crews from the Mihoro Air Corps, which had taken off late, and therefore had more fuel remaining, or from the Kanoya Air Corps, which had delivered the last devastating torpedo attacks on *Prince of Wales* and *Repulse*. The Japanese airmen realized that there was now little danger from the anti-aircraft guns of the sinking British capital ships and still no sign of British fighter aircraft. They circled to watch the drama still unfolding below.

It was one flight of these aircraft that had swept low over the scene of *Repulse*'s sinking when the survivors believed that they were about to be machine-gunned. But the Mitsubishis had flown over their heads without opening fire, and one *Repulse* survivor is certain that he saw a Japanese pilot saluting the spot where *Repulse* had sunk. The Japanese could certainly have caused a large number of casualties among the trained and valuable seamen then in the water, but neither then nor at any time later were survivors fired upon. Commander C. W. May, captain of *Electra*, later submitted this report.

Several formations of Japanese aircraft were in the vicinity until about 13.10 but no attempt was made to bomb or machine-gun destroyers and survivors. Possibly no bombs remained but it is certainly considered that enemy aircraft purposely refrained from any hostile act during rescue work.

This restraint on the part of the Japanese is interesting because it is out of character with many other Japanese acts in the opening months of the war. The reason for it is not known. Perhaps these Japanese professional naval officers and men had some regard for their British contemporaries; perhaps they were so stunned by the complete success of their recent attacks that the idea of continuing the fight against the men in the water never occurred to them. A large number of the British survivors confidently told the authors of this book that one Japanese aircraft had even signalled to the rescuing destroyers, 'CEASE FIRING. PICK UP SURVIVORS'; and that some sort of truce had then followed. The wording of the reputed signal in many accounts was always the same. This would have made a good story, but unfortunately there is no truth in it and there was never any communication between the two sides in the battle.

Midshipman Hoashi, who had flown off to Kuantan airfield to drop his two small bombs there, returned soon after *Repulse* had gone to the bottom and resumed his duty of signalling reports of the action to Saigon. He reported that *Repulse* had sunk, that *Prince of Wales* was clearly sinking, and then details of the rescue work, adding his opinion that there would not be room on the three destroyers for all the *Repulse* survivors and that the *Prince of Wales* survivors would fail to be rescued.

This leisurely Japanese viewing of the scene was rudely interrupted at about 13.20, about three minutes before *Prince of Wales* sank, by the arrival on the scene of the Australian-piloted Brewster Buffalo fighters that had taken off from Sembawang airfield an hour earlier. One of the Buffaloes had been forced to turn back with engine trouble soon after leaving Sembawang, but the other ten, led by Flight Lieutenant Tim Vigors, all reached the scene of the recent battle. The departure from Sembawang had been so hurried that there had been no briefing; Vigors was simply told to fly to a position sixty miles south-south-east of Kuantan and find the British ships which were under Japanese air attack. There was no time to tell the other pilots anything, and they simply took off and followed Vigors. Vigors has written the following impression of his arrival on the scene.

When we reached the scene everything was a hell of a mess. The *Repulse* had been sunk long before. I just saw the last of the *Prince of Wales* as she put her nose in the air and slid in backwards. The scene was fairly sickmaking particularly as I realized the immensity of the disaster and knew that it need never have occurred. If I had been allowed to keep a standing patrol over the Fleet we could have kept the shadow aircraft away. Even had the Japanese been able to establish an exact position without shadow aircraft, their torpedo bombers had no fighter escort and were very heavily laden. Even six Buffaloes could have wrought merry hell with them and certainly prevented a lot of the torpedo strikes. The *Repulse*, which was much less heavily armoured, would probably have bought it anyway, but I have no doubt in my mind that we could have saved the *Prince of Wales* and got her back to Singapore.

One or two of the Buffalo pilots saw Hoashi's Mitsu-bishi, but the Japanese made off at high speed and, although the Buffaloes were slightly faster, Hoashi's aircraft soon disappeared into a cloud. The other Japanese aircraft in the area may have left by then, or they may have made their escapes like Hoashi, but they were not seen by the Buffaloes. Vigors split his formation into smaller groups to patrol at various heights in case any more Japanese planes appeared, but he took his own plane down low and flew around the desolate scene of the recent sinkings. He could see the hundreds of men in the sea quite plainly, and the men in the sea could see him. What the shipwrecked sailors and the pilot thought of each other is of some interest.

A few sailors, uninjured and more resilient than most, may well have waved and cheered when Vigors flew over their heads, but the majority saw in the belated arrival of these few fighter aircraft the cause of all their troubles and of the loss of the two great ships that had, until a few minutes earlier, been their homes, but which were now the tombs for so many of their shipmates. They jeered, booed and swore at the solitary pilot circling above. Able Seaman R. H. James, late of the *Prince of Wales*, sums up the feelings of so many men at this moment.

If, as I sincerely hope, the pilot of that aircraft is still alive, his ears must still be burning. Not that he was in any way to blame but, for a moment, he merely became the focal point of all the despair and frustration felt by the bulk of the survivors at the complete lack of support from the air.

This resentment at the fighter pilots was not felt only by the survivors of the sunken ships; a *Prince of Wales* man on *Express* noted that 'if the gun crews on the destroyer had had their way they would have opened fire on the Buffaloes'.

Flight Lieutenant Vigors completely misinterpreted his reception from the men in the water, but this will be more conveniently described later. After almost an hour over the rescue scene, the Buffaloes had to leave because of fuel shortage. No more Japanese aircraft had been seen. The fighters investigated the steamer *Haldis* while on their return flight, and then flew on to land safely back at their airfield.

The first stage of the rescue work was carried out with the destroyers *Electra* and *Vampire* working at the scene of *Repulse*'s sinking, and *Express* at that of *Prince of Wales*. This was a sensible arrangement. While there had been more *Prince of Wales* survivors to be picked up, their ship had gone down slowly and boats, Carley floats and much floatable gear had been got into the water. *Express* had, moreover, taken aboard a number of crew directly from *Prince of Wales* before she sank. Many survivors believe that the two ships went down within a mile of each other, or two miles at most, but the wreck of *Prince of Wales* now lies nearly eight miles to the south-east of that of *Repulse*. The final actions had taken place about four miles apart, with *Repulse* sinking while still turning to starboard and away from *Prince of Wales*, and the tidal current probably carried *Prince of Wales* a further two miles away during the fifty minutes between the sinking of the two ships.

The *Repulse* men in the water, or already aboard *Electra* or *Vampire*, had seen *Prince of Wales*'s bow rise into the the air and then watched as the great ship sank. The event was viewed with mixed feelings by some of the *Repulse* survivors; they had always regarded *Prince of Wales* as a 'Jonah', and on *Electra* 'there was a mass exodus to the upper deck where a hearty cheer bade her farewell'. One survivor aboard *Electra* has 'a very vivid memory of an almost naked man dancing up and down and screaming for a camera' to photograph the sinking battleship. This may have been the American reporter, Cecil Brown of C.B.S., but whoever it was never got his picture of a lifetime and the sinking of neither ship was photographed, though the Japanese took one or two indistinct photographs of the battle that have survived and Sub-Lieutenant P. F. C. Satow took one excellent one from the bridge of his ship, *Express*, while still alongside *Prince of Wales*.

When *Prince of Wales* sank, Commander C. W. May of *Electra* became Senior Officer Force Z. Although *Electra* was working at the scene of *Repulse*'s sinking, *Electra* had been broadcasting signals on behalf of the flagship since 13.00. May sent this last simple, but world-shattering, signal from *Electra* at 13.18:

H.M.S. PRINCE OF WALES SUNK.

This was received in the War Room at G.H.Q. Singapore three minutes later. Nine signals had been sent in all; not one had requested the assistance of the R.A.F.*

The many swimmers from both ships had mostly made their way to the Carley floats or to the few ship's boats that had been got away and awaited their turn to be picked up by the destroyers.

I kicked my shoes off whilst in the water and swam around in the oil fuel for about an hour making my way forward to one of the Carley floats with men already on it. The only fear that was in my mind at that moment was the sharks. When I got to the float, I hung on to the side to get my wind back. I noticed the Warrant Bosun was hanging on to a piece of wood twenty yards from the float. He was

* Appendix Three gives the full text of these signals.

delirious through consuming oil fuel. I swam towards him and brought him back on the Carley float. He said, 'If I'm too much trouble, let me go back in the water and drown.' I held him between my legs up on the float and, with the float rolling and my knees sticking into his stomach, it made him bring all the oil fuel up. Within ten minutes, he was as right as rain. (Marine J. Powell, H.M.S. *Repulse*)

After nearly being knocked senseless by a booted man who had jumped on top of me, I managed to swim to an empty Carley float but could not get in it as it floated too high out of the water, so I held on to the lifelines, then two bluejackets reached the float and their combined weight brought one end down; they got in and hauled me in also. We picked up many swimmers, including one midshipman with a stomach wound; his blood was colouring the water which was waist high for the taller men and armpit high for smaller men. A movement on the raft caused the water, blood and oil to splash our faces. We picked up a few dead sailors, but slid them back into the sea to make way for the living. As senior rank on the raft, I went to the wounded midshipman, who could only mutter, 'Thank you sir, I'll be all right.' I heard the poor lad died next day. (Lieutenant H. Abrahams, H.M.S. *Repulse*)

There was one chap up the front of the raft paddling like mad and he kept screaming for everybody else to paddle to the nearest land (which we could just see in the distance). Nobody was paying much attention to him, except to tell him to shut up. (Boy Seaman B. N. Millard, H.M.S. *Prince of Wales*)

The impression that remains uppermost in my own mind about the affair – it was strong then and it is equally strong now over thirty years later – was the incredible calmness and good humour with which the lads took to the water. Although we were all covered from head to foot in thick black oil, and many of us were in pain, I heard nothing but wry joking from the chaps who shared my crowded Carley float. One of them was grumbling lugubriously because the so-and-so's had chosen 'tot-time' [the time when the rum issue was normally made] to launch their attack and the Navigating Officer was dispassionately telling us roughly what our position was at the time of the sinking. Another chap, a signalman, was balancing himself precariously on the heaving raft and making a semaphore message to the nearest destroyer to say that we had one or two casualties among us, including myself on whom that same resourceful signalman had already tied a crude but effective splint made from a spar of wood and some strips of torn shirt. (Leading Telegraphist B. G. Campion, H.M.S. *Prince of Wales*)

The man semaphoring to the destroyer was the resilient Signalman Cole, who had earlier been seen standing calmly on the flat bottom of *Prince of Wales* still with his white hat on and trusting to his lifebelt to float him safely off.

Lieutenant Ian Forbes of *Prince of Wales* joined up with his Gunnery Officer, Lieutenant-Commander Colin Mc-Mullen, on a Carley float.

We had an agreeable time there for, perhaps, two hours as rescue operations were conducted by the escorting destroyers. We were fully aware that the Japanese planes would not return (why should they?) and so there was an air of pleasurable release, sitting in a warm and sunlit sea. A British aircraft flew over from time to time, which was greeted with waving and ribald remarks. This, I believe, was reported as being a sign of wonderful 'morale'. I don't suppose our morale was any different from the rest of the Fleet but, when released from such an event, no one solemnly considers, at that moment, the vast historic implications, such as the fall of Singapore, the total ending of all Colonial possessions, etc. All hands are happy to be alive and to wave and cheer accordingly.

Perhaps the most bizarre story to come out of the Carley floats is that of Able Seaman Alexander White, a radar operator from *Prince of Wales*.

When I joined the Navy, an aunt presented me with the caul that covered my grandfather at birth and which had been saved. Apparently there is an old seafarers' superstition that he who carries a caul will never drown. This was attached to a covering letter which I carried in my wallet which happened to be in the pocket of my trousers when I went over the side. While in the float I found the letter floating – the wallet and the caul having disintegrated. I still have the letter with the ink smeared by the water!*

* CAUL: The amnion or inner membrane enclosing the foetus before birth. This, or a portion of it sometimes enveloping the head of a child at birth, is regarded as lucky and supposed to be a preservative against drowning' – *Shorter Oxford English Dictionary*

The three destroyers worked hard to get all the survivors out of the water. The calm sea, warm weather and absence of Japanese aircraft made this a straightforward operation for trained seamen rescuing their colleagues. Scrambling-nets were let over the sides and the fit men climbed aboard. Lines were thrown to single swimmers who were not near to scrambling-nets, but these lines were very difficult to grasp for oil-soaked men.

I even had my own moment of humour when *Electra* (and how superb those destroyers were that day) found time to get around to my vicinity where I was trying to help a very large, unconscious Royal Marine, wounded and clogged with oil. Expertly handled, *Electra* glided alongside me and threw me a rope. Wrestling to get it underneath the man's armpits and prematurely anticipating success, I shouted 'Haul away' a little too eagerly only to find that the noose had slid up round his neck. Just in time. There were ribald comments on my performance by friends in the water and already on deck, and then we were both safe. (Lieutenant J. O. C. Hayes, H.M.S. *Repulse*)

Unfortunately there were several men who made it to the bottom of the nets or to the lines, but, who then reaching the limit of their strength, fell back and disappeared.

The most badly wounded on the destroyers were taken below for treatment, but most survivors were unceremoniously hauled away from the side and dumped on the decks to be left while further men were saved from the water. There were soon dozens of exhausted men laying out on the hot metal decks, retching and coughing the oil out of their lungs. Rum was found to be an excellent remedy for swallowed oil; a stiff tot often brought forth a violent sickness and prompt recovery. Once survivors had recovered, they started to rub the worst of the foul-smelling oil off their skins, to wander around looking for missing pals, to search for a drink or a cigarette. Many recovered survivors helped with further rescue work. On all the rescuing destroyers it was noticed that survivors usually gravitated towards familiar positions to offer help. For example, *Repulse*'s Royal Marines manned the after guns on *Electra* in case of further air attack and thus released the destroyer's seamen gunners for rescue work.

Able Seaman James from *Prince of Wales* was one of the survivors who tried to help in rescue work.

I finished up on the fo'c'sle of the *Express* and there made what was probably my one constructive contribution to the proceedings. Three of us heaved a man aboard from the ratlines over the side and he promptly collapsed on the deck. The three of us took it in turns to apply artificial respiration, and I was amazed how much water came out of this man, forming a small continuous stream running down to the gunwale. After what must have been at least twenty minutes, he finally sat up and said, 'Thanks mate. Got a cigarette?' This we were able to provide, thanks to the generosity of the Canteen Manager on *Express*, who was distributing them freely by the packet.

Officers' Cook Wilf Greenwood of *Repulse* was rescued by *Electra*.

I remember lying on the deck and looking at the clouds and sky and thanking God for still being alive. The Steward aboard the *Electra* was a grand little chap; he assisted some survivors down into the wardroom mess and tried his best to comfort us, helping us in many ways. It was quite a sight in the messroom – bodies were everywhere. I remember seeing one big chap laid on a table, oil was coming from his mouth. Another chap who was a Chief Petty Officer looked all in and wasn't a young chap; he said, 'I've had enough of this, this is the third time for me.' Another sailor came in and said laughing, 'I've lost my bleeding teeth.' While all this was going on the radio was playing 'Ah, Sweet Mystery of Life'. It made me think.

There were many distressing scenes in the destroyers' wardrooms, for it was here that the badly wounded men were being treated. Many scalded or flash-burned men had managed to survive this far, but were now suffering from delayed shock. There was little the doctors could do for these cases except to give them morphia to relieve the pain. On each of the rescuing ships there was soon a pitiful row of blanket-covered bodies in a quiet corner of the upper deck.

Ordinary Seaman W. E. England of *Prince of Wales* went below in *Express* to see if he could find some way of helping.

I found a messmate lying on a stretcher with his head packed in cotton wool. All the skin from his face and body had been burned off. He was, I believe, a stoker or gun-layer A.B. in the regular R.N. He told me that he had just come out of a doorway into the 'waist' of *Prince of Wales* when the flash from the last bombs caught him. He gave me his money and his watch (which was scorched and had stopped), and he asked me if I would write to his wife when I got back. I tried to comfort him and said that he was safe now and it would not be long before we were in Singapore and he was in hospital. He cheered up a bit and asked for a drink. I went off to find the bathroom on the destroyer and eventually came back with a cup of water, but I was too late. Bob had ended his story of 'life in the Navy' and passed peacefully away. I lifted his head to see what damage had been done and found his skull wide open. How had he managed to talk to me about his wife in that condition? His wife had her first child three months later.

Lieutenant J. O. C. Hayes had been 'Snotty's Nurse' in *Repulse*. One of his boys was now lying on one of the two bunks that was all that *Electra* had by way of a sick bay.

One of our young doctors was among the survivors, in no great shape himself but tackling his overwhelming task as one would expect. He came to seek me out and told me that he had a little midshipman in one of the bunks, that he was dying from bullet wounds in the groin, although sedated he was in great pain and asking to see me if I was on board. There was another dying man in the other bunk.

Among his thirty gunroom colleagues, this midshipman had hitherto appeared the least developed. Immature for his age and often in trouble – through no intention of his, but there are those who cannot avoid it – he had seemed and looked a near child and therefore had needed careful handling. He was insufficiently fledged to have an Action Station of any import and I had therefore alloted him something to do with the secondary armament, at which station he had been wounded by a machine-gun bullet.

Scarcely recognizable myself, I asked to be alone with him and took his hand. He gave me a brave smile which knifed into my heart and conscience for any previous admonishment I had had to bestow. He held on to my hand with a firm little grip as though trying to express his last tangible feeling in the young life he must have known was slipping from him. I have never before or since seen death, or the awareness of death, in that moment of truth so transform youth to man, suddenly adult, brave and silently perceptive of the tragedy in which we were both enmeshed. He died that evening.

By 14.00, nearly one and a half hours after *Repulse* had sunk, the work of rescuing her survivors was nearly over. Commander May ordered *Vampire* to carry out one last search while he took *Electra* over to the scene of *Prince of Wales*'s sinking. No other rescue ships had arrived on the scene and *Express* had been working quite alone. She was now so full of survivors as to be dangerously top-heavy. Although there were still 300 or so *Prince of Wales* men in the water awaiting rescue, Commander May ordered Lieutenant-Commander Cartwright of *Express* to make straight for Singapore while *Electra* took over the rescue work. An hour later, *Vampire* had satisfied herself that the last live *Repulse* man had been taken from the sea. She came across to *Electra*, picking up on the way two *Prince of Wales* men who had drifted out of the main rescue area. *Vampire* too was then released by Commander May to return to Singapore.

Electra stayed a further forty-five minutes, and the last few *Princes of Wales* survivors were got on board. Among the last to be picked up was a group of men who had taken refuge on one of *Prince of Wales*'s waterlogged cutters. This, although entirely below the surface, had had enough buoyancy to support the men standing in it. They were quite cheerful, and one rating was 'still mad enough to sing in defiance' until rescued. One exhausted boy seaman, however, when he had to climb *Electra*'s scrambling-net, found it 'like climbing the peak of Everest'.

At 16.00 Commander May took his ship over to the last survivors he could see, a float with a small group of men, one of whom cheerfully rolled up a trouser leg and 'thumbed a lift'. Then *Electra*'s lookout reported 'a man swimming or a drifting coconut astern'. Commander May took his ship round in one last wide sweep, and indeed found this final survivor and picked him up. *Electra* increased speed and turned towards Singapore.

·   ·   ·

The three destroyers had picked up 2,081 men who would
survive the short voyage to Singapore as well as several
corpses and some badly wounded who would die on the
way. The smallest destroyer, the Australian *Vampire*, was
the only one of the three to record the exact numbers she
had picked up – from *Repulse*, nine officers including Captain Tennant, 213 ratings and one civilian war correspondent, O'Dowd Gallagher of the *Daily Express*, and two
ratings from *Prince of Wales*. *Express*, which had worked
alone for so long at the scene of *Prince of Wales*'s sinking,
is believed to have rescued about 1,000 men, leaving
Electra with nearly 900, of whom 571 were from *Repulse*
and the remainder from *Prince of Wales*.

To mark the scene of a momentous battle there were
left behind great sheets of stinking oil, drifting boats,
Carley floats, flotsam of every description and many
corpses, either floating face down and anonymous or
bobbing about supported by their lifejackets.

14

The Aftermath

News of the disaster was becoming known in many places throughout the world even while *Electra*, *Express* and *Vampire* were still picking up survivors. Among the first to hear were the British warships in the Far East whose wirelesses had been tuned to the frequency on which the signals from Force Z had been broadcast. These messages had been decoded at once and passed to the ships' respective captains. The cruiser *Exeter* was just approaching Singapore – the first British naval reinforcement for the Eastern Fleet since the outbreak of the Japanese war. Lieutenant-Commander G. T. Cooper recounts how he received the news.

I was on the forecastle preparing the anchors and cables when the Commander came up and touched me on the shoulder.

'Had a good lunch, Number One?' he asked.

'Not particularly,' I replied.

'You better have,' he whispered. '*Repulse* sunk. *Prince of Wales* hit.'

In his own imperturbable way he moved on, leaving me standing there absolutely stunned. He obviously did not mean me to convey this information to the sailors working under me, so I continued with the cables without saying a word.

A few minutes later, I felt another nudge on the shoulder. It was the Commander again.

'*Prince of Wales* sunk too,' he said, and moved away.

A short time after, we secured alongside the dockyard wall in the Naval Base. It was not a very pleasant situation. Here we were, an 8,000-ton cruiser left as the spearhead of the British Navy against the whole naval might of Japan.

In the Operations Room at the Naval Base, Rear-Admiral Palliser was faced with the unpleasant task of having to inform the Admiralty. At 13.45, just over twenty minutes after *Prince of Wales* went down, he sent a simply worded signal informing the Admiralty that *Prince of Wales* and *Repulse* had both been sunk 'by torpedoes'; later signals gave more detail. When Lieutenant Richard Dyer of H.M.S. *Tenedos* reported to Palliser later that evening, he found Admiral Phillips's Chief of Staff 'completely stunned and virtually inarticulate; he seemed to have lost his voice and could barely nod or shake his head'. It was not known at that time whether or not Admiral Phillips had survived, and the Admiralty sent instructions that Vice-Admiral Layton, the former Commander-in-Chief China Station who had just left Singapore on the liner *Dominion Monarch*, was to be recalled to assume temporary command of the Eastern Fleet.

The authorities at Singapore had the delicate problem of how to handle the news of the sinkings, particularly in view of the existing doubts over the morale of the native populations in the Far Eastern possessions. It was assumed that the Japanese would waste no time in announcing their great victory, and it was known that three destroyers would arrive at the Naval Base later that day and discharge their hundreds of survivors – an event that could hardly be concealed from the many civilian dockyard workers. It was decided that Mr Duff Cooper, M.P., who had been the British War Cabinet's representative in Singapore since early September, should broadcast that evening on the local radio. He did so and announced the loss of the two ships without attempting to minimize the scale of the tragedy.

This is not the first time in our long history of glory that we have met with disaster and have surmounted it. Indeed there is something in our nature and of our fathers before us, that only disaster can produce.*

The local press followed this up next morning. The *Singapore Free Press* printed this editorial:

Sometimes there is news which no one will at first believe. This has happened twice during the past three days. First there was the air

* *Singapore Free Press*, 11 December 1941.

attack on Singapore early on the morning of Monday. It took everyone by surprise. Last night there was the news of the sinking of *Prince of Wales* and *Repulse*. Such grievous news, it seemed, could not possibly be true. Yet true it is, alas, and the heavy blow will long be felt by us in the Far East, by the whole British Empire and by the Royal Navy in particular. No words that can be printed here will lighten the blow and no one would dare to minimize the seriousness of the loss . . . We must face the fact that two of our best heavy warships have been sunk by the Japanese within the first three days of the fighting in this part of the world; we must admit that the pride of the Eastern Fleet is no more.

It was a realistic and dignified piece of journalism, but it came all too late. British prestige in the Far East and morale in the fighting services there had been dealt a blow from which they would never recover.

The Japanese had actually been the first to broadcast the news when, at 14.35 (Singapore Time), the Imperial Navy Headquarters in Tokyo issued this statement.

From the outbreak of hostilities the movements of the two British capital ships have been closely observed. Yesterday afternoon they were discovered by one of our submarines carrying out a reconnaissance in co-operation with Naval surface ships and the Naval Air Force. At 11.30 this morning our submarine again confirmed the position of the British ships, off Kuantan on the east coast of Malaya. Without losing a moment the Naval Air Force entered into a dauntless and daring attack and in a twinkling of the eye attacked at about 12.45. The *Repulse* was seriously damaged by the first bombs dropped and shortly afterwards the *Prince of Wales* was hit and developed a heavy list to port. The *Repulse* sank first and, shortly after, at ten minutes to three, the *Prince of Wales* blew up and finally sank.

The third day of hostilities has resulted in the annihilation of the main strength of the British Far Eastern Squadron.*

It was an accurate statement in all respects save that the Navy had credited the sighting off Kuantan that morning to a submarine and not to Midshipman Hoashi's aircraft

* Masanobu Tsuji, *Singapore, the Japanese Version*, Constable, London, 1962, p. 97.

and *Prince of Wales* had not blown up before sinking. This splendid news for the Japanese was immediately broadcast on Tokyo Radio, and at 15.53, while *Electra* was picking up the last of the survivors from the sea, the Japanese Domei News Agency broadcast an English-language report on its China Zone Service.

The British Foreign Office Radio Monitoring Station at Beaconsfield was one of the many places throughout the world where this report was picked up. The time was a little after 08.00 in London. The news item was immediately flashed to the Admiralty and to the Prime Minister's Office in Downing Street, but it did no more than confirm what was already known from Rear-Admiral Palliser's earlier signal. A telephone at his bedside had already woken Winston Churchill, and Sir Dudley Pound, the First Sea Lord, had given the terrible news. At first Churchill could not understand what Admiral Pound was saying, but once the message finally became clear, Churchill, as he later wrote in his memoirs, 'turned over and twisted in bed and the full horror of the news sank in on me'. Britain had lost capital ships before in this war, but never two in one day and not in such a humiliating and one-sided battle. It had been Churchill himself who had insisted that *Repulse* and *Prince of Wales* go out to the Far East.

As in Singapore, it was decided that nothing could be gained by attempting to conceal the loss from the public. Mr Churchill went down to the House of Commons, and at 11.32, immediately after prayers, he rose and made the following straightforward statement.

I have bad news for the House which I thought I should impart at the earliest moment. A report has been received from Singapore that H.M.S. *Prince of Wales* and H.M.S. *Repulse* have been sunk while carrying out operations against the Japanese attacks on Malaya. No details are yet available except those contained in the Japanese communique which claims both ships were sunk by air attack. *

* *Evening News* (London), 10 December 1941.

At the same time, an Official Admiralty communiqué gave much the same information to the radio and press. Such was the speed of world-wide communications that virtually everyone in England heard the news from the B.B.C.'s lunchtime news broadcasts before any of the survivors of the sinkings had reached Singapore. That afternoon it was the front-page item in all the London evening papers.

The three rescue ships were still on their way to Singapore when Winston Churchill was addressing the House of Commons. Rescuers and rescued had settled down to make the best of their eight-hour voyage to the Naval Base. Many of the survivors had to remain on deck, and only the wounded could be sure of a place below, though one old 'three-badger' rescued from *Repulse* recovered sufficiently to be observed in *Electra*'s galley calmly drying out his £1 notes. Shell-shock and reaction sometimes set in; one of *Express*'s stokers handed a cigarette to an oil-covered survivor, and was surprised to find the man was an officer who remarked bitterly, 'Don't you thank God that you weren't on *Prince of Wales*. At least you've still got your ship.'

But many of the survivors soon recovered their spirits, especially after liberal tots of rum – or whisky on the Australian *Vampire* – had been issued. *Express* was carrying the greatest load of survivors, and the issue of rum caused a queue to form along one side of the ship so that an 'alarming list' developed. Lieutenant J. R. A. Denne rushed down from the bridge, 'wondering what further disaster had hit us'. All became well after the queue had been 'wound round the funnel and the ship came upright again'. As soon as the late afternoon brought cooler conditions clothes were shared out. One *Repulse* survivor on *Vampire* was given an Australian Naval Rugby Team shirt – 'it was Number 7 and became my most treasured possession'. Food was issued, though when soup was taken to the seamen's messdeck in *Express* the younger seamen couldn't find their appetites as someone had left the body of a dead sailor laid out on the messdeck table.

Cleaned up, fed and with a tot of rum inside them, the survivors could do no more but wait for the crowded destroyers to reach Singapore. There was much fear that the Japanese aircraft would return and bomb the destroyers; casualties would have been fearful had this happened, but the Japanese were not seen again. Leading Supply Assistant Leonard Sandland, a *Repulse* survivor aboard *Electra* probably sums up well the scene at this stage.

I took a walk round the ship, seeing if I could find anyone I knew. The whole deck was covered with exhausted men, but it was difficult to recognize anybody at all because of the oil. I did eventually find one or two of my mates, but in each case I recognized them only by their voices or their outline as they walked.

I had intended to do something when and if I eventually left the Service and that was to paint a picture of some of the survivors sitting round the well of the forward gun turret for warmth – some with just a vest on, some with just underpants on, some with nothing at all on, just a row of bare bottoms sitting round that well – filthy, dead tired, but glad to be alive. It's engraved indelibly on my memory. I've never got around to painting it yet, but I will.

Vampire met again the steamer *Haldis* during the return voyage, and inquired whether any assistance was required, but the merchant ship was not in any trouble and continued with her plodding voyage to the safety of Singapore.*

Express met five destroyers heading north. These were the four American ships – *Alden, Edsall, John D. Edwards* and *Whipple* – that had arrived at Singapore that morning, and the fifth ship was H.M.S. *Stronghold*. They had all been sent out from Singapore in answer to Admiral Phillips's request for destroyer assistance. The United States Navy had thus come this close to being involved in a famous

---

* *Haldis* survived the war and sailed again in the Far East until July 1948 when she was blown ashore in a gale at Hong Kong and wrecked.

naval action. *Express* informed the destroyers that the action was over and that there was nothing they could do to help, though the five destroyers remained at sea for several hours. The four Americans searched the area where *Prince of Wales* and *Repulse* had sunk to make sure that there were no more survivors, but all they found was oil, debris and floating bodies. Early the next morning the Americans sighted what they believed to be the tracks of torpedoes fired at them, but they were not hit and no sign was found of the submarine that might have fired the torpedoes. Soon after this the U.S.S. *Edsall* found and boarded a Japanese fishing trawler, the *Shofu Fu Maru,* which had four small boats in tow. These were almost certainly the small ships seen by Force Z off Kuantan the previous morning. The *Edsall* took the Japanese ships back to Singapore where they were closely examined both by the Americans and by some British officers from H.M.S. *Mauritius* who had been out with the Americans as liaison officers. There was no sign whatsoever that the Japanese ship was other than a normal fishing trawler, with the smaller boats being used for line fishing, and the Japanese were interned. There seems to be no connection between the *Shofu Fu Maru* and the bullet-riddled boat containing Japanese army equipment found near Kuantan which had been the basis of the false report that the Japanese were landing there. *

                        .   .   .

* Three days later the four American destroyers left Singapore hurriedly, on orders from Admiral Hart at Manila, much to the disappointment of the British. *Edsall* had the most exciting time in the next few weeks. She was the first U.S. Navy destroyer to take part in the sinking of a full-sized Japanese submarine when, with three Australian corvettes, she sank I.124 off Darwin, Northern Australia, on 20 January 1942. At the end of March 1942, *Edsall* and *Whipple* were in company with the famous American ship *Langley* when it was bombed and sunk by the same Japanese naval bombers that had sunk *Prince of Wales* and *Repulse.* After transferring *Langley*'s survivors to another American ship at Christmas Island, *Edsall* had the misfortune to meet two Japanese battleships, the *Hiei* and the *Kirishima,* and was sunk in a hopeless action. *Alden* and *John D.*

Express, with her huge load of *Prince of Wales* survivors, was the first of the rescue ships to reach Singapore. Despite numerous signals sent earlier, giving the estimated time of her arrival, the destroyer found that she could get no reply from the Signal Station at Changi Point. To proceed up Johore Strait without first being 'booked in' at Changi was forbidden and would incur the risk of being shelled by coastal artillery. Lieutenant-Commander Cartwright fumed as his signaller tried in vain to get a reply to his flashing lamp signals.

We came in absolutely packed with survivors and had to stand off Changi Signal Station for nearly twenty-five minutes before we could get a reply. If I'd had any ammunition left, I'd have put a shell right through them. I was furious.

Changi eventually woke up and allowed *Express* to proceed. The destroyer reached the Naval Base at 23.10 and secured alongside. *Vampire* soon followed, and then Commander May brought *Electra* in and berthed at exactly midnight.

Survivors of shipwreck always seem to have a dazed, anonymous appearance when landing and the men of *Prince of Wales* and *Repulse* were no exception. Many were only partially dressed, few had badges of rank, most were exhausted and filthy from the fuel oil. They came ashore by the hundreds on to the quayside of the Naval Base; one wonders whether the planners and naval strategists had ever envisaged such an ignominious scene as this one.

There was, of course, the greatest sympathy and much help for the survivors. The crew of the recently arrived H.M.S. *Exeter* – another Devonport-manned ship – were prominent at the scene, as were the permanent staff of the Naval Base. The wounded came off on stretchers; the

Edwards both fought in the Battle of the Java Sea and, with *Whipple*, eventually returned to the United States. These three ships spent most of the remaining war years as escorts on Atlantic convoys.

H.M.S. *Stronghold* was sunk by Japanese warships on 4 March 1942 while attempting to escape to Australia after the Japanese invasion of Java.

dazed were helped ashore or even carried pick-a-back. One filthy survivor, walking gingerly barefoot over the gravel chippings of the quayside, was offered a lift by an officer. The survivor protested that the officer would ruin his spotless white uniform '. . . . the uniform. Get up on my back.' A lonely figure on the quayside was the young Midshipman Leach, searching for his father.

When *Express* pulled in to secure, someone had shouted up from the quayside, 'How big was the Jap Fleet you clued up with?' The reply, from someone on the destroyer, was, 'A bloody big air fleet.' And, when *Electra*'s load of survivors were going ashore, one of her crew shouted, 'Come back tomorrow, you shower of B's, and clean our ship of oil fuel'; but another man remembers that the landing was carried out 'in a grim sort of silence with no laughing or yelling'. The last survivors were soon ashore and the crews of the destroyers were allowed to rest; most fell at once into a deep sleep, and the authorities were sympathetic enough not to disturb them for twelve hours. One *Express* crew member remembers the desolate scene aboard his ship – 'The breeze blowing discarded bandages flapping from the upper superstructure, blood smeared across paintwork, and that smell of anaesthetic everywhere.'

Once ashore, the survivors were given sandwiches, cigarettes and more rum, the latter in almost unlimited quantities, perhaps in order to force men to vomit again and get rid of the last of the oil they had swallowed. The staff of the base had set up a row of tables and chairs under arc lights and had been waiting for the survivors. Each survivor made his way to this reporting centre and gave his rank, name and service number. All this activity was taking place in the middle of the night after the most traumatic day in the lives of most of them, and many were now near the end of their tether. One disillusioned member of the base staff describes them as 'a drunken, oil-sodden, undisciplined rabble but this was not surprising in view of the events'; and an officer from H.M.S. *Mauritius*, who was helping, observed among the survivors 'a feeling of shame and, in a few cases, some tears'.

After giving in their names, the survivors were led away to the Fleet Shore Accommodation and put to bed.

The contrast between the mood at Singapore and that among the Japanese involved in the recent action can easily be imagined. As long as the action had continued, there had been furious activity with the Japanese directing their submarines and surface vessels to the scene of the battle off Kuantan. Plans were actually made to rearm the returning aircraft and carry out a second strike at the British ships. The Japanese had been desperately anxious to finish off *Prince of Wales* and *Repulse* in any way possible so that their operations could be resumed in the way intended before the untimely arrival of the two British ships at Singapore.

It was a stroke of good fortune for the Japanese that the Buffaloes of 453 Squadron did not arrive on the scene a few minutes before they did; Midshipman Hoashi had just had time to see *Prince of Wales* capsize and float bottom upwards before escaping into the cloud. He knew there could be no survival for the battleship and was thus able to signal to his base that both the British capital ships had been destroyed. Had the Buffaloes arrived a little earlier, this valuable piece of information would not have reached Saigon. The Japanese would thus have had to continue with their efforts to finish off *Prince of Wales*, but Hoashi's report released them from this anxiety. The submarines and surface warships were recalled; the merchant ships supplying the Japanese invasion forces were ordered to resume work; the plan for the second aircraft strike was abandoned. The whole of the Japanese naval effort in this area could now be directed without fear of interference on the next stage of their war plan. This was the first fruit of the victory the airmen had achieved off Kuantan.

These airmen had also picked up Hoashi's signal while flying back to Saigon. They could hardly believe what they

heard – these two great warships both sunk by their aero-
planes in just one series of attacks! The feelings of jubilation among the Japanese aircrews may also easily be
imagined.

Saigon had ordered that any returning aircraft short of
fuel could divert to the recently captured R.A.F. airfield
at Kota Bharu, and several pilots took advantage of this.
The remainder flew on to Indo-China and landed there to a
great welcome from the ground staffs. One Mitsubishi
Betty of the Kanoya Air Corps, seriously damaged by
British anti-aircraft fire during the last hectic series of
torpedo attacks, crashed on landing and was completely
wrecked, though there is no record of casualties among its
crew. Midshipman Hoashi was one of the last to land, his
Nell having been in the air for thirteen hours! This young
pilot and his crew had certainly served their Emperor well.
There were great parties on the Japanese airfields that
night. Two small statements have filtered through the
intervening years: one, that 'the victory was celebrated
against the current background of hatred for the British
and the West'; the other that the airmen all got 'roaring
drunk'.

There was one surprising sequel to the Japanese victory.
Next morning, Lieutenant Iki of the Kanoya Air Corps
flew again over the scene of the sinkings and dropped a
wreath at the spot where so many men had died a few
hours earlier. This wreath has been recorded as being a
tribute by Lieutenant Iki to the bravery of the British
sailors who had fought their ships to the end. It will be
shown later that there were connections between the
Japanese Naval Air Force and the Royal Navy, and there
is no need to doubt Iki's sincerity. However, the crews of
the two aircraft flying alongside Iki in his attack on the
Repulse had both been shot down and killed before his eyes,
and the Japanese pilot was almost certainly honouring
these dead comrades as well as his British adversaries.

It was obvious that many high-level questions about the

recent action would soon be asked in Britain, and there was much writing of reports to be done before the survivors of the two ships were allowed to disperse. Of the *Repulse* men, it was only some of the officers who had to sit down and write out their memories of the action; it was realized that the loss of an old 1916 battle cruiser after being hit by five torpedoes was not exceptional. But the loss of *Prince of Wales*, and especially the fact of the extensive damage caused by the first torpedo hit, was not going to be passed off so lightly, and hence many of her senior ratings had also to make reports. This work was coordinated by Lieutenant-Commander A. G. Skipwith, who had been first lieutenant in *Prince of Wales* and who was her senior surviving executive branch officer. It took six days for Skipwith to take these preliminary statements, and he sent copies off to London by two different routes to ensure that at least one copy arrived safely. Skipwith's covering letter expressed the hope that these statements would 'provide valuable data for future constructions'. The documents were preserved and are now in the Public Record Office in London. They were only the first of a great mass of paperwork concerning the loss of this battleship that would eventually accumulate.

Another man busy making out a report was Flight Lieutenant Tim Vigors who had led the belated attempt by 453 Squadron to provide Force Z with fighter cover. The day after the sinkings he sat down and, on his own initiative, wrote this letter.

> R.A.A.F. Station, Sembawang.
> 11/12/41.

To Commander-in-Chief,
Far Eastern Fleet.

Sir,
I had the privilege to be the first aircraft to reach the crews of the *Prince of Wales* and the *Repulse* after they had been sunk. I say the privilege for, during the next hour while I flew low over them, I witnessed a show of that indomitable spirit for which the Royal Navy is so famous. I have seen a show of spirit in this war over Dunkirk,

during the 'Battle of Britain' and in the London night raids, but never before have I seen anything so comparable with what I saw yesterday. I passed over thousands who had been through an ordeal, the greatness of which they alone can understand, for it is impossible to pass on one's feelings in disaster to others.

Even to an eye so inexperienced as mine it was obvious that the three destroyers were going to take hours to pick up those hundreds of men clinging to wreckage and swimming around in the filthy oily water. Above all this, the threat of another bombing and machine-gun attack was imminent. Every one of those men must have realized that. Yet, as I flew around, every man waved and put his thumb up as I flew over him.

After an hour, lack of petrol forced me to leave but during that hour I had seen so many men in dire danger waving, cheering and joking as if they were holidaymakers at Brighton waving at a low flying aircraft. It shook me, for here was something above human nature. I take off my hat to them, for in them I saw the spirit which wins wars.

I apologize for taking up your valuable time, but I thought you should know of the incredible conduct of your men.
I have the honour to be,
Sir,
Your obedient servant,
Signed T. A. Vigors Flt/Lt
O.C. 453 Squadron.

This letter went first to Air Headquarters, from where it was sent to Naval Headquarters with a covering letter from Air Vice-Marshal Pulford which stated that 'the whole of the personnel under my command would like to join in' the tribute paid to the sailors by Flight Lieutenant Vigors. Vigors's letter too was preserved and was eventually published in the British Official History. When this appeared in 1957, many men who had been in the water or on Carley floats when Vigors had flown just over their heads were amused or slightly contemptuous to see that the pilot had taken their shaking fists and shouted abuse to be friendly greetings.

Flight Lieutenant Vigors had felt particularly bitter that his pilots had not been allowed to take off until long after the Japanese air attacks on the British ships had started. He had intended to carry out a more detailed investigation into this failure for his own interest rather than for official use, but he was shot down and badly burned a few days later. Until he was contacted for the research for this book, he was still firmly convinced that there had been a fifty-minute delay in passing on *Repulse's* first signal, about being under Japanese aircraft attack, to Sembawang. The actual time-lapse was only fifteen minutes.

Half a world away there was more paperwork, but here of a far sadder nature. Petty Officer Wren Muriel Saunders was in charge of seven or eight Wrens in the Casualty Office at H.M.S. *Drake*, the naval shore establishment at Devonport which had originally provided the crews for both *Repulse* and *Prince of Wales*.

For some reason I cannot now recall, I had gone to lunch at my mother's house at the far side of Plymouth. We had the radio on and I was completely shocked to learn from an announcement by the B.B.C. that the *Prince of Wales* and *Repulse* had been sunk by the Japanese. Within half an hour, while I was still wondering what to do, a dispatch rider arrived, having been sent by the Drafting Commander to recall me to Barracks. I remember the pillion ride across town – a little unorthodox in those days. On arrival at the Barracks it was quite evident what devastating repercussions the radio announcement was to have on anxious relatives and friends of those serving in the two vessels. As for us, we could only gather together the record cards and look at the names of those involved in the action and pray. There were names of many on those cards well known to us in our section and even colleagues of previous months were on board.

The telephone lines were jammed and, indeed, I recall a family whose anxiety brought them immediately from Liverpool to stand by the barrack gates and wait.

We waited too and I remember the signals eventually arriving from Admiralty and the mounting horror, as we read the names of survivors picked up or landed at Singapore, at the magnitude of the disaster. From those survivor lists we did our grim subtraction from the total complement on board and, harassed from all sides, the pressure was then upon us. I recall the Drafting Commander putting our department out of bounds to all except the seven or eight Wrens while we plied our sorry task of typing hour after hour, over and over again, the words 'missing on war service'.

We had the Welfare Office next to our domain and at that time I trod the covered way between the two departments all too frequently. I recall meeting there a young woman some time after the next of kin had been informed who appeared to have had no news at all of a certain rating. She showed me a picture of herself with him and their children. I checked of course and my immediate suspicions were confirmed. His real wife somewhere in the North had already been told and it was evident that he had contracted a bigamous marriage. Her distress in the double disaster with which she was now faced was harrowing to say the least. I recall that he was one of those we 'presumed dead' many years later. I remember many other incidents – but perhaps my pen runs away with me and none of these recollections of mine may be of interest to you at all.

15

An Analysis

Many questions about the sinkings were being asked by
British politicians and press. Why had two capital ships
been sent from England to the Far East without an aircraft
carrier? Why, once war had broken out, had these two
ships been sent out without adequate land-based air cover?
Why had the two ships and their escorts failed so miserably
to defend themselves against the aircraft of a nation that
had been considered so inferior in the art of waging war?
How had the modern *Prince of Wales* been crippled so
easily?

These were all valid questions to which the politicians
and the press did receive some immediate answers and to
which more detailed answers can be given here. Before
doing so, however, it may be useful to summarize the
factual losses of both sides in that action off Kuantan.

Within a few hours Britain had lost one First World War
battle cruiser and one modern battleship. This was the
first occasion since Jutland that the Royal Navy had lost
two capital ships on one day. If we count aircraft carriers
as capital ships, *Repulse* and *Prince of Wales* were the seventh
and eighth such ships to be lost by Britain during this war.
In fact it had been a disastrous few weeks for the navy
because, with the aircraft carrier *Ark Royal* and the battleship *Barham* both torpedoed by German submarines in
the Mediterranean in the previous month, four capital
ships had now been lost in just four weeks, although the
loss of *Barham* had not yet been publicly announced. In
purely material terms, Britain could perhaps afford to lose
the old *Repulse*; there still remained nine First World War
battleships or battle cruisers. But the loss of *Prince of
Wales* was a great setback as only three modern or semi-

modern battleships were left in service – *King George V*, *Nelson* and *Rodney* – though three more of the King George V Class would soon be available.

The two ships lost had been carrying 2,921 men when they had been sunk, and of these 840 had lost their lives (Table 1 below gives a more detailed break down). The

Table 1.

	Aboard	Lost	Percentage lost
Repulse			
Officers	69	27	39·1
Ratings	1,240	486	39·2
Total	1,309	513	39·2
Prince of Wales			
Officers	110	20	18·2
Ratings	1,502	307	20·4
Total	1,612	327	20·3

overall fatal casualty rate was 28·8 per cent, and, surprisingly perhaps, a higher proportion of officers had survived than ratings. This occurred mainly in *Prince of Wales*, and may be partly explained by the presence aboard the flagship of Admiral Phillips's staff officers – men who were without responsibility for departments and most of whom were well above deck in the armoured conning tower and were released by Phillips well before *Prince of Wales* actually sank.

Repulse's crew had suffered almost twice as heavily as had that of *Prince of Wales*. This can be accounted for by the simple fact that *Repulse* had sunk quickly after being first struck by torpedoes, crew members still being at

Action Stations a few minutes before the ship heeled over and went down. *Prince of Wales* had been virtually a hulk for some time before sinking, and a great many men had been able to come up from their posts below deck and take part in a more leisurely escape. Although Force Z had suffered several strokes of cruel luck that morning, all the factors affecting the rescue operation had been favourable. The sea was warm and calm, the Japanese aircraft had not interfered in any way with the rescue work, and there had been just enough destroyers to pick up all survivors before dark. The Japanese had estimated that the rescue work would not be so successful, and a report recorded in their Official History had concluded that the greater part of the two ships' companies would be drowned.

The warm seas into which *Repulse* and *Prince of Wales* sank are the home of several species of man-eating sharks, particularly the Great White Shark or White Pointer (*Carcharoden carcharias*). The sailors knew of this danger and there had been much apprehension over the possibility of being taken by sharks. In fact, one officer's report in the Public Record Office mentions the fins of sharks being seen and men heard screaming. The subject of sharks and the possibility that some of the survivors may have lost their lives in this way has been investigated closely by the authors, but we have not been able to find one witness who actually saw one of his friends attacked or who saw live sharks on that day. It is thought almost certain that, however many different ways in which men did perish on that day, no one died in this repulsive manner, though some dead bodies not covered in oil may later have been savaged.

A man's post above or below deck had much influence upon his chance of survival, and the most fortunate of the larger groups were probably the men of the Royal Marine detachments whose duties were mainly in gun positions on deck. No Royal Marine officer became a casualty in either ship, and only twenty-seven out of 192 marines in *Prince of Wales* died – a casualty rate well below the normal for the battleship. Age may also have been a survival factor. Only four of fourteen warrant officers aboard *Repulse* managed to survive, though, at the other extreme, thirty boy seamen from both ships and one Royal Marine boy bugler were lost. Particularly tragic were the deaths of one of the two sets of twins aboard *Prince of Wales*. Boys 1st Class Robert and James Young, only seventeen years old, had joined the Navy from a Cheltenham orphanage. The *Gloucestershire Echo*, reporting their deaths, told of the swimming and lifesaving badges the two lads had once held, but these had not saved their lives. This newspaper also reported the loss in *Prince of Wales* of Signalman R. A. Jones, the first member of the newspaper's staff to die in this war.

The youngest casualties of all were two sixteen-year-olds, Canteen Assistant George Henderson of Edinburgh, lost in *Repulse*, and Boy Bugler Gilbert Stapleton of *Prince of Wales*. The oldest casualty was fifty-four-year-old Able Seaman W. H. Jeffery, a Cornishman in *Prince of Wales*, and close behind was the Commander-in-Chief himself, Admiral Sir Tom Phillips, aged fifty-three.

The two press correspondents and the Admiralty photographer aboard *Repulse* all survived. Cecil Brown and O'Dowd Gallagher wrote their own books on the action, and, after the war, Lieutenant Horace Abrahams went, of all places, to Japan as a Keystone Press Agency photographer. In 1958, at a Tokyo hotel, Abrahams and Cecil Brown met Lieutenant Sadao Takai who had led one of the Genzan Air Corps squadrons that had attacked *Repulse* but without scoring any torpedo hits. The Japanese was at first reluctant to come, but the strange reunion went well.

The destroyers had suffered no casualties apart from the man injured when *Tenedos* had been bombed – though many miles from the main action – and the one seaman in *Express* who had become shell-shocked by the gunfire of his own ship.

Seldom can a major battle have been so one-sided in its

casualty lists. In addition to their reconnaissance planes, the Japanese had launched eighty-five Nell and Betty attack aircraft into the operation. Eighteen of these had failed to attack the main British force: nine bombers had wasted their bomb loads on *Tenedos*; nine more had released their bombs in error just short of Force Z; and one torpedo-carrying aircraft had turned back with engine trouble. Table 2 gives the performances and casualties of the attacking forces.

Table 2.

Air Corps	Took off	Attacked	Hits scored	Shot down	Damaged
A. *Torpedo Attack Aircraft*					
Genzan	17	16*	2	1	7
Kanoya	26	26	9	2	10
Mihoro	8	8	0	0	0
Totals	51	50	11	3	17
B. *Bomber Attack Aircraft*					
Genzan	9	0	0	0	0
Mihoro	25	16*	2	0	11†
Totals	34	16	2	0	11

* One Genzan aircraft's torpedo release and one Mihoro's bomb release failed to function, but they are counted here as having attacked.

† One Mihoro aircraft crashed on landing.

Eighteen airmen, all petty officers or ratings, had died in the three aircraft shot down. The Japanese Official History states that these were the result of attempted suicide attacks made by aircraft whose crews knew that their planes had been too badly hit to survive. This may be true of the first plane shot down, which crashed close alongside *Prince of Wales*, but the last two were shot down by *Repulse*'s pom-poms and crashed straight into the sea. Considering their hatred for the British at that time, their warrior code and love of Emperor, the crews of all three planes probably died happy men. Some British documents of the period mistakenly claimed seven Japanese aircraft shot down, others five. Of the Japanese aircraft that returned, one crashed on landing and twenty-seven were damaged, but all except three of these were only slightly damaged and were capable of local repair. It is not recorded that any of the crews of the returning aircraft suffered casualties.

As we have already remarked, the Japanese Official History, published in 1969, persisted in the view that no less than twenty-one of the forty-nine torpedoes launched against *Prince of Wales* and *Repulse* had scored hits, despite the fact that the British Official History, published twelve years earlier, had given a figure of ten torpedo hits – five on each ship. It is now thought that *Prince of Wales* was hit six times, counting the torpedo which exploded just a few feet away from the port side in the first attack, and eleven torpedo hits in all is probably the correct figure. The Japanese also claimed three bomb hits, though there were only two.

Despite their overclaiming – not uncommon in all forms of warfare involving hectic action – the Japanese airmen had done extraordinarily well. Russia's President Stalin, in a letter to Churchill, was convinced that aircraft flown by Japanese crews could not have achieved this great success and believed that these aircraft were either German planes that had somehow been got out to Japan in time for the opening of hostilities in the Far East, or were, at least, Japanese aircraft flown by German crews. Stalin had recently noted a lack of German air activity on the Russian Front and had been told by his advisers that Germany had sent 1,500 aircraft to Japan! It is more likely that the scarcity of German aircraft seen in Russia was the result of the Luftwaffe's troubles in coping with their first Russian winter; there were no German aircraft in the Far East.

The Japanese success had, however, been achieved by a narrow margin. Rear-Admiral Matsunaga's last-minute decision to switch one squadron of aircraft from torpedo to bomb attack had nearly caused a failure. Matsunaga had probably made the change in an attempt to neutralize the British anti-aircraft fire still further and thus give his torpedo attackers a better chance to get in close, but the high-level bombers had turned out to have very little influence on the action and every last available torpedo aircraft had been needed to achieve the two sinkings. Had there been a few more misses among the earlier torpedo attacks, then the torpedoes of that diverted squadron would really have been needed. But the lucky hit on the stern of *Prince of Wales* crippled the battleship early on in the action and thus redressed the balance. Matsunaga's switch to the old-fashioned bomb attack had had no serious ill-effects.

The Japanese Official History compares the operation against *Prince of Wales* and *Repulse* with the results of pre-war training exercises. Against target battleships steaming at 14 knots and taking vigorous evasive action, the hit rate in practice torpedo attacks had been 70 per cent. The Japanese expected that under conditions of live action this would fall by one half. The actual hit rate in this action – against ships sometimes steaming at 25 not 14 knots – was eleven out of forty-nine, only 22 per cent. Their bombing practice results – again against targets steaming at 14 knots – had been only 12 per cent and was expected to fall to 6 or even 4 per cent in action. But the actual bomb hits on *Prince of Wales* and *Repulse* was two out of twenty-three; at nearly 9 per cent this was better than had been expected.

In the end it was the Bettys of the hard-driving Kanoya Air Corps squadron, with nine torpedo hits scored in three minutes at a cost of two aircraft shot down, that really settled the issue. These were the aircraft sent to Saigon, from the Philippines attack force stationed in Formosa, when the Japanese learnt that *Prince of Wales* and *Repulse* had reached Singapore. Rarely in warfare can the diversion of such a modest force from one campaign to another have paid off so handsomely. On the other hand, if there was one Japanese activity which almost brought them failure, it was their signals procedure, which over and over again failed at crucial times.

It is absolute irony that the Japanese Naval Air Service had originally been helped into being by an American and a Briton. In 1919, a rich American, who insisted on remaining anonymous, gave the Japanese government a large sum of money to buy aircraft and train pilots as he felt that Japanese had all the right attributes to make fine aviators. Five years later, the British sent to Japan a Naval Mission headed by Commander Forbes-Sempill – Lord Sempill, known also as the Master of Sempill. He was a veteran naval pilot of the First World War, and his task was to help Japan, a country still friendly at that time, to establish its first small naval air arm. After the Second World War, a British officer was told by the famous Japanese naval airman, Commander Minoru Genda, the man who had planned the Pearl Harbor attack, that, 'Of course, it was the grandsons of the Master of Sempill who sank the *Prince of Wales* and *Repulse*.'

Although the Japanese Navy was as guilty as the other Japanese services in committing what the West would regard as war atrocities between 1941 and 1945, the crews of the Genzan, Mihoro and Kanoya Air Corps had perhaps carried forward some of the Master of Sempill's British traditions. They had fought a clean battle with no machine-gunning of survivors or any interference with the rescue work of the destroyers. Lieutenant Iki's wreath-dropping ceremony at the scene of the sinkings on the morning after the battle was a rare incident of chivalry in the Far Eastern war.

Having detailed the factual losses – two ships, so many

aircraft, so many men – there is more to be gained by a study of the larger issues such as the War Cabinet decision to send two capital ships East at that stage in the war, the decision by Admiral Phillips to sail from Singapore and his judgement concerning the danger to his ships from the Japanese aircraft known to be at Saigon. And, once the ships had sailed from Singapore, should the operation have been handled differently and could the individual ships in Force Z have been fought any better once they were attacked? What were the immediate and then the long-term effects of the loss of the only British capital ships in the Far East?

But one thing must be stated clearly: the authors of this book are fully aware of the huge advantages given to them by hindsight and by the ability to study at leisure problems which wartime commanders had to solve under pressure and always with only partial knowledge of any given situation. These wartime men had often to guess and gamble and then stake their reputations and sometimes their lives on the result. The comments that follow now acknowledge the privilege of the post-war historian's position, and any criticisms made are academic ones and have no intention of diminishing the stature of wartime leaders.

This book started by describing the changing nature of Japan in the years following the First World War when she ceased to be an active ally of Britain and the United States, and when, through jealousy, ambition and the results of Western insults, Japan moved to a position from which she threatened the Far Eastern interests of Britain, the United States and Holland. It is difficult to assess whether more skilful diplomacy between the wars could have arrested this deterioration in Japan's relations with the West; perhaps diplomacy could have slowed the process down, but it is more likely that appeasement would have been taken for weakness (as it was so taken by Hitler in the same years), and that a clash with Japan was inevitable, although the proud posture of the West and the racial insults handed out to the Japanese were unprovoked and were certainly the cause of much of the trouble.

Britain's decision to build a base at Singapore to protect her legitimate interests in the Far East as well as the peoples of Australia and New Zealand drew a bitter reaction from Japan, though it probably did no more than accelerate the inevitable decline in relations; on its own, the Singapore Naval Base was not a *causus belli*. But, once the European war had broken out, the dilemma of the War Cabinet over the use and defence of the Naval Base, the planned linch-pin of the Far Eastern defences, was a cruel one. The homeland was in real danger of defeat in 1940, and that danger had not yet fully receded in 1941. Every man, tank, gun, ship or aeroplane dispatched to the East was sent at the risk of the homeland's own safety.

But there is scope for an examination of the resources available to the three services at that time. By War Cabinet decision in August 1940, the R.A.F. had been given the main responsibility for defending Malaya and Singapore and was asked to re-equip the Far East squadrons with modern aircraft before the end of 1941 if possible. By late 1941, however, Britain was sending large quantities of modern fighters – though only a few pilots – to Russia; Fighter Command was maintaining a huge force of fighter squadrons in England in case the Luftwaffe came back and tried a second Battle of Britain; and Bomber Command was consuming ever-increasing quantities of aircraft and aircrews for the strategic bombing campaign against Germany for which Churchill and the 'bomber barons' had such high hopes. Not one modern aircraft was sent to the Far East. The R.A.F., faced with a real war in Europe and the dream of ending a modern war there by the relentless use of the heavy bomber against the industrial heartland of the enemy, chose to keep their main strength and all their modern aircraft at home. It must be emphasized that this policy had the full and active support of Churchill himself.

In supporting this policy, the Air Ministry must bear some responsibility for the failures in the Far East. When the R.A.F. was asked to take over the main responsibility for the defence of Malaya, the Army committed its main strength to the defence of airfields. A few squadrons of Spitfires or Hurricanes could have slaughtered the Mitsubishis which so casually bombed the R.A.F. out of those airfields. Modern heavy bombers could have bombed both the invasion convoys and the Japanese airfields around Saigon. That was supposed to have been the cornerstone of the new policy for the defence of Malaya. The service that was the ultimate loser by the Air Ministry's reluctance to provide modern aircraft for the Far East was the unfortunate Army – caught deployed for the defence of airfields which had no effective aircraft flying from them and which were often evacuated by the R.A.F. in the early stages.

Once the R.A.F. had virtually released themselves from their Far Eastern obligations by their failure to implement the War Cabinet decision, the War Cabinet was bound to fall back on the possibility of sending capital ships to the Far East as soon as the war clouds started gathering there in mid-1941. This was, after all, why the Singapore Naval Base had originally been built and subsequently maintained at considerable expense. And, if the ships could be got out to the East early enough and in sufficient strength, their presence might persuade the Japanese not to attack. This – the deterrent effect – was the main purpose of the dispatch of capital ships.

The next question was how many ships and of what type. The decision eventually arrived at has been detailed in an earlier chapter and may be passed over quickly. The choice of *Prince of Wales*, *Repulse* and *Indomitable* was as good as any. The choice of *Repulse* did not represent a great sacrifice to the Navy's responsibilities in the European war; she was one of many old battleships and battle cruisers – albeit faster than most – that the Navy was finding some difficulty in keeping usefully employed. It was more of a hardship to part with the modern *Prince of Wales*, but later events were to show that Churchill was correct in insisting that the absence of *Prince of Wales* would have no serious effect on the Navy's problems in Europe. The Germans never did send *Tirpitz* out in bold manner, and in purely material terms *Prince of Wales* was never missed from European waters.

In all the considerations of this affair it must never be forgotten that the Admiralty *had* allocated one of its modern aircraft carriers for the Singapore-bound force. It was the cruellest misfortune that *Indomitable* should have gone aground in the West Indies. Her repairs only took twenty-five days, but the loss of those days was never retrieved. It is fascinating to speculate how the battle off Kuantan might have turned out had *Indomitable*, with her nine Hurricane fighters, been in company with *Prince of Wales* and *Repulse*. It is significant that, as soon as war did break out in the Far East, the R.A.F. was able to find fifty Hurricanes and their pilots to put aboard *Indomitable* at Port Sudan for the belated reinforcement of Malaya.

The deterrent purpose of sending the ships East was a complete failure. The all-pervading under-estimation of Japanese ability and strength, and the fact that the Japanese were hell-bent on war, however many ships Britain sent out to Singapore, meant that there was really no naval deterrent force that Britain could have spared at that time that would have made any difference. It is true that the local Japanese commanders in the Malayan operation were concerned about the British naval reinforcements and were certainly relieved when these were disposed of, but there is no evidence that the Japanese central leadership ever seriously reconsidered their war plans on this account. Whether they would have thought twice if Britain had earlier sent Spitfires, Hurricanes and modern heavy bombers to Malaya is another matter. This is a hypothetical question to which there is no ready answer.

The sightings of the Japanese invasion convoys on 6

December 1941 provided the visible evidence that the deterrent aspect of the British ships' presence had failed. The study of events therefore now focuses on the decision to sail *Prince of Wales*, *Repulse* and their destroyer escorts in the attempt to catch and destroy the Japanese troopships. Because of the command set-up at Singapore, with the Royal Navy being excluded from the province of Commander-in-Chief Far East, and because the Admiralty in London found it difficult to control operations in an area nearly half a world away, Admiral Sir Tom Phillips was, for a naval commander, in the unique position of having almost absolute freedom in the way he handled his powerful forces. It is ironic that a man who had so often occupied the long-range control seat at the Admiralty in so many naval operations since 1939 should now be the first commander at sea able to play a lone hand in a major action. The study of events from this point until the death of Admiral Phillips must inevitably become a study of this officer's attitude to the situation in which he found himself and of the decisions he made.

The Admiralty had urged Phillips to get one or both of his ships away from Singapore before war commenced, though this was probably to lessen the risk of the ships being caught in harbour by aircraft attack or bottled up by submarines. Once the Japanese attacks in the Far East commenced, Phillips had no option but to sail from Singapore and seek out the Japanese landing forces. He had good intelligence about the Japanese mines, submarines, warships and aircraft. The mines his ships could and did avoid, submarines also. His big ships would have thrashed the Japanese surface warships if encountering them in reasonable conditions. But the air – that was the less certain element.

Again we come back to the known facts of the time: that, despite Billy Mitchell's pre-war trials, despite the warnings of R.A.F. officers, *no major warship had yet been sunk by aircraft attack while at sea and many had survived such attacks*. And the prize? If his two big ships could have got in among the Japanese shipping off the invasion beaches, there would have been a veritable slaughter, a great victory for the Navy and possibly salvation for Malaya and Singapore. Such a result would have been the complete vindication of years of naval policy. It is probable that Air Chief Marshal Brooke-Popham did try to stop Phillips, whose rank was junior to his own, but Brooke-Popham had no authority to order a naval operation to be cancelled. It might have been better if he had; the Navy could not then have been accused of failing to try their best if their local commander had been overruled.

It is clear from Japanese documents, however, that the decision taken on the morning of 8 December to sail that evening was already too late. As the Japanese quotation about the situation on the 9th, when Force Z was still eighteen hours' steaming from the invasion beaches, stated: 'Even if the British attacked from now onwards, there would be no damage done to the military units already landed and any damage would only be to empty ships and to a small quantity of supplies . . . The British naval force had lost their best chance.' The best time to sail would have been late on the 6th or on the 7th, soon after the Japanese convoys had been sighted while still at sea. But *Repulse* was away on its voyage to Australia and Phillips was at Manila conferring with the Americans. The very latest time to have sailed from Singapore and still to have had a chance of influencing the outcome of the Japanese landings would have been at dawn on the 8th, followed by a direct dash north through the Japanese minefield. But to criticize the delay until the evening departure of the 8th is to take undue advantage of hindsight; no one at Singapore guessed that the Japanese would complete the landings so swiftly.

What is more debatable is the role played in this operation by the R.A.F. and the general attitude of Admiral Phillips towards air cover. Before sailing, Phillips had asked for fighter cover and aerial reconnaissance. The latter was provided and is not the subject of any dispute, but the story of fighter cover is central to the tragedy of *Repulse* and *Prince of Wales*. The R.A.F. had earmarked the Australian 453 Squadron as 'Fleet Defence Squadron', and its commander discussed the problems and opportunities available with the Air Liaison Officer on Admiral Phillips's staff before Force Z sailed. Flight Lieutenant Vigors estimated that, if his squadron could use the airfields on the east coast of Malaya, 'I could keep a standing patrol of six aircraft over the fleet at all times during daylight providing the fleet did not go more than 100 miles north of Kota Bharu and not further than sixty miles from the coast at any time.' But this plan had not been adopted, much to Vigors's disgust. Admiral Phillips was clearly not prepared to restrict his freedom of action by staying so close to the coast – there was, after all, the Japanese minefield to consider – and not willing to risk the breaking of radio silence that might be made necessary by such cooperation. It was probably the Navy's refusal to agree on these important points that caused the R.A.F. to send, a few hours after Force Z had sailed, that well-known signal informing Phillips that fighter cover could not be guaranteed, although the heavy casualties then being suffered by the R.A.F.'s squadrons and the damage being inflicted on their up-country airfields were also factors.

So Force Z sailed into the blue, all the time keeping strict wireless silence. The coastal airfields that Flight Lieutenant Vigors had hoped to use came under even further Japanese attack; and because of this, as well as a lack of knowledge of the movements of Force Z, the R.A.F. never sent 453 Squadron to these airfields so as to shorten the flight to Force Z should the ships be attacked and call for help. The Buffaloes were kept at the disposal of the Navy, at constant daylight readiness, but at the airfield at Sembawang on Singapore Island. R.A.F. Malaya would be reduced to fifty-nine serviceable aircraft *of all types* by the morning of 10 December, and while Admiral Phillips could not have known the full details of the R.A.F.'s worsening situation in the days after he sailed, it is reasonable to assume that he knew there were some fighter aircraft available should he call for them. This point is of the utmost importance and will be referred to later.

There are few comments to be made about the first twenty-four hours of Force Z's voyage. By judicious routing, the Japanese minefield was avoided. By bad luck, the British ships were spotted by I.65, though the Japanese were slow to profit from their knowledge. But once the British ships were sighted again and shadowed by the three Japanese seaplanes on the evening of the 9th, the game was as good as up, and it seems surprising that Admiral Phillips did not turn back at that moment. Instead, he continued to sail deeper into the Gulf of Siam that night in the hope of finding Japanese shipping off the beaches next morning. But such a course was just like 'sailing the Home Fleet into the Kattegat', as had been stated at his conference aboard *Prince of Wales* just before sailing, and, moreover, with the enemy having certain knowledge that the British ships were there. The Japanese Official History contains an interesting comment upon this stage of the operation.

What was the objective of the northward moves of the British ships? Was it to hinder our landing in the Kota Bharu area? Was it to cause confusion in our rear and look for prey there? Or was it a manifestation of the British Navy's principles of war to manoeuvre the enemy cleverly into an unfavourable position? It was up to us to go and find this out. Did they know or not know that we had torpedo aircraft and a number of large cruisers and destroyers? . . . Did they think that a large number of our attack aircraft in southern Indo-China were unserviceable?

The movement of the British ships might have been reckless but its audacity was to be admired. *

It was certainly a reckless move on the part of Phillips to steam on after having been so carefully shadowed by the three Japanese seaplanes. Phillips persisted with this for a

* Japanese Official History, p. 484.

further two hours, and it is highly significant that he only gave up his course of action after seeing the flare dropped by the Japanese bomber over the Japanese cruiser *Chokai*. It was this flare, believed by Phillips to be a sign of Japanese surface warship activity, that finally caused him to turn back. It is probable that Phillips would not have persisted in his plan to raid the invasion areas next morning even if that flare had not been seen; his next signal to *Repulse* said that he had given up because of the Japanese seaplanes seen before dark. The popular view is that he had decided to give up the operation after realizing that the Japanese seaplanes had reported him before dark and that he had been intending to turn south to return to Singapore at midnight. But the two hours' further steaming towards the invasion beaches were taking Force Z ever farther from home and safety. It was a dangerous course of action, and his turn away to the south, after seeing the flare, was long overdue.

The whole affair was then complicated by the signal of a Japanese landing at Kuantan. There are no grounds for criticism in Phillips's decision to sail towards that area on his way back to Singapore; he was not to know that the report was based on false information, and he could hardly have returned without investigating.

The first of four major errors was, however, committed off Kuantan next morning. Force Z was now close enough to land to be well within the reach of any R.A.F. fighter cover, yet, when the suspected Japanese plane was seen at 06.45, no signal requesting such cover was sent. Whether or not that particular plane was really Japanese is not known, but it would certainly have been prudent at this stage to ask for air cover. Secondly, once the Walrus aircraft had reported no sign of Japanese activity in the Kuantan area, there was absolutely no need to hang about longer. Indeed, the hour lost by sending the destroyer *Express* close inshore to investigate further was to prove critical. Then, thirdly, the turn north-east by the whole of Force Z to investigate one small vessel towing a few barges was a further error. One of the three destroyers or one of the two Walrus aircraft still available could easily have done the task. The time lost in this way did not amount to much since Midshipman Hoashi's reconnaissance plane turned up a few minutes later, but the decision was none the less a bad one.

It is sometimes suggested that Rear-Admiral Palliser, Phillips's Chief-of-Staff at Singapore, was the one to blame for the disaster that followed, having failed to read his commander's mind and arrange for air patrols to be over Force Z at Kuantan that morning. We cannot agree with this view. Palliser and Phillips had been together for six weeks, and Phillips had had ample opportunity to ensure that Palliser was 'tuned in' to his likely movements and needs. No one in *Prince of Wales* has ever stated that Admiral Phillips showed any sign of disappointment that Palliser had failed to provide fighters for him that morning.

The errors committed so far were, however, nothing to what was to follow, and it was with the appearance of Hoashi's aircraft that the fourth miscalculation was made and the disaster to come sealed. There was little doubt in anyone's mind that this Mitsubishi could easily be the forerunner of the considerable force of aircraft known to be available to the Japanese and which could be expected to be out looking for Force Z that morning. Phillips did then leave the tug and barges, turn Force Z south and order his ships to man their anti-aircraft armament; but still he made no effort to summon the R.A.F. fighters that he knew were allocated to him, even though there was no need for Force Z to maintain radio silence any longer. Why did Admiral Phillips not call for the fighters? It remains the biggest question about the whole operation, and the answer to it indicates the root cause of the disaster that followed.

To answer this question it is necessary to examine two things: first, the knowledge that was available to Admiral Phillips at that time, and secondly, his general attitude to the threat of air attack.

The basic fact was that it was not really a question of the method an enemy might use to deliver explosive charges against a ship, but the form of the charges themselves. A shell and a bomb could have very similar effects upon a capital ship, and such ships were built with armoured protection around their vital compartments to withstand a considerable battering. It did not matter, therefore, whether Force Z was attacked by Japanese warships, by high-level bombers or even dive-bombers. In fact, Japanese aircraft carrying bombs were probably the least of the dangers threatening *Prince of Wales* and *Repulse*. *Prince of Wales*, particularly, had a fine outfit of high-level anti-aircraft armament, and previous experience indicated that a large proportion of any bombs dropped would miss. The actual performance later that morning of the four Japanese squadrons allocated by Rear-Admiral Matsunaga to the high-level bomber role bore this out perfectly.

What every naval officer really feared – if fear is the right word to use – was the torpedo. A bomb or shell could cause damage, and often fearful casualties, on the upper decks, but a torpedo hit will open up the side of a ship and let in water. Although their ships had anti-torpedo bulges and elaborate systems of watertight compartments to minimize the effect of one or two torpedo hits, the sailors knew that no big ship was proof against sustained torpedo attack. Such an attack could come from submarines, small fast surface vessels or torpedo-carrying aircraft. A good destroyer screen and a constant high speed was the best defence against submarines, and as we saw in earlier chapters, two Japanese submarine attacks on Force Z failed. An attack by Japanese destroyers in daylight would have been no more than suicide for the attackers, and the fine climatic conditions of that morning gave Force Z complete protection from such a threat.

That left the torpedo-carrying bomber as the one important hazard about which Admiral Phillips should have been concerned. He had excellent intelligence on the number of Japanese aircraft at the Saigon airfields. He knew that some of these aircraft had reached and bombed Singapore on the first night of the war. Did he not then wonder whether such aircraft could also carry torpedoes and might be homing in on the signals of the spotter aircraft? Should he not have known that this was possible?

To the average Royal Navy officer of Phillips's generation, torpedo aircraft were mainly slow planes of limited range that had to be borne on aircraft carriers. The standard British aircraft of this type – the Swordfish – had put paid to three Italian battleships at Taranto, *in harbour*, and within the last few days the Japanese carrier-borne torpedo aircraft had surprised the United States Pacific Fleet in Pearl Harbor. The intelligence information available to Admiral Phillips was fairly definite that no Japanese aircraft carriers were within range of Force Z, and this intelligence was quite correct. But what about land-based torpedo aircraft, which could take off from long runways with the heavily laden fuel tanks that gave a greater range than that of carrier-borne aircraft? It was known that the Italians had such aircraft – the Savoia-Marchetti Types 79 and 84 had been seen often enough in the Mediterranean convoy battles. *Prince of Wales* had actually seen them in action in the 'Halberd' operation less than three months earlier. But the Savoias had not attacked *en masse* and had suffered severely from naval anti-aircraft fire; their torpedoes had scored few successes and their performance had not impressed the Royal Navy.

The British had also developed a land-based torpedo aircraft, the Bristol Beaufort. This twin-engined plane had roughly the same performance as the Nells and Bettys at Saigon and had already been in service with Coastal Command for a year. Unfortunately, Britain was feeling her way very slowly with this warfare technique and there were many inter-service difficulties to hinder its development. The R.A.F. was more interested in the strategic bomber, the Navy in conventional warships; caught between the two, Coastal Command had not flourished. But there had been an interesting operation in June 1941 when, in cooperation with the Admiralty, Coastal Command Beauforts flying from Scotland had attacked the German pocket battleship *Lützow* off Norway. The *Lützow* was surprised by three Beauforts and severely damaged by one torpedo hit. By the time a fourth Beaufort reached the scene, German fighter protection had arrived and this Beaufort was promptly shot down. *Lützow* was in dock for seven months.

All this happened while Admiral Phillips was at the Admiralty, and he must surely have known of the operation even if he had not been directly involved. Perhaps he would have taken more notice if *Lützow* had been sunk, but this incident, together with the Italian operations in the Mediterranean, should have shown Phillips that it was perfectly feasible for land-based Japanese torpedo aircraft to operate in the area off Kuantan in which *Prince of Wales* and *Repulse* were so leisurely steaming that morning. But it is clear from Phillips's remark, when the first Japanese torpedo bombers were seen coming in to make their attack, that he considered the possibility of the Japanese having developed such aircraft to be impossible. 'No,' said Phillips. 'There are no torpedo aircraft about.'

Admiral Phillips was not the only officer in Force Z to hold this view. Many of the surviving officers, younger and possibly more aviation-minded than Phillips, speak of their astonishment when these twin-engined aircraft carried out their first torpedo attack. The reasons for their amazement were two-fold: the failure of the Navy generally to appreciate that the land-based torpedo bomber was now an operational reality, and the more widespread belief that the Japanese were so far behind the West that they could not yet have developed an aircraft like the Beaufort or the Savoia-Marchetti. In fact, while Britain, Italy and later the Germans had been moving slowly in developing the land-based torpedo bomber, the Japanese had quietly out-thought everyone and were about to put their theories into action in a thoroughly convincing demonstration.

It is just possible that Naval Intelligence had established, possibly from the American deciphering service, that the Japanese aircraft known to be in Indo-China could carry torpedoes. There had been the peculiar signal to Admiral Phillips from the First Sea Lord warning of the danger of aerial attack against Force Z while in harbour. There is also hearsay evidence that the Intelligence Officer on Admiral Phillips's staff found, on his return to Singapore after the sinkings, that the naval staff ashore had known of the presence of Japanese torpedo bombers in Indo-China while Force Z had been at sea but had not thought it necessary to send a warning signal. Unfortunately the truth of this cannot be established because the officer involved is now dead.

So far it can be shown that Admiral Phillips was no more in error about the presence of torpedo bombers than many of his officers, apart from the fact that he had access to the latest intelligence on torpedo bomber development in Europe and must have known of the Beaufort operations against the *Lützow*. If it had stopped there, and if Admiral Phillips's attitude had been no more mistaken than his contemporaries, something might yet have been saved. But, throughout the operation, Phillips continued to show a disregard, almost a contempt, for the dangers of any type of air attack. It is possible (and no more than possible, for there is no hard evidence) that Phillips had quarrelled with Brooke-Popham over the potential danger from the air. It is probable that he had made difficulties over co-operating with the R.A.F. on 453 Squadron's provision of standing patrols. It is certain that, on that morning, at a time when nothing further could be gained by keeping his presence off Kuantan a secret, he did not call for the air cover which he could so easily have had.

It is true that, just after sailing from Singapore, Force Z had received a signal stating that the R.A.F. could not supply fighter protection on 10 December. But this signal had been the answer to the requests, made by Admiral Phillips before sailing, for various types of R.A.F. assistance – reconnaissance on 9 December, reconnaissance *off Singora* (in the Gulf of Siam) at first light on 10 December and fighter protection *off Singora* during daylight on the 10th. Rear Admiral Palliser, who had sent the signal, had not felt it necessary to add the two words 'off Singora' when telling Phillips that the R.A.F. could not provide the fighter cover there. Did Phillips interpret this signal as meaning that the R.A.F. could not provide any fighter cover, anywhere, not even off Kuantan which was within 160 miles of four airfields in southern Malaya and Singapore? Did Phillips think that the Buffalo squadron allocated to him before the operation would no longer be available, that the R.A.F. could find no help at all, that it was not even worth while sending a signal asking for help? It is more likely that Admiral Phillips was confident that his ships could defend themselves and that he was determined not to ask for the help of another service.

So Force Z continued to maintain radio silence after Midshipman Hoashi had settled down to shadow and report Force Z, and even when the first high-level bombers appeared at 11.00. It was only an incredible fifty-eight minutes later that Captain Tennant of *Repulse* finally got away the first signal. *Prince of Wales* never did signal, until she was virtually sinking, and even then all Phillips's signals asked for destroyers or tugs – purely *naval* answers to all his problems! Never ever an appeal for aircraft!

While these may seem harsh findings, the facts speak for themselves: two great ships and many good men were lost because one stubborn old sea-dog refused to acknowledge that he had been wrong. Consider the following two timetables, the first being the actual timing of events that morning, the second the timetable that would have been possible had Phillips called for air support three minutes after Midshipman Hoashi settled down to shadow Force Z.

Actual timetable

10.15   Japanese shadowing plane spotted by Force Z.

11.13   First high-level bombing attack commences.

11.40   First torpedo attack.

11.58   *Repulse* signals to Singapore.

12.20   453 Squadron takes off.

12.35   *Repulse* sinks.

13.20   453 Squadron arrives.

13.23   *Prince of Wales* sinks.

Possible timetable

10.15   Japanese shadowing plane spotted by Force Z.

10.18   Force Z requests fighter support.

10.30   453 Squadron takes off.

11.13   First high-level bombing attack commences.

11.30   453 Squadron arrives.

11.40   First torpedo attack.

There is nothing spurious about this second timetable. The
only variable is the time of the first signal from Force Z;
everything else would have followed as detailed. The
Buffaloes could, in practice, have arrived after *Repulse* had
been hit by just one 250-kg. bomb and before the disastrous
first torpedo attack that crippled *Prince of Wales*. It will
never be known what effect the eleven Buffaloes could have
had on the eventual outcome, but the Japanese bombers
had no fighter support and Vigors and his Australians
could certainly have done something to break up their
attacks. The Japanese airman were determined, even
fanatical, and some torpedoes would no doubt have struck
home, but surely not the great number that finally overwhelmed the two ships.

There is not much to be said about the manner in which the
British ships were fought once the Japanese attacks com-
menced. The initial handling of the Force by Admiral
Phillips had been too rigid, but he soon realized his mistake

and allowed his ships freedom of manoeuvre, after which it became a series of single-ship actions.

Prince of Wales was desperately unlucky in being crippled so early in the action, and neither Captain Leach nor his crew had much chance to show what they were worth after that. Her 5·25-in. guns were a menace to the Japanese aircraft to the end, and their Official History pays this tribute.

> The anti-aircraft fire of the British ships was extremely fierce and the damage suffered by the aircraft bombing from a straight and level approach at high altitude was very great. Consider just the Takeda squadron of eight aircraft which bombed last, when *Prince of Wales* had already reduced speed to about 6 knots and was sinking. Five of Takeda's aircraft were hit. *

This damage was caused by just two turrets, S1 and S2; how effectively might the full complement of these guns have performed had they not been robbed of power and denied a level platform by the early damage and the resulting list of *Prince of Wales*.†

It is sometimes suggested that the internal organization and morale in *Prince of Wales* broke down too quickly after the first torpedo hits, and it is true that this is how it might have appeared. But here was a ship that had never claimed to have been fully worked up, that was badly under-ventilated even when all power supplies were functioning, and which had suffered a loss of power and, above all, of communications that had never been envisaged and for which no drills had prepared the crew. While there was certainly some evidence of a lack of morale among this mainly wartime-conscripted crew, this was before the battle and there are no cases of outright failure of duty during the action other than the early departure from the ship by a few men who had probably been driven from their

---

* Japanese Official History, p. 478.

† Appendix Four contains the post-action report of Lieutenant-Commander C. W. McMullen, Gunnery Officer in *Prince of Wales*.

place of duty below an hour before and when the ship was clearly about to sink. Any weakness in the organization of *Prince of Wales* caused by the lack of a proper working-up period, or possibly by patchy morale, made no difference in the end to the way she was fought. No gun was left unmanned, no vital position was left unattended. The end, when it came, was quite inevitable. Instead of harping too much upon the few deficiencies in *Prince of Wales*, it would be more just to remember the many acts of gallantry seen to be performed by her crew.

The only thing that might just have delayed the sinking of *Prince of Wales* was a realization by Damage Control that the efforts of the electrical repair parties would have been better spent trying to cure the root cause of the electrical failure in the ring-main-breaker system and redistributing the available supply instead of spending their time attempting to rig up emergency supplies to such out-lying services as the gun turrets. But it was a vicious circle; the communications failure caused by the loss of electricity prevented the correct appreciation and allocation of re-sources, and to criticize here would again be an unfair use of hindsight.

Captain Tennant and the crew of *Repulse* never put a foot wrong. Their ship, poorly armed against aircraft attack, had fought to the end and simply been overwhelmed. The lack of any further comment here is simply because this gallant ship and her crew had done their best and could have done no more. *Repulse* should never have been put in the position of having to fight off repeated air attacks without friendly air cover when that cover was so easily available. Not only was her loss tragic, it was unnecessary.

The destroyers had few chances to shine. Before the action, they had twice failed to detect Japanese submarines that had fired torpedoes and then reported Force Z's position; but these were failures resulting from a lack of advanced Asdic equipment rather than deficiencies of training or spirit. The destroyers' pop-gun armament had been quite inadequate to deal with the swarm of attacking

Japanese aircraft. Their hour came with the rescue work, which was carried out with a fine display of seamanship, and they undoubtedly helped to keep down the casualty toll.

I think that, given the design of *Prince of Wales*, with certain inbuilt vulnerabilities, and with (as with the *Bismarck* earlier) a hit in the most sensitive and vulnerable area, there was no more that we on board could have done to keep her afloat and bring her in. This does not mean that there was no room for speculation and subsequent inquiry. There was. (Lieutenant D. B. H. Wildish)

Far higher authority than Lieutenant Wildish thought that certain questions about his ship should be answered. The British press were the first to be critical. The *Daily Herald* seemed remarkably well informed in alleging a delay by Admiral Phillips in asking for fighter support, as did the *Sunday Express* in criticizing the tradition by which Admiral Phillips had gone down with his ship. There followed, on 19 December, a secret debate in the House of Commons at which there were rumblings about the original decision to send the ships East, about the failure to provide an aircraft carrier or land-based aircraft cover, about the ineptitude of the authorities generally. Churchill was by then away in the United States meeting President Roosevelt to discuss the implications of the recent outbreak of war with Japan, and it was left to Mr A. V. Alexander, the First Lord, to answer the criticisms. Alexander gave a reasoned statement of the events leading up to the disaster, but never mentioned that *Indomitable* had been earmarked for the Far East but had gone aground.

More enlightened questions were being asked in the War Cabinet and the Admiralty as to why the modern *Prince of Wales* had succumbed so easily to the first torpedo attack. The British have a neat way of dealing with such problems – they refer them to an independent judicial inquiry. Mr Justice Bucknill seemed to specialize in naval disasters, and it was he who was appointed to head the inquiry to identify the failure in *Prince of Wales* and to suggest improvements to other vessels of her class. What

became known as the Second Bucknill Committee started
its sittings at Grosvenor Gardens House on 16 March 1942.
This was Mr Bucknill's third naval inquiry; the First
Bucknill Committee had investigated the accidental loss
of the submarine *Thetis* off Liverpool in 1939, and a more
recent inquiry, not designated as a full committee, had
investigated the failure, in February 1942, of the Navy and
the R.A.F. to stop the passage of the German ships
Scharnhorst, *Gneisenau* and *Prinz Eugen* through the
English Channel from Brest to Germany.

There were two more members of Mr Bucknill's
committee: Rear-Admiral W. F. Wake-Walker, who had
been in the cruiser *Norfolk* during the hunting of the
Bismarck, and Sir Maurice Denney, a celebrated marine
engineer. Several of the officers and two senior ratings who
had been in *Prince of Wales* were returned to England to
give evidence. They attended in turn and submitted to
questioning by the members of the committee in the quiet
London rooms that were such a contrast to the conditions
of the action being investigated. Besides questioning the
Prince of Wales men, the committee studied the reports
taken at Singapore from other survivors immediately after
the sinkings, asked questions about the amount of water
that had entered *Prince of Wales* when the German bomb
exploded near her while she was being fitted out at
Birkenhead in 1940, called for Sir Stanley Goodall, the
Director of Naval Construction, and other specialists, and
went to Wallsend-on-Tyne to see *Prince of Wales*'s sister
ship *Anson* being completed at the Swan-Hunter yards
there.

The Bucknill Committee met for some twenty days. The
result of all their effort was a mass of documents that was
kept secret until 1972. For the technically minded, there is
now a small pot of gold in the Public Record Office.* For
the more general reader, the following résumé will probably suffice.

* Public Record Office ADM 116/4554.

The two main questions that concerned the committee were:

1. How had the first torpedo hit, presumed to be by the torpedo whose explosion had been seen on *Prince of Wales*'s port side near Y Turret, caused so much damage farther to the rear of the ship and permitted such a vast quantity of water to enter the ship?

2. Why had the ship's electrical installations failed so drastically?

On the first question, there was much discussion about a certain pre-war experiment, Job 74, in which a mock-up of the side protection of the King George V Class battleships and the aircraft carrier *Ark Royal* had been subjected to an underwater explosion equivalent to a torpedo with a warhead of 1,000 lb. of explosive. The riveted construction of the torpedo protection later used in *Prince of Wales* was found to withstand the trial explosion better than the welded construction used in *Ark Royal*. The committee estimated that the Japanese torpedoes had carried a warhead of 867 lb. Why, then, had so much damage to *Prince of Wales*'s side protection occurred?

The committee could not have known two things: first, that the Japanese torpedoes contained only 330 or 450 lb. of explosive charge (which knowledge would only have increased their dilemma), and secondly, that the extensive damage and flooding had been caused not by the explosion seen on *Prince of Wales*'s port side but by the unseen torpedo hit underneath the stern. This was the torpedo that tore the 'A' bracket of the port-outer shaft away from the hull, distorted the shaft itself, and permitted the vast inrush of water. It is small wonder that the committee was baffled and that Sir Stanley Goodall could only point out lamely the urgent demands for up-to-date battleships and the restraints on contruction caused by the pre-war treaties and budgets. It was not until after the war, when *Prince of Wales*'s hull was examined, that the truth became known.

So the committee mistakenly presumed that the riveted

construction had failed despite the tests done on Job 74. It was recommended that future ships should have an extra strengthened bulkhead isolating the known vulnerability of the stern area more securely from the rest of the ship; and that, if possible, the three-shaft system of propulsion, known to be favoured by German naval constructors, be adopted in the machinery of future capital ships. (The three-shaft system was, however, never implemented.)

The Bucknill Report contains wads of material on the electrical failure in *Prince of Wales*. It transpired that the Controller of the Admiralty had laid down, in July 1938, eighteen points of principle for electrical installations in naval vessels, but because of the urgency in the building of the King George V Class ships, these had not been fully complied with. The major electrical overhauls and amendments that the remaining King George V Class ships underwent later in the war were a direct result of the failures highlighted in *Prince of Wales*.

There were many minor items. It was recommended that the officer in charge of Damage Control should have the 'prestige' to ensure that his decisions on priorities were accepted and his orders obeyed despite the claims on his organization from other departments. It was recommended that 'in future, no consideration of weight or cost should be allowed to stand in the way of making communications as safe from failure as possible'. There were comments on working-up periods and on the routing of ventilation shafts and cable passages – through which much water had passed in *Prince of Wales* – and much more. On the other hand, there was little criticism of the machinery other than a recommendation that the auxiliary services for machinery compartments should be self-contained to each compartment and the size of each engine room be reduced by placing the gearing in a separate compartment. These measures were asked for so as to restrict the effects of flooding on a ship's primary machinery.

Mr Bucknill submitted his Report and the inquiry closed. It is not known whether anyone lost his job or pension because of the failures highlighted in *Prince of Wales*, but many valuable lessons had been learnt. If the remaining King George V Class battleships had been involved in serious action later in the war, many members of their crews would have owed their lives to the experiences of *Prince of Wales*, but these other battleships were lucky in that none was ever subjected to the battering suffered by their unfortunate sister ship.

And so the action off Kuantan took its place in history. The loss of *Repulse* and *Prince of Wales*, coming so soon after the Americans had been trounced at Pearl Harbor, had far-reaching effects upon the new war. Not only had the Americans, and now the British, lost or had put out of action their entire battle fleet in the Pacific and the Far East, but these great Western nations had been publicly humiliated in an area where to lose 'face' was as serious as to lose a battle. The Allies had thus lost the respect and some of the support they might otherwise have expected from their colonial possessions. This was particularly so for the British who had the greater influence and the larger empire. For the humble natives of these countries, there could no longer be respect for a power which colonized you and traded with you, but that could not defend either herself or you when challenged by an enemy which had always been depicted as inferior. The thrashing administered in those few hours off Kuantan knocked the bottom out of British prestige in the Far East. It never recovered. This was true also in the white countries of Australia and New Zealand, though the effects were slower to appear here. These countries fought on at Britain's side loyally throughout the remainder of the war, but there was a distinct change in the post-war years and a steady move away from the close ties with Britain.

And the nature of naval warfare had changed. What Billy Mitchell and the lesser prophets had foreseen had at last come to pass. The lesson was finally learnt that the expensive battleship with a crew of one and a half thousand men had serious limitations. It could only move in two dimensions and at a speed of 30 knots at most. The cheap mass-produced aeroplane with a crew of half a dozen men could move in three dimensions, at ten times the speed of the battleship, and could deliver its load of high explosive as accurately as the battleship. There was little the battleship could do that the aeroplane could not do more efficiently, especially if that aeroplane was carrier borne. And the battleship had been proved so vulnerable; it could no longer move anywhere without constant air cover. For the Royal Navy and for navies everywhere the battleship had become obsolete. The next generation of capital ship would be the aircraft carrier, and the lifespan of even that vessel would expire while some of the survivors of *Repulse* and *Prince of Wales* were still comparatively young men.

These conclusions may be resented by some professional sailors, but surely they are the self-evident truths of the Kuantan action. It was Admiral Tom Phillips's bad luck that he had to be the one in the wrong place at the wrong time who had to learn these truths for his fellows. The fighters might have saved him, but his old dictum 'that properly-handled capital ships can defend themselves' had been proved false. For dedicated members of the Senior Service it was a bitter pill to swallow. Did Admiral Phillips think of all this as he stood on the bridge of the sinking *Prince of Wales*? Did he decide that he could not live with the shattering of all his beliefs and illusions? We shall never know, but it seems not unlikely.

It is not often that two historical milestones are reached in one day. The men of Force Z had been involved in the beginning of the break-up of an empire and in the end of the useful lifespan of the battleship. Had the Americans at Pearl Harbor not already seen the revelation of Japan as a modern military power, there would have been a third milestone to add to the list.

Those few days in December 1941 were truly historic.

16

The Years that Followed

The morning after the sinking, the officers and ratings who had survived from *Repulse* and *Prince of Wales* assembled on the parade ground at the Singapore Naval Base. They were addressed first by Captain Tennant, who told the survivors he had been ordered to fly to England to report upon the disaster and that he would do what he could to get the remains of the two ships' companies home as soon as possible for the usual survivors' leave. He was cheered by the 2,000 men on the parade ground as he left. He reached England within a few days and was never blamed for anything that had happened.*

Unbeknown to Captain Tennant, a decision had already been taken that most of the survivors were to be retained in the Far East. This policy was probably initiated by Admiral Layton, now confirmed as Commander-in-Chief Eastern Fleet, and it became his task to inform the survivors that most would not be going home. It is generally agreed by the men on the parade ground that he made a lamentably poor job of it, and there was much murmuring in the assembled ranks of survivors. After Admiral Layton had stepped down from the platform the parade was dismissed. At that moment the ship's companies of H.M.S. *Repulse* and H.M.S. *Prince of Wales* ceased to exist as formal

---

* Within two months, Captain Tennant had been promoted to Rear-Admiral and was flying his flag at sea in the cruiser *Newcastle*, escorting convoy WS. 16 out to Egypt via the Cape. In 1944 he was given the tasks of getting the components for the Mulberry Harbours across the Channel and assembled after D-Day and of supplying the invasion armies with petrol. The Naval Official History comments that he commanded 'the most oddly assorted fleet which can ever have fallen to a flag officer'. Tennant later achieved full admiral's rank and, after retirement, became Lord Lieutenant of Worcestershire. He died in July 1963.

units of the Royal Navy. It was a very unhappy and demoralized batch of sailors who drifted away to await whatever uncertain fate was in store for them in the Far East.

The survivors remained in this limbo for the next few days, mostly packed into the Fleet Shore Accommodation of the Naval Base. Commander R. J. R. Dendy was the senior officer remaining from the two lost ships. He was sent to Java to consult with the Dutch Vice-Admiral Helfrich, who had requested that some of the *Prince of Wales* and *Repulse* survivors be sent to help man the Dutch cruiser *Sumatra*, two submarines and some motor torpedo boats. But Dendy's talks with the Dutch did not proceed smoothly. The official story is that Dendy found the mechanical condition of the Dutch ships so poor that nothing could be done, but he himself states the real reason to have been that Admiral Helfrich would only allow the British seamen to sail in Dutch ships under a Dutch captain and under a Dutch flag if he received orders to that effect from Queen Wilhelmina in exile in London. The negotiations collapsed and Commander Dendy returned to Singapore to find the breaking-up of the *Repulse* and *Prince of Wales* crews already well advanced.

Two days after the sinkings, Admiral Layton received more detailed instructions from the Admiralty about the future employment of the survivors. The help to the Dutch – which had come to nothing – had been the first priority. Layton's staff were then allowed to choose officers or ratings to fill essential gaps in local naval units or in the few ships remaining in Eastern Fleet, 'or to relieve those men who had been abroad over two years'. After these outlets had been exhausted, surplus officers could be returned to England, but surplus ratings had to be found some local employment if possible.

During the next few weeks a few picked men were posted to top up the complements of the few warships at Singapore. Those who went to the cruiser *Mauritius* were the most fortunate; her firemain was badly corroded and she was sent straight home to England for major repair. Others went to *Exeter*, to suffer a less happy experience, and the destroyers and smaller naval craft at Singapore all took a few men.

Others, in various categories, were selected to be sent to England. Many of the officers were so earmarked, as were most of the specialist ratings. The younger of the boy seamen were told, 'You will be sent where you belong – near your mothers'; they were delighted. Another group of men to be warned for home were the C.W. ratings.* 'C.W. candidates were not exactly popular with their mess-mates, and we could not help feeling guilty because of the preferential treatment we were now accorded. But we were not sorry to go.' All these happy groups, 900 men in all, were packed into a dirty old transport, the *Erinpura*, which sailed for Colombo on 21 December.

Morale fell badly among those left behind. They bitterly resented having to replace men who had served 'cushy' years amid the luxuries of Singapore while they had been in wartime England or involved in the sea war with Germany, to say nothing of the recent ordeal of the sinking of their ships. Many were formed into military-type units, and, with only the hastiest of training, were expected to fight as ground troops. They saw, all around them, the apathy and disorganization of a country unprepared for war and suffered the results of a service administration under severe pressure. But it was no good protesting. 'There was much muttering among the lads, who felt they were getting a rough deal, but those organizing the drafts made it known that they did not want to hear the word "survivors" again; all they were interested in was date left U.K.' The War Diary of the Eastern Fleet makes this comment:

Among naval personnel on shore and, in particular among the survivors of the *Prince of Wales* and *Repulse* who had to be ruthlessly

* C.W. ratings were named after the Navy's Commissions and Warrants Branch and these men were serving their trial periods as ratings before going on to train as officers.

re-employed on shore as soon as they were fit, morale was patchy. The survivors had, of course, had a severe shock and, by the time bombing of their accommodation at Singapore had become frequent, many were at the end of their tether.*

One small party of former *Prince of Wales* men became involved in an incident, little publicized but serious enough for those concerned. Three sub-lieutenants and some ratings were dispatched to Prai, on Malaya's west coast, to man three small ferryboats operating between Penang Island and the mainland after their civilian crews had done a bunk. The *Prince of Wales* men worked hard in the most difficult conditions of bombing, panic and disorganization, but the five or six men on one boat, the S.S. *Violet*, eventually left their posts. The sub-lieutenant in charge could not get them to return; they complained they were 'dead beat', joined a party of soldiers in a lorry and drove off to Singapore. The officer had little option but to follow them.

The Naval Officer in Charge at Penang, an elderly retired captain, had already been replaced as it was thought that he was not in sufficient control, and now the Navy decided to court martial the *Prince of Wales* officer and his men. 'Desertion' and 'desertion in the face of the enemy' were among the charges, but it is not known whether 'mutiny' was included – the papers of courts martial are not released for a hundred years. It is known that Lieutenant-Commander C. W. McMullen, the former gunnery officer of the *Prince of Wales*, defended the accused ratings, and that Surgeon-Lieutenant S. G. Hamilton, formerly of *Repulse*, had to examine the accused officer and found him medically fit. Hamilton felt annoyed at 'all this gold-braid sitting about; why weren't they doing something about the Japanese coming down the peninsula?' The accused were all found guilty, but given minimum sentences.

After the case, Admiral Layton sent this message to

* Public Record Office ADM 119/1185.

Rear-Admiral Spooner who was in charge of the Royal Navy in Malaya.

> This is not at all inspiring. Officers and men do not seem to realize that war is not always a very pleasant game and setbacks and dangerous experiences must be met with fortitude. Officers and men at Hong Kong had a very unpleasant and nerve-shaking experience which lasted for fourteen days but it did not impair their fighting spirit. I wish to hear no more sentimental rubbish about survivors not being fit for the next job that comes along – they should be only too ready to get their own back. *

This minor affair still rankles, and former *Prince of Wales* officers have asked that it not be mentioned here, or at least placed in its correct context. They say that this was no organized mutiny but a tiny band of men, no longer part of an organized crew, who were at the end of their tether. At least one of the ratings involved later petitioned the Queen for a review of the case and for the removal of details of it from his otherwise perfect service record sheet.

The largest bodies of men to remain together from the two ships were their Royal Marine detachments. The marines had been trained in the basics of soldiering and were obviously capable of making a useful contribution to the defence of Malaya. Few if any of the marines were returned to England, and about two hundred, with their original *Prince of Wales* and *Repulse* officers, were eventually merged with the remnants of an army battalion, the 2nd Argyll and Sutherland Highlanders, who had been badly cut up in the jungle fighting in northern Malaya. The new composite battalion was officially called 'The Marine Argyll Battalion', but it immediately took on a far better remembered name. The marines had all come from Plymouth Marine Barracks, and it was inevitable that the new unit should become known as 'The Plymouth Argylls' after that city's football club. The marines formed two

---

* Public Record Office ADM 199/357.

companies of the new battalion, one of them made up entirely of *Prince of Wales* men under the command of Captain C. D. L. Aylwin, and the second mainly *Repulse* men under Captain R. G. S. Lang. The marines also provided the men for an armoured-car platoon and the battalion's machine-gun and signals section.

Singapore fell ten weeks after the sinking of *Repulse* and *Prince of Wales*. The Admiralty ordered all naval personnel to get away before the final defeat, and those left behind were mostly Royal Marines and wounded seamen. At least thirty-eight *Prince of Wales* and *Repulse* men were killed in the final stages of the fighting in Singapore, most being marines of the Plymouth Argylls who fought at least as well as the regular army units and whose exploits were to become part of Royal Marine folklore.* The survivors then passed into the hands of the Japanese when the garrison surrendered on 15 February 1942 and thus faced the horror of three and a half years in Japanese prison camps.

Among those who got away before Singapore fell was Vice-Admiral Layton and the staff of Eastern Fleet. Layton had decided that he could do no good at Singapore and sailed for Colombo. On his departure, he left this message for the naval personnel at Singapore:

I have gone to collect the Eastern Fleet. Keep your heads high and your hearts firm until I return.

It has been described as 'one of the most badly phrased signals ever to be sent during the war'. One man who was left behind writes that 'the sailors' comments were unprintable'.

Admiral Layton left Rear-Admiral Spooner, a former captain of *Repulse*, in charge at Singapore. Two nights

* Both the Royal Navy and the Army had their youngest Second World War deaths in the final fighting at Singapore. Boy 1st Class Michael Foran from Camborne, Cornwall, was only fifteen years old, and Boy W. Martin from Ipswich was a sixteen-year-old soldier in the 1st Manchester Regiment.

before the island fell Spooner arranged for every available vessel to sail from Singapore with as many service personnel and civilians as could be packed aboard them. Spooner himself, with Air Vice-Marshal Pulford (who was ordered to leave by General Percival, the senior service officer then remaining in Singapore), sailed the same night in a naval launch. Most of the ships in that last desperate exodus ran into Vice-Admiral Ozawa's cruisers and destroyers which had so nearly clashed with Force Z the night before *Repulse* and *Prince of Wales* were sunk. Ozawa's guns slaughtered the defenceless ships and forty of them were sunk. The launch in which Spooner and Pulford were attempting to escape was bombed and wrecked and their party was left stranded upon a small island. They died of starvation.

Of the six destroyers that had escorted *Prince of Wales* from England or that had sailed with Force Z in its last action, five were sunk during the next few weeks. *Electra* and *Jupiter* were both lost in the Battle of the Java Sea on 27 February 1942. *Encounter* went the next day, the same day as the famous cruiser *Exeter*. Japanese carrier-borne aircraft sank *Tenedos* off Ceylon on 5 April, and two days later *Vampire* received the same treatment while in company with the old British aircraft carrier *Hermes*. *Express*, which had come alongside *Prince of Wales* just before she sank, was the only destroyer associated with that ill-fated operation to survive the war. In 1943 she went to the Royal Canadian Navy – under the name of *Gatineau* – and lived on to end up in a Vancouver breaker's yard in 1956.

The Australian pilots of 453 Squadron who survived the Malayan campaign were evacuated from Singapore on the old cruiser *Danae*, one of the three original China Station cruisers that had been considered too weak to go out with Force Z. *Danae* ended the war with the Free Polish Navy, but *Dragon* and *Durban* were ignominiously sunk to help form one of Admiral Tennant's breakwaters off the Normandy beaches soon after D-Day. 453 Squadron was disbanded in Adelaide in March 1942, but a new 453 Squadron, still Australian, was formed in Scotland three months later and flew Spitfires over Europe for the remainder of the war. The squadron was finally disbanded in May 1945. Flight Lieutenant Tim Vigors, who had been badly burnt ten days after *Repulse* and *Prince of Wales* were sunk, survived the war and later became a successful racehorse breeder.

The Japanese airmen who had been so successful that morning had a hard war. The Nell turned out to be a sturdy aircraft, capable of taking much punishment, but the Bettys were found to be highly inflammable; American pilots who often met them in the air battles of the Pacific campaign called them the 'one-shot lighters'. Few of the Genzan, Kanoya and Mihoro airmen survived the war, many being killed in the battles around the Solomon Islands in August 1942.

The nature of sea warfare changed dramatically after the battle off Kuantan. There were still occasional clashes between battleships, as when *Prince of Wales*'s sister ship, *Duke of York*, with a force of cruisers and destroyers caught and sunk the German *Scharnhorst* in December 1943; but such actions were the exception rather than the rule in the second half of the war. It was the R.A.F.'s 617 Squadron, with the aid of a super-bomb designed by Barnes Wallis, who put paid to the *Tirpitz* in November 1944 and finally relieved the Admiralty of the need to keep an eye on this menace. R.A.F. bombers also took care of the remainder of the German battleship force – *Gneisenau, Admiral Scheer* and *Lützow*.

But it was in the vast reaches of the Pacific that the new type of naval battle developed. This was the battle fought between rival fleets whose main hitting power were the air squadrons aboard their aircraft carriers. These great carrier battles, in which the rival Japanese and American fleets never saw each other and in which battleships became little more than embarrassing encumbrances, settled the outcome of the naval war in the Pacific. In revenging the

Japanese naval successes of 1941 and early 1942, American planes, mostly carrier-borne naval planes, sank six Japanese battleships, seventeen aircraft carriers and a host of minor vessels including every one of Vice-Admiral Ozawa's cruisers which had hunted *Prince of Wales* and *Repulse*.* Even the monster Japanese battleships *Yamato* and *Musashi*, each of 64,000 tons and with their upperworks covered with anti-aircraft armament, succumbed to the torpedo attacks of tiny American carrier-borne aircraft.

The battleships of Germany and Japan were swept away by air power. Those of Britain and America became little more than floating artillery batteries, as which they performed sterling work off many an invasion beach but only as long as air superiority had been won for them in advance.

The Royal Navy was not left behind in this new type of naval warfare. Within a few weeks of the loss of *Repulse* and *Prince of Wales*, the building of an entire new class of light fleet aircraft carriers was authorized. These were the ten vessels of the Colossus Class – small, fast carriers, each with forty-eight aircraft aboard. But, with the German Navy confining itself mostly to submarine warfare in the closing years of the war, the British carriers had little opportunity to shine in European waters. When Germany fell, the Royal Navy started to move its best ships East to take its place with the Americans in the war against Japan, but with the dropping of atom bombs on Hiroshima

---

* Vice-Admiral Ozawa's cruisers were disposed of as follows:

Mikuma in the Battle of Midway by aircraft of U.S.S. *Enterprise* and U.S.S. *Hornet*, 6 June 1942.

Yura in the Battle of Santa Cruz by U.S. aircraft, 24 October 1942.

Chokai (by aircraft of U.S.S. *Natoma Bay*), *Suzuya* (by aircraft of U.S.S. *Kitkun Bay*), *Mogami* (by aircraft of U.S. 7th Fleet carriers) and *Kinu* (by aircraft of U.S. 3rd Fleet carriers and U.S.A.A.F.) were all sunk in the Battle of Leyte Gulf, 25–6 October 1944.

Kumano was sunk off Luzon by aircraft of U.S. 3rd Fleet carriers, 25 November 1944.

and Nagasaki in August 1945, this war collapsed before the British really worked up to full strength in the Pacific.

The Royal Navy never lost another battleship after *Prince of Wales*. It did ask the taxpayer to provide it with one more new battleship, the 42,000-ton *Vanguard*, which was completed in 1946 at a cost of £9 million to say nothing of the cost of maintaining it until it was scrapped in 1960. It is difficult to see what role the Navy saw for *Vanguard* in wartime, but fortunately she never had to face that test.

The *Prince of Wales* and *Repulse* men who had managed to escape from Singapore spread through the ships and shore establishments of the Navy where the very fact that they had taken part in that momentous action marked them as men whose stories were worth listening to. Thus the sinking of these two ships gradually passed into the history of the Royal Navy. If it had been a victory, there would have been honours and decorations for the more worthy of the participants, but, the Admiralty obviously decided, this would not be appropriate here, despite the many acts of outstanding heroism that had been witnessed. One *Repulse* officer tried to get awards for two of his midshipmen who had lost their lives in the bravest of circumstances, but was told that 'in a disaster of such magnitude no recommendations for awards can be considered'. It was not until October 1942 that the Admiralty published a list of twenty-four men, fifteen from *Repulse* and nine from *Prince of Wales*, who had been 'Mentioned in Dispatches' – the lowest degree of recognition for courage or outstanding service that can be given to a serviceman. Thirteen of the 'Mentions' were posthumous.* There was no award for Captain Tennant, whose ship had performed so well, and many *Prince of Wales* survivors were disappointed that Lieutenant-Commander Cartwright of *Express* was not

* Appendix Five gives full details of the twenty-four Mentions in Dispatches.

decorated for the magnificent handling of his destroyer alongside their sinking ship, but perhaps such ability was expected as a matter of course from destroyer captains.

The war ended, the British returned to Singapore and the men who had fought off Kuantan and survived the remainder of the war mostly went home, some of the old Regulars retiring for a second time, the Hostilities Only men gladly becoming civilians again. None would ever forget that morning, and for nearly all it would be the highpoint of their lives.

At the time of writing, the wrecks of *Prince of Wales* and *Repulse* remain intact and undisturbed at the original sites of their sinkings. They have been inspected several times but, as far as is known, never entered. The Japanese were the first visitors early in 1942. The wrecks were located by their minesweepers and then buoyed. *Prince of Wales* was found to be eight miles east-south-east of *Repulse*. The Japanese salvage ship *Seishu* was involved in this work, and it is believed that the Japanese were trying to recover the radar equipment of the British ships but had little success. In June 1943 a Tokyo radio broadcast stated that Japanese engineers were attempting to refloat the *Repulse*, which lay in only thirty fathoms of water compared with thirty-six fathoms of *Prince of Wales*, but this venture did not succeed either.

In 1954 the destroyer H.M.S. *Defender* made the first of several post-war British surveys. The positions established varied very little from those recorded by the Japanese, but considerably from those reported by the destroyers of Force Z at the time of the action. The 1941 position of *Prince of Wales* was found to be two miles in error, and that of *Repulse* was eight miles out. The exact positions, fixed by H.M.S. *Dampier* using Decca radar in 1959, are:

Repulse	03° 37′ 18″ North, 104° 20′ 36″ East
Prince of Wales	03° 34′ 12″ North, 104° 27′ 48″ East

Both ships were found to be in remarkably sound and clean

condition. *Repulse* was almost completely heeled over to port, with her highest part, the starboard bilge keel, only 105 feet below the surface. *Prince of Wales* was almost upside down with her starboard bilge keel again the highest point, 155 feet below the surface. It was these post-war surveys that revealed for the first time the unsuspected torpedo hole near the *Prince of Wales*'s stern which had been the cause of the massive initial flooding.* Both ships can be seen from the air under favourable conditions. The British government regards them as Crown property and as the official war graves of the 840 men who were lost. Naval divers regularly replace the White Ensigns which are attached to rigid steel wires on a propeller shaft of each ship. Several applications for permission to salvage the ships have been refused, the most persistent applicants being the Japanese, who apparently have little idea of the offence such requests cause. But, when the question of salvage was raised in the House of Lords in October 1975, Lord Winterbottom for the government did not rule out the possibility of salvage, 'provided the bodies of the dead were reverently treated'. Many would hope that the wrecks will never be disturbed.

The men lost in *Prince of Wales* and *Repulse* are commemorated on the impressive Memorial to the Missing of the Royal Navy's Devonport Division on Plymouth Hoe, close by the depot which provided the original crews. A few men have individual graves. There are eighteen in the Kranji Military Cemetery at Singapore: sixteen of them who died aboard the rescuing destroyers or who died of injuries soon after being landed at Singapore, and two more who died later as prisoners of war. Twelve more graves have been identified in cemeteries in Siam; these were marines who were taken prisoner with the Plymouth Argylls and who died while working on the infamous Burma–Siam Railway.

* Appendix Six contains a report describing an examination of *Prince of Wales* made in 1966.

There is another memorial, in St Andrew's Cathedral, Singapore.

TO THE GLORY OF GOD
AND IN MEMORY OF
ADMIRAL SIR TOM SPENCER VAUGHAN PHILLIPS
K.C.B.
LIEUTENANT JOHN FORRESTER BROWNRIGG
RICHARD ALEXANDER HUNTING
AND ALL THOSE WHO GAVE THEIR LIVES IN
H.M.S. PRINCE OF WALES AND H.M.S. REPULSE
DECEMBER 10TH 1941

An altar cross and a set of candlesticks are also part of the memorial. The authors of this book spent some time looking for a possible connection between the three names on the one plaque. Lieutenant Brownrigg turned out to be an army officer in the 1/5th Sherwood Foresters, a battalion of the ill-fated British 18th Division which was sent to Singapore as a reinforcement in the final fighting. 'Jack' Brownrigg was the stepson of Admiral Sir Tom Phillips, being the son of Lady Phillips by a previous marriage. He was among the wounded in Singapore's Alexandra Military Hospital when Japanese troops broke in and massacred two hundred wounded and medical personnel. Lady Phillips gave money for a memorial to her lost son and husband.

Richard Alexander Hunting was Lieutenant Dick Hunting who had commanded the close-range anti-aircraft guns on *Repulse*. He was seen alive when *Repulse* was sinking, but never after that. Hunting was a member of the family which built up the shipowning and aviation business of that name, and his brother, while on a post-war visit to Singapore, also gave money for a memorial. There was no other connection between the Hunting and Phillips families.

What are the thoughts today of the men who survived that historic action?

Each year I spend my holidays at Plymouth and lay a wreath on the Cenotaph where the names of my comrades – sailors and marines – are inscribed. These kind of men don't live today. (Marine G. Kennedy, H.M.S. *Repulse*)

Why put the blame on anyone? We were short of ships, aircraft, soldiers because of other campaigns. Decisions were made at that time bearing this in mind. Thank God decisions were taken, wrong though some of them were with hindsight, but we might have tried to muddle through and that would have been worse. (Paymaster Sub-Lieutenant A. F. Compton, H.M.S. *Prince of Wales*)

I have, during my later years in the service, been twice over the spot where the grand old lady is resting and each time wished I could just dive and retrieve a few things from my locker, for I feel certain I would know exactly where I had to go to get to it. (Boy Seaman 1st Class C. F. T. Heydon, H.M.S. *Repulse*)

She was a great ship. (Lieutenant D. B. H. Wildish, H.M.S. *Prince of Wales*)

I found time, in hospital, to wonder – 'How?' 'Why?' and to grieve. Afterwards, I served in other ships and other theatres of war, good, efficient ships and, apart from one, they weren't sent to the bottom, but *Repulse* always did and always has seemed to be the best of ships and carried on board the best 'crowd' of men it was my privilege to serve with. (Able Seaman T. Barnes, H.M.S. *Repulse*)

I'm going to ask you a question I've asked myself for over thirty years. 'WHY ME?' Have I to live with the spectre of these men I lived with and learned to love, and say, 'There by the Grace of God go I.' I ask you 'Why?' I've been out today and drank myself out of my wife's favour but I can't forget. (Chief Mechanician P. Matthews, H.M.S. *Prince of Wales*)

Prince of Wales Compass Platform Narrative*

11.13.   Opened fire on eight high level bombers which attacked
          Repulse. *Repulse* was straddled by bombs and reported some
          damage and small fire from two near misses.

11.41½.   Opened fire on nine torpedo bombers coming to attack
          from port side.

11.44.   Hit by torpedo on port side aft of the bridge. (Exact
          position not known.)

11.44½.   One aircraft shot down, falling in sea close on the star-
          board side.

11.45.   Close miss past the starboard quarter by torpedo passing
          from forward to aft.

11.49½.   *Repulse* attacked by one aircraft which dropped one
          torpedo.

11.50½.   Reported – one aircraft crashed in sea Green 140. At this
          stage a heavy list to port had developed.

11.57½.   Opened fire on six aircraft on the starboard side thought to
          be attacking *Repulse*.

11.58   Ceased fire.

11.59.   Aircraft seen to have turned away.

12.05.   Man overboard port side.

12.06½.   *Vampire* ordered to pick him up.

12.10.   Hoisted 'Not Under Control.'

12.13½.   Out of touch with X Engine Room. (Out of touch with
          Damage Control Headquarters since shortly after hit.)

12.20.   Seven aircraft on the starboard bow.

12.21½.   Opened fire.

12.23.   Two hits by torpedoes on starboard side, a few seconds
          apart. One very near the stem, the other in the after part
          of the ship.

12.24½.   One hit starboard side under compass platform, by torpedo.

12.26½.   *Repulse* shot down two aircraft.

12.27.   *Repulse* observed to be listing to port. ? hit by two torpedoes.

12.28.   Destroyers ordered to close *Repulse*.

12.30.   Nine high level bombers on port bow.

* Public Record Office ADM 199/1149.

12.30.	X Engine Room only working.
12.32.	*Repulse* sinking.
12.33.	*Repulse* sunk.
12.41.	Opened fire on eight high level bombers on port bow.
12.44.	Hit by one bomb. (Reported as being starboard side catapult deck.)
12.50.	Asked Singapore for tugs.
13.10 (Approx.)	Order to inflate lifebelts ordered.
13.15 (Approx.)	List to port began to increase rapidly.
13.20 (Approx.)	Ship sank, capsizing to port.

W. H. Blunt
Paymaster-Lieutenant

Medical Officer's Report on the Action on
10 December 1941 when H.M.S. Repulse was
sunk by Enemy Action. *

Owing to the nature of the incident, the communication is best made
in the form of a personal account.

The general medical arrangements for dealing with casualties will
be known from former medical journals. Briefly, there was [sic] two
main Medical Distributing Stations, both below the armour deck
which in the *Repulse* is two decks below the main mess decks. The
Forward M.D.S. was situated between A and B Turrets, and the
Aft M.D.S. just forward to Y Turret. The Medical parties were
made up thus:

FORWARD	AFT	RESPONSIBILITY
Surg. Cdr Newbery*	Surg. Lt Hamilton	In charge
Surg. Lt Cavanagh*	Surg. Lt (D) Major	Anaesthetics
S.P.C.P.O. Trusscott	S.B.P.O. Stevens*	Instruments
L.S.B.A. Newall*	S.B.A. (D) Morgan*	Asst Instruments
L.S.B.A. Ashworth*	R.P.O. Trudgeon	Labels etc.
S.B.A. Bridgewater	P.O.Ck Hobbs	Food, water
M.A.A. Cummins*	Sy P.O. Allum	Telephones
Ch. Stwd Robertson*	Ck Blades	Emergency lighting
Ldg Wtr Marsh*	Wtr Rees	Dressings
Ldg Wtr Jackson*	Wtr Griffiths*	Dirty dressings, pans etc.
Ldg Stwd James*	Stwd Miller*	Splints
Ch. Ck Williams*		

* Became fatal casualties.

The idea was that after or during a lull in an action, the Commander would tell us which Mess deck was most suitable to convert into

* From papers kindly provided by Dr S. G. Hamilton.

a casualty ward. The necessary implements would be set up and work would commence in the shortest possible time. In theory all would stay below armour till then.

The Medical Officers, however, and the Sick Bay staff had First Aid bags ready for use should the occasion arise, to attend casualties where they might occur. From my experience, I found that these should contain simple First Aid dressings, a few larger ones made up ready for use (i.e. not rolls of gauze and wool), a bottle of flavine, triangular and ordinary bandages, and several padded splints about 18 inches long. Rubber tubing for tourniquets is more practical than the St John's type. Morphia would be carried by the Medical Officers, and it was found that rubber-capped bottles are far more convenient than ampoules. A torch or head lamp is essential.

In addition to these arrangements, First Aid boxes were available at the Gun positions and in the Engine, Condenser and Boiler Rooms and in many other parts of the ship. The Gunnery Officer, the Senior Engineer and the Padre each had morphia and a syringe and had received instruction in their use. As far as I know, only the Padre was able to make use of this facility. All men working on deck had received anti-flash gear and had been instructed to wear shirts with long sleeves, long trousers tucked into their socks, and boots or leather shoes, instead of the normal light tropical rig. Many wore boiler suits, which are very satisfactory.

At 11.00 hours on December 10th 1941, Air Raid Alarm was sounded. Action continued for one hour and twenty minutes; then the ship sank.

When the Action began I was forward in the Sick Bay with some of the Sick Bay Attendants. We had only one serious case on board viz, Sub-Lieutenant W. R. D. Page R.N.V.R. who on the previous morning had sustained a comminuted fracture-dislocation of his left wrist and bruising of his back. The forearm was in plaster of Paris. We helped him to the Forward M.D.S. and I then carried on to my station Aft.

On arrival I found all the rest of the party present. S.B.P.O. Stevens was calmly setting out medical supplies from the cupboards; the others were at their posts. The Forward M.D.S. was informed by telephone that all was correct. Very soon a loud explosion was heard. As we were over Y Magazine and smoke was beginning to enter the space from the deck above, I ordered the armoured hatch to be closed. Loudspeakers then announced that a bomb had fallen through the catapult and Marines' Mess deck and had exploded, and caused fire to break out.

Tapping was heard on the armoured hatch and we opened it to admit five casualties. The first was dead from severe head injuries so was removed again. The others, who were all frightened, consisted of a man with a lacerated wound of the forearm, a boy with a large haematoma of the buttock, caused by his being thrown to the deck by the bomb exploding near him, and two severe cases of burns. The two former were given first aid treatment, and the two cases of burns were given morphia and retained below after tannafax had been applied to the burnt areas.

One of the telephones in direct communication with Y Turret asked for help. Surg. Lieut (D) Major was despatched by way of the handling room. He found A.B. W. J. Hewitt with a compound fracture of the arm from a bullet. He applied dressings and a splint and gave morphia. Subsequently this man survived and did well in hospital.

While this was happening a warrant officer came to inform us that several casualties had collected in the Captain's lobby flat, so I proceeded there via the quarter deck and triple gun deck. I realized afterwards that it would have been better and saved time if I had taken an S.B.A. or Writer with me. On arrival we found about a dozen men; some were burnt and scalded, one had a fractured leg, another had sustained severe lacerations of the thigh and calf, and a few were more frightened than hurt and needed encouragement. Morphia and other necessary treatment were given, but the cases were not labelled because I found it took too long to do it myself, and I had hoped to return to do this. The Ward Room flat just below was full of smoke and steam but fortunately this did not come up.

Then I returned overdeck to fetch more supplies and to find out if any message had come in. En route I saw the Padre on the quarter deck and told him of the casualties and he went to see to them.

On arrival at the medical station messages came telling of the casualties in the Ward Room Cabin flat just above us, and on the half deck. Surg. Lieut Major and S.B.P.O. Stevens were despatched to investigate and deal with these.

I then telephoned to the Forward M.D.S. and heard that they were busy with about twenty casualties, mostly burns, and that Surg. Cdr Newbery with S.B.A. Ashworth were out attending casualties on the upper deck.

Then a loud explosion shook the ship, so I ordered the armoured hatch to be closed, thinking that bombs were again falling. Actually it was a torpedo somewhere amidships.

A few minutes later another bigger explosion occurred, which I considered to be a bomb through the quarter deck just aft of Y Turret. Again, in fact, it was a torpedo. The ship shook violently and lights momentarily went out.

About one and a half minutes later a still greater explosion occurred. One or two of the lights went out. Correctly we thought that this was a torpedo near us. The ship began to list, so I decided to investigate and ordered the armoured hatch to be opened by means of the winch. Water started to pour down into the station, so I ordered the hatch to be opened at full speed and everyone out. It was only just possible to climb the vertical ladder against the fall of water. Writers Griffiths and Rees, whose duty was to turn the winch, did not lose their heads and continued till there was enough space for the men to scramble out.

We proceeded to the quarter deck which was listing heavily to port to such an extent that it was difficult to reach the starboard rails. Many men had already jumped into the sea.

It has been estimated that the ship sank within seven minutes. Lifebelts were blown up though it was not very easy to do so in a hurry, and many men jumped from the starboard side of the ship and injured their heels on the bulkheads. As the ship was still moving forward, those who jumped soon were left clear, but there must have been some danger from the propellers.

Destroyers soon started to pick men up, and I was fortunate to be picked up by H.M.S. *Electra* fairly soon, and so was able to help Surg. Lieut Seymour organize resuscitation parties and afterwards to sort, treat and label the patients till we arrived in Singapore some ten hours later. S.B.A. Anderson (of *Electra*) and S.B.A. Bailey (*Repulse*) were tireless and invaluable during these hours. There were over 800 additional to the normal complement of the destroyer on board.

Most of the casualties rescued were burns, cuts and fractures. There were, in addition, men suffering from the effects of the swallowing and inhalation of oil. Two cases of severe burns died during the voyage. Fractures of the Os Calcis were frequent, caused by jumping onto the bulkhead or the ship's side. One, however, was a fractured Femur which was put in a Thomas's splint. One midshipman had a perforating bullet wound of the abdomen and required frequent doses of morphia. He was operated on by Mr Julian Taylor F.R.C.S. on arrival, but died three days later of peritonitis resulting from multiple perforation of the jejunum.

In the crowded ship we made the patients as comfortable as possible, giving morphia when required. We saw that supplies of water and hot sweet tea were continually taken round, and dressings and splints were applied and adjusted.

Although many suffered for a few days from the effects of swallowing oil fuel, there were few lasting sequels from it. Many of the men were partly naked but the warmth of the climate no doubt helped to prevent pneumonia and to lessen shock.

It was a pity that many of the men were unable to swim, as I feel that fewer lives would then have been lost.

I understand that Surg. Lieut Seymour of H.M.S. *Electra* has a full account of the casualties and the measures taken to help them in his Medical Journal.

In conclusion, I should like to express my sorrow at the loss of so many of our medical staff. From many months of loyal co-operation in all sorts of conditions I know them to have been exceptionally keen and reliable in their work.

S. G. Hamilton
Surgeon Lieutenant R.N.V.R., M.A., M.B., B.CHIR., M.R.C.S., L.R.C.P.

Log of Signals Received in Singapore from Force Z*

SECRET
MICROGRAM.
Non-Urgent.

The British Naval Commander-in-Chief, Eastern Fleet.
26th December 1941.

No. 741/4724.
The Secretary of the Admiralty.

LOSS OF PRINCE OF WALES AND REPULSE.
LOG OF MESSAGES.

In continuation of my submission No. 730/4742 of 17th December 1941, I enclose a log of the messages received in the War Room at Singapore in connection with the operations on 10th December 1941.

G. Layton VICE-ADMIRAL. COMMANDER-IN-CHIEF.

Time of receipt in War Room	From	To	Report
12.04	REPULSE	Any British Man of War.	Enemy aircraft bombing My position 134 N Y T W 22 x 09. (11.58).
12.40	PRINCE OF WALES		*Emergency* Have been struck by a torpedo on port side. N Y T W 022 R 06 4 torpedoes. Send Destroyers. (12.20.)

* Public Record Office ADM 199/1149.

Time of receipt in War Room	From	To	Report
13.04	SENIOR OFFICER, FORCE Z	Any British Man of War.	*Emergency.* Send all available tugs. My position 003° 40′ N, 104° 30′ E. (12.52.)
13.10	ELECTRA.	Any British Man of War.	*Most Immediate.* H.M.S. PRINCE OF WALES hit by 4 torpedoes in position 003° 45′ N, 104° 10′ E. REPULSE sunk. Send Destroyers. (05.30z)*
13.17	COMMANDER-IN-CHIEF, EASTERN FLEET.	CHIEF OF STAFF, Singapore.	*Most Immediate.* Am disembarking men not required for fighting ship. Send – ? – ? – fast as possible. (13.11.)
13.10	SENIOR OFFICER, FORCE Z.	Any British Man of War.	*Most Immediate.* H.M.S. PRINCE OF WALES disabled and out of control. (13.00.)
13.11	PRINCE OF WALES.	Any British Man of War.	*Emergency.* Send all available tugs. My position now is EQTW 40(?). (05.31z.)
13.17	ELECTRA.	Any British Man of War.	*Most Immediate.* My 05.30z send tugs.
13.21	ELECTRA.	Any British Man of War.	*Most Immediate.* H.M.S. PRINCE OF WALES sunk. (05.48z.)

* The 'Z' times are Greenwich Mean Time, 7½ hours ahead of the Singapore Time used elsewhere in these signals and in the narrative of the book.

Post-Action Statement by Gunnery Officer of H.M.S. Prince of Wales.

Lt. Cdr C. W. McMullen, H.M.S. *Sultan*, Singapore, 14 Dec 1941 Draft of Gunnery Officer's letter to Senior Surviving Officer of *Prince of Wales*. *

Sir,

   I have the honour to forward the following gunnery report of events leading to loss of H.M.S. *Prince of Wales*. I attach many statements taken from officers in various positions.

1. Attack No. 1. Nine bombers were observed ahead in close formation. Fire was opened by Starboard Fore Group and then Port Fore Group as own ship altered course to starboard. Finally fire was opened by Starboard Fore Group as own ship altered course back to port *Repulse* was straddled and hit by the pattern of this formation.

2. Attack No. 2. At 11.41½. About nine torpedo bombers were engaged on the starboard side and then on the port side by Starboard Fore Group and both Port Groups of 5·25-inch guns and close range weapons. One hit port side and severely shook the ship.

A good barrage was developed but this in no way deterred the enemy.

Oerlikon tracer appeared effective. Two of these machines crashed on the disengaged side after they had dropped their torpedoes. Ship assumed an 11½ degree list to port and loss of efficiency resulted in gunnery material as follows:

S3 Turret. Not possible to train in hand.

S4 Turret. Power failed and an oil leak was caused somewhere under left gun. Not possible to train uphill in hand.

P1 Turret. List of ship caused turret to jamb due to turret settling sideways onto a hydraulic pipe – this was cleared before the next attack but would not train in power against the list.

   * Based on Public Record Office ADM 1/12181.

P2 Turret. Power failed to turret. Emergency leads brought power on but turret would not train until after second attack when list was reduced.

P3 Turret. Power failed and then came on again for about two minutes. It then failed for good. It was not possible to train the turret in hand.

P4 Turret. Guns continued to elevate in power but turret would not train due to list. Power then failed.

S1 and S2 not possible to depress below 5 degrees of elevation.

Ship handling. The ship could not alter course.

Between attack No. 2 and attack No. 3, fire was opened from S1 and S2 Turrets at aircraft which were attacking *Repulse*.

3. Attack No. 3. About nine torpedo bombers attacked from the starboard side. These were engaged by S1 and S2 Turrets at 12.20 and by close range weapons. Ship was at this time unmanoeuvrable and she was hit by two torpedoes three minutes later, one hitting the bow. One aft starboard side. A minute and a half later the ship was hit by a third torpedo abreast B Turret.

4. The damage caused by this attack removed power from P1 pom-poms which had become jambed in training, probably due to distortion of the roller path. Two enemy aircraft were seen to crash on the disengaged side.

5. Attack No. 4. Eight or nine high-level bombers carried out a formation attack approaching from ahead. These were engaged by P2 and S1 and S2 Turrets. The fire from S1 and S2 was not effective as an estimated height had to be used due to the rangetaker being wounded in the right eye. The 'pattern' of these bombers straddled the ship and, in addition to near misses, one bomb hit the catapult deck and exploded on the armour deck below. S1 and S2 Turrets were the last quarters to fire in *Prince of Wales*.

6. Due to the lack of an A.A. destroyer and cruiser screen, fighter escort and the determination and skill with which the enemy pressed home their attacks, it is doubtful if anything could have prevented torpedo bombers achieving their object.

The following serious deficiencies in gunnery material, however, should be put right in all ships fitted with similar equipment to that in *Prince of Wales*.

(A) Some 5·25-inch turrets failed to train in power or hand with a list of 11½ degrees on the ship (see Para 2).

(B) All pom-poms suffered from a large number of stoppages due to the shell and cartridges becoming separated, this defect showed itself in Operation Halberd but not to the same extent. Since Operation Halberd ammunition has been frequently checked for loose shells and cases.

(C) The tracer from the Bofors gun and Oerlikons was definitely seen to make some attacking aircraft jink. The pom-poms, although they were seen to hit the enemy, did not frighten him during his approach due to lack of tracer.

(D) All close range weapons should have at least 15 degrees of depression.

7. The Bofors gun on the quarterdeck fired without a stoppage. The tracer is most effective and it is considered that in KGV Class these guns should be mounted as follows:
two on top of B Turret, two on Y Turret (all on the fore and aft line) and as many as possible on the boat deck, fo'c'sle and quarterdeck in addition to the Oerlikons.

It is considered that a Bofors with tracer ammunition in local control is a more valuable weapon than an 8-barrelled pom-pom in director control without tracer, added to which a Bofors in no way relies on power and fires one-eighth of the ammunition.

8. Japanese tactics.
Torpedo bombing No. 1. Formation approached in close formation at heights between 5,000 and 7,000 feet. When at extreme gun range they formed line astern on the starboard bow and went into a shallow dive on a course at right angles to the ship and crossed from starboard to port. When on the port bow they turned to port losing height the whole time and flew on a course on the port beam reciprocal to that of the ship. Then they appeared to do a series of 'blue turns' and waves of two or three came towards the ship at a time in a rough line abreast. The deflection was at all times great up to the final moment when they turned towards the ship. They approached and dropped their torpedoes at high speed from heights of at least 100 feet from ranges of between 1,000 and 2,000 yards.
Due to the high speed of the machines, the time between their turn to a firing course and torpedo release was very small. The machines passed very close to the ship and some used their machine-guns as

they passed. A large amount of Oerlikon appeared to hit these machines.

Attack No. 2. Similar to attack No. 1 but attack from the opposite side and the number of waves is doubtful.

High level bombing attacked from a height of about 10,000 to 12,000 feet in close formation. They attacked from right ahead and released one good salvo. Similar tactics were used against *Repulse*. Before bombing they were seen to drop a salvo into the sea about 4 miles away. It is possible that this was some form of 'sighter', on the other hand it may have been a damaged aircraft jettisoning its bombs. It is not thought that the bombs were bigger than 500 pounds but this is not certain.

Type of aircraft.
The torpedo bombers were fine, robust looking craft with twin engines and rudder. They looked rather like Hudsons but larger.

9. Remarks by a Gunnery Officer on general recommendations after a year's experience as Gunnery Officer of a modern battleship in time of war.

The two statements below are not made as a result of this action but after six months' thought. I have not considered it wise to voice them before as it would be easy to be accused of 'vested interests'. Such a remark cannot now be made so here they are:—

(a) I consider that, in a ship of the K.G.V. Class, the Gunnery Officer should be a Commander (or Acting Commander) and should have a similar status to the Commander (E). It is believed that this became the practice in big ships in the last war. It is noted also that BISMARCK had a Gunnery Commander and at least three gunnery officers under him.

(b) I consider that it is wrong for 'Damage Control' to be the sole responsibility of the Engineer Officer. It should be an executive responsibility and it would be advisable to adapt the French system of *L'Officier de L'Intérieur* who is responsible for co-ordinating all matters relating to the inside of the hull both from a domestic and fighting point of view, i.e. Messdecks, ventilation, Fire Parties, Repair Parties, Watertight doors, and to be responsible in action to the second in command for Damage Control.

As his assistants he should have an Engineer Officer, the Shipwright Officer, an Electrical or Torpedo Officer and the Commissioned Gunner.

10. I wish to state that there was one bright spark in an otherwise depressing and disastrous day and that was the excellent morale and discipline of the gunnery quarters that I saw of *Prince of Wales*. Every H.A. director, pom-pom director and pom-pom requested permission before falling out. Pom-poms and 5·25-inch crews remained in action as long as possible and the working chambers crews of S1 finally went down with the ship.

I was particularly impressed by the leadership of the following officers:

Lieutenant-Commander G. C. J. Ferguson, R.N.V.R., who was in charge of the Air Defence Position and did not manage to survive.

Sub-Lt R. C. Ripley, R.C.N.V.R., Assistant Air Defence Officer.

Lieutenants E. J. Kempson, J. B. Womersley (not a survivor), E. V. Dawson and D. C. Hopkinson, all R.N.V.R. officers in charge of H.A. Directors.

Lt W. M. Graham, R.N.V.R., who was in charge of pom-pom decks.

Lt R. C. Beckwith, 2nd Gunnery Officer, who made tremendous endeavours to get 5·25-inch Turrets back into action finally trying to train those who jambed by block and tackle.

Lt (E) A. J. Cawthra and Ord.Lt E. Lancaster who did their best to bring 5·25-inch guns back into action.

Sub-Lt A. G. C. Franklin, R.N.V.R., who organized secondary supply arrangements to P3 and P4 Turrets.

The conduct of the following Petty Officers was magnificent:

P.O. Paget and P.O. Paley, who were in charge of pom-poms. Neither survived.

C.P.O. Mantle, who was Chief Gunner's Mate on the Pom-Pom Deck.

Leading-Seaman Coles, in charge of S1 pom-pom and P.O. Stevens in charge of B pom-pom.

A.B. MacNelly (not a survivor), who manned an Air Defence Position telephone to the pom-poms until ordered to take it off as the ship started to capsize.

P.O. Spencer (not a survivor), who was in charge of lookouts and did not leave Air Defence Position until too late.

Mr F. Luxton, Commission Gunner, who organized the pom-pom supply which was kept going until the last moment when the ship started to list heavily to port. He was also a great leader in keeping people cool and cheerful below.

There were many other cases of high morale and leadership which cannot be recorded but I wish to repeat that the spirit shown by H.M.S. *Prince of Wales*'s officers and men fighting the guns during the action and at the end was in the highest tradition of the Royal Navy.

I have the honour to be sir,
Your obedient servant,

C. McMullen, Lt-Cdr R.N.

Appendix 5

Citations for Mentions in Despatches
in H.M.S. Prince of Wales and H.M.S. Repulse,
10 December 1941*

Sick Berth Attendant W. Bridgewater   H.M.S. *Repulse*

For remaining down below in the fore medical station for several minutes after the order 'everyone on deck' in order to help a wounded man on deck. Although he failed in this he only abandoned this attempt when the ship had a very heavy list and was about to sink.

Midshipman A. C. R. Bros, R.N.   H.M.S. *Repulse*   Posthumous

For showing great calmness and leadership in causing the 15″ T.S. to be evacuated in an orderly manner when the order 'everyone on deck' was given. It is considered that Midshipman Bros thereby saved many lives.

Lieutenant-Commander K. R. Buckley, R.N.   H.M.S. *Repulse*

For outstanding calmness in action under trying circumstances.

Chief Stoker Cameron   H.M.S. *Repulse*   Posthumous

Was outstanding in maintaining the efficiency of the damage control throughout the action. He is not a survivor.

Corporal W. R. Chambers, R.M.   H.M.S. *Prince of Wales* Posthumous

The successful supply of ammunition to the 2-pdr guns was largely due to the efforts of this N.C.O. and his ability, coolness and example were outstanding. When conditions between decks became very difficult he continued to carry on, closing down magazines and shell rooms in the final effort to keep the ship afloat. His work in assisting to limit the spread of water when S3 and 4 magazines were flooded were most useful. He was lost with the ship.

Chief Petty Officer F. T. Crittenden   H.M.S. *Repulse*

Was outstanding in maintaining supply of H.A. ammunition under difficult circumstances owing to bomb damage.

* Based on Public Record Office ADM 1/12315.

Midshipman R. I. Davies, R.A.N.   H.M.S. *Repulse*   Posthumous

This very gallant young officer was last seen firing an Oerlikon gun at enemy aircraft when he and the gun mounting were slowly submerging.

Commander R. J. R. Dendy, R.N.   H.M.S. *Repulse*

For outstanding calmness in action under trying circumstances.

Writer J. I. Griffiths   H.M.S. *Repulse*   Posthumous

When the ship was listing heavily and about to sink, showed great calmness in continuing steadily to wind the winch to raise the armoured hatch over Y Space leading to the after medical station. Water was pouring down the hatch, his coolness under trying conditions enabled eleven men to escape of whom nine are survivors.

Lieutenant-Commander H. B. C. Gill, R.N.   H.M.S. *Repulse*

For outstanding calmness in action under trying circumstances.

Surgeon Lieutenant S. G. Hamilton, R.N.V.R.   H.M.S. *Repulse*

For outstanding devotion to duty on board when in action in tending the wounded and in continuing to do so for some nine hours in the destroyer *Electra* after he had been picked up.

Chief Petty Officer W. E. Houston   H.M.S. *Prince of Wales*

This Chief Petty Officer showed fine qualities of leadership in charge of an electrical repair party. He carried on his work to the end under conditions of extreme difficulty, setting a fine example to those under him. He was wounded in the last bombing attack, but is a survivor.

Lieutenant Commander (E) R. O. Lockley H.M.S. *Prince of Wales*

This officer displayed great initiative and coolness under action conditions and it was due to him that many essential services were maintained. He showed great powers of leadership and example under arduous conditions. Although wounded, he was of great assistance in helping survivors and maintaining the high standard of morale after the ships had sunk.

Chief Mechanician Lugger   H.M.S. *Repulse*   Posthumous

Was outstanding in maintaining the efficiency of the Damage Control throughout the action. He is not a survivor.

Commissioned Electrician E. H. Marchant   H.M.S. *Prince of Wales*   Posthumous

This officer displayed great devotion to duty in conditions of extreme difficulty. He showed fine qualities of leadership and continued his electrical repair work to the end. He was last seen in an exhausted condition between decks.

Boy W. T. O'Brien   H.M.S. *Prince of Wales*

The ability, courage and coolness of this boy during the action was outstanding and his work in assisting to get up ammunition when conditions below deck were both serious and difficult, was an example to senior ratings. He remained to assist in closing down the magazines under most trying circumstances, finally taking charge of ladders and controlling the traffic leading to the upper deck. He survived and is believed to have reached Australia.

Gunner J. B. Page, R.N.   H.M.S. *Repulse*   Posthumous

As the ship was about to sink, Mr Page found Ordinary Seaman J. MacDonald on the upper deck and without life-saving belt. Mr Page took off his own belt and put it on MacDonald. Mr Page was not picked up.

Writer W. Rees   H.M.S. *Repulse*

When the ship was listing heavily and about to sink showed great calmness in continuing steadily to wind the winch over Y Space leading to the after medical station. Water was pouring down the hatch, his coolness under trying conditions enabled eleven men to escape of whom nine are survivors.

Chief Stoker S. J. Ridgeway   H.M.S. *Prince of Wales*   Posthumous

Always a man of untiring energy and devotion to duty, this Chief Petty Officer showed great qualities of leadership during the action. He was invaluable in taking charge of pumping operations and in the supply of good fuel to boilers in spite of damaged tanks and trying conditions. He continued his efforts to the end and went down with the ship.

Chief Stoker A. Russell   H.M.S. *Repulse*   Posthumous

Volunteered to enter D Boiler Room and fan flat to shut off steam in a steam-filled compartment. He is not a survivor.

Petty Officer J. S. Spencer   H.M.S. *Prince of Wales*   Posthumous

This Petty Officer was in charge of lookouts and remained at his post to the end, going down with the ship. By his example and leadership he was instrumental in maintaining the high standard of concentration displayed by the air lookouts under trying conditions.

Shipwright 1st Class A. B. Squance   H.M.S. *Prince of Wales*

This shipwright was sent to the scene of the greatest damage from his station forward. He displayed great resourcefulness and skill in stopping leaks and in organizing repair parties. By his inspiring energy, example and initiative, he proved himself a fearless leader. After the action, although wounded, he continued to further morale by his cheerfulness and morale.

Lieutenant (E) L. F. Wood, R.N.   H.M.S. *Repulse*   Posthumous

Was outstanding in maintaining the efficiency of the damage control throughout the action. Not a survivor.

Chief Shipwright L. J. Woolons   H.M.S. *Prince of Wales*
Posthumous

This Chief Petty Officer was in charge of No. 3 Shipwright Repair Party and displayed great initiative and skill in the ordering and carrying out of the shoring of hatches and the stopping of leaks. He set a fine example of leadership and carried on to the last moment despite his exhaustion. He was not saved.

Statement by Lieutenant-Commander D. P. R. Lermitte, R.N., Far East Fleet Clearance Diving Team, Following External Survey of H.M.S. Prince of Wales in 1966.*

The *Prince of Wales* was located on Sonar and marked with two mooring buoys prior to the start of the operation.

The Far East Fleet Clearance Diving Team backed up by Clearance Divers from H.M.S. *Sheraton* and the Royal Australian Navy's Clearance Diving Team No. 1, carried out the survey involving six days on a task between 25th April and 6th May this year. Diving was initially carried out from the *Sheraton*, but half way through she had to be withdrawn for operational reasons, and the team transferred to H.M.S. *Barfoil* for the remainder of the time available.

A total of sixty-four dives were carried out between 160 and 180 feet involving an overall time of thirty-three hours underwater. Most of the dives were carried out in SDDE (Surface Demand Diving Equipment – a diving suit), but the SABA (Swimmer's Air Breathing Apparatus – an aqualung) was used on a few occasions, particularly for towed diver searches from the Gemini dinghies. DUCS (Diver's Underwater Communications System) was used throughout and, when it worked effectively, found to be invaluable. The weather was fine but the ocean current, although not strong, was unpredictable and at times hindered the operation and made positioning of the diving support ship above the wreck difficult.

The *Prince of Wales* lies on a heading of 020 degrees, and bar about 15 or 20 degrees, is upside down. The shallowest part of the ship is in the vicinity of her starboard bilge keel at a depth of 155 feet. The large flat expanse of the ship's bottom is remarkably free from marine growth and, apart from the occasional sea egg, weed or small clam, is only covered with a fine layer of silt. However, the vertical surfaces and those in the dark underhanging part of the ship was well covered with small clams, weed and similar encrustation.

Owing to the vast size of this awesome ship and the problems concerned with mooring the diving support vessel above her it was only

* This is a personal statement, and we are grateful to Lieutenant-Commander Lermitte for permission to reproduce it.

possible, in the limited time available, to dive on three separate zones of the *Prince of Wales*, namely, amidships in the vicinity of the Engine Rooms, right forward on the stem and right aft in the vicinity of the propellers and rudders.

Further, owing to the sensitive nature of such an operation, our terms of reference were that we were not to enter or disturb the wreck in any way, and this fact, combined with being confined to the depth limit of 180 feet, restricted operations to the external area of the hull alone.

During the course of the survey the following evidence of war damage was seen:

(a) A large and jagged hole about twenty feet in diameter in the forepeak passing right through the ship and in one place fracturing the stem post.

(b) The starboard outer shaft crosses over the starboard inner and its propeller wedged between the inner shaft and the hull. There is a jagged hole some six feet in diameter slightly forward of where the two shafts cross over.

(c) The port outer propeller is missing entirely and the bare shaft has pulled away from the ship, snapping the 'A' bracket in the process. A few feet forward of the 'A' bracket stub is a large hole about twelve feet in diameter with the ship's side plating jaggedly bent inwards.

Diving conditions were generally good with at least a maximum horizontal visibility of forty feet on the wreck, but this would reduce to some fifteen feet when silt was stirred up by the effect of the ocean current. The wreck abounds with marine life and one was constantly accompanied by shoals of fish of all varieties. Apart from one very large and lethargic whale shark, no other kinds of shark were seen; large shoals of barracuda were frequently in attendance and on a few occasions large grouper or Jew fish were sighted. As one ascends away from the wreck and out of the milky blanket that covers her one comes into crystal clear water and visibility in excess of 120 feet.

Acknowledgements

Before all others we would like to thank the following men who were serving aboard the ships of Force Z in the action of 10 December 1941, and the men and women who were in various other positions at that time and who all helped by sending personal contributions for our research. Without this generous and always friendly help, this book could never have been written in its present form. (Contributors are listed in alphabetical order. Ranks shown are those held on 10 December 1941.)

H.M.S. *Prince of Wales*

Able Seaman H. H. Ashurst, Leading Seaman G. H. Barstow, Paymaster Lieutenant J. G. Baskomb, Stoker R. H. Bealey, Able Seaman F. W. Bennett, Petty Officer Telegraphist A. E. C. Best, Able Seaman A. J. Bidewell, Petty Officer W. G. Bigmore, Sub-Lieutenant G. A. G. Brooke, Cook P. Byrne, Surgeon Lieutenant-Commander E. D. Caldwell, Leading Telegraphist B. G. Campion, Ordinary Seaman J. Cockburn, Leading Seaman W. Dawber, Stoker Petty Officer S. Dingle, Able Seaman A. H. V. Elliott, Leading Seaman C. B. Elsmore, Ordinary Seaman W. E. England, Able Seaman R. H. Errington, Ordinary Seaman J. Everson, Lieutenant I. D. S. Forbes, Lieutenant W. M. Graham, Engine Room Artificer A. Guy (died 1974), Lieutenant-Commander R. F. Harland, Sick Berth Petty Officer W. M. Harrigan (died 1974), Able Seaman D. G. Heath, Petty Officer F. J. Hendy, Engine Room Artificer E. Holbrook, Leading Seaman G. F. Holehouse, Leading Seaman E. Housman, Ordnance Artificer D. Hunter, Ordinary Seaman J. S. Ivers, Able Seaman R. H. James, Ordinary Telegraphist W. King, Ordnance Artificer H. W. Latto, Petty Officer L. V. Leather, Ordinary Seaman H. A. Lindsay, Telegraphist J. Macmillan, Telegraphist J. A. McCall, Lieutenant-Commander C. W. McMullen, Stoker W. Malkin, Leading Sick Berth Attendant W. Mann, Boy Seaman G. D. Marks, Leading Writer J. Marsh, Chief Mechanician P. Matthews, Able Seaman J. E. Melling, Boy Seaman B. N. Millard, Able Seaman G. Mooney, Artisan Rating L. Morley, Able Seaman P. Paterson, Stoker F. Powell, Yeoman of Signals E. A. Randall, Chief Petty Officer Writer J. H. Richards, Surgeon-Lieutenant J. E. Richardson, Leading Stoker H. Rogers, Stoker Petty Officer W. A. Roseveare, Able Seaman F. Rowe, Able Seaman G. Schofield, Boy Seaman W. S. Searle, Lieutenant-Commander A. G. Skipwith, Able Seaman P. Smalley, Shipwright A. B. Squance, Shipwright Petty Officer S. R.

Stephenson, Leading Officers' Cook D. W. Thomas, Stoker D. Ulrick, Able Seaman W. Webster, Able Seaman A. F. S. White, Lieutenant D. B. H. Wildish, Officers' Steward I. E. Wilkinson, Able Seaman R. Wilkinson, Leading Signalman J. H. Willey, Ordinary Seaman D. F. Wilson, Boy Seaman R. Wilson, Engine Room Artificer R. A. Woodhead, Chief Petty Officer H. E. Wright. *Royal Marines:* Captain C. D. L. Aylwin, Marine V. T. Barnes, Marine R. Bellwood, Marine D. S. Brown, Marine E. G. Dart, Marine P. G. Dunstan, Marine G. H. Locker, Marine R. W. Seddon, Marine R. Swain, Marine R. B. Wade, Corporal R. T. Warn, Marine T. A. Webber, Marine G. F. Whitman, Marine J. Wignall, Sergeant F. Winstanley.

Fleet Air Arm: Midshipman G. A. Trevett.

Staff of Commander-in-Chief Eastern Fleet: Paymaster Sub-Lieutenant J. G. Blackburn, Commander H. N. S. Brown (Fleet Gunnery Officer), Paymaster Sub-Lieutenant A. F. Compton, Telegraphist C. V. House, Officers' Steward J. A. Murray, Commander H. Norman.

H.M.S. *Repulse*

Lieutenant H. J. Abrahams (attached from the Admiralty Press Division), Sub-Lieutenant G. K. Armstrong, Able Seaman D. W. Avery, Stoker Mechanic G. T. Avery, Able Seaman T. Barnes, Able Seaman S. C. Baxter, Able Seaman H. Boyd, Sick Berth Attendant W. Bridgewater, Able Seaman S. E. Brown, Able Seaman S. Burgess, Ordinary Seaman H. Cain, Petty Officer J. Davey, Commander R. J. R. Dendy, Ordinary Seaman S. C. Dimmack, Ordinary Seaman R. W. Fraser, Stoker R. G. Gage, Lieutenant-Commander H. B. C. Gill, Able Seaman F. W. Green, Officers' Cook W. Greenwood, Midshipman G. R. Griffiths, R.A.N., Ordinary Seaman H. J. Hall, Surgeon-Lieutenant S. G. Hamilton, Cook J. Harbinson, Lieutenant J. O. C. Hayes, Leading Seaman N. Heap, Boy Seaman C. F. T. Heydon, Blacksmith J. A. Howe, Ordinary Seaman T. D. Jaffray, R.N.Z.N., Cook J. H. Larthwell, Able Seaman H. G. D. Lawrence, Able Seaman G. A. McCulloch, Petty Officer A. E. Mooney, Able Seaman R. Moore, Signalman G. Morris, Able Seaman E. L. Nevin, Stoker J. Parkinson, Petty Officer B. Pester, Lieutenant R. A. W. Pool, Stoker H. Radcliffe, Chief Petty Officer R. R. Rendle, Leading Seaman J. Robson, Leading Supply Assistant L. Sandland, Petty Officer A. T. Skedgell, Leading Stoker J. Slater, Chief Petty Officer Ordnance Artificer E. L. Smith, Able Seaman

J. S. Smith, Boy Telegraphist W. C. Tinkler, Leading Seaman I. G. Tucker, Steward W. Ward, Coder R. Watson, Boy Telegraphist E. Woodworth, Able Seaman H. Wynn.

Royal Marines: Lieutenant R. J. L. Davis, Marine A. Dodgson, Marine F. W. Endacott, Marine H. W. Farrell, Sergeant J. H. Gammon, Marine J. Hayes, Lieutenant G. A. Hulton, Marine G. Kennedy, Sergeant H. A. Nunn, Marine J. Powell, Sergeant S. A. Prevett, Corporal L. T. Townsend, Marine G. Turner.

H.M.S. *Electra*

Leading Seaman J. Ashton, Petty Officer C. W. Braley, Leading Seaman J. P. McGrady, Leading Stoker H. S. Mantle, Leading Seaman P. H. Perkins, Radar Operator B. V. Roberts, Able Seaman J. R. Russell, Surgeon-Lieutenant W. R. D. Seymour, Petty Officer Telegraphist A. J. Smith, Stoker Petty Officer D. J. Smith.

H.M.S. *Express*

Surgeon-Lieutenant T. E. Barwell, Stoker K. J. R. Birtwistle, Stoker R. Burnett, Lieutenant-Commander F. J. Cartwright (died 1974), Stoker R. J. Collier, Lieutenant J. R. A. Denne, Sick Berth Attendant A. Dudman, Able Seaman J. M. Farrington (died 1974), Leading Signalman J. A. Fear, Able Seaman C. L. Fox, Stoker Petty Officer G. C. Gillett (died 1973), Lieutenant A. V. Hickley, Able Seaman W. H. Jeffery, Ordinary Seaman A. Newton, Sub-Lieutenant P. F. C. Satow, Ordinary Seaman G. Slater, Stoker A. E. Smith, Able Seaman A. Taylor.

H.M.S. *Tenedos*

Lieutenant R. Dyer, Chief Stoker H. Hodson.

H.M.A.S. *Vampire*

Leading Seaman V. Sotheren.

*

Service personnel connected with the sailing of *Prince of Wales* and *Repulse* to the Far East, or who were in Singapore or Malaya at the time of events described in the book, or who were otherwise connected with the sinking of the ships.

United Kingdom to Singapore

95 Squadron R.A.F., Freetown, Sierra Leone: Sergeant D. S. Fowler,

No. 1 Mobile Naval Base Defence Organization Royal Marines, Addu Atoll: Sergeant E. Winter.

Naval Personnel at Singapore

Shore based: Telegraphist S. C. Ball, Lieutenant-Commander D. F. Chandler, Ordinary Seaman C. L. Jones, R.N.Z.N., Ordinary Seaman J. C. Leslie, Sub-Lieutenant H. J. Lock (formerly of *Prince of Wales*), Writer G. F. Palmer, Able Seaman M. C. Robertson, R.N.Z.N. U.S.S. *Alden:* Lieutenant B. J. Anderson (temporarily transferred from H.M.S. *Mauritius*). H.M.S. *Dragon:* Chief Shipwright G. Barritt. H.M.S. *Durban:* Leading Stoker A. H. C. Rogers. H.M.S. *Exeter:* Petty Officer T. A. Andrews, Lieutenant Commander G. T. Cooper, Stoker G. Darley. H.M.S. *Mauritius:* Midshipman H. C. Leach, Lieutenant A. H. Webber. Patrol Boat 328: Engineer W. Misso.

R.A.F. Personnel at Singapore

453 Squadron R.A.A.F.: Sergeant V. A. Collyer, Sergeant S. G. Scrimgeour, Flight-Lieutenant T. A. Vigors. R.A.F. H.Q.: Leading Aircraftman A. J. Smith. R.A.F. Station Tengah: Flight-Lieutenant J. A. D. Anderson.

Army Personnel in Malaya

Signalman H. G. Rowe, 9th Indian Division Signals (in Observation Post at Kuantan, and possibly the last man on shore to see *Prince of Wales* and *Repulse*). Lieutenant G. F. Hamilton, 2/3rd Australian Reserve Motor Transport Company (at Penang Ferries).

Casualty Office, H.M.S. Drake, Devonport

Petty Officer Wren Muriel Saunders (now Mrs Holland).

PERSONAL ACKNOWLEDGEMENTS

We would like to express our thanks to people and organizations in several countries for their generous help with the preparation of this book. We think it would be invidious to attempt to place these in order of merit and hope they will forgive the following groupings by countries and in alphabetical order.

Britain

T. F. (Freddie) Abbott, of Boston, for naval advice; Group Captain H. T. Bennett, Mr T. Umehara and Mr H. Yamaguchi of London, for diligent translation of Japanese documents; Captain

N. J. M. Campbell, Ryde, Isle of Wight, for technical advice; Tommy Dean, Wickford, Essex, for initial encouragement and assistance to Patrick Mahoney, and also to his daughter Mrs Sue Bunney of Garmouth, Morayshire; Professor D. J. Gee of Leeds University; Mike Hodgson of Mareham, near Boston; Tom L. Iremonger of London; the Japan Society of London; Geoffrey F. Keay of Scarborough; Stephen Knight of the *Ilford Recorder*; Lieutenant-Commander David Lermitte of Godalming; Janet Mountain and Cherry Robinson of Boston, Lincs., for their usual efficient typing for Martin Middlebrook; Alfred Price of Uppingham; Antony Preston, editor of *Warship Profiles*; Mrs K. H. L. Painter of Camberley and Brigadier J. L. A. Painter, widow and son of the late Brigadier G. W. A. Painter, who commanded the 22nd Indian Infantry Brigade at Kuantan, for the loan of personal papers; Captain Sir Anthony Thorold, Bart, R.N. Retired, of Syston, near Grantham; Commander J. F. H. Wheeler of Alderney; Mr J. Whitton of Siebe Gorman & Co. Ltd, Chessington.

We also thank the staffs of the Ilford Central, Seven Kings and Boston Public Libraries and the Library of Australia House, the Commonwealth War Graves Commission, Imperial War Museum, the London and the Devon and Cornwall Branches of the Far Eastern Prisoner of War Association, B.B.C. Monitoring Service, Caversham (Mr S. A. G. Cook), Australian High Commission in London (Rear-Admiral C. V. Gladstone), Embassy of Japan, London (Captain H. Sato, Defence Attaché), National Maritime Museum (Mr D. J. Lyon), British Museum (Peter J. Whitehead of the Natural History Department) and Cammell Laird Ltd of Birkenhead.

We are also grateful to the following departments of the Ministry of Defence: Naval Historical Branch, Naval Home Division, Department of Naval Secretary, Department of Ships, Hydrographic Department and the Air Historical Branch.

Singapore

We would like to thank the following, mostly in connection with Patrick Mahoney's visit to Singapore in September 1974: Mr T. W. Chatterton of the Commonwealth War Graves Commission, Mr D. E. S. Chelliah, Doctor C. T. Cheng, Tim Hunt of U.K. Joint Service Public Relations, Mr B. Nair of the Ministry of Culture, Squadron-Leader D. A. Rolph, R.A.F., Peter Scanlon of the British High Commission and Miss Mary J. Yapp. The staff of the Alexandra Hospital and Singapore General Hospital, Outram Road, kindly allowed an inspection of the premises that were the scene of historic events in February 1942. Two Australian pilots, Greg McKern and Mel Dougherty of the Singapore Flying Club, together with Corporal P. R. Willett, a photographer loaned by the Royal New Zealand Air Force, made every effort to help Patrick Mahoney see and photograph the wrecks of *Repulse* and *Prince of Wales*, but sight of the wrecks was unfortunately prevented by weather conditions.

U.S.A.

Our thanks are due to William H. Garzke Jr, a naval architect of Deer Park, New York, for his valuable advice on naval construction problems; and to the Naval Historical Center, Washington Navy Yard, and the General Services Administration for the provision of official records.

Japan

We are grateful to the Senshi-Shitsu (War History Division) of the Japanese Defence Agency, Mr Shiro Ihara of Mitsubishi Heavy Industries Ltd and to Mr W. G. Jackson of Times Publishing, Tokyo.

We wish also to acknowledge the help of the Australian War Memorial, Canberra, the Historical Section of the Australian Department of the Navy, Melbourne, and the Historical Section of the Netherlands Naval Staff, The Hague.

*

Acknowledgement for permission to include quotations from certain publications is gratefully given as follows: from the *Official History of the Second World War* to the Controller of H.M. Stationery Office; from the *Japanese Official History* to the publishers, Asagumo-Shinbunsha Co. Ltd of Tokyo; from *Zero! The Story of the Japanese Navy Air Force* to the authors, Masatohe Okumiya and Jiro Horikoshi with Martin Caidin and to E. P. Dutton and Co. Inc.; from *Singapore, the Japanese Version* to Constable Publishers; from *Japan Must Fight Britain* to Hutchinson Publishing Group Ltd; from *The Memoirs of General The Lord Hastings Ismay* to William Heinemann Ltd; and, for quotations from the London *Evening News*, the *Liverpool Daily Post*, the *Cape Times* and the *Singapore Free Press*, to the proprietors of those newspapers.

The cartoon by David Low is reproduced by arrangement with the Trustees and the London *Evening Standard*.

The authors would also like to thank those newspapers in the United Kingdom, South Africa, Australia, New Zealand, Singapore, Malaysia and Japan who published Patrick Mahoney's appeals for participants of the actions described in the book.

Bibliography

Official Histories

Japanese Defence Agency's Research Section, *The Book of Military History, The Malayan Area*, Tokyo, 1969.

Kirby, Major-General S. Woodburn, *The War Against Japan*, vol. I, H.M.S.O., London, 1957.

Morison, S. E., *History of United States Naval Operations in World War II*, vol. II, Oxford University Press, 1948–56.

Roskill, Captain S. W., *The War at Sea*, 3 vols., H.M.S.O., London, 1954–61.

Other Publications

D'Albas, Andrieu, *Death of a Navy*, Robert Hale, London, 1957.

Ash, Bernard, *Someone Had Blundered*, Michael Joseph, London, 1960.

Hough, Richard, *The Hunting of Force Z*, Collins, London, 1963.

Ishimaru, Lieutenant-Commander Tota, *Japan Must Fight Britain*, Paternoster Library, London, 1936.

Ismay, *The Memoirs of General The Lord Hastings Ismay*, Heinemann, London, 1960.

Leasor, James, *Singapore*, Hodder & Stoughton, London, 1968.

Lenton, H. T., and Colledge, J. J., *Warships of World War II*, Ian Allen, Shepperton, 1964.

Lockhart, Bruce, *The Marines Were There*, Putnam, London, 1950.

Okumiya, Masatake, and Horikoshi, Jiro, with Martin Caidin, *Zero! The Story of the Japanese Navy Air Force*, Cassell, London, 1957.

Storry, Richard, *A History of Modern Japan*, Penguin Books, Harmondsworth, 1960.

Toland, John, *The Rising Sun*, Cassell, London, 1970.

Tsuji, Masanobu, *Singapore, The Japanese Version*, Constable, London, 1962.

Watts, A. J., *Japanese Warships of World War II*, Ian Allen, Shepperton, 1966.

Index

* The references to *Electra* and *Express*, after they had been chosen
to accompany *Prince of Wales* and *Repulse* to the Far East, are so
numerous that further indexing is considered unhelpful.

* The numerous references to *Prince of Wales* and *Repulse*, after they had been chosen for dispatch to the Far East, have not been indexed.

† General references to Singapore are too numerous to be usefully indexed.

READ MORE IN PENGUIN

In every corner of the world, on every subject under the sun, Penguin represents quality and variety – the very best in publishing today.

For complete information about books available from Penguin – including Puffins, Penguin Classics and Arkana – and how to order them, write to us at the appropriate address below. Please note that for copyright reasons the selection of books varies from country to country.

In the United Kingdom: Please write to *Dept. JC, Penguin Books Ltd, FREEPOST, West Drayton, Middlesex UB7 OBR*

If you have any difficulty in obtaining a title, please send your order with the correct money, plus ten per cent for postage and packaging, to *PO Box No. 11, West Drayton, Middlesex UB7 OBR*

In the United States: Please write to *Penguin USA Inc., 375 Hudson Street, New York, NY 10014*

In Canada: Please write to *Penguin Books Canada Ltd, 10 Alcorn Avenue, Suite 300, Toronto, Ontario M4V 3B2*

In Australia: Please write to *Penguin Books Australia Ltd, 487 Maroondah Highway, Ringwood, Victoria 3134*

In New Zealand: Please write to *Penguin Books (NZ) Ltd, 182–190 Wairau Road, Private Bag, Takapuna, Auckland 9*

In India: Please write to *Penguin Books India Pvt Ltd, 706 Eros Apartments, 56 Nehru Place, New Delhi 110 019*

In the Netherlands: Please write to *Penguin Books Netherlands B.V., Keizersgracht 231 NL–1016 DV Amsterdam*

In Germany: Please write to *Penguin Books Deutschland GmbH, Friedrichstrasse 10–12, W–6000 Frankfurt/Main 1*

In Spain: Please write to *Penguin Books S. A., C. San Bernardo 117–6° E–28015 Madrid*

In Italy: Please write to *Penguin Italia s.r.l., Via Felice Casati 20, I–20124 Milano*

In France: Please write to *Penguin France S. A., 17 rue Lejeune, F–31000 Toulouse*

In Japan: Please write to *Penguin Books Japan, Ishikiribashi Building, 2–5–4, Suido, Tokyo 112*

In Greece: Please write to *Penguin Hellas Ltd, Dimocritou 3, GR–106 71 Athens*

In South Africa: Please write to *Longman Penguin Southern Africa (Pty) Ltd, Private Bag X08, Bertsham 2013*

READ MORE IN PENGUIN

HISTORY

The Guillotine and the Terror Daniel Arasse

'A brilliant and imaginative account of the punitive mentality of the revolution that restores to its cultural history its most forbidding and powerful symbol' – Simon Schama.

The Second World War A J P Taylor

A brilliant and detailed illustrated history, enlivened by all Professor Taylor's customary iconoclasm and wit.

Daily Life in Ancient Rome Jerome Carcopino

This classic study, which includes a bibliography and notes by Professor Rowell, describes the streets, houses and multi-storeyed apartments of the city of over a million inhabitants, the social classes from senators to slaves, and the Roman family and the position of women, causing *The Times Literary Supplement* to hail it as a 'thorough, lively and readable book'.

The Anglo-Saxons Edited by James Campbell

'For anyone who wishes to understand the broad sweep of English history, Anglo-Saxon society is an important and fascinating subject. And Campbell's is an important and fascinating book. It is also a finely produced and, at times, a very beautiful book' – *London Review of Books*

The Making of the English Working Class E. P. Thompson

Probably the most imaginative – and the most famous – post-war work of English social history. 'A magnificent, lucid, angry historian ... E. P. Thompson has performed a revolution of historical perspective' – *The Times*

The Habsburg Monarchy 1809–1918 A J P Taylor

Dissolved in 1918, the Habsburg Empire 'had a unique character, out of time and out of place'. Scholarly and vividly accessible, this 'very good book indeed' (*Spectator*) elucidates the problems always inherent in the attempt to give peace, stability and a common loyalty to a heterogeneous population.

READ MORE IN PENGUIN

HISTORY

Citizens Simon Schama

The award-winning chronicle of the French Revolution. 'The most marvellous book I have read about the French Revolution in the last fifty years' – Richard Cobb in *The Times*

To the Finland Station Edmund Wilson

In this authoritative work Edmund Wilson, considered by many to be America's greatest twentieth-century critic, turns his attention to Europe's revolutionary traditions, tracing the roots of nationalism, socialism and Marxism as these movements spread across the Continent creating unrest, revolt and widespread social change.

Jasmin's Witch Emmanuel Le Roy Ladurie

An investigation into witchcraft and magic in south-west France during the seventeenth century – a masterpiece of historical detective work by the bestselling author of Montaillou.

Stalin Isaac Deutscher

'The Greatest Genius in History' and the 'Life-Giving Force of socialism'? Or a despot more ruthless than Ivan the Terrrible and a revolutionary whose policies facilitated the rise of Nazism? An outstanding biographical study of a revolutionary despot by a great historian.

Aspects of Antiquity M. I. Finley

Profesor M. I. Finley was one of the century's greatest ancient historians; he was also a master of the brief, provocative essay on classical themes. 'He writes with the unmistakable enthusiasm of a man who genuinely wants to communicate his own excitement' – Philip Toynbee in the *Observer*

British Society 1914–1945 John Stevenson

'A major contribution to the *Penguin Social History of Britain*, which will undoubtedly be the standard work for students of modern Britain for many years to come' – *The Times Educational Supplement*

BY THE SAME AUTHOR

also by Martin Middlebrook in Penguin:

The Peenemünde Raid 17–18 August 1943

Bomber Command launched a unique operation to destroy a secret research establishment located in a remote part of Germany. A meticulously researched book which brings all the action and drama of this event vividly alive.

The Berlin Raids R.A.F. Bomber Command 1943–44

This fascinating and meticulous study draws on eyewitness accounts from both sides and previously unreleased documents to recreate the most sustained – and controversial – bombing offensive of the Second World War.

The Nuremburg Raid 30–31 March 1944

What should have been a routine raid on the city turned into a major disaster, with Bomber Command suffering its heaviest losses of the war.

'Martin Middlebrook's skill at description and reporting lift this book above the many memories that were written shortly after the war' – *The Times*

BY THE SAME AUTHOR

also by Martin Middlebrook in Penguin:

The First Day on the Somme 1st July 1916

It was the blackest day of slaughter in the history of the British Army, with 60,000 casualties – one for every eighteen inches of the front.

'A particularly vivid and personal narrative' – *The Times Literary Supplement*

The Kaiser's Battle

The last great battle of the First World War began in March 1918 when the German armies struck a massive blow against the weakened British troops.

'The clever blending of written and oral accounts makes the book an extremely convincing reconstruction – *Sunday Times*

forthcoming:

The Somme Battlefields
(with Mary Middlebrook)

BY THE SAME AUTHOR

also by Martin Middlebrook in Penguin:

Convoy
The Battle for Convoys SC. 122 and HX. 229

In March 1943, two convoys set off from New York across the Atlantic with supplies for the United Kingdom. But this was at the height of the Battle of the Atlantic – 'the only thing that really frightened me', as Churchill said. Martin Middlebrook portrays the climax of that hard, drawn-out struggle with grim accuracy.

The Battle of Hamburg

Operation Gomorrah was Bomber Command's code name for the devastating fire raids on Hamburg in July 1943.

'Controversy will persist for generations; Mr Middlebrook's book will provide useful raw material to feed the fires of debate' – Max Hastings

The Schweinfurt-Regensburg Mission

On 17 August 1943, the entire strength of the American heavy bomber forces in England struck deep into Southern Germany for the first time. The outcome was the American air forces' worst defeat of World War II.

'As always Martin Middlebrook brings a clear eye, a clear mind and a clear pen to his meticulously detailed description and analysis' – *Economist*

also published:

Task Force: The Falklands War, 1982
The Fight for the 'Malvinas'